Effective Teaching Strategies for Dyscalculia and Learning Difficulties in Mathematics

Effective Teaching Strategies for Dyscalculia and Learning Difficulties in Mathematics provides an essential bridge between scientific research and practical interventions with children. It unpacks what we know about the possible cognitive causation of mathematical difficulties in order to improve teaching and therefore learning.

Each chapter considers a specific domain of children's numerical development: counting and the understanding of numbers, understanding of the base-10 system, arithmetic, word problem solving, and understanding rational numbers. The accessible guidance includes a literature review on each topic, surveying how each process develops in children, the difficulties encountered at that level by some pupils, and the intervention studies that have been published. It guides the reader step-by-step through practical guidelines of how to assess these processes and how to build an intervention to help children master them.

Illustrated throughout with examples of materials used in the effective interventions described, this essential guide offers deep understanding and effective strategies for developmental and educational psychologists, special educational needs and/or disabilities coordinators, and teachers working with children experiencing mathematical difficulties.

Marie-Pascale Noël is professor of psychology at the UCLouvain University in Belgium and senior researcher at the National Research Fund of Belgium. She has been interested in numerical development and math learning difficulties for many years. She teaches this matter in Belgium and abroad. She is also the head of a clinical centre in child neuropsychology.

Giannis Karagiannakis is a mathematician and a fellow researcher at the University of Athens. For many years he has been interested in numerical cognition, publishing related work. He leads training courses for educators worldwide on differentiation for learning maths. He is Chief Scientific Officer of the MathPro Education.

Effective Teaching Strategies for Dyscalculia and Learning Difficulties in Mathematics
Perspectives from Cognitive Neuroscience

Marie-Pascale Noël and Giannis Karagiannakis

LONDON AND NEW YORK

Cover image: © Getty Images

First published 2022
by Routledge
4 Park Square, Milton Park, Abingdon, Oxon OX14 4RN

and by Routledge
605 Third Avenue, New York, NY 10158

Routledge is an imprint of the Taylor & Francis Group, an informa business

© 2022 Marie-Pascale Noël and Giannis Karagiannakis

The right of Marie-Pascale Noël and Giannis Karagiannakis to be identified as authors of this work has been asserted by them in accordance with sections 77 and 78 of the Copyright, Designs and Patents Act 1988.

All rights reserved. No part of this book may be reprinted or reproduced or utilised in any form or by any electronic, mechanical, or other means, now known or hereafter invented, including photocopying and recording, or in any information storage or retrieval system, without permission in writing from the publishers.

Trademark notice: Product or corporate names may be trademarks or registered trademarks, and are used only for identification and explanation without intent to infringe.

British Library Cataloguing-in-Publication Data
A catalogue record for this book is available from the British Library

Library of Congress Cataloging-in-Publication Data
A catalog record has been requested for this book

ISBN: 9781032151434 (hbk)
ISBN: 9781032151427 (pbk)
ISBN: 9781003242703 (ebk)

DOI: 10.4324/b22795

Typeset in Bembo
by Deanta Global Publishing Services, Chennai, India

Contents

General introduction vi
Acknowledgments viii

1 The bases of a cognitive intervention for math learning difficulties or dyscalculia   1

2 Basic numerical skills   36

3 Base-10 representation   72

4 Arithmetic   106

5 Word problem solving   195

6 Rational numbers   236

Index   295

General introduction

This book is the fruit of the collaboration of two experts interested in the problem of learning disabilities in mathematics and dyscalculia: a child neuropsychologist and a mathematician. Each of them has developed a career combining scientific research and interest in the clinical field.

The aim of this book is to build bridges between, on the one hand, what science has been able to highlight concerning children's numerical development and the difficulties linked to this development and, on the other hand, clinical practice. It is aimed at anyone who has to assist children with learning difficulties in mathematics, whether or not they have been diagnosed as 'dyscalculic'. They may be mathematics teachers working in special education, therapists, educational psychologists, or neuropsychologists. We will therefore regularly use the term math coach to refer to these different support professionals. It should be noted, however, that our approach is based on a detailed cognitive analysis of the processes involved and that a basic training in this field is therefore necessary to understand the content of this book.

The book has six chapters. The first chapter outlines effective instruction or remediation. The second chapter focuses on basic numerical skills such as counting and enumerating. Chapter 3 focuses on the mastery of symbolic numerical codes, i.e. verbal numbers and Arabic numbers, exploring in particular the transcoding and understanding of the base-10 structure underlying these two systems. Chapter 4 focuses on the basic arithmetic operations: addition-subtraction and multiplication-division. Chapter 5 focuses on word problem solving. Chapter 6 deals with rational numbers, i.e. fractions and decimal numbers. A similar structure underlies Chapters 2 to 6. Each chapter consists of a theoretical part and a practical part. The theoretical part includes an explanation of the processes involved and their development, and the difficulties and challenges encountered in this development are presented, especially for people with dyscalculia or learning difficulties in mathematics. Then, a synthesis of intervention studies aimed at remedying these difficulties is presented. The last two sections are more oriented towards clinical or educational practice. Firstly, a short section focuses on the evaluation of these processes with the idea of helping the math coach to assess whether or not it is necessary to provide help at this level to the child he or she is assisting, but also to evaluate the effectiveness of his or her treatment, if necessary. Finally, each chapter ends with a clear and concrete proposal for an intervention programme to support children in the development of the process in question. These programmes are based on the scientific knowledge presented in the theoretical part of the chapter but also on the clinical experiences of the two authors of the book.

Through this book, we want to equip coaches with the tools they need to intervene more effectively in their support of children with learning difficulties and to help these children through their difficulties.

Acknowledgments

The authors thank all the children who have participated in their studies or they individualised intervention sessions over the past years.

They also thank Alice De Visscher for her contribution to the writing of Chapter 4.

Special thanks to Ms Cooreman and Eureka. Several of the methods and the ideas presented in this book are inspired by the RekenTrapperS methodology which has been developed by Anny Cooreman for Eureka Leuven in Belgium. The mathematical methodology RekenTrapperS is used at the Eureka school as an exclusive math method. It has been implemented for more than 20 years at other schools, by professionals and by families at home to remediate mathematical difficulties. The second author of this book has been collaborating with Ms Cooreman over the last years to share good practices for intervention in mathematics.

Finally, the first author also thanks the National Research Fund of Belgium (FNRS) for its financial support.

1 The bases of a cognitive intervention for math learning difficulties or dyscalculia

1.1 What is dyscalculia or math learning disability?

Educational systems all over the world put a lot of emphasis on developing children's numerical skills as having some mathematical abilities is crucial for success in modern societies (Ancker & Kaufman, 2007). Yet, not everyone is able to master even the basics of mathematics. For instance, in Minnesota, 21% of 11-year-olds leave primary school without reaching the mathematics level expected of them, and 5% fail to attain even the numeracy skills expected of a 7-year-old (Gross, 2007). These difficulties are usually called 'Mathematical learning difficulties' or 'Math learning disabilities'. When these difficulties are severe, persistent, and not due to poor intelligence or inadequate schooling, they are called 'developmental dyscalculia'.

The prevalence of dyscalculia is about 6%. For instance, Gross-Tsur, Manor, and Shalev (1996) tested 3,029 Israeli fourth-grade children and detected dyscalculia using 2 main criteria: having an intelligence within the normal range and scoring on a math test lower than the average performance obtained by children 2 years younger (i.e., second-grade children). They found that 6.5% of the children met these criteria. Similarly, in a recent study of 2,421 primary school children, Morsanyi, Bers, McCormack, and McGourty (2018) identified persistent and severe difficulties with mathematics in 6% of the sample. Yet, many of these learning difficulties remain undetected (Barbaresi, Katusic, Colligan, Weaver & Jacobsen, 2005).

Most of the time, these problems are persistent. For instance, Shalev, Manor, Auerbach, and Gross-Tsur (1998) followed the fourth-grade children who were detected as dyscalculic in the study mentioned above over a period of three years. They found that nearly all of them still scored low on a math achievement test (below the 25th percentile) and about half of them had still very severe difficulties (they scored below the 5th percentile). These mathematical learning difficulties persist even into adulthood, and it is estimated that a fifth of adults from England have numeracy skills below the basic level needed for everyday situations (Williams et al., 2003). The difficulties encountered by people with dyscalculia are multiple and may concern, among other things, the mastery of the numerical codes (reading and writing Arabic

DOI: 10.4324/b22795-1

numbers, understanding the base-10 system), the storage of arithmetic facts in long-term memory (for example, remembering that 5 + 4 = 9, 8 × 3 = 24), performing the calculation procedures, or solving mathematical word problems. In their everyday life, most of them complain about difficulties such as checking the money returned or giving the correct amount (coins) of money in shops, following the proportions indicated when following a cooking recipe, or converting between measurement units such as understanding that quarter to 6 pm is the same time as 5:45 pm.

1.2 What are the causes of these learning difficulties?

Besides global factors such as low socio-economic status, affective difficulties, low intelligence, and so on, research in cognitive science has tried to identify the most basic numerical processes that are the corner stones of all further mathematical learning and which, if impaired, could lead to mathematical learning difficulties.

1.2.1 A basic number processing deficit

One of the most dominant hypotheses in the field is an impaired 'approximate number system' (also called ANS). Indeed, babies are born with an innate ability to detect, in an approximate way, the numerosity or the number of items in a set (see Chapter 2). The underlying representation is called the approximate number system. This is a non-verbal representation that supports an intuitive and approximate sense of number in humans as well as in many other animal species (e.g., rats, chimps). According to Wilson and Dehaene (2007) and Piazza et al. (2010), impairment at the level of this approximate number system would explain the appearance of mathematical learning difficulties as this would be the basis of all further numerical development. One way to measure this is to show two collections of objects (e.g., dots) arranged randomly and for a brief moment only (e.g., less than two seconds) in order to prevent any counting and ask the person to select the larger collection among the two. Research has found that the ability to detect the larger set among two (without counting) measured in preschool selectively predicts performance on school mathematics at six years of age (Mazzocco, Feigenson & Halberda, 2011a). Second, it has also been shown that children with mathematical learning difficulties or dyscalculia have lower performance than typically achieving children in such tasks (e.g., Piazza et al., 2010; Mazzocco, Feigenson & Halberda, 2011b). Yet, several other researches failed to replicate these results (for a review, see De Smedt, Noël, Gilmore & Ansari, 2013).

Then, other research argued that it is not so much this approximate number system that is the basis of further learning in mathematics but rather, the child's ability to connect number symbols (e.g., number words such as 'five' or Arabic numbers such as '5') to their meaning, i.e., to the numerical magnitude they represent (Rousselle & Noël, 2007; Noël & Rousselle, 2011). Indeed, symbolic numbers allow us to go beyond an approximate representation of the numbers' magnitude and to activate a precise number representation, and mathematics requires such a precise representation. Many studies have found that performance in math tests correlates more strongly with the ability to detect among two Arabic numbers which is the bigger than to do a similar task but on sets of items, also called non-symbolic items. In particular, Schneider, Beeres, Coban, Merz, Schmidt, Stricker, and De Smedt (2017) reviewed the studies measuring the association between symbolic (Arabic digits) and non-symbolic (dots) magnitude comparison tasks and math performance and found a stronger association with the symbolic than with the non-symbolic tasks. Also, several studies have reported that people with dyscalculia are especially impaired in symbolic number comparison relative to their typically achieving peers, and not so much in non-symbolic comparison (see for instance, the meta-analysis of Schwenk, Sasanguie, Jörg-Tobias, Kempe, Doebler & Holling, 2017).

Another type of number magnitude processing that has been invoked as a possible cause of dyscalculia is subitizing. Subitizing refers to the fast and accurate identification of the number of items in a small set (usually, between one and four items). A few studies have indeed observed impairment in this process in children with mathematical learning difficulties (e.g., Moeller, Neuburger, Kaufmann, Landerl & Nuerk, 2009; Schleifer & Landerl, 2011; Ashkenazi, Mark-Zigdon & Henik, 2013).

Finally, recent research has been considering another basic aspect of numbers: their ordinal value. This refers to the order of the numbers in the counting sequence. Thus, children with mathematical learning difficulties are slower than typically achieving children to recite the number sequence (Landerl, Bevan & Butterworth, 2004). Furthermore, the ability to judge whether three numbers are presented in ascending order (e.g., 2 3 6), descending order (e.g., 6 3 2), or not in order (e.g., 3 2 6) is a very strong predictor of mathematical achievement, even stronger than number magnitude comparison tasks (Lyons & Beilock, 2011; Morsanyi, O'Mahony & McCormack, 2017), and people with dyscalculia seem to be impaired in this process (Rubinsten & Sury, 2011). Yet, more recent research suggests that this difficulty is not specific to the numerical domain. Indeed, non-numerical order tasks, such as judging the order of months or letters, also correlate with math performance in adults (Vos, Sasanguie, Gevers & Reynvoet, 2017 or Morsanyi, O'Mahony & McCormack, 2017) and can predict first-grade children's math abilities one year later (O'Connor, Morsanyi & McCormack, 2018). Finally, difficulties in both numerical and non-numerical order tasks are observed in people with dyscalculia (Morsanyi, van Bers, O'Connor & McCormack, 2018). These order difficulties would also be observed in short-term memory as people with dyscalculia are particularly impaired in the retention of the serial order of the items rather than the retention of the items themselves (Attout, Salmon & Majerus, 2015; De Visscher, Szmalec, Van der Linden & Noël, 2015).

Yet, more and more recent works point to the fact that dyscalculia is not a homogeneous profile characterized by a single underlying cause but rather that different profiles of dyscalculia exist. For instance, Skagerlund and Träff (2016) showed that some mathematical learning difficulties result from weaknesses with symbolic number processing, others with both symbolic and non-symbolic number processing, and that more general cognitive deficits can also be the cause of some mathematical learning difficulties (Träff, Olsson, Östergren & Skagerlund, 2017). Szucs (2016) distinguished people with mathematical learning difficulties depending on whether or not they have associated reading problems: people with learning difficulties both in mathematics and in reading would be characterized by weak verbal short-term and working memory while isolated mathematical learning difficulties would be linked to weak visual-spatial short-term and working memory. Using another way to distinguish among people with mathematical learning difficulties, De Visscher, Szmalec, Van der Linden, and Noël (2015) found that a hypersensitivity to similarity interference in memory could be the cause of pure arithmetic fact dyscalculia (i.e., people who have difficulties storing in memory the answer of small calculations) while impaired order processing would lead to more global dyscalculia. Other researchers did not make any a-priori distinction but ran cluster analyses (i.e., a certain type of statistical analysis) to find different subgroups of people with mathematical learning difficulties. Thus, Bartelet, Ansari, Vaessen, and Blomert (2014) found six distinguishable clusters of children with mathematical learning difficulties: (1) those with a weak mental number line, (2) those with a weak approximate number system, (3) those with spatial difficulties, (4) those with difficulties in accessing number magnitude from symbolic numbers, (5) those without any numerical cognitive deficit, and (6) a garden-variety group.

Currently, many authors agree with the idea that numerical development is built on multiple neurocognitive components and that impairment in any of these can compromise this learning (Fias, Menon & Szucs, 2013). Accordingly, heterogeneity of mathematical learning difficulties is expected (see also, Andersson & Östergren, 2012).

We have started by underlining that different basic number processes are important for math learning. These core number processes are the approximate number system, subitizing, access to the number magnitude from symbolic numbers, and the processing of order. A deficit in any of them could possibly lead to some kind of mathematical learning difficulties. Besides those core number processes, general cognitive processes are also important for good numerical development. The role of these general cognitive processes will be explained in the next section.

1.2.2 A deficit in one or several general cognitive processes

1.2.2.1 Language

One of these general cognitive processes is language. Indeed, babies are born with a sensitivity to the number magnitude dimension, but the child's first numerical learning is the counting sequence, in which number words have to be learned and produced according to their correct order in the counting sequence. Numerous articles have shown that children with a specific language disorder show great difficulties in this learning (Fazio, 1994; Donlan, Cowan, Newton & Lloyd, 2007). Subsequently, they also show difficulties in other numerical learning, such as the enumeration process or calculation. Overall, the mathematics level of children with specific language disorders corresponds to their language level (Durkin, Mok & Conti-Ramsden, 2013). However, it seems that this delay is present for the exact number processing but not for the approximate number magnitude processing of non-symbolic material (Nys, Content & Leybaert, 2013).

This relationship between language skills and mathematics is also observed in typical populations where phonological abilities have been shown to predict numerical and mathematical development. Thus, several studies have shown significant correlations between children's arithmetic performance and their phonological awareness (the awareness of the sounds or phonemes that make up words) (see Leather & Henry, 1994; Hecht, Cowan, Newton & Lloyd, 2001). These phonological awareness abilities (measured at the age of four or five) predict the subsequent mathematical skills of children one or two years later (Alloway, Gathercole, Adams, Willis, Eaglen & Lamont, 2005; Simmons & Singleton, 2008). However, Krajewski and Schnieder (2009) show that the phonological awareness abilities measured at age five correlate significantly with mathematical performance at age eight when it comes to basic abilities (counting and reading Arabic numbers) but much less when it comes to tasks requiring understanding of the quantity expressed by numbers.

Numerous studies have also looked at people with dyslexia, since this is a disorder characterized by low phonological awareness. A review of the question shows that people with dyslexia often have poor performance in mathematics, particularly in the retrieval of arithmetic facts in memory (Simmons & Singleton, 2008), that is the answers of small calculations such as $5 + 3$ or 6×3 for instance. Researchers have also studied dyslexic participants with no associated developmental dyscalculia. Again, it was found that these people especially have difficulties in the constitution of an arithmetic facts network in long-term memory (for example, Cirino, Ewing-Cobbs, Barnes, Fuchs & Fletcher, 2007; Hanich et al., 2001; Boets & De Smedt, 2010). According to Göbel (2015), the association between a phonological deficit and difficulties in building an arithmetic facts network in memory is due to the fact that the same brain structure, in particular, the left angular gyrus, is involved in these two processes.

1.2.2.2 Memory

A second domain of importance is the memory. Indeed, mathematics requires memorizing information and retrieving it from long-term memory such as the number words and their order in the count list, or the solution of small arithmetical operations (i.e., the arithmetical facts). One study found that children with math learning difficulties were slower than their peers in reciting the count list (Landerl, Bevan & Butterworth, 2004), and several others have found that children with mathematical learning difficulties have problems memorizing the arithmetical facts (e.g., Garnett & Fleischner, 1983; Geary, Hoard & Hamson, 1999). The difficulties in memorizing arithmetical facts would not be explained by globally weak long-term memory capacities (Mussolin & Noël, 2008; De Visscher & Noël, 2014a and 2014b) but by exaggerated sensitivity to similarity interference in memory (De Visscher & Noël, 2014a and 2014b, see Chapter 4). A difficulty in sequence memory has also been shown to correlate with poor arithmetic fact processing in undergraduate students (Holmes & McGregor, 2007).

Many more studies dealt with short-term memory capacities based on the idea that storing in long-term memory the result of small calculations, such as 4 + 2 = 6, requires that these three numbers are first coactivated in the short-term memory. Studies found that all working memory components (including inhibition, shifting, and updating) are associated with mathematical performance, with the highest correlation being with verbal updating (see the meta-analysis of Friso-van den Bos, van der Ven, Kroesbergen & van Luit, 2013). Moreover, when contrasting the different numerical domains, working memory capacities correlate more strongly with word-problem solving and calculations (see the meta-analysis of Peng, Namkung, Barnes & Sun, 2016). Finally, several studies have shown that children with mathematical learning difficulties have poor verbal and visual-spatial working memory (WM) (see the meta-analysis of Swanson & Jerman, 2006).

1.2.2.3 The visual-spatial processes

A third general cognitive domain that seems to be involved in numerical development is the visual-spatial domain. Indeed, mathematics obviously requires visual-spatial processing for geometry but also for understanding the place-value system of Arabic numbers or for solving vertical multi-digit calculations. Visual-spatial processes also seem to support word-problem solving as a higher performance in word-problem solving correlates with the more frequent use of visual images (Van Garderen, 2006). Furthermore, the number magnitude representation itself is supposed to be oriented in space (see Chapter 2 and Hubbard, Piazza, Pinel & Dehaene, 2005). Indeed, in Western cultures, the small numbers would be represented on the left of a mental number line and the larger numbers on the right. A famous task to measure the mapping of numbers onto space is the number line estimation: the child is presented with a non-graduated horizontal line with one number written on each extremity (e.g., 0 and 100) and is asked to position a given number on this line. The meta-analysis of Schneider et al. (2018) shows that precision in this task significantly correlates with broader mathematical competence, thus underlining, again, the importance of connecting space and number in numerical development.

Some studies have found that capacities in mathematics correlate with spatial skills (Mix & Cheng, 2012 or Osmon, Smerz, Braun & Plambeck, 2006, for a review; see Crollen & Noël, 2017), and Rourke and his colleagues (Rourke & Finlayson, 1978; Rourke, 1993; Rourke & Conway, 1997) identified one type of mathematical learning difficulties as due to visual-spatial difficulties. In support of this, Mammarella and colleagues observed that children with impaired visual-spatial abilities but intact verbal abilities had poorer performance than typical peers in geometry (Mammarella, Giofrè, Ferrara & Cornoldi, 2013), in written calculation, and in number ordering (Mammarella, Lucangeli & Cornoldi, 2010). Crollen and colleagues (Crollen & Noël, 2015 and Crollen, Vanderclausen, Allaire, Pollaris & Noël, 2015) went further and showed that in children with visual-spatial impairment, number magnitude representation is less precise and its left-right orientation is less strongly established. Yet, not all mathematical learning difficulties are due to poor visual-spatial skills. For instance, Szucs, Devine, Soltesz, Nobes, and Gabriel (2013) did not find any significant difference between children with mathematical learning difficulties and control children in two visual-spatial tasks (mental orientation and spatial symmetry) but found poorer visual-spatial short-term and working memory.

1.2.2.4 Reasoning

Finally, reasoning skills are obviously important for solving at least some of the more complex mathematical problems. Some studies indeed found that non-verbal reasoning measured (with the matrices test) in first or third grades predicted mathematic word-problem solving or math achievement one year later (Fuchs, Compton, Fuchs, Paulsen, Bryant & Hamlett, 2005; Nunes, Bryant, Evans, Bell, Gardner, Gardner & Carraher, 2007; Fuchs, Fuchs, Compton, Powell, Seethaler, Capizzi, Schatschneider & Fletcher, 2006). Across a wide age range (6 to 21 years), Green, Bunge, Chiongbian, Barrow, and Ferrer (2017) found that fluid reasoning was a significant predictor of math outcomes 1.5 and 3 years later. Moreover, Morsanyi, Devine, Nobes, and Szucs (2013) as well as Schwartz, Epinat-Duclos, Léone, Poisson, and Prado (2018) found that children with mathematical learning difficulties have lower reasoning skills (in this case, transitive reasoning) than typically achieving children. Finally, Nunes, Bryant, Evans, Bell, Gardner, Gardner, and Carraher (2007) found that training children in logical reasoning led to greater progress in mathematics than a control group who did not receive this training, which supports the idea of a causal link between logical reasoning and mathematical learning.

In conclusion, numerical development and math learning are based on several core number processes but also on many general cognitive skills, including language, memory, visual-spatial, and reasoning skills. Accordingly, impairment in any of these can lead to some specific difficulties in the numerical domain. Further research will try to make these different mathematical learning difficulties profiles more precise, but all clinicians, special education teachers, or math coaches working with a child with mathematical learning difficulties or dyscalculia should be aware of this heterogeneity and try to understand the specific profile of the child s/he is working with to be more efficient in the intervention s/he will propose.

1.3 Effective instruction practices

Addressing the need for improved mathematics achievement for all students will be an undeniable challenge. Currently, school mathematics oscillates between more traditional teacher-directed teaching practices and more innovative student-directed approaches. Teacher-directed practices have students work on a set of problems and encourage students to use strategies that in most cases they have memorized. Then teachers tend to move students as quickly as possible to practice through worksheets that are completed individually with limited or no communication between students. Student-centred instruction gives preeminent value to the development of students' personal mathematical ideas. Student-centred activities provide students with opportunities to be actively involved in the process of generating mathematical knowledge (Clements & Battista, 1990). Students learn multiple strategies for explaining and solving mathematics problems. This type of instruction places greater emphasis on understanding underlying mathematical concepts than on acquiring procedural fluency. Opportunities to communicate their mathematical understanding should strengthen students' metacognitive reasoning. Both, however, occur in a 'one size fits all' classroom with little attention to the vast differences in background experience, knowledge, and entry skills of students of a given grade (Ketterlin-Geller, Chard & Fien, 2008).

Typically achieving students may be more able to benefit from student-centred instructional practices due to the greater organizational, social, verbal, and task demands of this approach, whereas teacher-directed practices may be particularly helpful to students experiencing mathematical learning difficulties. This is because the later practices often place less demand on attention, working memory, language, and general cognitive resources where deficits or delays often take place. Procedural fluency for students with mathematical learning difficulties may be especially appropriate as they begin to master basic knowledge and skills (e.g., number recognition, fact retrieval) requiring relatively less abstract reasoning or other higher order strategies (Kroesbergen & Van Luit, 2003; Kroesbergen, Van Luit & Maas, 2004).

Morgan, Farkas, and Maczuga (2014) used longitudinal data to investigate the relation between mathematics instructional practices used by first-grade teachers in the United States and the mathematics achievement of their students. The results indicated that only the practice-and-drill teacher-directed instruction was significantly associated with the achievement of students with mathematical learning difficulties. In contrast, for students with no learning difficulties in math, teacher-directed and student-centred instruction had approximately equal, and positive effects. These authors recommend increasing the use of teacher-directed instruction in order to raise the mathematics achievement of students with difficulties in mathematics.

On the other hand there are promising findings supporting the suggestion that students with mathematical learning difficulties could also benefit from the presentation of multiple strategies placing emphasis on understanding. For example, Bottge and Hasselbring (1993) compared the performance of two groups of adolescents with mathematical learning difficulties in problem solving in two conditions, one involving standard word problems and the other using contextualized problems on videodisc. Although both groups improved their performance, the students in the contextualized problem group did significantly better on the post-test and were able to use their skills in two transfer tasks that followed instructions. The characteristic of the contextualized approach is to stress real-world applications, focus on understanding underlying concepts of authentic problems, and discuss these concepts with the students that have mathematical learning difficulties. The instruction sought to teach students about mathematical thinking, arguing that a more vigorous emphasis on concept development was critical to mathematics success and would lead not only to a deeper understanding of math but also to computational proficiency (Baker, Gersten & Lee, 2002).

Unfortunately, mathematics instruction for students with mathematical learning difficulties has not received the same level of consideration from the research community, policy makers, and school administrators as the field of reading. Although research about 'what works better' in mathematics instruction for students with mathematical learning difficulties is limited, there are some meta-analyses suggesting the most effective evidence-based intervention practices for these students. According to the meta-analysis conducted by Gersten and his colleagues (2009) seven remediation strategies emerge as the most efficient for students with math learning difficulties: (1) *explicit instructional*, (2) *visual representation*, (3) *student verbalization*, (4) *using multiple instructional examples*, (5) *use of heuristic/multiple strategies*, (6) *providing on-going feedback*, (7) *peer-assisted mathematics instruction*. The analysis suggested that the aforementioned instructional strategies with the highest impact were the explicit instructional strategy and the use of heuristic/multiple strategies. The explicit instructional strategy provides step-by-step modelling and opportunities for practice with targeted feedback, whereas the use of heuristic/multiple examples follows a more generic approach for solving a problem that involves multiple ways to solve a problem including discussion to evaluate proposed solutions. Other reviews also support the effectiveness of explicit instruction (e.g., Chodura et al., 2015; Ketterlin-Geller et al., 2008; Kroesbergen & Van Luit, 2003) and the use of heuristic/multiple strategies (Kroesbergen & van Luit, 2002).

Recently, Stevens, Rodgers, and Powell (2017) conducted a meta-analysis of 25 years of mathematics intervention for students with mathematical learning difficulties in 4th through 12th grade. The purpose was to determine the effects of mathematics intervention on students' mathematics outcomes. They found an extreme variability in the magnitude and direction of the effects. The mean effects found were lower than in prior reviews of interventions focusing exclusively on primary school students (e.g., Chodura et al., 2015; Gersten et al., 2009), suggesting that remediating mathematical learning difficulties in older students might be more challenging than remediation in younger students. This makes sense, considering that older students probably have more knowledge gaps and misconceptions across mathematical topics given the hierarchical structure of math lessons. The results in terms of intervention content revealed that students might not respond favourably to interventions targeting a specific content domain with existing knowledge gaps in previous skills. This is also supported by Ma (1999) arguing that students' misconceptions and concomitant difficulties in mathematics are likely a result of being taught rules and algorithms in early mathematics that are not precise or are not supported conceptually. As a result, she suggested that mathematical interventions for struggling students should serve a corrective function and involve re-teaching fundamental mathematical concepts and principles. Therefore, there may be value in investigating interventions that build in complexity or target multiple content areas. The latter will let students manipulate more advanced mathematical tasks since they are required to analyse and to solve a variety of problems, exhibiting higher level mathematics reasoning (Stevens et al., 2017).

1.4 From research to practice

The previous section made it clear that explicit instructions and the use of heuristics (a more teacher-directed approach) as well as multiple strategies and conceptual instruction (a more student-directed approach) seem to be the most efficient instructional strategies for students with mathematical learning difficulties. For this reason, we will first underline extensively the principles of (1) *explicit instruction*, (2) *the use of heuristics*, and (3) *math flexibility instruction* including features of the rest of the instructional strategies: *visual representation, student verbalization, use multiple instructional examples, providing on-going feedback*, and *peer-assisted mathematics instruction*, which will be briefly described next. We chose the term *math flexibility* to make clear that it describes an instructional strategy, which incorporates multiple instructional strategies, deep understanding, and decision making about the strategy that best fits each student.

Before proceeding to the description of the different types of evidence-based instruction, we would like to address a main drawback of these intervention studies from our point of view. Indeed, typically in these studies, researchers have recruited the samples of students with mathematical learning difficulties mainly by using a mathematical achievement test and then selecting the students whose performance fell under some cut-off point. Yet, Murphy, Mazzocco, Hanich, and Early (2007) found that the commonly used cut-offs (10th percentile and 25th percentile) identified groups of students with different cognitive profiles. Therefore, a main limitation of the efficacy of the intervention studies for students with mathematical learning difficulties is the heterogeneity of the participants of the samples. Thus, a specific instructional strategy that could be beneficial for one child with mathematical learning difficulties would not necessarily work for another one who would display different strengths and weaknesses in terms of mathematical skills. So, in practice, clinicians, teachers, or math coaches should be aware of the different needs of each student in order to provide her/him with the corresponding instructional practice. As Ball, Lubienski, and Mewborn (2001) claim, knowing how to teach math well to students with differing abilities seems to be much more important than having math teachers who possess strong backgrounds in mathematics. There is a general agreement that teachers in the elementary and middle grades have not been sufficiently prepared both in terms of their own knowledge of mathematics and on how to teach it to provide effective instruction to their students (Ball, Hill & Bass, 2005). This effort becomes more challenging when the mathematics instruction has to meet the needs of students with mathematical learning difficulties who are exhibiting heterogeneous mathematical profiles.

Therefore, a key point for regular classroom teachers but even more importantly for the special educators, clinicians, or any math coach is how to tailor their guidance to the students with mathematical learning difficulties they are working with and plan the courses of their intervention taking into account the mathematical profile of each student with mathematical learning difficulties. Trying to meet this challenge after explaining the three instruction strategies (*explicit, use of heuristics, math flexibility*), we are going to suggest specific decision-making criteria about how to plan individual intervention courses by deriving elements from all the aforementioned instructional strategies. What we propose is not to select exclusively one instructional strategy but to compose the intervention cocktail that best fits the mathematical profile of each student.

So, although all the intervention courses will contain characteristics from all three strategies (explicit, use of heuristics, math flexibility), the allocation between them will differ among different mathematical profiles of mathematical learning difficulties. This is in line with the intervention conducted by Fuchs et al. (2016), who showed that combining explicit instruction with high-quality explanations resulted in improved content understanding, particularly for students with limited working memory. To describe the instructional strategy that would differently favour each of its components on the basis of the mathematical profile of each student with mathematical learning difficulties, we will introduce the term 'Flexplicit intervention strategy'. So, we will first describe extensively the principles of the 'Flexplicit intervention strategy', and then we will provide recommendations on how to apply it to students with different profiles of mathematical learning difficulties.

1.4.1 Components of the Flexplicit intervention strategy

1.4.1.1 Explicit instruction

Explicit instruction is a mainstay feature of many special education programmes. It is an evidence-based practice that provides teachers with a practical and feasible framework for delivering effective and systematic instruction. It includes teaching components such as:

- clear modelling of the specific steps to solve the problem by thinking aloud and using unambiguous explanations and demonstrations;
- pre-teaching prerequisite skills, presenting multiple instructional examples of the problem, and applying their solutions;
- providing immediate on-going and corrective feedback to the students on their accuracy.

Typically, teacher's models are delivered at the beginning of instruction when a new procedure or concept is first introduced. Effective teacher models show students *exactly* what math content they will learn and how they will apply it. So, when teaching a new procedure or concept, teachers should think aloud by using clear and unambiguous language to guide students through the steps required to solve the problem (for example, 'Today, I'm going to show you how to solve subtraction problems that have two-digit numbers', see Box 1.1). While modelling the steps in solving the problem on the board, the teacher should verbalize the procedures, note the symbols used and what they mean, and explain any decision-making and thinking processes (for example, 'This problem says fifty-eight minus twenty-three' (pointing to the minus sign), 'First we take away the tens, …', see Box 1.1). During the demonstration, the teacher engages students in the model (for example, 'Can you break apart fifty-eight and twenty-three', see Figure 1.1). It is very important for the students to be actively involved in instruction because their motivation to learn new content is likely to increase (Archer & Hughes, 2010). Students' involvement also allows the teacher to sense if the task is easy or challenging for the group or for a particular student. If the task is relatively easy, the teacher should praise the students for their involvement (Well done! Nice work!), and two or three instructional examples might suffice. In contrast, if the teacher's model seems complex and students lack prerequisite skills and knowledge, they will need additional support. In this case, the teacher can include in his/her model concrete materials (for example real euro coins, see Figure 1.7) or visuals (for example Montessori overlapping numbercards, see Figure 1.6), to support both students who find it difficult to follow the teacher's model or who do not have the necessary prerequisites skills (for example how to split up a two-digit number into tens and units). Guided practice by selecting supplementary materials will help students with difficulties to concentrate more and keep them on track.

> **BOX 1.1 Example of basic-level explicit instruction: the teacher introduces the decomposition strategy of subtraction between two-digit numbers by using the bubbles structure (Cooreman & Bringmans, 2004)**
>
> - "Today, I'm going to show you how to solve subtraction problems that have two-digit numbers by using bubbles. This strategy will lead you to do two-digit subtractions mentally".
> - "This problem says fifty-eight minus twenty-three" (pointing the minus sign). 58 – 23 = ◯ ◯ = ▢
> - "Can you break up fifty-eight and twenty-three?"
> - "Fifty-eight is made up of fifty and eight" (pointing to 58), "and twenty-three is made up of twenty and three" (pointing to 23).
> - "First we take away the tens, that is fifty minus twenty is thirty, writing the result in the first bubble". 58 – 23 = (30) ◯ = ▢
> - "Now I'm going to subtract the units, so if from eight I take away three I have left five. That's why I write plus five in the second bubble" (pointing to the + sign). 58 – 23 = (30) (+5) = ▢
> - "Finally, I'm going to find what I have left in total, that is thirty plus five is thirty-five, writing the final answer in the box at the end." 58 – 23 = (30) (+5) = |35|
> - "So, to solve the problem fifty-eight minus twenty-three by using the bubbles, first I subtracted the tens, putting the result in the tens bubble, then I subtracted the units, putting the result in the units bubble, and finally I added them to find the answer."

During initial learning and practice, the teacher provides immediate feedback to prevent mistakes in learning and allows students to ask questions for clarification. Consistent academic feedback reduces the potential for misunderstanding and helps deepen students' understanding of math concepts and skills (Doabler et al., 2012). Teachers should provide timely feedback since errors are easier to repair the earlier they are acknowledged (Stein, Silbert & Carnine, 2006). For example, when students answer 305 for the problem 58 − 23 = (Box 1.1), the teacher would ask them to represent both 30 and 5 numbers through the Montessori overlapping number-cards (see Figure 1.6) in order to help students understand their mistake and find out the correct answer. After that, positive feedback from the teacher lets students know that they are doing well so they can keep up their efforts successfully.

Once students can solve fluently similar easy subtraction problems (without regrouping, like 47 − 15 = or 64 − 31 =) by using the decomposition strategy (see also Chapter 4), the teacher can proceed to the demonstration of more complex problems following the same instructional steps. He/she could go one step further and for example either instruct how to solve subtraction problems with three-digit numbers without regrouping (for example 679 – 423) or with two-digit numbers with regrouping (see Box 1.2).

BOX 1.2   Example of basic-level explicit instruction: the teacher introduces the decomposition strategy to a more complex subtraction problem with two-digit numbers by using the bubbles structure (Cooreman & Bringmans, 2004)

- "But what happens when the units that I have to take away are more than what I have? Let's see such an example together."
  72 – 43 = ◯ ◯ = ☐
- "This problem says "seventy-two minus forty-three" (pointing to the minus sign).
- "First we take away the tens, that is seventy minus forty is thirty, writing the result in the first bubble." 72 – 43 = (30) ◯ = ☐
- "Now I'm going to subtract the units. I have two units and I need to take away three."
- "How many units am I missing?" 72 – 43 = (30) (-1) = ☐
- "I am missing one unit. So I write minus one in the units bubble" (pointing to the – sign). 72 – 43 = (30) (-1) = | 29
- "Finally, I'm going to find what I have left in total, that is thirty minus one is twenty-nine, writing the final answer in the box at the end."
- "So, when you subtract two-digit numbers by using the bubbles model either you write the plus sign (+) in the second bubble indicating the units you have left or the minus sign (–) to indicate the units that you are missing, then you do addition when you have units left and subtraction when you are missing units."

Doabler and Fien briefly summarized the highlights of the instructional sequence of explicit instruction as the following:

1. States clear expectations at the start of instruction
2. Starts instruction with a relatively easy instructional example
3. Limits the number of instructional examples
4. Uses consistent wording throughout the activities
5. Provides clear demonstrations and step-by-step explanations
6. Provides frequent practice opportunities
7. Uses math manipulatives to build conceptual understanding

8. Offers ongoing academic feedback
9. Provides cumulative review at the end of the third activity
(Doabler & Fien, 2013, p. 284)

Explicit instruction should be followed by a drill and practice phase. The goal of the drill and practice is for students to rehearse and practice math skills to improve fluency and automation. The provision of multiple opportunities to practice skills supports the automaticity of recall and proficiency, which leads to mastery (Fuchs et al., 2008). This could be done by using flashcards or computerized practices. Lessons should also incorporate a cumulative review (VanDerHeyden & Witt, 2005). Review can be in various forms: warm-up activities, computerized practice, and paper-and-pencil review (Fuchs et al., 2008).

An analysis of 34 intervention studies found explicit instruction to be more successful in 32 of the 34 studies reviewed (Adams & Engelmann, 1996). This is the case for students with mathematical learning difficulties as well. According to the Final Report of the National Mathematics Advisory Panel (2008), explicit systematic instruction improves the performance of students with mathematical learning difficulties and their transferring of known skills to novel situations. However, the panel noted that while explicit instruction has consistently shown better results, no evidence supports its exclusive use for teaching students with learning disabilities. The panel recommends that all teachers of students with learning disabilities teach explicitly and systematically on a regular basis to some extent and not necessarily all the time (Jayanthi, Gersten & Baker, 2008). Explicit instruction by itself may not allow students the opportunity to benefit from problem-solving discussions with teachers and peers. Math coaches, educators, or clinicians might consider ways to embed discussion within step-by-step instruction to provide opportunities for students to explain their mathematical reasoning. High-quality explanations may support content understanding and expose students to various solutions, thus leading to flexibility in mathematical thinking (Stevens et al., 2017).

1.4.1.2 Using heuristics

A heuristic is a method that exemplifies a generic approach for problem solving, solving an equation, computational skills, etc. Instruction in heuristics, unlike explicit instruction, is not problem specific. Heuristic models can be used in organizing information and solving a range of math problems. For example, a heuristic model to solve word problems can include specific steps such as 'Circling, Organizing, Sketching, Modelling, Operating, Scanning' (COSMOS) (Figures 1.1 and 1.2 for an illustration). This COSMOS model (Karagiannakis, 2015; see more in Chapter 5) can be used to solve any word problem. The heuristics models usually include student discourse and reflection about the step s/he is on or the next step that s/he should take.

C	Circle	the student (after having read the problem) circles the important information of the problem.
O	Organize	the student separates the knowns from the unknowns.
S	Sketch	the student visualizes the problem by drawing an image (sketch, diagram or table)
M	Model	the student invents a mathematical model, that will include the appropriate operations in order to lead to the solution.
O	Operate	the student executes the arithmetic operations included in the mathematical model created at the previous step.
S	Scan	the student checks the validity of the result reflecting on his/her sketch.

Figure 1.1 Example of a heuristic model of word-problem solving (Karagiannakis, 2015).

Another example of use of heuristics is the steps older students could follow to simplify arithmetic expressions, that is the order of operations: brackets, exponents, multiplication and division, addition and subtraction (BEMDAS). Figure 1.3 presents the steps that should be followed to simplify any arithmetic procedure by using the BEMDAS acronym.

The use of heuristics helps students to memorize the steps in solving a problem and can therefore help students who are struggling to organize their thinking, to know where to start; it can also help in decision making.

1.4.1.3 Math flexibility

Instruction in math flexibility is part of a contemporary trend in mathematics education. A key learning outcome in problem-solving domains is the development of flexible knowledge, where learners know multiple strategies and apply them adaptively to a range of situations (Star & Rittle-Johnson, 2007). For children with mathematical learning difficulties, it is unclear whether the same goals can and should be set. Some researchers and policy makers advise teaching these children only one solution strategy; others advocate stimulating the flexible use of various strategies, as for typically developing children. Peters, De Smedt, Torbeyns, Verschaffel, and Ghesquière (2014) investigated the use of the subtraction by addition strategy to mentally solve two-digit subtractions in children with mathematical learning difficulties. With this strategy, one can solve 81 − 79 very efficiently by determining how much needs to be added to 79 to make 81 (79 + 1 = 80, 80 + 1 = 81, so the answer is 1 + 1 = 2). They found that children with mathematical learning difficulties – similar to their typically developing peers – switch between the traditionally taught direct subtraction strategy (in which the smaller number is subtracted from the larger number) and subtraction by addition, based on the relative size of the subtrahend. These findings support the view that students with mathematical learning difficulties, or at least some of them (for example those with poor memory

The bases of a cognitive intervention 17

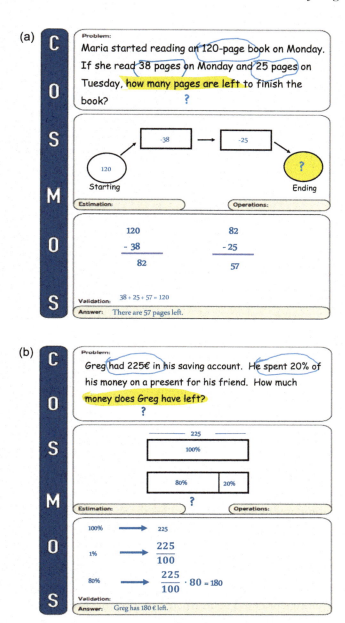

Figure 1.2 Example of use of COSMOS heuristic model to solve (a) a two-step change word problem using schema and (b) a percentage word problem using Singapore bars (see Chapter 5).

18 The bases of a cognitive intervention

$2 \cdot (4 \cdot 6 - 3 \cdot 5) + 24 \div (3 + 3^2) - 4 \cdot 2^2 + 1^3 =$	(B) E M-D A-S	**Highlight** & execute the operations within the **Brackets** respecting the order of operations
$2 \cdot (24 - 15) + 24 \div (3 + 9) - 4 \cdot 2^2 + 1^3 =$	(B) E M-D A-S	**Highlight** & execute the operations within the **Brackets** respecting the order of operations
$2 \cdot 9 + 24 \div 12 - 4 \cdot 2^2 + 1^3 =$	B̶ (E) M-D A-S	**Highlight** & execute the **Exponents**
$2 \cdot 9 + 24 \div 12 - 4 \cdot 4 + 1 =$	B̶ E̶ (M-D) A-S	**Highlight** & execute the **Multiplications & Divisions**
$18 + 2 - 16 + 1 =$	B̶ E̶ M̶-D̶ (A-S)	**Highlight** & execute the **Additions & Subtractions** from the left to the right
$20 - 16 + 1 =$	B̶ E̶ M̶-D̶ (A-S)	**Highlight** & execute the **Additions & Subtractions** from the left to the right
$4 + 1 =$	B̶ E̶ M̶-D̶ (A-S)	**Highlight** & execute the **Additions & Subtractions** from the left to the right
5	B̶ E̶ M̶-D̶ A̶-S̶	

Figure 1.3 Example of use of the BEMDAS heuristic model to simplify an arithmetic expression.

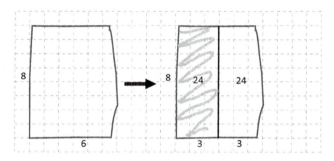

Figure 1.4 Find times tables facts by using visuals.

but average or high reasoning skills), can benefit from multiple strategies, challenging typical special education classroom practices, which only focus on the routine mastery of the direct subtraction strategy.

When a teacher demonstrates multiple strategies, he/she should lead the discussion in the direction of using strategies and facilitate discussion of the solutions provided by the students. Each student should be free to select a strategy for use, but the teacher should assist the child in discussing and reflecting on the choices made. For example when students are taught times tables, teacher can introduce alternative strategies for the students who are not able to store the facts in memory. The student could be instructed to solve the product 6 × 8 by visuals (Figure 1.4). A possible solution in that case is first the calculation of one-half, that is 'three eights' (3 × 8 = 24), and then doubling it to find the solution (24 + 24 = 48).

Alternatively, they could reflect on a table like the one presented in Figure 1.5, where it is highlighted that multiplication is repeated addition. So to calculate for example 6 × 8, that is 'six eights', you can start with an easy fact like 'five eights' on the number line, adding one more 'eight' or

The bases of a cognitive intervention 19

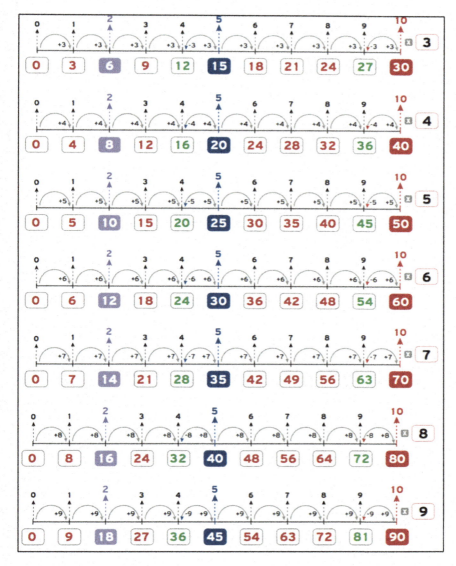

Figure 1.5 Find times tables facts based on the simple products (Karagiannakis, 2015).

jumping on one 8 to the right (6 × 8 = 40 + 8 = 48). Subsequently, let's assume that a student wants to calculate the product 8 × 9, that is 'eight nines'. Being aware of the commutative property of multiplication, she/he knows that 8 × 9 = 9 × 8. So, instead of trying to find 'What are eight nines?' she/he could try to find 'What are nine eights?' She/he knows that 10 × 8 = 80, so to find 9 × 8 (9 eights), she/he could subtract one 8 (jumping on one 8 to the left) from 80 (8 × 9 = 80 − 8 = 72). This approach is based on building relations between the simple number facts (e.g., times tables of 2, 5, 10) and the more difficult facts, so that solutions are built upon known (simple) facts rather than retrieved from the long-term memory (for children who have difficulties in memorizing facts).

Central to this intervention is the use of student think aloud. Students describe the reasoning behind the mathematical procedures they use each time to solve a problem. During the activities, students model appropriate mathematical thinking and verbalize their conceptual understanding of the material, thereby encouraging deep understanding and allowing teachers to provide formative feedback.

1.4.1.4 Other dimensions to integrate

In the Flexplicit approach described above, it is important to consider and integrate other components, in particular, using visual representations, students' verbalization, using multiple examples, giving feedback, fostering peer exchange and support, and supporting motivation in learning. This is what we will discuss below.

1.4.1.4.1 VISUAL REPRESENTATION

Visual representations (drawings, graphic representations) have been used intuitively by teachers to explain and clarify problems and by students to understand and simplify problems. When used systematically, visuals have positive benefits for students' mathematic performance (Jayanthi et al., 2008). Researchers have demonstrated that a graduated instructional sequence that proceeds from concrete to representational to abstract benefits struggling students and students with disabilities in elementary and secondary schools (Witzel, 2005). Visuals should be incorporated in the explicit instruction in order to make clear the procedure as well as to support students who lack prerequisite skills. For example, for the subtraction problem '58 − 23 =' presented above, the teacher could use Montessori overlapping number-cards to show how to decompose a two-digit number (Figure 1.6). By using the cards, the student can easily realize, both in a visual and a kinaesthetic manner, that 58 is made up of 50 units and 8 units and 23 of 20 units and 3 units.

Alternatively, the teacher could use concrete materials, for example real coins, to support students who still struggle with subtraction of whole tens and units or who find difficult to understand whether they have units left (Figure 1.7a) or units missing (Figure 1.7b).

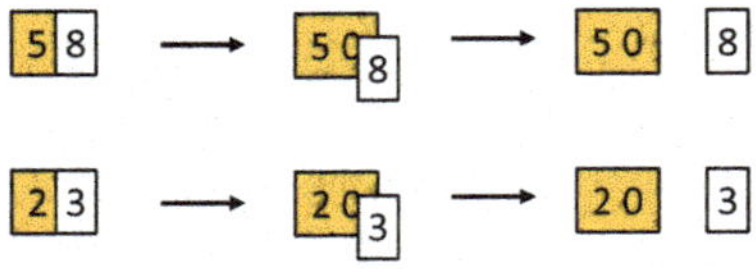

Figure 1.6 Example of using visuals: the teacher demonstrates how to decompose two-digit numbers by using Montessori overlapping number-cards.

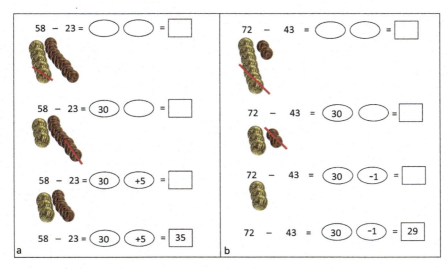

Figure 1.7 Example of concrete materials: the teacher demonstrates the bubbles structure to subtract two-digit numbers (Cooreman & Bringmans, 2004).

1.4.1.4.2 STUDENT'S VERBALIZATION

Encouraging students to verbalize or think aloud the steps of a procedure or their decisions and solutions is very important because it allows students to share their mathematical thinking and understanding (Kilpatrick, Swafford & Findell, 2001). Students can verbalize the steps of a specific problem (e.g., 'Fifty-eight made up from fifty and eight', see Box 1.1) following an explicit instruction or a generic approach (e.g., 'First I circle the numbers and important words of the problem and then…', see Figure 1.2) using a heuristic model. This can be achieved by prompting students to answer math-related questions (e.g., 'John, tell us why you put minus one (−1) in the second bubble', see Box 1.2). Verbalization can be used during the initial learning phase as well as when the students are solving or have solved the problem. The latter is very important when students solve word problems because the prompt to verbalize their solution motivates them to check if their solution makes sense. Many students with mathematical learning difficulties behave impulsively (especially when time limits put more pressure on them) and when faced with multi-step problems frequently attempt to solve them by randomly combining numbers rather than by implementing a solution strategy step-by-step. Verbalization may help to anchor skills and strategies both behaviourally and mathematically. Verbalizing steps in problem solving may address students' impulsivity directly and may facilitate students' self-regulation during problem solving (Jayanthi, Gersten & Baker, 2008). Teachers, as part of explicit instruction, should allow students to think aloud about the decisions they make while solving problems (National Mathematics Advisory Panel, 2008).

1.4.1.4.3 USE MULTIPLE INSTRUCTIONAL EXAMPLES

Math coaches or teachers should plan their mathematics instructions or remediation by selecting and sequencing their instructional examples. The goal is to select a range of multiple examples of a problem type. The underlying intent is to expose students to many of the possible variations and at the same time highlight the common but critical features of seemingly disparate problems (Jayanthi, Gersten & Baker, 2008). For example, while teaching students to subtract by using the bubbles structure (see explicit instruction), a variety of problems can be presented that differ in terms of numerical size (two-digit, three-digit numbers, ...), highlighting the common feature of subtracting and adding each time the numbers with the same place value (Figure 1.8a) as well as whether the amount of units are left, are missing or equal to zero (Figure 1.8b). The judicious selection of instructional examples that are easier to understand will especially help students with mathematical learning difficulties and ease them into more advanced math content. Teachers and math coaches are recommended, as part of explicit instruction, to carefully sequence problems to highlight the critical features of the problem type (National Mathematics Advisory Panel, 2008).

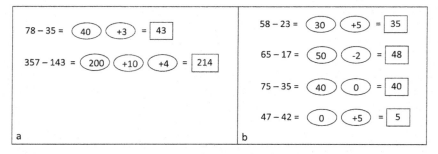

Figure 1.8 Illustration of use of multiple examples to teach subtraction through decomposition by using the bubbles structure (Cooreman & Bringmans, 2004).

1.4.1.4.4 PROVIDING ON-GOING FEEDBACK

One consistent finding is that providing teachers, clinicians, and math coaches with specific information on how each student is performing seems to enhance mathematics achievement consistently (Baker, Gersten & Lee, 2002). Providing an on-going formative assessment of students' level in mathematics to teachers can help them to monitor the progress of their students as well as to find the proper way to meet each student's needs. This can be done by implementing a range of formal and informal assessment procedures conducted by teachers/coaches during the learning process in order to modify teaching and learning activities to improve student attainment. Gersten and his colleagues (2009) found that providing teachers with specific information on how each student was performing enhanced student math achievement. Furthermore, giving formative feedback to special educators produced even stronger effects. Maybe this is because then special education teachers are prepared to use detailed student performance data to sketch out targeted intervention programmes. Taking into account the heterogeneity of students with mathematical learning difficulties, providing teachers with precise information on specific areas of students' strengths and weaknesses in mathematics has beneficial effects on their mathematics performance. However, greater benefits for student's performance will be observed if the formative assessment is accompanied with instructional suggestions about how to teach the next topics or fill the previous gaps (Jayanthi, Gersten & Baker, 2008).

1.4.1.4.5 PEER-ASSISTED MATHEMATICS INSTRUCTION

Cross-age tutoring (a student in a higher grade functions primarily as the tutor for a student in a lower grade) appears to work more effectively than within-class peer-assisted learning (Gersten et al., 2009). One reason for that may be that the older tutor is better able to engage the learner in meaningful mathematical discourse. However, practically, cross-age tutoring is more difficult to implement. In general, research shows that the use of peers to provide feedback and support improves low achievers' computational abilities and holds promise as a means to enhance problem-solving abilities. If nothing else, having a partner available to provide immediate feedback is likely to be of great benefit to a low achiever struggling with a problem (Baker, Gersten & Lee, 2002). Tutors also make sure to stress the strategies they used, both while students are working on the problem and after it has been completed (Woodward, Monroe & Baxter, 2001).

1.4.1.4.6 MOTIVATION FACTORS

In any case, a motivational environment promotes high levels of learning among all students (Fuchs & Fuchs, 2001). Unfortunately, students with mathematical learning difficulties (especially older students) have experienced failure and difficulty many times, which may cause some of them to avoid participating in the intervention. This partly explains the findings that students with mathematical learning difficulties benefit more from a teacher-directed approach where the student has to provide less effort. Thus, incorporating tangible (e.g., stickers, prizes) and intangible (e.g., motivating statements, positive feedback) motivators and reinforcements is key to successful intervention. As students become more capable and feel better about their math abilities, their confidence increases and they are more motivated to persevere, which increases their chances of success (Pool, Carter, Johnson & Carter, 2013).

To close this section, we will quote the conclusions proposed by Fuchs, Fuchs, Powell, Seethaler, Cirino, and Fletcher (2008), who define seven principles for effective intervention.

The first of these principles is instructional explicitness. Indeed, according to Fuchs et al., students with mathematical learning difficulties do not profit from programmes which rely on a constructivist, inductive instructional style. Rather, they need an explicit, didactic form of instruction, in which the coach shares all the required information for the child to learn.

Second, the remediation programme should be designed to minimize the learning challenge. The coach should be aware of all possible tricks that students might use or misunderstandings and avoid them by anticipating them and providing precise explanations following carefully sequenced and integrated sessions so that the achievement gap can be closed as early as possible.

Third, instruction should provide a strong conceptual basis for the procedures that are taught. The child needs to really understand the processes; otherwise s/he will forget them as soon as s/he is not using them anymore. For that purpose, the use of adequate manipulatives, of schemas, of number lines, etc., can be of great help.

Fourth, when a procedure is learned, it should be used many times to allow the student to really master it. So drills and practice are very important.

Fifth, end each of your training sessions with a cumulative review.

Sixth, students with mathematical learning difficulties have experienced repeated failure, and some of them have even developed math anxiety. It is thus very important to motivate the child. You can use graphs where they can see their progress, and you can use stars or other types of rewards. Your objective is to help self-motivation and self-regulation, i.e., helping the child to focus his/her attention on what s/he is doing.

Seventh, although some programmes have been shown to be effective in experimental study, it does not necessarily mean that they will be efficient for the particular child you are coaching. Therefore, on-going progress monitoring is key. It will help you to adjust the intervention to the specific needs of the child who is working with you so that the programme is in fact effective for that student.

This leads us naturally to the next section of this chapter that deals with the different profiles of students with mathematical learning difficulties and how interventions should be tailored to lead the student they are designed for to repeated success by building on his/her strengths as a way to compensate her/his weaknesses, while avoiding repetitive tasks that cause repetitive failure experiences (Karagiannakis & Cooreman, 2014).

1.4.2 Mathematical profiles

As described above, math learning disabilities can be caused by difficulties in basic numerical processing or in general cognitive areas such as language, memory, visual-spatial processes, or reasoning. Some numerical tasks place greater demands on some domains than others. For example, solving small calculations quickly requires having stored the answers in long-term memory and therefore calls upon the memory dimension, whereas solving a complex calculation based on the proposed answer for another calculation (for example, if I know that 35 × 6 = 210, what is 6 × 35?) requires reasoning skills instead.

In this context, Karagiannakis, Baccaglini-Frank, and Roussos (2017) created an evaluation battery in which different numerical tasks were proposed; each one was supposed to be more sensitive to one of the causal factors or domains mentioned above. For example, a task for positioning numbers on a numerical line was used to measure the influence of visual-spatial processes in numerical processing, whereas the mnemonic aspects were more solicited in a task of single-digit calculation verification (see Table 1.1). They administered this battery to a sample of 165 pupils in 5th and 6th grade, among whom 9 children had math learning disabilities and 12 others had poor performance. Analysis of these data showed that the tasks were well distributed in different factors, corresponding to the areas mentioned above, and that the children with low performance or math learning disabilities were distributed in different groups, thus showing that the causes of their difficulties were varied (see also, Karagiannakis, Baccaglini-Frank & Papadatos, 2014). An improved version of this battery has been recently published (Karagiannakis & Noël, 2020). This is the MathPro test, an online test with automatic correction (https://mathpro.education).

Table 1.1 Domains of the four-pronged model and sets of mathematical skills associated with each domain

	Mathematical skills associated with the domain
Core number	Estimating accurately a small number of objects (up to four); estimating approximately quantities; placing numbers on number lines; managing Arabic symbols; transcoding a number from one representation to another (analogical-Arabic-verbal); counting principles awareness.
Memory (retrieval and processing)	Retrieving numerical facts; decoding terminology (numerator, denominator, isosceles, equilateral); remembering theorems and formulas; performing mental calculations fluently; remembering procedures and keeping track of steps.
Reasoning	Grasping mathematical concepts, ideas, and relations; understanding multiple steps in complex procedures/algorithms; grasping basic logical principles (conditionality – 'if ... then ...' statements – commutativity, inversion); grasping the semantic structure of problems; (strategic) decision making; generalizing.
Visual-spatial	Interpreting and using spatial organization of representations of mathematical objects (for example, numbers in decimal positional notation, exponents, geometrical 2D and 3D figures or rotations); placing numbers on a number line; understanding Arabic numerals and mathematics symbols; performing written calculation when position is important (e.g., borrowing/carrying); interpreting graphs and tables.

Source: Karagiannakis, Baccaglini-Frank & Roussos, 2017.

The purpose of this type of tool is therefore to inform teachers, clinicians, and math coaches about the specific profile of the student they are coaching in order to help them adapt their intervention to this specific profile (Fletcher, Lyon, Fuchs & Barnes, 2007; Watson & Gable, 2013).

However, it is important to note that often, complex numerical tasks actually involve several domains at the same time. For example, research has shown that positioning numbers on a number line involves visual-spatial processes, understanding the number being presented, and reasoning (Gunderson, Ramirez, Beilock & Levine, 2012 or Simms, Clayton, Cragg, Gilmore & Johnson, 2016).

Table 1.1 thus presents different mathematical skills each associated with the domain that corresponds most to them, distinguishing here between basic or elementary numerical processes, the domain of memory, and the domain of reasoning, specifying the possible association of an important visual-spatial component. Although we are aware that, often, several domains are involved in the deployment of a skill, or even other cognitive functions not mentioned here, and that this involvement may change during the course of schooling (for example, solving a small addition problem involves reasoning in young students and then more memory in older ones), we think that this is a good starting point to encourage clinicians, teachers, and math coaches to consider a broad area of math skills in order to sketch the mathematical profile of each student.

1.4.3 Recommendations

Table 1.2 provides an overview of the components of the Flexplicit intervention instruction (see Section 1.4.1). The middle column briefly indicates the

Table 1.2 Overview of the components of the Flexplicit intervention instruction

Components	Use it to:	Support with:
A. **Explicit instruction**	• Clearly model the steps to solve a specific problem after pre-teaching any prerequisite skills	1. Concrete materials manipulation 2. Visual representations 3. Student's verbalization
B. **Using heuristic**	• Organize and memorize the steps to solve a range of problems • Facilitate decision making	4. Use multiple instructional examples 5. Provide on-going feedback 6. Peer-teaching
C. **Math flexibility**	• Facilitate the selection of the easiest/most efficient option between multiple strategies • Stimulate deep understanding and justification	7. Motivation factors

criteria for selection between the three main components whereas the last column includes supplementary instruction strategies that support any of the main components of the Flexplicit intervention instruction.

Table 1.3 shows, in a simplified way, different cognitive profiles of students with math learning difficulties. For each of these profiles, it is important to implement the three dimensions of the Flexplicit strategy. However, the emphasis placed on each may differ depending on the student's profile.

Table 1.3 Characteristic cognitive profiles of students with math learning difficulties

	Memory ↑	Memory ↓
Reasoning ↑	1	3
Reasoning ↓	2	4

- In profile 1, students have good reasoning and memory skills. If academic performance in mathematics in general is poor, see if the child has visual-spatial impairment that might negatively impact the processing of number magnitude or, if this is not the case, then look at reasons outside the cognitive sphere (e.g., lack of motivation, difficulties in the relationship with the teacher or with his/her teaching approach, etc.).
- In profile 2, students have good memory skills but a weakness in reasoning. For these students, begin by applying essentially explicit instructional strategies. The explicit instruction should be built through authentic materials (coins, tape measure, playing cards) and simple everyday scenarios to build meaning and experience success as fast as possible. Then use heuristic models to help decision making by using cues if needed. Stimulate generalization by presenting multiple examples. Although the traditional approach starts with simple examples, progressively increasing the difficulty level, in this case you could occasionally try the opposite. When for example a mathematical task contains many steps (for example simplify an arithmetic expression), present first a complicate example, which requires all the possible steps of the solving procedure. After the student masters them, it may be easier to solve simpler examples where fewer steps of the procedure are needed.
- In profile 3, students have good reasoning skills but poor memory. In this case use instruction to stimulate math flexibility. Focus on deep understanding of the procedures by using mnemonics, visuals, and/or manipulation of concrete materials kinaesthetically. Present multiple strategies stimulating decision making for the most economical choice. Then use

heuristic models to cumulate the multiple strategies supporting their weak memory skills. Promote the application of the school math topics on everyday problems, discussing with them 'how it works' and 'why it works', so that you attract their curiosity.

- For profile 4 children with weaknesses both in memory and in reasoning, follow the instructions of profile 2, that is, use explicit instruction built through authentic materials (coins, tape measure, playing cards) and simple everyday scenarios to stimulate basic numerical skills needed for everyday life. Present the strategy that is consistent and always works even if it takes longer than the optimal one. Use heuristic models to help decision making by using explicit cues. Stimulate generalization by presenting multiple examples. Although the traditional approach starts with simple examples, progressively increasing the difficulty level, in this case you could try the opposite. Present first complicate examples, which require all the possible steps of the solving procedure. After the student masters them it may be easier to solve simpler examples where fewer steps of the procedure are needed. Do not hesitate to give mnemonic tools to the pupils to help them to pass their exams.

Regarding the core number skills (see Table 1.1), students with good reasoning skills (profile 1 and profile 3) usually perform well on the corresponding tasks. Weak core number skills may be due to slow processing speed or to the fact that the students put in less effort or were less attentive when performing these basic tasks. Low performance on basic numerical skills together with efficient reasoning skills could also be due to deficient visual-spatial skills (see Crollen & Noël, 2015; Crollen, Vanderclausen, Allaire, Pollaris & Noël, 2015; Crollen & Noël, 2017). On the other hand, poor performance in core number tasks combined with weak reasoning skills (profile 2 and profile 4), indicates severe difficulties in understanding the meaning of Arabic numerals and in understanding the base-10 structure of the numerical system. In this case decrease the level of difficulty expected for the student's age and try to re-teach basic mathematical concepts and procedures to fill in the gaps; otherwise the student will always be delayed due to the hierarchical structure of mathematical knowledge.

Finally for students with weak performance on mathematical tasks where visual-spatial skills are mainly required (see Table 1.1), try to use compensatory material to support their difficulties. For example, use squared paper or structured worksheets to execute vertical additions and subtractions (for example, see Chapter 4, Figures 4.25 and 4.29) in order to facilitate the alignment of the numbers, use different colours for the different positional ranks of the digits in the number, etc. Highlight on 2D or 3D geometrical shapes those components the problems requests students to focus on (for example the diameter or the radius of a circle or a particular linear segment or angle of a geometrical shape). Provide support when instruments, such as a protractor, compass, or ruler, are used, where hand–eye coordination is involved (Karagiannakis & Cooreman, 2014).

References

Adams, G. L., & Engelmann, S. (1996). *Research on direct instruction: 25 years beyond DISTAR.* Seattle, WA: Educational Achievement Systems.

Alloway, T. P., Gathercole, S. E., Adams, A. M., Willis, C., Eaglen, R., & Lamont, E. (2005). Working memory and phonological awareness as predictors of progress towards early learning goals at school entry. *British Journal of Developmental Psychology, 23*(3), 417–426.

Ancker, J. S., & Kaufman, D. (2007). Rethinking health numeracy: A multidisciplinary literature review. *Journal of the American Medical Informatics Association JAMIA, 14*(6), 713–721.

Andersson, U., & Östergren, R. (2012). Number magnitude processing and basic cognitive functions in children with mathematical learning disabilities. *Learning and Individual Differences, 22*(6), 701–714.

Archer, A. L., & Hughes, C. A. (2010). *Explicit instruction: Effective and efficient teaching.* New York: Guilford Press.

Ashkenazi, S., Mark-Zigdon, N., & Henik, A. (2013). Do subitizing deficits in developmental dyscalculia involve pattern recognition weakness? *Developmental Science, 16*(1), 35–46.

Attout, L., Salmon, E., & Majerus, S. (2015). Working memory for serial order is dysfunctional in adults with a history of developmental dyscalculia: Evidence from behavioral and neuroimaging data. *Developmental Neuropsychology, 40*(4), 230–247.

Baker, S., Gersten, R., & Lee, D. (2002). A synthesis of empirical research on teaching mathematics to low-achieving students. *Elementary School Journal, 103*(1), 51–73.

Ball, D. L., Hill, H. C., & Bass, H. (2005). *Developing measures of mathematics knowledge for teaching.* Ann Arbor, MI: University of Michigan Press.

Ball, D. L., Lubienski, S. T., & Mewborn, D. S. (2001). Research on teaching mathematics: The unsolved problem of teachers' mathematical knowledge. In V. Richardson (Ed.), *Handbook of research on teaching* (4th ed., pp. 433–456). Washington, DC: American Educational Research Association.

Barbaresi, W. J., Katusic, S. K., Colligan, R. C., Weaver, A. L., & Jacobsen, S. J. (2005). Math learning disorder: Incidence in a population-based birth cohort, 1976–82, Rochester, Minn. *Ambulatory Pediatrics, 5*(5), 281–289.

Bartelet, D., Ansari, D., Vaessen, A., & Blomert, L. (2014). Cognitive subtypes of mathematics learning difficulties in primary education. *Research in Developmental Disabilities, 35*(3), 657–670.

Boets, B., & De Smedt, B. (2010). Single-digit arithmetic in children with dyslexia. *Dyslexia, 16*(2), 183–191.

Bottge, B. A., & Hasselbring, T. S. (1993). A comparison of two approaches for teaching complex, authentic mathematics problems to adolescents in remedial math classes. *Exceptional Children, 59*(6), 556–566.

Chodura, S., Kuhn, J. T., & Holling, H. (2015). Interventions for children with mathematical difficulties A meta-analysis. *Zeitschrift für Psychologie, 223*(2), 129–144. doi: 10.1027/2151-2604/a000211

Cirino, P. T., Ewing-Cobbs, L., Barnes, M., Fuchs, L. S., & Fletcher, J. M. (2007). Cognitive arithmetic differences in learning disability groups and the role of behavioral inattention. *Learning Disabilities Research and Practice, 22,* 25–35.

Clements, D. H., & Battista, M. T. (1990). Constructivists learning and teaching. *Arithmetic Teacher, 38,* 34–35.

Cooreman, A. & Bringmans, M. (2004). *Rekenen remediëren: droom of haalbare kart?.* Anvers: De Boeck.

Crollen, V., & Noël, M. P. (2015). Spatial and numerical processing in children with high and low visuospatial abilities. *Journal of Experimental Child Psychology, 132*, 84–98.

Crollen, V., & Noël, M. P. (2017). How does space interact with numbers? In M. S. Khine (Ed.), *Visual-spatial ability in STEM education. Transforming research into practice* (pp. 241–263). Ville: Springer International Publishing.

Crollen, V., Vanderclausen, V., Allaire, F., Pollaris, A., & Noël, M. P. (2015). Spatial and numerical processing in children with non-verbal learning disabilities. *Research in Developmental Disabilities, 47*, 61–72.

De Smedt, B., Noël, M. P., Gilmore, C., & Ansari, D. (2013). How do symbolic and non-symbolic numerical magnitude processing skills relate to individual differences in children's mathematical skills? A review of evidence from brain and behavior. *Trends in Neuroscience and Education, 2*(2), 48–55.

De Visscher, A., & Noël, M. P. (2014a). Arithmetic facts storage deficit: The hypothesis of hypersensitivity-to-interference in memory. *Developmental Science, 17*(3), 434–442.

De Visscher, A., & Noël, M. P. (2014b). The detrimental effect of interference in multiplication facts storing: Typical development and individual differences. *Journal of Experimental Psychology: Genera, 143*(6), 2380–2400.

De Visscher, A., Szmalec, A., Van der Linden, L., & Noël, M. P. (2015). Serial-order learning impairment and hypersensitivity-to-interference. *Cognition, 144*, 38–48.

Doabler, C. T., & Fien, H. (2013). Explicit mathematics instruction: What teachers can do for teaching students with mathematics difficulties. *Intervention in School and Clinic, 48*(5), 276–285.

Doabler, C. T., Strand Cary, M., Jungjohann, K., Fien, H., Clarke, B., Baker, S. K., … Chard, D. (2012). Enhancing core math instruction for students at-risk for mathematics disabilities. *Teaching Exceptional Children, 44*(4), 48–57.

Donlan, C., Cowan, R., Newton, E. J., & Lloyd, D. (2007). The role of language in mathematical development: Evidence from children with specific language impairments. *Cognition, 103*(1), 23–33.

Durkin, K., Mok, P. L. H., & Conti-Ramsden, G. (2013). Severity of specific language impairment predicts delayed development in number skills. *Frontiers in Psychology, 4*, article 581, 1–10. doi: 10.3389/fpsyg.2013.00581

Fazio, B. (1994). The counting abilities of children with specific language impairments: A comparison of oral and gestural tasks. *Journal of Speech and Hearing Disorders, 37*(2), 358–368.

Fias, W., Menon, V., & Szucs, D. (2013). Multiple components of developmental dyscalculia. *Trends in Neuroscience and Education, 2*(2), 43–47.

Fletcher, J. M., Lyon, G. R., Fuchs, L. S., & Barnes, M. A. (2007). *Learning disabilities: From identification to intervention*. New York: Guilford Press.

Friso-van den Bos, I., van der Ven, S. H. G., Kroesbergen, E. H., & van Luit, J. E. H. (2013). Working memory and mathematics in primary school children: A meta-analysis. *Educational Research Review, 10*, 29–44.

Fuchs, L. S., Compton, D. L., Fuchs, D., Paulsen, K., Bryant, J. D., & Hamlett, C. L. (2005). The prevention, identification, and cognitive determinants of math difficulty. *Journal of Educational Psychology, 97*(3), 493–513.

Fuchs, L. S., & Fuchs, D. (2001). Principles for the prevention and intervention of mathematics difficulties. *Learning Disabilities Research and Practice, 16*(2), 85–95.

Fuchs, L. S., Fuchs, D., Compton, D. L., Powell, S. R., Seethaler, P. M., Capizzi, A. M., … Fletcher, J. M. (2006). The cognitive correlates of third-grade skill in arithmetic, algorithmic computation, and arithmetic word problems. *Journal of Educational Psychology, 98*(1), 29–43.

Fuchs, L. S., Fuchs, D., Powell, S. R., Seethaler, P. M., Cirino, P. T., & Fletcher, J. M. (2008). Intensive intervention for students with mathematics disabilities: Seven principles of effective practice. *Learning Disability Quarterly, 31*(2), 79–92.

Fuchs, L. S., Malone, A. S., Schumacher, R. F., Namkung, J., Hamlett, C. L., Jordan, N. C., & Changas, P. (2016). Supported self-explaining during fraction intervention. *Journal of Educational Psychology, 108*(4), 493–508.

Garnett, K., & Fleischner, J. E. (1983). Automatization and basic fact performance of normal and learning disabled children. *Learning Disability Quarterly, 6*(2), 223–230.

Geary, D. C., Hoard, M. K., & Hamson, C. O. (1999). Numerical and arithmetical cognition: Patterns of functions and deficits in children at risk for a mathematical disability. *Journal of Experimental Child Psychology, 74*(3), 213–239.

Gersten, R., Chard, D. J., Jayanthi, M., Baker, S. K., Morphy, P., & Flojo, J. (2009). Mathematics instruction for students with learning disabilities: A meta-analysis of instructional components. *Review of Educational Research, 79*(3), 1202–1242.

Göbel, S. (2015). Number processing and arithmetic children and adults with reading difficulties. In R. C. Kadosh & A. Dowker (Eds.), *The Oxford handbook of numerical cognition* (pp. 696–720). Oxford: Oxford Library of Psychology.

Green, C. T., Bunge, S. A., Chiongbian, V. B., Barrow, M., & Ferrer, E. (2017). Fluid reasoning predicts future mathematical performance among children and adolescents. *Journal of Experimental Child Psychology, 157*, 125–143.

Gross, J. (2007). Supporting children with gaps in their mathematical understanding: The impact of the National Numeracy Strategy (NNS) on children who find mathematics difficult. *Educational and Child Psychology, 24*(2), 146–154.

Gross-Tsur, V., Manor, O., & Shalev, R. S. (1996). Developmental dyscalculia: Prevalence and demographic features. *Devevelopmental Medicine and Child Neurology, 38*(1), 25–33.

Gunderson, E. A., Ramirez, G., Beilock, S. L., & Levine, S. C. (2012). The relation between spatial skill and early number knowledge: The role of the linear number line. *Developmental Psychology, 48*(5), 1229–1241.

Hecht, S. A., Torgesen, J. K., Wagner, R. K., & Rashotte, C. A. (2001). The relations between phonological processing abilities and emerging individual differences in mathematical computation skills: A longitudinal study from second to fifth grades. *Journal of Experimental Child Psychology, 79*(2), 192–227.

Holmes, V. M., & McGregor, J. (2007). Rote memory and arithmetic fact processing. *Memory and Cognition, 35*(8), 2041–2051.

Hubbard, E. M., Piazza, M., Pinel, P., & Dehaene, S. (2005). Interactions between number and space in parietal cortex. *Nature Reviews. Neuroscience, 6*(6), 435–448.

Hanich, L. B., Jordan, N. C., Kaplan, D., & Dick, J. (2001). Performance across different areas of mathematical cognition in children with learning difficulties. *Journal of Educational Psychology, 93*, 615–626.

Jayanthi, M., Gersten, R., & Baker, S. (2008). *Mathematics instruction for students with learning disabilities or difficulty learning mathematics: A guide for teachers.* Portsmouth, NH: RMC Research Corporation, Center on Instruction.

Καραγιαννάκης, Γ. (2015). *Οι αριθμοί πέρα απ' τους κανόνες. Αθήνα: Διερευνητική μάθηση.*

Karagiannakis, G., Baccaglini-Frank, A., & Papadatos, Y. (2014). Mathematical learning difficulties subtypes classification. *Frontiers in Human Neuroscience, 8,* 57.

Karagiannakis, G., Baccaglini-Frank, A., & Roussos, P. (2017). Detecting strengths and weaknesses in learning mathematics through a model classifying mathematical skills. *Australian Journal of Learning Difficulties, 21*(2), 115–141.

Karagiannakis, G., & Cooreman, A. (2014). Focused intervention based on a classification MLD model. In S. Chinn (Ed.), *The Routledge international handbook of dyscalculia and mathematical learning difficulties* (pp. 265–276). London: Routledge.

Karagiannakis, G., & Noël, M.-P. (2020). Mathematical profile test: A preliminary evaluation of an online assessment for mathematics skills of children in grades 1–6. *Behavioral Sciences (Basel, Switzerland)*, *10*(8), 126. doi: 10.3390/bs10080126

Ketterlin-Geller, L. R., Chard, D. J., & Fien, H. (2008). Making connections in mathematics. Conceptual mathematics intervention for low-performing students. *Remedial and Special Education*, *29*(1), 33–45.

Kilpatrick, J., Swafford, J., & Findell, B. (2001). *Adding it up: Helping children learn mathematics*. Washington, DC: Mathematics Learning Study Committee.

Krajewski, K., & Schnieder, W. (2009). Exploring the impact of phonological awareness, visual-spatial working memory, and preschool quantity-number competencies on mathematics achievement in elementary school: Findings from a 3-year longitudinal study. *Journal of Experimental Child Pyschology*, *103*(4), 516–531.

Kroesbergen, E. H., & van Luit, J. E. H. (2002). Teaching multiplication to low math performers: Guided versus structured instruction. *Instructional Science*, *30*(5), 361–378.

Kroesbergen, E. H., & Van Luit, J. E. H. (2003). Mathematics interventions for children with special educational needs: A meta-analysis. *Remedial and Special Education*, *24*(2), 97–111.

Kroesbergen, E. H., Van Luit, J. E. H., & Maas, C. M. (2004). Effectiveness of explicit and constructivist mathematics instruction for low-achieving students in the Netherlands. *Elementary School Journal*, *104*(3), 233–251.

Landerl, K., Bevan, A., & Butterworth, B. (2004). Developmental dyscalculia and basic numerical capacities: A study of 8–9-year-old students. *Cognition*, *93*(2), 99–125.

Leather, C. V., & Henry, L. A. (1994). Working memory span and phonological awareness tasks as predictors of early reading ability. *Journal of Experimental Child Psychology*, *58*(1), 88–111.

Lyons, I. M., & Beilock, S. L. (2011). Numerical ordering ability mediates the relation between number-sense and arithmetic competence. *Cognition*, *121*(2), 256–261.

Ma, L. (1999). *Knowing and teaching elementary mathematics: Teachers' understanding of fundamental mathematics in China and the United States*. Mahwah, NJ: Lawrence Erlbaum.

Mammarella, I. C., Giofrè, D., Ferrara, R., & Cornoldi, C. (2013). Intuitive geometry and visuospatial working memory in children showing symptoms of nonverbal learning disabilities. *Child Neuropsychology: a Journal on Normal and Abnormal Development in Childhood and Adolescence*, *19*(3), 235–249.

Mammarella, I. C., Lucangeli, D., & Cornoldi, C. (2010). Spatial working memory and arithmetic deficits in children with nonverbal learning difficulties (NLD). *Journal of Learning Disabilities*, *43*(5), 455–468.

Mazzocco, M. M. M., Feigenson, L., & Halberda, J. (2011a). Preschoolers' precision of the approximate number system predicts later school mathematics performance. *PLOS ONE*, *6*(9), e23749.

Mazzocco, M. M. M., Feigenson, L., & Halberda, J. (2011b). Impaired acuity of the approximate number system underlies mathematical learning disability (dyscalculia). *Child Development*, *82*(4), 1224–1237.

Mix, K. S., & Cheng, Y. L. (2012). The relation between space and math: Developmental and educational implications. In J. B. Benson (Ed.), *Advances in child development and behavior* (Vol. 42, pp. 197–243). San Diego, CA: Academic Press.

Moeller, K., Neuburger, S., Kaufmann, L., Landerl, K., & Nuerk, H. C. (2009). Basic number processing deficits in developmental dyscalculia: Evidence from eye-tracking. *Cognitive Development, 24*(4), 371–386.

Morgan, P., Farkas, G., & Maczuga, S. (2014). Which instructional practices most help first-grade students with and without mathematics difficulties? *Educational Evaluation and Policy Analysis, 37*(2), 184–205.

Morsanyi, K., Devine, A., Nobes, A., & Szucs, D. (2013). The link between logic, mathematics and imagination: Evidence from children with developmental dyscalculia and mathematically gifted children. *Developmental Science, 16*(4), 542–553.

Morsanyi, K., O'Mahony, E., & McCormack, T. (2017). Number comparison and number ordering as predictors of arithmetic performance in adults: Exploring the link between the two skills, and investigating the question of domain-specificity. *Quarterly Journal of Experimental Psychology, 70*(12), 2497–2517.

Morsanyi, K., van Bers, B. M. C. W., McCormack, T., & McGourty, J. (2018). The prevalence of specific learning disorder in mathematics and comorbidity with other developmental disorders in primary school-age children. *British Journal of Psychology, 109*(4), 917–940.

Morsanyi, K., van Bers, B. M. C. W., O'Connor, P. A., & McCormack, T. (2018). Developmental dyscalculia is characterized by order processing deficits: Evidence from numerical and non-numerical ordering tasks. *Developmental Neuropsychology, 43*(7), 595–621.

Murphy, M. M., Mazzocco, M. M. M., Hanich, L. B., & Early, M. C. (2007). Cognitive characteristics of children with mathematics learning disability (MLD) vary as a function of the cutoff criterion used to define mathematical learning difficulties. *Journal of Learning Disabilities, 40*(5), 458–478.

Mussolin, C., & Noël, M. P. (2008). Specific retrieval deficit from long-term memory in children with poor arithmetic facts abilities. *Open Psychology Journal, 1*, 26–34.

National Mathematics Advisory Panel. (2008). *Foundations for success: The final report of the National Mathematics Advisory Panel.* Washington, DC: United States Department of Education.

Noël, M. P., & Rousselle, L. (2011). Developmental changes in the profiles of dyscalculia: An explanation based on a double exact-and-approximate number representation model. *Frontiers in Human Neuroscience, 5*, 165. doi: 10.3389/fnhum.2011.00165

Nunes, T., Bryant, P., Evans, D., Bell, D., Gardner, S., Gardner, J., & Carraher, J. (2007). The contribution of logical reasoning to the learning of mathematics in primary school. *British Journal of Developmental Psychology, 25*(1), 147–166.

Nys, J., Content, A., & Leybaert, J. (2013). Impact of language abilities on exact and approximate number skills development: Evidence from children with specific language impairment. *Journal of Speech, Language and Hearing Research, 56*(3), 956–970.

O'Connor, P. A., Morsanyi, K., & McCormack, T. (2018). Young children's non-numerical ordering ability at the start of formal education longitudinally predicts their symbolic number skills and academic achievement in maths. *Developmental Science, 21*(5), e12645.

Osmon, D. C., Smerz, J. M., Braun, M. M., & Plambeck, E. (2006). Processing abilities associated with math skills in adult learning disability. *Journal of Clinical and Experimental Neuropsychology, 28*(1), 84–95.

Peng, P., Namkung, J., Barnes, M., & Sun, C. (2016). A meta-analysis of mathematics and working memory: Moderating effects of working memory domain, type of mathematics skill, and sample characteristics. *Journal of Educational Psychology, 108*(4), 455–473.

Peters, G., De Smedt, B., Torbeyns, J., Verschaffel, L., & Ghesquière, P. (2014). Subtraction by addition in children with mathematical learning disabilities. *Learning and Instruction, 30*, 1–8.

Piazza, M., Facoetti, A., Trussardi, A. N., Berteletti, I., Conte, S., Lucangeli, D., ... Zorzi, M. (2010). Developmental trajectory of number acuity reveals a severe impairment in developmental dyscalculia. *Cognition, 116*(1), 33–41.

Pool, J. L., Carter, G. M., Johnson, E. S., & Carter, D. R. (2013). The use and effectiveness of a targeted math intervention for third graders. *Intervention in School and Clinic, 48*(4), 210–217.

Rourke, B. P. (1993). Arithmetic disabilities, specific and otherwise: A neuropsychological perspective. *Journal of Learning Disabilities, 26*(4), 214–226.

Rourke, B. P., & Conway, J. A. (1997). Disabilities of arithmetic and mathematical reasonning: Perspectives from neurology and neuropsychology. *Journal of Learning Disabilities, 30*(1), 34–46.

Rourke, B. P., & Finlayson, M. A. J. (1978). Neuropsychological significance of variations in patterns of academic performance: Verbal and visual-spatial abilities. *Journal of Abnormal Child Psychology, 6*(1), 121–133.

Rousselle, L., & Noël, M. P. (2007). Basic numerical skills in children with mathematics learning disabilities: A comparison of symbolic vs non-symbolic number magnitude processing. *Cognition, 102*(3), 361–395.

Rubinsten, O., & Sury, D. (2011). Processing ordinality and quantity: The case of developmental dyscalculia. *PLOS ONE, 6*(9), e24079.

Schleifer, P., & Landerl, K. (2011). Subitizing and counting in typical and atypical development. *Developmental Science, 14*(2), 280–291.

Schneider, M., Beeres, K., Coban, L., Merz, S., Schmidt, S. S., Stricker, J., & De Smedt, B. (2017). Associations of non-symbolic and symbolic numerical magnitude processing with mathematical competence: A meta-analysis. *Developmental Science, 20*(3), e12372.

Schneider, M., Merz, S., Stricker, J., De Smedt, B., Torbeyns, J., Verschaffel, L., & Luwel, K. (2018). Associations of number line estimation with mathematical competence: A meta-analysis. *Child Development, 89*(5), 1467–1484.

Schwartz, F., Epinat-Duclos, J., Léone, J., Poisson, A., & Prado, J. (2018). Impaired neural processing of transitive relations in children with math learning difficulty. *NeuroImage: Clinical, 20*, 1255–1265.

Schwenk, C., Sasanguie, D., Jörg-Tobias, K., Kempe, S., Doebler, P., & Holling, H. (2017). (Non-) symbolic magnitude processing in children with mathematical difficulties: A meta-analysis. *Research in Developmental Disabilites, 64*, 152–167.

Shalev, R. S., Manor, O., Auerbach, J., & Gross-Tsur, V. (1998). Persistence of developmental dyscalculia: What counts? Results from a three-year perspective follow-up study. *Journal of Pediatrics, 133*(3), 358–362.

Simmons, F. R., & Singleton, C. (2008). Do weak phonological representations impact on arithmetic development? A review of research into arithmetic and dyslexia. *Dyslexia, 14*(2), 77–94.

Simms, V., Clayton, S., Cragg, L., Gilmore, C., & Johnson, S. (2016). Explaining the relationship between number line estimation and mathematical achievement: The role of visuomotor integration and visuospatial skills. *Journal of Experimental Child Psychology, 145*, 22–33.

Skagerlund, K., & Träff, U. (2016). Number processing and heterogeneity of developmental dyscalculia: Subtypes with different cognitive profiles and deficits. *Journal of Learning Disabilities, 49*(1), 36–50.

Star, S. & Rittle-Johnson, B. (2008). Flexibility in problem solving: The case of equation solving, *Learning and Instruction*, *18*(6), 565–579.
Stein, M., Silbert, J., & Carnine, D. (2006). *Designing effective mathematics instruction: A direct instruction approach*. Upper Saddle River, NJ: Merrill.
Stevens, E. A., Rodgers, M. A., & Powell, S. R. (2017). Mathematics interventions for upper elementary and secondary students: A meta-analysis of research. *Remedial and Special Education*, *39*(6), 327–340.
Swanson, H. L., & Jerman, O. (2006). Math disabilities: A selective meta-analysis of the literature. *Review of Educational Research*, *76*(2), 249–274.
Szucs, D. (2016). Subtypes and comorbidity in mathematical learning disabilities: Multidimensional study of verbal and visual memory processes is key to understanding. *Progress in Brain Research*, *227*, 277–304.
Szucs, D., Devine, A., Soltesz, F., Nobes, A., & Gabriel, F. (2013). Developmental dyscalculia is related to visuo-spatial memory and inhibition impairment. *Cortex*, *49*(10), 2674–2688.
Träff, U., Olsson, L., Östergren, R., & Skagerlund, K. (2017). Heterogeneity of developmental dyscalculia: Cases with different deficit profiles. *Frontiers in Psychology*, 7, article 2000, 1–15. doi: 10.3389/fpsyg.2016.02000
van Garderen, D. (2006). Spatial visualization, visual imagery, and mathematical problem solving of students with varying abilities. *Journal of Learning Disabilities*, *39*(6), 496–506.
VanDerHeyden, A. M., & Witt, J. C. (2005). Quantifying context in assessment: Capturing the effect of base rates on teacher referral and a problem-solving model of identification. *School Psychology Review*, *23*, 339–361.
Vos, H., Sasanguie, D., Gevers, W., & Reynvoet, B. (2017). The role of general and number-specific order processing in adults' arithmetic performance. *Journal of Cognitive Psychology*, *29*(4), 469–482.
Watson, S. M. R., & Gable, R. A. (2013). Unraveling the complex nature of mathematics learning disability: Implications for research and practice. *Learning Disability Quarterly*, *36*(3), 178–187.
Williams, J., Clemens, S., Oleinikova, K., & Tarvin, K. (2003). The skills for life survey: A national needs and impact survey of literacy, numeracy and ICT skills. DfES Research Report No. 490. Colegate, UK: Crown and co. Retrieved from https://webarchive.nationalarchives.gov.uk/20130323042246/https://www. Retrieved from education.gov.uk/publications/eOrderingDownload/RR490.pdf
Wilson, A. J., & Dehaene, S. (2007). Number sense and developmental dyscalculia. In D. Coch, G. Dawson & K. W. Fischer (Eds.), *Human behavior, learning, and the developing brain: Atypical development* (pp. 212–238). New York: Guilford Press.
Witzel, B. S. (2005). Using CRA to teach algebra to students with math difficulties in inclusive settings. *Learning Disabilities: A Contemporary Journal*, *3*(2), 53–64.
Woodward, J., Monroe, K., & Baxter, J. (2001). Enhancing student achievement on performance assessments in mathematics. *Learning Disability Quarterly*, *24*(1), 33–46.

2 Basic numerical skills

In this book, we consider that basic numerical processes correspond to those that develop during the first five or six years of a child's life, that is, before he or she receives real mathematics instruction at school. In particular, we will consider the approximate number system (ANS), the subitizing, the verbal numerical chain, the counting, the understanding of the cardinal value of number words, and then, of Arabic numerals. We will explain these different processes and how they develop. We will examine the difficulties that may be encountered at these levels in children with a mathematics learning difficulty or dyscalculia. We will then synthesize the scientific work on interventions or the teaching of these processes. Finally, we will address the more clinical aspects, in particular, the evaluation of these processes and the concrete management of difficulties at these levels. A similar structure will be followed in the other chapters of this book.

2.1 The development of basic numerical skills

2.1.1 The approximate number system (ANS) and the object tracking system

Research has shown that many animal species, for example, monkeys (Brannon & Terrace, 2000), birds (Brannon, Wusthoff, Gallister & Gibbon, 2001), fish (Agrillo, Dadda, Serena & Bisazza, 2009), and even insects such as bees (Gross et al., 2009) show some sensitivity to numerical quantity. It has been hypothesized that this sensitivity has been selected by evolutionary processes because it allows animals, for example, to select the location (e.g., trees or flowers) with the most food or to judge whether a group of adversaries can be confronted or, on the contrary, whether to flee because there are too many of them (Dehaene, 1997).

In humans, habituation paradigms have shown that babies are able to distinguish between collections of objects of different numerical size. Indeed, they are able to distinguish between small quantities such as 1 versus 2 or sometimes 2 versus 3 (Antell & Keating, 1983), but also large quantities such as 8 versus 16, whereas they do not distinguish between a collection of 8 items and one of 12 (Xu & Spelke, 2000).

DOI: 10.4324/b22795-2

What explains these capacities and limitations? Current research suggests that two different mechanisms are at work. The first mechanism is called the object tracking system. According to Trick and Pylyshyn (1994), we have at our disposal spatial markers that allow us to locate elements in space and to follow, in parallel, their trajectory. This object tracking system would only allow us to track a limited number of objects in parallel (±4). This system would allow the baby to precisely discriminate between small collections (less than four elements) of n and $n \pm 1$ objects, probably by a term-to-term matching between the trace of objects in one of the collections (for example, 0_1, 0_2, 0_3 for three objects) and the trace of objects in the other collection (for example, 0_1, 0_2 for two objects) without representing the numerical quantity as such.

Later on, this mechanism would allow the implementation of the subitizing process, i.e., the direct and precise apprehension of the cardinal of small collections without recourse to counting (Kaufman, Lord, Reeve & Volkmann, 1949). Indeed, when small collections are presented, response times are typically short and almost constant for numbers from 1 to 4 and then, beyond 4, they increase linearly with the size of the collection. Indeed, we have the ability to perceive, in an almost direct and instantaneous way, the quantity of elements in small collections, whereas for larger collections (beyond four), we have to shift our attention to each object in turn and count them. On the other hand, if the collections are presented for an extremely brief time (for example, 200 ms), people are typically able to give the exact cardinal for collections of four objects or less, whereas for larger collections, the answers become less and less precise. For example, Starkey and Cooper (1995) showed that two-year-olds can correctly discriminate between collections of one to three objects even when one of them is presented for only 200 ms. This ability extends to collections of four items for three- to five-year-olds.

A second mechanism differentiates between larger collections through an Approximate Number System ANS (Dehaene, 1997). As the name implies, this representation is approximate. For example, Xu and Spelke (2000) observed that 6-month-old infants differentiate between 8 and 16 dots but not between 8 and 12. It appears that a difference of eight is not the criterion for distinguishing the two sets, but that the minimum difference is relative rather than absolute. In fact, young babies discriminate between two collections if they have a relation of 1:2 with each other (thus, n and $n \times 2$). Thus, young babies cannot discriminate between 16 and 24 dots but are able to discriminate between 16 and 32 or between 8 and 16. Some recent data indicate that this minimal ratio of discrimination evolves during development. For instance, in the auditory modality, 6-month-old babies discriminate 8 from 16 sounds (ratio of 1/2), but not 8 from 12 (ratio of 2/3), whereas 9-month-old babies discriminate 8 from 12 sounds (ratio of 2/3) but not 8 from 10 (ratio of 4/5) (Lipton & Spelke, 2003). Studies with children of different ages used tasks of quick comparison of two collections without counting and observed that children became increasingly able to compare collections of close magnitude

(Halberda & Feigenson, 2008). In adults, the largest discriminable ratio is of the order of 7/8, which allows them, for instance, to adequately compare collections of 14 and 16 dots without counting.

According to some authors, this ANS is the basis for subsequent numerical developments, and the degree of precision of this system, also called the acuity of the ANS, determines the degree of ease in this development (Libertus, Feigenson & Halberda, 2013).

2.1.2 Verbal counting: acquisition and elaboration

Around two years of age, the child will produce his/her first number words. S/he is learning a first number symbolic code: the verbal number system. This learning process is special because, in addition to knowing the words themselves, the child must also learn to recite them in a particular order to form the verbal numerical chain. During this development, the numerical chain will become increasingly longer; the child will be able to count further and further. This learning is done on the basis of memorization of the words but also, for larger numbers, from the discovery of the rules for combining the number words to form all the numbers (i.e., the syntax). In young children up to about six years of age, the comparison of successive counting trials produced by the same child reveals three parts in the sequences produced (Fuson, Richards & Briars, 1982, see box 2.1); a first part called '*stable and conventional*' is produced identically from one trial to another and corresponds to the expected conventional sequence (for example, 'one, two, three, four, five, six'), a second part called '*stable but unconventional*' is produced identically in all the trials by the child but the elements produced are not in the expected order or some of them are missing (for example, 'eight, ten, eleven'), and finally, a third part that is '*unstable and unconventional*', where the numbers are produced out of order and this part is not constant from one trial to the next (for example, during a first count the child would say 'thirteen, twenty' and another time, 'fifteen, thirty'). The acquisition of the verbal numerical chain up to about twenty thus results in the progressive increase of the stable and conventional part.

BOX 2.1 The different parts of the counting chain

Trial 1: *one, two, three, four, five, six, eight, ten, eleven, thirteen, twenty*
Trial 2: *one, two, three, four, five, six, eight, ten, eleven, fifteen, thirty*
Trial 3: *one, two, three, four, five, six, eight, ten, eleven, ten*

In blue, the stable and conventional part, in green, the stable and unconventional part, and in red, the unstable and unconventional part of the sequence.

Beyond twenty, learning changes in nature and is built on the discovery of the linguistic composition laws of the sequence of number names. In particular, the child understands that in order to produce numbers beyond twenty, one should say the word of the ten (or decade) and then a unit name starting from one to nine, and then move on to the word for the next decade and so on. At this point, it is common to observe typical errors such as omitting a whole ten (for example, counting correctly to thirty-nine and then saying fifty, fifty-one…) or to observe that children stop at a number ending in nine (for example, thirty-nine), not knowing what comes next. If you tell them the next number (in our example, 'forty'), they are then able to continue counting to the end of that decade (at least up to forty-nine in the example cited) (Siegler & Robinson, 1982).

In parallel to this acquisition of the sequence of number words constituting the verbal numerical chain, the child will also develop what is called the *elaboration of the verbal numerical chain* which will allow him/her to go from a verbal numerical chain where the words are undifferentiated to a more evolved verbal numerical chain. Fuson et al. (1982) described five levels in this development.

The first of these levels is called the *string level*; the numerical sequence corresponds to a sequence in which the words are not differentiated from each other. It is more of a litany 'onetwothreefourfive…'. At this stage, the number words have no meaning for the child.

The second level is called the *unbreakable chain*. This time, the words are differentiated (one two three four), and the child can match them with objects in a counting activity. This level is called the 'unbreakable chain' because the child must always start counting from 'one'. If you ask them to count from seven, for example, they will whisper the numbers from one to six before they can continue counting at seven and above. At this level, the highest ability the child can achieve is to count up to a given number. This activity is, of course, more complex than simply counting 'as far as you can go', since in this case, it is a matter of retaining the number presented as the upper limit and stopping once the recitation has reached it.

In the *breakable chain* level, the child can enter the verbal number chain from a number other than 'one'. For example, s/he can count from 'six' and recite 'six, seven, eight, etc.'. At this level, the child is also able to give the number word following another ('what comes after seven?'). S/he can also count from a lower to an upper bound; this type of task also involves remembering the upper bound and stopping the count at the right place. At this point, the child is slowly introduced to backward counting. Most of the time, s/he will use a loud or whispered recitation of all or part of the numerical chain forward to find the portion of the numerical chain containing the number n and, therefore, discover the number $n - 1$. For instance, to count backward from 5, the child first says 'five' and then counts 'one, two, three, four, five' and then says 'four!'. Then s/he again counts 'one, two, three, four', then says 'three!' and so on. These various trial-and-error steps will gradually allow him/her to count backwards more and more easily. Finally, at this stage, the child is also able to indicate which number comes before or after another, which allows him/her to determine ordinal relationships between numbers.

In the *numerable level* of the string, the number words are entities that the child can count. Thus, s/he is now able to count n steps from a number, for example, to count three steps after six (seven, eight, nine) or to indicate how many counting steps there are between two numbers (for example, 'to go from four to nine, I have to do, five, six, seven, eight, nine, so five counting steps'). In these exercises, the child must keep track of his or her counting of the number words. Children can count their counting steps on their fingers or by using a visual image in their head (for example, to count three steps from six, they imagine the three points of the triangle), or some use a verbal trace ('seven is one, eight is two, and nine is three'). According to Fuson et al. (1982), all of these methods of maintaining the counting trace must be learned in school (except, possibly, the last one).

Afterwards, the child will also have to learn other numerical chains, such as counting by two, by ten, by five, etc. These acquisitions will be very important for entering into multiplication, but also (as far as counting by ten is concerned) for the understanding of base-10.

Finally, the chain is said to be *bidirectional* when it is fully automated both forwards and backwards and the child can change the direction of his or her count quickly and flexibly, thus solving a problem in the most appropriate way. For example, to solve the subtraction 21 − 3, it is more economical to count backwards from 21, 3 steps. On the other hand, for the subtraction 21 − 19, it is more efficient to count forward from 19 until reaching 21.

2.1.3 Enumeration and the counting principles

Mastery of the verbal counting chain will allow the possibility of enumerating a collection, i.e., matching the recitation of the verbal counting chain with the pointing to objects of a collection in order to determine precisely the cardinal of the collection. Enumeration activities are already observed at the age of two (Saxe, Guberman & Gearhart, 1987). Young children naturally use these enumeration activities to solve small calculations. For example, by age four or five, a child who has three candies and is given two more will count the collection of these two sets to obtain the sum of 3 + 2 (Baroody, 1987). According to Gelman and Gallistel (1978), five implicit principles underlie the counting of sets:

(1) the *stable order principle* according to which number names should always be produced in the same order;
(2) the *one-to-one correspondence principle* according to which a verbal label (a number name) is assigned to one and only one object (one cannot count the same object twice, omit one, or point successively at two objects while saying 'se − ven');
(3) the *cardinal principle* which indicates that the last numeral reached in a count represents the cardinal value of the enumerated set (and not the last element pointed out during the enumeration);

(4) the *abstraction principle* which means that the homogeneous or heterogeneous nature of the collections has no impact on the enumeration activity and its result. We can indeed count apples and pears!
(5) the *order irrelevance principle* which indicates that the enumeration result remains the same regardless of the order in which the elements of the collection have been counted (whether one starts by counting the green or red beads, the elements on the left or those on the right, etc.).

According to Gelman and Gallistel (1978), these principles are innate. However, Grégoire and Van Nieuwenhoven (1995) showed that the principles underlying counting are neither mastered nor coordinated by five-year-olds.

In young children, counting is generally accompanied by pointing one by one each object of the set with a finger. This allows the child to keep track of his or her activity, and to distinguish between 'objects already counted' and 'objects yet to be counted' as the enumeration progresses. Thus, at age four, if the child is prevented from pointing at objects with the finger, s/he produces more counting errors. At age six, on the other hand, finger pointing is no longer mandatory to guarantee the quality of the count; visual pointing (i.e., fixing each object successively with the eyes) is sufficient (Saxe & Kaplan, 1981). From seven years onwards, more elaborate strategies appear such as counting by *n* according to the spatial organization of the items in the collection (e.g., counting by two if the items are in pairs) or such as adding the cardinals of different sub-groups of objects (e.g., faced with a collection, the child could distinguish between a group of four and a subgroup of three and determine that the whole collection is of seven objects by adding three and four). These two last strategies are used in more than 20% of cases at age 11 and in nearly 50% of cases at age 13 (Camos, 2005). It should also be remembered here that correct enumeration requires, at the very least, an unbreakable verbal chain (and not a string level). Finally, it should be noted that the most common errors in enumeration are coordination errors where there is no precise synchronicity between the pointing at objects and the enunciation of the numerical chain (Gelman & Gallistel, 1978).

2.1.4 Learning the cardinal value of number words

According to Fuson (1992), it is around the age of four that most children move from a count where each number word corresponds to the label of the object being pointed at, to a representation in which the cardinal principle is integrated, i.e., the child understands that the last number word refers to the cardinal of the entire set. However, the transition from the cardinal to the set, assessed through the 'give me *n*' task (for example, 'give me three carrots') will occur in a still later stage. In this task, the child must understand the cardinal value of the number *n* and understand that counting will enable him or her to meet the demand. They should also keep in mind the target number (e.g., three) and stop counting once they have reached it.

To understand the cardinal value of the number words is to understand what precise quantities the number words 'two' or 'four', for example, refer to. Typically, this understanding is assessed by asking the child to give 'n' items. Curiously, young children (around two or three years old) who are able to enumerate collections of six or eight items are often unable to give two or three items on demand (Wynn, 1992), as if they had learned counting procedures by imitation without understanding the deeper meaning.

It had been hypothesized that this understanding of number words was naturally achieved by matching the words of the child's verbal number string to the representation of the numerical magnitude encoded on the ANS. If this was the case, once the numerical vocabulary had been acquired, this matching should be done relatively quickly. However, understanding the cardinal value of the number words that a child knows and is able to recite in order is a slow process that takes more than a year! Moreover, this matching is not done just anyhow. On the contrary, it follows a very precise order. The first level of this understanding is achieved by children who are able to give one object on request, but make mistakes when they are asked to give two or more objects. These children (around three years of age) are called *one-knowers* because they only know the cardinal value of the word 'one'. A few months later, these children will be able to give two objects on request. They will have reached the *two-knowers* stage. A few months later, they will understand the cardinal value of the word 'three' (*three-knowers*), and then again later, the cardinal value of the word 'four' (*four-knowers*). Finally, there comes a time when children understand what is called the function of succession, that is, they understand that every time they say a number word further up in the verbal number chain, the quantity to which that number refers is the same as the preceding number, plus one. At this point, the child is then able to understand the cardinal value of all the number words s/he can recite in the verbal number string. S/he has reached the stage of *counting-principle knower*, i.e., s/he has understood the principle of counting (around the age of four years). Finally, the child will be able to match these number words with the ANS and only then, will s/he be able to estimate (i.e., without counting) the cardinal of collections and give larger number words for larger collections (Le Corre & Carey, 2007). Thus, the mapping between the ANS and the number words is not the basis for understanding the cardinal value of the number words, but is the result of it. For Carey (2001, 2004) and Le Corre, Van de Walle, Brannon, and Carey (2006), the development of the cardinal meaning of the number words corresponds to the creation of a new numerical representation, conceptually superior to the initial quantitative representations of the baby: a precise numerical representation based on the succession function.

The creation of this representation is probably based on the object tracking system (since its development begins with the understanding of the small numbers one, two, three, etc.) as well as on the morphological properties of the language such as the singular/plural mark (see for example, Almoammer et al., 2013). This new representation based on the succession function would make

Basic numerical skills 43

it possible to accurately represent all numbers, even large ones (and be able, for instance, to know precisely that seven is different from eight).

2.1.5 Mapping numbers to a spatial layout: the number line

Many studies indicate that our mental representation of number magnitude is supported by a spatial medium which, in western cultures, would be oriented from left to right with small numbers on the left and larger numbers on the right. For this reason, the ANS is regularly referred to as the 'mental number line' (Dehaene, 1992). This hypothesis is based on the observation of the spatial numerical association of response codes (SNARC) effect. This effect was first observed in a parity judgement task (and later in other tasks such as number comparison) where a number is presented in the centre of the computer screen and the participant is asked to press a response key on the left and one on the right to indicate whether the number is even or odd. Each key is associated with a specific answer (e.g., 'even') in the first part of the experiment and then with the other answer (i.e., 'odd') in the second part. It has been shown that participants are relatively quicker to press the left key when the numbers to be judged are small and the right key when they are large (Dehaene, Bossini & Giraux, 1993), showing that the representation of small numbers is associated with the left part of the space and that of large numbers with the right part of the space.

To assess how the numerical magnitude would be encoded on this mental number line, the task of *positioning numbers on a number line* has been widely used: ungraded lines marked at each end by a number (e.g., 0 on the left and 100 on the right) are presented to the child along with a certain number (e.g., 27), and the child is asked to indicate the position that this number would occupy on this line (e.g., where would you put 27?, see Figure 2.1). It appears that over the course of development, children become increasingly accurate in these estimates and that this accuracy is greater for small scales than for large ones. Thus, on a scale from 0 to 10, the absolute percentage error (i.e., the distance between the position chosen by the child and the expected position divided by the scale used) is 14% at the end of first grade and only 4% at the end of second grade (Pettito, 1990). On a scale ranging from 0 to 100, the absolute percentage error is 19% at the end of the first grade and 8% in third grade. Finally, on a scale from 0 to 1,000, the absolute percentage of error is 21% in second grade, 14% in fourth grade, 7% in sixth grade, and only 1% in adults (Siegler & Opfer, 2003). This increase in precision is not only related to the numbers used but also to the size of the scale. Thus, children are much more accurate when they have to place the same numbers on a scale from 0

Figure 2.1 Positioning numbers on a number line.

to 100 than on a scale from 0 to 1,000 (Siegler & Opfer, 2003). Parallel to this increase in precision in the task, there is a change in the curves representing the relationship between the number to be positioned and the estimated position. This curve is initially logarithmic, with better accuracy for numbers near the scale boundaries than others. Then, gradually, this representation becomes linear. This change occurs at different points in the child's development, depending on the size of the number lines used. Thus, for lines from 0 to 100, the responses of kindergarten children correspond to a logarithmic representation, whereas those of second-grade children are linear (Siegler & Booth, 2004). However, these same second-grade students show a logarithmic representation for lines ranging from 0 to 1,000. On the other hand, from fourth grade onwards, pupils show a linear representation for this type of numerical line (Booth & Siegler, 2006; Opfer & Siegler, 2007; Siegler & Opfer, 2003).

Numerous studies have shown that the degree of linearity of a child's responses correlates significantly with his or her performance on a global math test (Booth & Siegler, 2006; Siegler & Booth, 2004). In a recent meta-analysis, this correlation is estimated at $r = 0.443$, which corresponds to a robust effect (Schneider et al., 2018).

Several authors have shown that accuracy in this task is strongly related to the ability to use proportional reasoning, i.e., to divide the scale and use anchor points (Ashcraft & Moore, 2012; Rouder & Geary, 2014). For example, a child who starts counting by 1 from 0 to position 24 will have significantly lower accuracy than one who considers the scale from 0 to 100 by first dividing it in half to find the position of 50, then in half again to find the position of 25, and finally positions 24 slightly to the left of this last marker. In addition, this task also involves visual-spatial processing. For example, Simms, Clayton, Cragg, Gilmore, and Johnson (2016) observe in ten-year-old children that the degree of linearity in this task correlates with the visual-spatial and visual-motor integration abilities of the children, and that the observed correlation between the degree of linearity in the numerical line task and a test of mathematical performance is fully explained by these visual-spatial and visual-motor integration abilities.

2.2 Difficulties encountered in dyscalculia

2.2.1 *The approximate number system*

As mentioned in the first chapter of this book, various researchers have hypothesized that an impaired approximate representation of the number magnitude is the cause of dyscalculia, since they believe that all mathematical learning is based on this representation. To support their argument, they subjected children with and without math learning difficulties or dyscalculia to tasks comparing two collections of dots that appear briefly (so as to prevent counting). Some of this research has shown significantly lower numerical acuity in children with dyscalculia or math learning difficulties than in typical children (Mazzocco,

Feigenso & Halberda, 2011; Piazza et al., 2010), but a range of studies failed to find this difference (for a review, see De Smedt, Noël, Gilmore & Ansari, 2013). It should nevertheless be noted that in this type of task, the numerosity (or number of elements) of the collection necessarily varies with other parameters such as the size of the elements, the external perimeter of the collection, and the density of the elements, and these visual-spatial dimensions impact numerical judgements (see Gebuis, Cohen Kadosh & Gevers, 2016). This raises the question of whether it is possible to measure true numerical acuity since it is necessarily related to the physical characteristics of the stimuli used.

Rousselle and Noël (2007) and Noël and Rousselle (2011) proposed that the deficit at the base of dyscalculia is not to do with ANS acuity but concerns the access to the representation of the numerical magnitude from symbolic codes (for example, Arabic and verbal numbers) or the development of an exact numerical representation as induced by the learning of symbolic numbers (Noël & Rousselle, 2011). To support their hypothesis, these authors showed that children with dyscalculia behaved in the same way as control children in dot collection comparison tasks (or non-symbolic comparisons), but were significantly less successful (slower and more error prone) in Arabic number comparisons (i.e., symbolic numbers, Rousselle & Noël, 2007). Other researchers have observed this same dissociation (e.g., De Smedt & Gilmore, 2011). A recent meta-analysis (Schwenk et al., 2017) indeed shows that the difference in performance between children with dyscalculia and typical children is significantly greater in tasks comparing the magnitude of symbolic numbers (Arabic numbers) than when comparing dot collections.

2.2.2 Subitizing

Several studies have also shown that people with math learning difficulties or dyscalculia show a dysfunction in the subitizing process. For example, when determining the cardinal of very small collections, the response time slope (as a function of the number of stimuli) of children with dyscalculia is higher than that of typical children (Schleifer & Landerl, 2011). These difficulties have been interpreted as indicative of a problem in the recognition of canonical patterns underlying the subitizing process (Ashkenazi, Mark-Zigdon & Henik, 2013). Using the eye tracker technique, it has been observed that children with dyscalculia had to count items from very small collections while typical children processed them in parallel and thus relied on the subitizing process (Moeller, Neuburger, Kaufmann, Landerl & Nuerk, 2009).

2.2.3 Counting and enumeration

Little work has been done on the counting and enumeration capabilities of children with dyscalculia. With respect to counting, Landerl, Bevan, and Butterworth (2004) found that 8–9-year-old children with dyscalculia (whether or not associated with dyslexia) were slower than typical children to count from 45 to 65, in steps of 2 to 20, or backwards from 20 to 1, whereas no difference was observed for simple counting from 1 to 20.

These authors also tested children's enumeration abilities by presenting them with small collections of up to ten dots. For collections above the subitizing rank, they observed a slightly steeper slope in response times (depending on the cardinal of the collection) for dyscalculic children than for control children (Landerl et al., 2004). However, this result was not replicated by Schleifer and Landerl (2011) with collections of up to eight points in second, third, and fourth-grade students.

Geary, Bow-Thomas, and Yao (1992) were more interested in the understanding of the counting principles. They asked first-grade children to judge whether a puppet counted collections correctly or not. They found that children with mathematical learning difficulties showed a delay in their ability to differentiate between essential and unessential features of counting. For example, in front of a row of mixed red and blue marbles, these children thought that counting first the red marbles and then the blue marbles was not correct and that they should necessarily count from one end of the row to the other. These children also had difficulty detecting errors in double counting one of the items in the collection, especially if it was at the beginning of the series of items to be counted (Geary et al., 1992; Geary, Hoard, Byrd-Craven, Nugent & Numtee, 2007).

2.2.4 Number positioning on a line

Several studies have compared the performance of children with mathematical learning difficulties or dyscalculia and typically developing children in tasks involving number positioning on a number line (see Figure 2.1). These have shown very consistent difficulties in children with mathematical learning difficulties; they are less accurate and their responses show longer logarithmic representations than typical children (Geary, Hoard, Nugent & Byrd-Craven, 2008; Sella, Lucangeli, Zorzi & Berteletti, 2013; van't Noordende, van Hoogmoed, Schot & Kroesbergen, 2016).

In conclusion, difficulties in these basic numerical processes have been observed in children with dyscalculia or mathematical learning difficulties.

2.3 Intervention studies

2.3.1 Should numerical or logical aspects be dealt with?

The scientific field of children's numerical development was marked by the work of Piaget and Széminska (1941), who emphasized the importance of mastering logical operations (e.g., seriation, classification, etc.) in order to develop a concept of number. From this point on, major rehabilitation schools of math learning difficulties based their work on the logical skills of children with mathematical learning difficulties.

Clements (1984) decided to confront therapeutic approaches inspired by these Piagetian theories with approaches more in line with current conceptions of the child's numerical development. They divided 45 4-year-old children into 3 training conditions: (1) a 'Logical' condition in which the logical operations of classification and seriation were worked on using non-numerical dimensions, such as colour, shape, size, etc., (2) a 'Numerical' condition in which numerical counting and enumeration skills were taught (without mobilizing the processes of seriation or classification in any way), and (3) a control condition. In the first 2 conditions, 3 30-minute intervention sessions were offered each week for 8 weeks. To measure their effects, the authors took measurements before and directly after these sessions with tasks testing logical operations (i.e., classification, seriation, and inclusion tasks on non-numerical dimensions such as shape, colour, length of objects, etc.), number processing (by counting tasks, comparing the numerical size of two collections or of two oral number words and calculations), and a number conservation task that had not been taught. The authors observed that only children in the two experimental conditions significantly improved their performance. With respect to logical operations, both groups progressed identically. With respect to the numerical tasks, both groups of experimental conditions improved, but the children in the Numerical condition performed better than the children in the Logical condition. Finally, for the logical task not worked on in the two programmes (the Number conservation task), the children in the Numerical condition performed better than the children in the Logical condition at posttest. Thus, if working on logical operations does lead to an improvement in logical and numerical skills, training focused on numerical activities is significantly more effective and should therefore be favoured. The authors conclude that the enumeration activity provides the structure and the representational tool with which to construct logical operations, including classification, seriation, and number conversation. Therefore, the approach we will propose here is to focus interventions on numerical dimensions and processes with the hypothesis, supported by the results of this research, that this type of intervention should also lead to improvements at the logical level.

2.3.2 Global numerical processing programmes

Programmes such as Rightstart (Griffin, Case & Siegler, 1994), Pre-K Mathematics (Starkey, Klein & Wakeley, 2004), and Building Blocks (Clements & Sarama, 2007) aimed at fostering early numerical development appear to be somewhat effective. These are school curricula or programmes that are explained to teachers so that they can implement them in their classrooms on a daily basis. Research testing the effectiveness of these programmes has generally been conducted with students from disadvantaged socio-economic backgrounds and has shown that this type of programme leads to better numerical skills than traditional school activities. In general, these programmes are based on research that has described the stages of a child's numerical development.

Activities related to developmental progression are offered to preschool children to help them move from one level of thinking to the next. For example, the Rightstart ('Head Start') programme helps children develop skills in counting, comparing quantities, and dealing with number changes (additions, subtractions, etc.), and then integrating these different skills. In the Building Blocks programme, the idea is to 'mathematize' daily life activities to help children develop the concept of numbers (including counting, subitizing), arithmetic operations, and spatial and geometric concepts. These are therefore fairly comprehensive programmes that are implemented over several months and, therefore, their description is beyond the scope of this book.

2.3.3 Targeted numerical interventions

2.3.3.1 Training the ANS: the Number Race

Wilson, Revkin, Cohen, Cohen, and Dehaene (2006) were the first to develop a training programme whose objective was to stimulate the ANS in order to help children with dyscalculia. These authors developed a computer game, the Number Race. It is an adaptive game: the activities proposed are of increasing complexity, and the programme automatically presents the child with activities that correspond to the optimal level of difficulty for him or her. While the original goal of the Number Race was to improve the ANS, in reality, this programme is quite varied. It includes comparisons of object collections, symbolic number comparisons, activities that link symbolic numbers to object collections, counting, addition and subtraction activities, and linking numbers to space. This programme therefore goes far beyond the 'pure' stimulation of the ANS. Several studies have tested the effectiveness of this programme. Some had methodological weaknesses, such as the lack of a control group or the use of a control group that did not include any numerical activity. For example, Sella, Tressoldi, Lucangeli, and Zorzi (2016) offered Number Race to five-year-olds and control training involving drawing to other children. Not surprisingly, these authors found a greater improvement in numerical skills in the group that played Number Race.

Two studies have compared the effects of Number Race with those of another numerical game. For example, Räsänen, Salminen, Wilson, Aunio, and Dehaene (2009) compared the effects of Number Race with those of GraphoGame-Math in six-year-old children with mathematical learning difficulties. In both cases, they found greater speed in comparing Arabic numbers after training. However, this improvement was greater with GraphoGame than with Number Race.

Obersteiner, Reiss, and Ufer (2013) compared Number Race to another version of the same game, which they called the 'exact version'. In both versions, the exercises proposed are the same, but the initial version favours the implementation of approximation (a typical ANS process) while the second version favours the precise processing of the number. For example, in matching collections of dots to an Arabic number, the initial version may present a collection of nine randomly arranged dots and the numbers 4 and 8; the child must then choose the one that best matches the collection presented. This type of activity therefore promotes the use of the ANS. Conversely, the exact version favours a precise processing of number magnitude. For example, a set of seven aligned dots is presented to the child who must choose, from the numbers 7 and 8, the one that corresponds (precisely) to the collection.

First graders were invited to play one of these number games for ten half-hour sessions. The authors observed that children's numerical performance improved under both conditions, and more significantly than what was observed in a group of control children playing language-stimulating activities. However, children in the approximate condition improved their performance in approximate numerical tasks, and children in the exact condition improved their performance in exact numerical tasks. The authors therefore concluded that these results support the idea that we have two systems of representing numerical magnitude, one approximate (ANS) and the other exact, precise. This conclusion supports the view presented at the beginning of this chapter that children are born with an ANS and then develop a precise magnitude representation based on the learning of the counting system.

In summary, current studies do not show conclusive results in favour of the effectiveness of Number Race compared to other numerical programmes. On the other hand, it appears that working on a precise representation of number is necessary to have an impact in tasks that require precise numerical processing, such as most exercises in a math class.

2.3.3.2 Specific training of the ANS

More recently, a series of studies have developed training that is much more focused on the ANS and have looked at the effects of this type of training on arithmetic skills.

Park and Brannon (2013) were the first to publish this type of research. They conducted two studies with adults. In the first one, a control condition is compared to an experimental condition consisting of ten sessions of approximate non-symbolic arithmetic exercises presented on a computer; a collection appears and is then hidden behind a screen, a subset of this collection is removed or a new collection is added to this initial collection, then a third collection appears, and the question is whether it is larger or smaller than the result of the addition or removal operation. The authors show that practising this task leads to an improvement in performance in a test of multi-digit number computations (additions and subtractions) while no progress is observed in the control condition.

In the second study, the same experimental condition is this time compared to another numerical training condition, the ordering of triplets of Arabic numbers, and to an active control condition (focused on the knowledge of new words). Again, the authors observe a better progression in the arithmetic task after the training in approximate non-symbolic arithmetic than after the other two trainings. On the other hand, training in triplet ordering leads to a better progression in a triplet order judgement task. The authors therefore conclude their research by saying that stimulating ANS has positive effects on calculation.

Inspired by this research, Hyde, Khanum, and Spelke (2014) conducted two studies to demonstrate that stimulating ANS has a positive impact on young children's ability to solve calculations. In the first study, six-year-olds were divided into one of the following four training conditions: (1) approximate non-symbolic addition (of the same type as described above in Park and Brannon, 2013), (2) addition of lengths (two lines are successively hidden behind a screen, then a third line appears and participants have to judge whether or not it is longer than the sum of the two others), (3) comparison of collections (a collection appears and then is hidden behind a screen; another one appears; participants have to judge whether this last one is larger or not than the first one), and (4) comparison of luminosity (a coloured zone appears and is then hidden behind a screen; another coloured zone appears; participants have to judge whether this last coloured zone is darker or lighter than the previous one).

In each condition, the child receives 60 practice attempts. The calculation capabilities are measured after the first 50 training attempts and then again after the last 10 training attempts. The authors observe faster response times to the addition task after the two numerical training conditions (approximate addition and collection comparison), but very little effect on accuracy. It should be noted, however, that in this experiment, there was no evaluation of the children's performance level prior to training.

In the second study, seven-year-olds were divided into two training conditions: non-symbolic approximate addition and brightness comparison. Again, there was no pre-test, but rather a measure of arithmetic and reading performance after 24 training items, then after another 12, and finally after another 12. The authors observed better performance in the arithmetic test in the numerical training condition than in the brightness training condition and no difference between groups on any reading task. Note that the authors observed no interaction between time and condition. They therefore did not show a greater progression in arithmetic after numerical training, but differences between groups that may have been there from the start.

As Szűcs and Myers (2017) point out, there is no reason to exclude that these results are simply due to the fact that these 'interventions' direct attention towards the numerical dimension, which could already have an impact on arithmetic performance.

Finally, it should be recalled that several studies have not been able to identify deficits in ANS in groups of people with dyscalculia or math learning difficulties. Furthermore, it seems that learning a numerical symbolic code and performing accurate numerical processing (for example, learning arithmetic) promote the development of better ANS accuracy (Suárez-Pellicioni & Booth, 2018).

2.3.3.3 Training the representation of the magnitude of symbolic or of non-symbolic number?

Some theoretical models assume that our unique representation of the numerical magnitude is the approximate number representation (the ANS), which is the result of evolutionary processes (Dehaene, 1997). Other authors, on the other hand, hypothesize that beyond this ANS, humans also develop another numerical representation that is exact and based on the succession function and thus linked to the learning of a symbolic counting system (such as verbal numbers and Arabic numbers) (Noël & Rousselle, 2011). Based on this theoretical alternative, Honoré and Noël (2016) have compared the effectiveness of two numerical intervention programmes; one dealing with non-symbolic collections and thus closely resembling the above-mentioned programmes promoting the development of ANS, and the other dealing with symbolic numbers, in this case, Arabic numbers. In both programmes, children aged five to six years practiced two games: one in which they had to order three numbers (presented in the form of dot collections or of Arabic numbers) and to position numbers (dot collections or Arabic numbers) on a number line. A third group served as a control and received story comprehension sessions. After ten practice sessions, it was observed that the two numerical training conditions lead to better numerical development of the children than the control condition. In addition, symbolic training (i.e., with Arabic numbers) led to significantly greater improvement in the children's arithmetic skills than non-symbolic training (i.e., with collections). These results therefore show the importance of working on the symbolic and precise aspects of numbers with children.

2.3.3.4 Number line training

According to Siegler and Opfer (2003), to assess the child's understanding of numbers and the magnitudes to which they refer, the best task is number positioning on a line. Indeed, the accuracy (and degree of linearity) in positioning numbers on a number line correlates significantly with performance in a math test in first to fourth grades.

In order to encourage the development of these processes, Ramani and Siegler (2008) invented a numerical game in which the numbers from 1 to 10 are aligned on a horizontal strip (see Figure 2.2). The child spins a

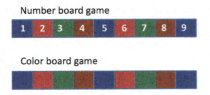

Figure 2.2 Number and colour board games similar to those used by Ramani and Siegler (2008).

roulette wheel (initially with only one area marked 1 and another marked 2) and must move his pawn as many squares on this strip as indicated by the wheel. As the child moves, he or she says aloud the number written on the squares he or she is using. For example, if his pawn is on square 4 and the roulette wheel indicates 2, the child says 'five, six' while moving his pawn to square 5 and then 6.

A large group of 4-year-olds was divided in 2 subgroups: one playing the Number board game for 5 sessions of about 15 minutes, and one playing the Colour board game in which the child turns the roulette wheel and moves his pawn to the next square of the same colour as indicated by the roulette wheel, while pronouncing the colours of the squares he touches on his way. The authors observed that playing the numerical game significantly improved (compared to playing the colour game) performance in a task of comparing the magnitude of two Arabic numerals, counting from 1 to 10 and naming Arabic numerals, as well as the accuracy of positioning the Arabic numerals on a number line marked 0 and 10 at each end. In addition, these effects were still visible nine weeks after the intervention.

The same types of game (a linear number game and a colour game) were used by Whyte and Bull (2008) with three- to four-year-old children and were compared to a non-linear number game. In this non-linear game, children used cards with collections of apples on the front and the corresponding Arabic number on the back; they had to estimate the number of apples, compare two collections, and then look at the corresponding Arabic numbers on the back to check their answer. Four 25-minute sessions were offered to the children. Only the two numerical interventions resulted in improved performance in counting, enumerating, reading, and comparing Arabic numbers. However, the intervention based on the linear number game was the only one to improve the quality of number positioning on a number line. The spatial dimension of the training therefore gave rise to an additional benefit.

Continuing this line of research, Siegler and Ramani (2009) examined the extent to which it is important for the number game to be spatially organized in a linear form by comparing three conditions of numerical stimulation: (1) the linear number game as presented in Figure 2.2, (2) the same number game, but presented this time in a circle device (with numbers from 1 to 10 inscribed as if on a clock), and (3) exercises in counting aloud, identifying Arabic numerals, and counting collections. Children aged 4 to 5 years, from underprivileged backgrounds, received 5 play sessions (approximately 15 minutes long). The authors observed that children's ability to read Arabic numerals from 1 to 9 increased significantly between the pre-test and post-test in both linear number games conditions, but not in the third condition. Furthermore, only children in the horizontal number game condition showed a significant improvement in their performance in comparing two Arabic numbers and in the number positioning on a line from 0 to 10.

2.3.3.5 Should we give priority to working on the number line?

Two studies have compared the effectiveness of an intervention based on the number line to another, based either on comparison or counting.

In the study by Maertens, De Smedt, Sasanguie, Elen, and Reynvoet (2016), training on the number line was compared to one based on comparison and two controlled conditions, one where children played a memory game and the other where they received no particular stimulation. It should be noted that the number line intervention involved placing an Arabic number on an ungraded number line, whereas the comparison-based intervention involved selecting from two Arabic numbers the one that corresponded to the largest magnitude. Five-year-old children received five ten-minute sessions of one of these games. The effects obtained were fairly moderate. They indicated a slight improvement in the children's numerical abilities following the two numerical training sessions and in the number line training only, an increase in precision in the number positioning on a line, i.e., in a task very similar to the one taught.

Friso-van den Bos, Kroesbergen, and Van Luit (2018) compared an intervention based on the number line to one based on counting. The first involved various activities such as positioning a number on a non-scaled number line or vice versa, saying the number corresponding to a certain position, and playing linear games of the type developed by Siegler in which the child moves his or her pawn on the game while speaking out loud the number indicated on the corresponding square. In the second training, based on counting, children are asked to count various elements (objects, clapping hands, etc.), perform counting exercises starting from a number different from one, etc. The pre- and post-tests included an addition task, comparing two Arabic numbers or two collections of dots, positioning symbolic (Arabic numbers) and non-symbolic (collections of dots) numbers on a number line, and counting tasks. Children (about five years of age) in the linear games condition showed no greater progression than the control group. On the other hand, children in the counting condition showed greater progression than the control group in counting, addition, and positioning Arabic numbers on a number line.

In summary, from these studies, there is not great evidence suggesting that number line training is the best and the only type to be used.

2.3.3.6 The importance of involving the body

Fischer, Moeller, Bientzle, Cress, and Nuerk (2011) have examined the importance of including a bodily, sensory-motor dimension in learning. They thus compared two training conditions proposed to young children aged five to six years old: one experimental condition integrating sensory-motor and spatial aspects and the other not. In the experimental condition, the children were in front of a dance floor on which was drawn a line marked 0 and 10 at the ends and 5 in the middle (in digits or dot collections). A digit or a dot collection appeared above the line and the children had to jump to the left of the mat, towards 0 if the magnitude was smaller than 5 or to the right if it was larger. In the other condition, children had to compare two Arabic numerals or collections of dots (one of which was 5) displayed on a tablet and press the one representing the larger quantity. Each practice consisted of 3 10–15-minute sessions. The authors observed better progression in the number positioning on a line from 0 to 10 in the experimental condition than in the control condition. However, there was greater proximity between this number positioning task and the sensory-motor training exercise than the control training exercise, which may partly explain the results.

In response to this criticism, Link, Moeller, Huber, Fischer, and Nuerk (2013) conducted another study in which they compared two trainings in number positioning on a line: one that largely included body movement, the other that did not. Indeed, in the 'body' condition, a 3 m long number line was stuck to the ground and the children had to walk on this line to indicate the position occupied by a number, whereas in the control condition, the children estimated the position of a number on a touch-sensitive tablet. A first analysis of the results of primary school children who participated in one of these two conditions indicated better benefits related to the body learning condition. However, a new analysis of these results showed that this difference was not significant (Link, Moeller, Huber, Fischer & Nuerk, 2015).

More recently, the importance of body involvement in learning has been tested by Crollen, Noël, Honoré, Degroote, and Collignon (2020). These researchers were interested in the kinesthetic dimension. They compared an intervention based solely on vision and another combining vision and touch. Small groups of 5-year-olds were given 3 sessions (20 minutes each) to learn how to solve small addition and subtraction problems. In the visual condition, the children saw the experimenter showing a first collection of marbles to which he added or subtracted a certain number, and the children had to find the result of this operation. In the condition combining vision and touch, the children themselves touched the marbles to make up the first collection, then removed or added the appropriate number of marbles and finally gave the answer to the calculation. In addition, in each of these conditions, half of the children were exposed to linearly arranged material and half to randomly arranged material. Results showed that after this intervention, children who handled the materials themselves showed significantly greater progression in their performance on an arithmetic task than children in the visual condition alone. The involvement of this kinesthetic aspect is therefore important to promote learning, at least in young children. However, the linear arrangement of the material did not really matter.

In summary, games such as those proposed by Ramani and Siegler (2008, see Figure 2.2), in which numbers are associated with a position in space, the Arabic number is associated with the corresponding verbal number, and where a counting of x steps from a number is taught, are useful, especially if their arrangement is linear. It is also possible that involving the body in these numerical exercises is beneficial. Finally, including the handling of materials with the hands is conducive to learning.

2.4 From research to practice: how to assess these processes?

Numerous tools are available to assess basic numerical abilities. For example, to test ANS acuity, Halberda, Mazzocco, and Feigenson (2008) developed an assessment tool, Panamath, which is freely available on the Internet (http://panamath.org/). The Symbolic Magnitude Processing Test is a paper-and-pencil tool that measures the comparison speed of two Arabic numbers (Brankaer, Ghesquiere & De Smedt, 2017), and the Numeracy Screener (Nosworthy, Bugden, Archibald & Ansari, 2013) includes both a fluency for comparing Arabic numbers and a fluency for comparing dot collections. The Examath 8-15 (Lafay & Helloin, 2016) also includes a dot comparison task. An accurate measure of subitizing is included in the TediMath Grands battery (Noël & Grégoire, 2015). Knowledge of the verbal numerical chain, assessment of its level of elaboration, enumeration quality, and knowledge of the underlying principles are included in the Tedi-math battery (Van Niewenhoven, Grégoire & Noël, 2002). The Zareki-R (Von Aster & Dellatolas, 2005) includes tasks for positioning numbers on a scale. The subtest 'Numeration', from the KeyMath-3, also includes some items assessing counting and enumeration (Connolly, 2007), and the Early Numeracy test (Wright, Martland & Stafford, 2006) is also a very valuable test. Several subtests from the MathPro test (Karagiannakis & Noël, 2020) are also of interest, in particular, the Dots Comparison (for measuring the approximate number sense), the Subitizing subtest, the Enumeration subtest (to test the child's skills in enumerating collections), the Single-Digit Number Comparison (to address the ability to understand the magnitude of symbolic numbers), the Next and Previous Number subtests (to assess the ordinal capacities), and the Number Lines. This list of tests is not exhaustive, and other tools will also allow you to evaluate some of these aspects.

2.5 From research to practice: a path to rehabilitation

Following the numerical development of the child, we will propose nine stages of intervention, knowing that it is important to verify where the child is in this development and to start guidance at the first level not perfectly mastered by the child.

2.5.1 The counting string

The first step concerns the counting string. It is not only a question of reinforcing the recitation of the sequence of number names with the child, but also of encouraging the progressive elaboration of this sequence. Indeed, a correct enumeration requires a level of elaboration corresponding at least to the level of the unbreakable numerical chain, i.e., the child is able to distinguish the various number words making up the numerical chain. Furthermore, in order for the enunciation of the numerical chain to be coordinated with object pointing, these two activities must follow a similar rhythm. To promote this acquisition, the child can be taught to recite the number chain by following a fairly slow metronome, or by following the rhythm of the math coach clapping hands or hitting feet on the ground.

2.5.2 Enumeration

Begin with the enumeration of small quantity arranged linearly with some space between items, so that the quality of the coordination between verbal counting and object pointing can be clearly observed. If the rhythms of the two activities do not match, work on the rhythm of each component separately. For example, have the child take turns pointing to each object at the regular rhythm of your handclaps. By working in this way, we were able to allow a six-year-old girl to correct her difficulties in verbal counting-pointing coordination (see Box 2.2).

BOX 2.2 A clinical example of an enumeration rehabilitation

In our clinical practice, we performed an intervention with a six-year-old girl in first grade who had difficulties in counting and enumeration for which she scored 0/10 and 5/11 respectively (i.e., scores below the cumulative percentage of 5) on the Tedi-math battery (Van Niewenhoven, Grégoire & Noël, 2002). A more detailed evaluation of these processes (see Table 2.1) showed some difficulties in object pointing, especially when the collections were arranged randomly, difficulties in counting both in terms of the acquisition of the counting string itself, but also in terms of its level of elaboration, and difficulties in enumeration, regardless of the sensory modality in which the stimuli were presented (visual or auditory).

We worked on these two components in isolation. At the counting level, the child was able to recite the verbal numerical chain up to 20, but we wanted to help her develop her level of elaboration. Thus, we asked her to recite the chain while inserting a gesture (clapping hands) between each number, then a longer gesture (clapping twice), then by inserting a sound between the words, longer and longer, then by reciting the verbal numerical chain in alternation with the math coach (the child says 'one', the math coach says 'two', the child says 'three etc').

To work on the pointing, we proposed exercises for pointing at objects in a collection after having dipped her finger in the paint, which made it possible to leave a visible trace on the objects already pointed at and to differentiate them from those which were not yet pointed at. The task was gradually made more complex by making the paint lighter and lighter and then not using it anymore, considering collections of increasing size

Table 2.1 Child's performance (number of correct trials out of the number of trials) before and after the intervention on counting, pointing, and enumeration tasks

Tasks	Before intervention	After intervention
Pointing		
• 10 to 20 linearly arranged stimuli	4/5	5/5
• 10 to 20 randomly arranged stimuli	3/5	5/5
Counting		
• Up to 20	0/5	4/5
• Starting from a number different than one	1/5	5/5
• Up to a given number	3/5	5/5
• From a number and up to another number	1/5	4/5
• Backwards	0/5	1/5
Enumeration		
• 10 to 20 linearly arranged stimuli	2/5	5/5
• 10 to 20 randomly arranged stimuli	0/5	4/5
• 10 to 20 regular sounds	2/4	3/4
• 10 to 20 irregular sounds	2/4	4/4
Total (%) accuracy in enumeration	33%	89%

and moving from linear arrangements of collections to arrangements in rectangles, circles, and then random.

We also worked on rhythm (clapping hands at the same rhythm as the coach, following a rhythm at the level of gesture, at the level of sounds).

Before and after the ten rehabilitation sessions, we measured the child's performance (see Table 2.1) and noted progress in the taught processes (i.e., object pointing and counting) but not in counting backwards, which was not worked on. Furthermore, it was observed that improvement in these two components led to an improvement in the enumeration process itself.

To promote understanding of the cardinality principle, offer small collections in the subitizing range and presented in canonical form (like the faces of a dice), so that the child can 'perceive' that the last word pronounced during its enumeration corresponds to the cardinal of the collection. After each count, ask the question, 'How many in total?' and make sure the child knows that the cardinal is the entire collection (the coach says: 'yes, there are four in total, there are four rabbits' while circling the entire collection) and not the last item pointed at.

58 *Basic numerical skills*

Once this principle has been learned, help the child understand the order irrelevance principle. Again, start with small collections. Have the child count the number of items in the collection (from left to right, from right to left, blue and then red, red and then blue) and check with the child that each time the cardinal remains the same.

Another possible difficulty in collection counting is the spatial marking of the elements, which makes it possible to distinguish elements already counted from elements not yet counted. This type of difficulty should not (or only slightly) be observed when items in the collection are lined up, but may occur when larger collections are randomly presented. In this case, you can suggest that the child cross out the items already counted with a felt marker to have a visible trace. You can also encourage the child to use more systematic collection scanning strategies to help visually mark items. This systematic scanning can go from left to right and bottom to top, or it can follow the 'imaginary' line of the collection that the child could draw with his or her finger beforehand (see Figure 2.3). The most important thing is that the child's count is correct. If the child has visual-spatial difficulties and the marking of items already counted remains problematic when the collections are arranged randomly, offer to always use an external aid such as crossing out each item already counted with a pencil and use collections of 3-D objects that can be moved around; this way, during the counting process, the child can physically set aside each item counted so as to clearly distinguish the objects already counted from those that are still to be counted.

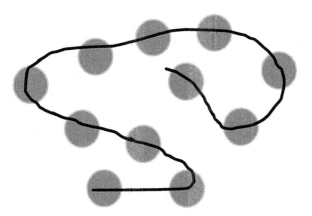

Figure 2.3 Organize the scanning of a randomly arranged collection along a path.

2.5.3 *The cardinal value of the number words*

Alternate counting exercises with give-me exercises. For the latter, it is important to start with very small numbers and gradually progress to larger numbers (up to ten). Encourage the child to memorize the target number (by repeating it several times) before beginning to count.

2.5.4 Fingers as a tool for number representation

Finger configurations are another code to represent numerical magnitudes. This code does not develop naturally in children (indeed, it is not present in the vast majority of people who are blind from birth, see Crollen, Noël, Seron, Mahau, Lepore & Collignon, 2014), and developing this code is important in early calculations (see Jordan, Kaplan, Ramineni & Locuniak, 2008).

Show the child how to count on the fingers of the hand. Several methods exist. In our cultures, counting is usually done by lifting the fingers and starting with the thumb. However, depending on the morphology of each person, the number 4 may correspond to a position that is not easy to take and maintain. A variation may be to raise the four long fingers and lower the thumb (see Figure 2.4). Again, it will be helpful to propose exercises where you ask the child to raise *n* fingers or to show *n* with his/her fingers or exercises where you show a configuration of fingers and the child has to tell you, as fast as possible, how many fingers are raised. Emphasize that when you go further up in the verbal numerical chain, it means you lift one more finger on your hand. The idea is to gradually promote a canonical numerical representation that allows the child to recognize 'directly' that you are showing *n* fingers without having to count them.

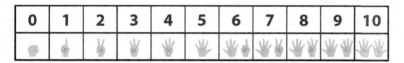

Figure 2.4 Number representation with the fingers.

Start with numbers from zero to five using only one hand. When the child is comfortable, i.e., can quickly and without counting determine the number of fingers raised and can easily lift the number of fingers requested, then you can introduce numbers up to ten. It is important to include the number zero as well so that the child understands that it is referring to a quantity representing 'nothing at all' or 'none'.

2.5.5 Connecting symbolic numbers with their number magnitude meaning

Using a variety of materials, promote the link between symbolic numbers (spoken verbal numbers and Arabic numerals) and the quantity they represent. For example, after counting a collection aloud, write the Arabic numeral corresponding to the cardinal. Also do the reverse exercise; give the child an Arabic numeral and ask him or her to read aloud the number and then to give this many items. For example, show the number '2' without saying the corresponding word and ask the child to read the number and give you 'this many' marbles. Work with one number at a time, starting with the smallest to the largest. As soon as you have worked with two different numbers (for example, 1 and 2), use the same exercises alternating between the two numbers; then work on 3. When the child has successfully completed the exercises, then mix the numbers 1, 2, and 3 in the following exercises, etc. Continue until all the numbers up to 10 are read correctly and understood by the child.

Playing cards can be used as good revision materials. First, once you have worked on the numbers from 1 to 5, select the cards corresponding to the values from 1 to 5 (using the ace to represent the 1). Shuffle this pack of 20 cards and ask the child to say the number written on the card as quickly as possible. This material is efficient because it corresponds to everyday material, but also because, if the child gets the name of the number wrong or doesn't know the name anymore, s/he can count the collection on the card. The arrangement of the number cards' symbols facilitates the cardinal principle whereas the fact that each number is represented through four different symbols (♣♦♥♠) supports the abstract principle. Measure the time and encourage the child to go as fast as possible without making mistakes. From day to day, s/he will be able to see his/her progress by looking at the graph of his/her response times you will create with him/her or by receiving a sticker each time s/he is faster than the previous time. Once the numbers from 1 to 10 have been worked on, then select the 40 cards corresponding to the values from 1 to 10 and perform this exercise on a regular basis. In addition to reading Arabic numbers, this exercise also gradually familiarizes the child with canonical configurations beyond the subitizing range (beyond four). These exercises therefore enable him/her to establish connections between the Arabic number, the collection, and the number word.

2.5.6 Relationships between numbers

Beyond the meaning of each symbolic number, it is also important to be able to establish relationships between these numbers: which one comes before or after a number? Which is the one that represents the greatest magnitude?

For the aspect of ordinality, you can write each Arabic number on the steps of a staircase so that the smallest number is the lowest and the numerical magnitudes increase as the corresponding stair steps get higher (see Figure 2.5). You can also use a horizontal strip of paper (possibly glued to the floor) with squares in which the Arabic numbers from the smallest to the largest are written, but our clinical experience suggests that the association between 'higher' and 'bigger number' is more meaningful to children than the association of 'right' and 'bigger number'. You can then play games in which you ask the child to go to the square or step corresponding to the number n (for example, step 5) and then to tell you, what is the number that comes next or just before. This will encourage the

Basic numerical skills 61

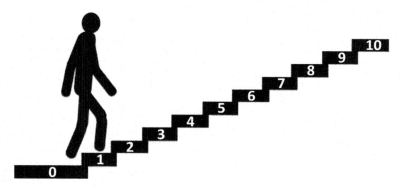

Figure 2.5 Presentation of numbers on the stairs.

construction of a breakable counting chain, an important prerequisite for more mature calculation strategies (see Chapter 3). You can then ask the child to stand on the step/number and then go up n steps by saying the corresponding numbers, or go down n steps by reciting the corresponding numbers. In this way, you gradually allow him to reach the level of the numerable chain. Counting backwards by going down the stairs is also very important, especially for performing subtractions (see Chapter 3). Going down the stairs faster and faster by reciting the corresponding number names gradually allows the automation of the countdown numerical chain.

When the child masters these exercises with ease, you can gradually remove certain numbers from the stair steps and thus gradually blur the clues. Afterwards, you can simply work on the desk by referring to the stairs (for example, 'if you are on step 5 and you go up three more steps, can you tell me the names of the corresponding numbers?'). One of the particular difficulties in exercises such as 'counting n from a number', or 'counting n downward from a number', is that it is double counting: counting the number of counting steps while reciting aloud the number chain. This way, you can start with small numbers of counting steps (± 1 or ± 2). Then you can explain to the child that the fingers can be used to keep track of his count.

You can also use horizontal number lines and play games such as those used by Siegler (see Figure 2.2) in which the child spins a wheel and moves forward as many squares in the game while saying the names of the numbers corresponding to the squares s/he passes over. Start with a wheel with just the numbers 1 and 2 marked; then after, you can use wheel with numbers from 1 to 4.

This aspect of ordinality can also be taught with card games. Give the child all the cards from 1 (ace) to 10 and ask him or her to arrange them in ascending order (see Figure 2.6). Ask them how they know that n is before $n + 1$ (for example, that 5 is before 6). The answer can be based on the ordinal aspect of the number sequence ('when you count you say "five" and then you say "six", so the five card is first and the six card is second'). Also invite him/her

62 *Basic numerical skills*

Figure 2.6 Arrangement of cards in ascending order.

to look at the collections and observe that $n + 1$ corresponds to the previous quantity (n) plus one. So in six, for example, I already have five and I still have one more.

With the cards, you can also practice the ordinality aspect by asking the child to give the number word after or before the number on the card. Shuffle the cards from 1 to 10 and ask the child to say the number above the number on the card as quickly as possible. If the child makes mistakes, ask them to return to the series of cards organized from 1 to 10. If the child can give correct answers, invite him/her to go faster and faster by measuring his/her time with a stopwatch and positively reinforcing each attempt where the previous time is beaten. Then you can play the reverse game by asking him/her to give the previous number each time. In this case, if the child does not know, offer to hide one of the symbols (a heart, square, clover, or spade icon) on the card and count the remaining number (see Figure 2.7). This explicit instruction will promote a correct response and a deeper understanding of this aspect of ordinality. Of course, it will penalize the response time, and the repetition of this exercise will be necessary to create an automation of the process.

Then propose comparison games using the cards. Give the pile of cards to the child with the exception of cards of a certain level (e.g., 5 cards). Place a card of that level (for example, the 5 of clubs) in the centre of the table. Shuffle the deck of cards (1 to 10) by asking the child to put the cards with smaller numbers

Figure 2.7 Find the previous number.

below card 5 and the cards with larger numbers above card 5 (see Figure 2.8). If the child is having difficulty, he or she can use drawings to help him or her see, for example, on card 7, that there are more than five icons. Change the reference card in the centre on a regular basis. If the child is again in difficulty, you can start with cards 1 to 5, using 3 for example, as the reference card in the centre of the table. More simply, you can also play 'battle' games where each in turn turns over the first card of his deck and the one with the highest value card wins both cards, letting, of course, the child judge on each try who is winning.

When the child is comfortable with all these exercises, you can also use cards on which the Arabic number alone is written and check that the child has good access to the magnitude of the symbolic numbers (when the corresponding collection is not drawn).

Figure 2.8 A comparison-to-five task with playing cards.

2.5.7 Decomposing numbers

To understand a number is to understand the cardinal value to which it refers, the numbers that precede it, and those that follow it, larger or smaller numbers, but also to understand that this number contains other numbers and that it can be decomposed in different ways. Children with mathematical learning difficulties often tend to think of numbers as the sum of separate units. For example, the number 5 is seen exclusively as 5 units. The goal here is to promote an understanding of this number as also being the sum of 3 and 2 or 4 and 1. You can support this learning by using play cards. For example, ask the child to find all the possible decompositions of 5 by looking at the icons of a playing card of 5. He can hide with his fingers or with another card some of the icons and find out how many are left (Figure 2.9a). You can then note these different possible decompositions. Also invite the child to become aware of the commutativity property of addition (for example, 5 is 3 and 2 or is 2 and

3). You can also ask them to recognize the smaller collections of icons contained in a card. Figure 2.9b shows, for example, the numbers included in 8.

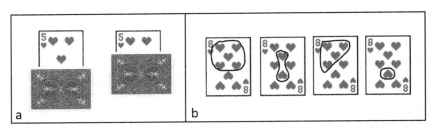

Figure 2.9 Find the decompositions of five by hiding part of the icons on the card (a) or recognize the smaller collections of icons included in 8 (b).

Fingers can also be used as a support to discover the decompositions of numbers, in particular, the decomposition of five, of ten, and of the sub-base five. Start with the number five on one hand and see all the possible decompositions. For the larger numbers, see with the child that the fingers naturally indicate the decomposition with five: six is five and one, seven is five and two, eight is five and three, etc. Then you can play to discover the decomposition of ten. If I raise one finger, then I have nine fingers down: ten is nine and one. If I raise two fingers now, then eight are down. I then realize that ten is also eight and two and so on (see Figure 2.10). The decompositions of ten are extremely important for the calculation as soon as the sums exceed ten.

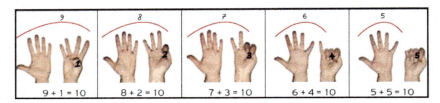

Figure 2.10 The decompositions of 10 with the support of the fingers.

2.5.8 Numbers up to 100

The verbal numerical chain must be developed well beyond ten. You can use a tape measure to facilitate this learning. Ideally, you should use a tape measure or a long number line stuck to the floor, with changes of colour at each change of ten. Since the Arabic numbers are visible on the tape measure, its usage is in line with the Number board game used by Ramani and Siegler (2008) but in an extended version. Ask the child to count from one as far as possible, touching the number he or she says each time. This exercise will allow the child to match the verbal number to the corresponding Arabic number while having an increment of movement on the ribbon. Later, you can also develop counting without the help of the tape. When counting from one is fluent, you can initiate counting from a number other than one (for example, counting from 12 or 28, etc.).

You can also hide certain numbers on the tape or on any other number line and ask the child to 'guess' the hidden number.

Again with the help of the tape measure, invite the child to count backwards, then suggest that he or she count *n* from a number, or to count down *n* steps from a number. Finally, you can also ask them to count in steps of two, in steps of ten, or other.

Then invite the child to locate as quickly as possible where a number is on the tape (for example, 3, 7, 10, 19, 35, 99, etc.). To go faster, invite him/her to first locate the ten corresponding to the number (focus on the colour changes and locate the coloured area corresponding to the target ten) and then find the precise target number in that area. Then ask them to indicate the neighbouring numbers (±1, see Figure 2.11a), then the round numbers (ending in 0) before and after that number (for example, 40 and 50 for target number 43, see Figure 2.11b).

Next, teach them to explicitly use the closest ten or so to better focus their search. For example, if I need to find 43, I must first look for 40 because 43 is closer to 40 than 50. On the other hand, if the target number is 47, then I have to find 50 first.

This tape measure can also be used as a support for number comparisons. Propose two numbers verbally or written in the Arabic code (in this case, ask the child to read both numbers aloud). Ask the child to indicate their respective positions on the ribbon (by pinning a clothespin to each location) and then indicate which of the two corresponds to the larger number.

Finally, to give a sense of the size of the numbers, you can also use the tape to measure the length of different objects. Consider only centimetres and do not emphasize this unit of measurement. Simply see with the child that different objects have different lengths and the larger objects are associated with larger numbers (cm) as well.

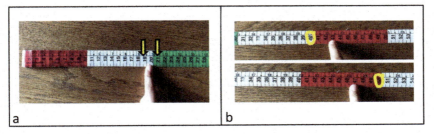

Figure 2.11 Find the position of a number on the tape measure: find the neighbours (a) and the nearest tens (b).

Observe with the child that numbers make sense in different contexts of daily life. For example, take a book and look at the numbers on the pages. Ask the child to find (without looking) the number on the next page or the number on the previous page. Then invite him or her to turn the page over to check his or her answer.

Consider the ages of different people in their family. See where these numbers are on the tape and make sure they are in order from the youngest to the oldest in the family.

Based on these different ideas and suggestions, feel free of course to create your own games and practice!

References

Agrillo, C., Dadda, M., Serena, G., & Bisazza, A. (2009). Use of number by fish. *PLOS ONE, 4*(3), e4786. doi: 10.1371/journal.pone.0004786

Almoammer, A., Sullivan, J., Donlan, C., Marusic, F., Zaucer, R., O'Donnell, T., & Barner, D. (2013). Grammatical morphology as a source of early number word meanings. *Proceedings of the National Academy of Sciences of the United States of America, 110*(46), 18448–18453.

Antell, S. E., & Keating, D. P. (1983). Perception of numerical invariance in neonates. *Child Development, 54*(3), 695–701.

Ashcraft, M. H., & Moore, A. M. (2012). Cognitive processes of numerical estimation in children. *Journal of Experimental Child Psychology, 111*(2), 246–267.

Ashkenazi, S., Mark-Zigdon, N., & Henik, A. (2013). Do subitizing deficits in developmental dyscalculia involve pattern recognition weakness? *Developmental Science, 16*(1), 35–46.

Baroody, A. J. (1987). The development of counting strategies for single-digit addition. *Journal for Research in Mathematics Education, 18*, 141–157.

Booth, J. L., & Siegler, R. S. (2006). Developmental and individual differences in pure numerical estimation. *Developmental Psychology, 42*(1), 189–201.

Brankaer, C., Ghesquière, P., & De Smedt, B. (2017). Symbolic magnitude processing in elementary school children: A group administered paper-and-pencil measure (SYMP Test). *Behavior Research Methods, 49*(4), 1361–1373.

Brannon, E. M., & Terrace, H. S. (2000). Representation of the numerosities 1–9 by rhesus macaques (Macacamulatta). *Journal of Experimental Psychology: Animal Behavior Processes, 26*(1), 31–49.

Brannon, E. M., Wusthoff, C. J., Gallistel, C. R., & Gibbon, J. (2001). Numerical subtraction in the pigeon: Evidence for a linear subjective number scale. *Psychological Science, 12*(3), 238–243. doi: 10.1111/1467-9280.00342

Camos, V. (2005). Développement et troubles des processus de quantification. In M. P. Noël (Ed.), *La dyscalculie: Trouble du développement numérique de l'enfant* (pp. 41–75). Marseille: Solal. [translation: Development and disorders of quantification processes. In M.P. Noël (ed.) *Dyscalculia: A child's numerical development disorder*]

Carey, S. (2001). Cognitive foundations of arithmetic: Evolution and ontogenesis. *Mind and Language, 16*(1), 37–55.

Carey, S. (2004). Bootstrapping and the origin of concepts. *Dœdalus, 133*(1), 59–68.

Clements, D. H. (1984). Training effects on the development and generalization of Piagetian logical operations and knowledge of number. *Journal of Educational Psychology, 76*(5), 766–776.

Clements, D. H., & Sarama, J. (2007). Effects of a preschool mathematics curriculum: Summative research on the building blocks project. *Journal of Research in Mathematics Education, 38*(2), 136–163.

Connolly, A. J. (2007). *KeyMath-3 diagnostic assessment: Manual forms A and B*. Minneapolis, MN: Pearson

Crollen, V., Noël, M-P., Honoré, N., Degroote, V. & Collignon, O. (2020). Investigating the respective contribution of sensory modalities and spatial disposition in numerical training. *Journal of Experimental Child Psychology, 190*, 104729.

Crollen, V., Noël, M. P., Seron, X., Mahau, P., Lepore, F., & Collignon, O. (2014). Visual experience influences the interactions between fingers and numbers. *Cognition, 133*(1), 91–96.

De Smedt, B., & Gilmore, C. K. (2011). Defective number module or impaired access? Numerical magnitude processing in first graders with mathematical difficulties. *Journal of Experimental Child Psychology, 108*(2), 278–292.

De Smedt, B., Noël, M. P., Gilmore, C., & Ansari, D. (2013). How do symbolic and non-symbolic numerical magnitude processing relate to individual differences in children's mathematical skills? A review of evidence from brain and behavior. *Trends in Neuroscience and Education, 2*(2), 48–55.

Dehaene, S. (1992). Varieties of numerical abilities. *Cognition, 44*(1–2), 1–42.

Dehaene, S. (1997). *La bosse des maths*. [Translation: *The number sense*]. Paris: Odile Jacob.

Dehaene, S., Bossini, S., & Giraux, P. (1993). The mental representation of parity and number magnitude. *Journal of Experimental Psychology: General, 122*(3), 371–396.

Fischer, U., Moeller, K., Bientzle, M., Cress, H., & Nuerk, H. C. (2011). Sensori-motor spatial training of number magnitude representation. *Psychonomics Bulletin Review, 18*(1), 177–183.

Friso-van den Bos, I., Kroesbergen, E. H., & Van Luit, J. E. H. (2018). Counting and number line trainings in kindergarten: Effects on arithmetic performance and number sense. *Frontiers in Psychology, 9*, 975. doi: 10.3389/fpsyg.2018.00975

Fuson, K. C. (1992). Relationships between counting and cardinality from age 2 to age 8. In J. Bideaud, C. Meljac & J. P. Fischer (Eds.), *Pathways to number. Children's developing numerical abilities* (pp. 127–149). Hillsdale, NJ: Lawrence Erlbaum.

Fuson, K. C., Richards, J., & Briars, D. J. (1982). The acquisition and elaboration of the number word sequence. In C. J. Brainerd (Ed.), *Children's logical and mathematical cognition: Progress in cognitive development research* (pp. 33–92). New York: Springer-Verlag.

Geary, D. C., Bow-Thomas, C. C., & Yao, Y. (1992). Counting knowledge and skill in cognitive addition: A comparison of normal and mathematically disabled children. *Journal of Experimental Child Psychology, 54*(3), 372–391.

Geary, D. C., Hoard, M. K., Byrd-Craven, J., Nugent, L., & Numtee, C. (2007). Cognitive Mechanisms underlying achievement deficits in children with mathematical learning disability. *Child Development, 78*(4), 1343–1359.

Geary, D. C., Hoard, M. K., Nugent, L., & Byrd-Craven, J. (2008). Development of number line representations in children with mathematical learning disability. *Developmental Neuropsychology, 33*(3), 277–299.

Gebuis, T., Cohen Kadosh, R., & Gevers, W. (2016). Sensory-integration system rather than approximate number system underlies numerosity processing: A critical review. *Acta Psychologica, 171*, 17–35.

Gelman, R., & Gallistel, C. R. (1978). *The child's understanding of number*. Cambridge, MA: Harvard University Press.

Grégoire, J., & Van Nieuwenhoven, C. (1995). Counting at nursery school and at primary school: Toward an instrument for diagnostic assessment. *European Journal of Psychology of Education, 10*(1), 61–75.

Griffin, S., Case, R., & Siegler, R. S. (1994). Rightstart: Providing the central conceptual prerequisites for first formal learning of arithmetic to students at risk for school failure. In K. McGilly (Ed.), *Classroom lessons: Integrating cognitive theory and classroom practice* (pp. 25–49). Cambridge, MA: The MIT Press.

Gross, H. J., Pahl, M., Si, A., Zhu, H., Tautz, J., & Zhang, S. (2009). Number-based visual generalisation in the honeybee. *PLOS ONE, 4*(1), e4263. doi: 10.1371/journal.pone.0004263

Halberda, J., & Feigenson, L. (2008). Developmental change in the acuity of the 'number sense': The approximate number system in 3-, 4-, 5-, and 6-year-olds and adults. *Developmental Psychology, 44*(5), 1457–1465.

Halberda, J., Mazzocco, M. M. M., & Feigenson, L. (2008). Individual differences in non-verbal number acuity correlate with maths achievement. *Nature, 455*(7213), 665–668.

Honoré, N., & Noël, M. P. (2016). Improving preschoolers' arithmetic through number magnitude training: The impact of non-symbolic and symbolic training. *PLOS ONE, 11*(11), e0166685. doi: 10.1371/journal.pone.0166685

Hyde, D. C., Khanum, S., & Spelke, E. S. (2014). Brief non-symbolic, approximate number practice enhances subsequent exact symbolic arithmetic in children. *Cognition, 131*(1), 92–107.

Jordan, N. C., Kaplan, D., Ramineni, C., & Locuniak, M. N. (2008). Development of number combination skill in the early school years: When do fingers help? *Developmental Science, 11*(5), 662–668.

Karagiannakis, G., & Noël, M.-P. (2020). Mathematical profite test: A preliminary evaluation of an online assessment for mathematics skills of children in grades 1–6. *Behavioral Sciences, 10*, 126.

Kaufman, E. L., Lord, M. N., Reese, T. W., & Volkmann, J. (1949). The discrimination of visual number. *American Journal of Psychology, 62*(4), 498–525.

Lafay, A., & Helloin, M.-C. (2016). *Examath 8–15*. Editions Happy Neuron (sur internet).

Landerl, K., Bevan, A., & Butterworth, B. (2004). Developmental dyscalculia and basic numerical capacities: A study of 8–9-year-old students. *Cognition, 93*(2), 99–125.

Le Corre, M., & Carey, S. (2007). One, two, three, four, nothing more: An investigation of the conceptual sources of the verbal counting principles. *Cognition, 105*(2), 395–438. doi: 10.1016/j.cognition.2006.10.005

Le Corre, M., Van de Walle, G., Brannon, E. M., & Carey, S. (2006). Re-visiting the competence/performance debate in the acquisition of the counting principles. *Cognitive Psychology, 52*(2), 130–169.

Libertus, M. E., Feigenson, L., & Halberda, J. (2013). Is approximate number precision a stable predictor of math ability? *Learning and Individual Differences, 25*, 126–133.

Link, T., Moeller, K., Huber, S., Fischer, U., & Nuerk, H. C. (2013). Walk the number line – An embodied training of numerical concepts. *Trends in Neuroscience and Education, 2*(2), 74–84.

Link, T., Moeller, K., Huber, S., Fischer, U., & Nuerk, H. C. (2015). Corrigendum to 'Walk the number line – An embodied training of numerical concepts' [Trends Neurosci. Educ. 2(2) (2013) 74–84]. *Trends in Neuroscience and Education, 4*(4), 112.

Lipton, J. S., & Spelke, E. S. (2003). Origins of number sense: Large-number discrimination in human infants. *Psychological Science, 14*(5), 396–401.

Maertens, B., De Smedt, B., Sasanguie, D., Elen, J., & Reynvoet, B. (2016). Enhancing arithmetic in pre-schoolers with comparison or number line estimation training: Does it matter? *Learning and Instruction, 46*, 1–11.

Mazzocco, M. M., Feigenson, L., & Halberda, J. (2011). Impaired acuity of the approximate number system underlies mathematical learning disability (dyscalculia). *Child Development, 82*(4), 1224–1237.

Moeller, K., Neuburger, S., Kaufmann, L., Landerl, K., & Nuerk, H. C. (2009). Basic number processing deficits in developmental dyscalculia: Evidence from eye-tracking. *Cognitive Development, 24*(4), 371–386.

Noël, M. P., & Grégoire, J. (2015). *TediMath Grands, Test diagnostique des compétences de base en mathématiques du CE2 à la 5e*. Montreuil, France: Editions du centre de psychologie appliquée.

Noël, M. P., & Rousselle, L. (2011). Developmental changes in the profiles of dyscalculia: An explanation based on a double exact-and-approximate number representation model. *Frontiers in Human Neuroscience, 5*, article 165, 1–4. doi: 10.3389/fnhum.2011.00165.

Nosworthy, N., Bugden, S., Archibald, L. E., & Ansari, D. (2013). A two-minute paper-and-pencil test of symbolic and nonsymbolic numerical magnitude processing explains variability in primary school children's arithmetic competence. *PLOS ONE, 8*(7), e67918. doi: 10.1371/journal.pone.0067918. Print 2013.

Obersteiner, A., Reiss, K., & Ufer, S. (2013). How training on exact or approximate mental representations of number can enhance first-grade students' basic number processing and arithmetic skills. *Learning and Instruction, 23*, 125–135.

Opfer, J. E., & Siegler, R. S. (2007). Representational change and children's numerical estimation. *Cognitive Psychology, 55*(3), 169–195.

Park, J., & Brannon, E. M. (2013). Training the approximate number system improves math proficiency. *Psychological Science, 24*(10), 2013–2019.

Pettito, A. L. (1990). Development of number line and measurement concepts. *Cognition and Instruction, 7*(1), 55–78.

Piaget, J., & Széminska, A. (1941). *La genèse du nombre chez l'enfant*. Ed. Delachaux & Niestlé S. A. Neuchatel - Paris.

Piazza, M., Facoetti, A., Trussardi, A. N., Berteletti, I., Conte, S., Lucangeli, D., … Zorzi, M. (2010). Developmental trajectory of number acuity reveals a severe impairment in developmental dyscalculia. *Cognition, 116*(1), 33–41.

Ramani, G. B., & Siegler, R. S. (2008). Promoting broad and stable improvements in low-income children's numerical knowledge through playing number board games. *Child Development, 79*(2), 375–394.

Räsänen, P., Salminen, J., Wilson, A. J., Aunio, P., & Dehaene, S. (2009). Computer-assisted intervention for children with low numeracy skills. *Cognitive Development, 24*(4), 450–472.

Rouder, J. N., & Geary, D. C. (2014). Children's cognitive representation of the mathematical number line. *Developmental Science, 17*(4), 525–536.

Rousselle, L., & Noël, M. P. (2007). Basic numerical skills in children with mathematics learning disabilities: A comparison of symbolic vs non-symbolic number magnitude processing. *Cognition, 102*(3), 361–395.

Saxe, G. B., Guberman, S. R., & Gearhart, M. (1987). Social processes in early number development. *Monographs of the Society for Research in Child Development, 52*(2), Series No. 216, 3–162.

Saxe, G. B., & Kaplan, R. (1981). Gesture in early counting: A developmental analysis. *Perceptual and Motor Skills, 53*(3), 851–854.

Schleifer, P., & Landerl, K. (2011). Subitizing and counting in typical and atypical development. *Developmental Science*, *14*(2), 280–291.
Schneider, M., Merz, S., Stricker, J., De Smedt, B., Torbeyns, J., Verschaffel, L., & Luwel, K. (2018). Associations of number line estimation with mathematical competence: A meta-analysis. *Child Development*, *89*(5), 1467–1484.
Schwenk, C., Sasanguie, D., Jörg-Tobias, K., Kempe, S., Doebler, P., & Holling, H. (2017). Non-symbolic magnitude processing in children with mathematical difficulties: A meta-analysis. *Research in Developmental Disabilites*, *64*, 152–167.
Sella, F., Lucangeli, D., Zorzi, M., & Berteletti, I. (2013). Number line estimation in children with developmental dyscalculia. *Learning Disabilities: A Contemporary Journal*, *11*(2), 41–49.
Sella, F., Tressoldi, P., Lucangeli, D., & Zorzi, M. (2016). Training numerical skills with the adaptive videogame 'The Number Race': A randomized controlled trial on preschoolers. *Trends in Neuroscience and Education*, *5*(1), 20–29.
Siegler, R. S., & Booth, J. L. (2004). Development of numerical estimation in young children. *Child Development*, *75*(2), 428–444.
Siegler, R. S., & Opfer, J. (2003). The development of numerical estimation: Evidence for multiple representations of numerical quantity. *Psychological Science*, *14*(3), 237–243.
Siegler, R. S., & Ramani, G. B. (2009). Playing linear number board games – But not circular ones – Improves low-income preschoolers' numerical understanding. *Journal of Educational Psychology*, *101*(3), 545–560.
Siegler, R. S., & Robinson, M. (1982). The development of numerical understandings. In H. Reese & L. P. Lipsitt (Eds.), *Advances in child development and behavior* (Vol. 16, pp. 241–312). New York: Academic Press.
Simms, V., Clayton, S., Cragg, L., Gilmore, C., & Johnson, S. (2016). Explaining the relationship between number line estimation and mathematical achievement: The role of visuomotor integration and visuospatial skills. *Journal of Experimental Child Psychology*, *145*, 22–33.
Starkey, P., & Cooper, R. G. (1995). The development of subitizing in young children. *British Journal of Developmental Psychology*, *13*(4), 399–420.
Starkey, P., Klein, A., & Wakeley, A. (2004). Enhancing young children's mathematical knowledge through a pre-kindergarten mathematics intervention. *Early Childhood Research Quarterly*, *19*(1), 99–120.
Suárez-Pellicioni, M., & Booth, J. R. (2018). Fluency in symbolic arithmetic refines the approximate number system in parietal cortex. *Human Brain Mapping*, *39*(10), 3956–3971.
Szűcs, D., & Myers, T. V. (2017). A critical analysis of design, facts, bias and inference in the approximate number system training literature: A systematic review. *Trends in Neuroscience and Education*, *6*, 187–203.
Trick, L. M., & Pylyshyn, Z. W. (1994). Why are small and large numbers enumerated differently? A limited-capacity preattentive stage in vision. *Psychological Review*, *101*(1), 80–102.
Van Niewenhoven, C., Grégoire, J., & Noël, M. P. (2002). *Tedi-math: Test diagnostique des compétences de base en mathématiques*. Paris: Editions du centre de psychologie appliquée.
van't Noordende, J. E., van Hoogmoed, A. H., Schot, W. D., & Kroesbergen, E. H. (2016). Number line estimation strategies in children with mathematical learning difficulties measured by eye tracking. *Psychological Research*, *80*(3), 368–378.
Von Aster, M., & Dellatolas, G. (2005). *Zareki-R: Batterie pour l'évaluation du traitement des nombres et du calcul chez l'enfant*. Paris: Editions du centre de psychologie appliquée.

Whyte, J. C., & Bull, R. (2008). Number games, magnitude representation, and basic number skills in preschoolers. *Developmental Psychology, 44*(2), 588–596.

Wilson, A. J., Revkin, S. K., Cohen, D., Cohen, L., & Dehaene, S. (2006). An open trial assessment of 'The number Race', an adaptive computer game for remediation of dyscalculia. *Behavioral and Brain Functions, 2*(1), 1–16.

Wright, R. J., Martland, J., & Stafford, A. K. (2006). *Early numeracy. Assessment for teaching & intervention*. London: SAGE Publications.

Wynn, K. (1992). Children's acquisition of the number words and the counting systems. *Cognitive Psychology, 24*(2), 220–251.

Xu, F., & Spelke, E. S. (2000). Large number discrimination in 6-month-old infants. *Cognition, 74*(1), B1–B11.

3 Base-10 representation

3.1 Theoretical considerations and development

3.1.1 The numerical systems

To express the infinity of numerical magnitude, most human societies have developed symbolic number systems, including the verbal numbers. As it would not be possible to memorize a specific word denoting each of the possible quantities, languages have developed a limited numerical lexicon and rules for combining these words, i.e., syntax. Most of the languages in Western and Oriental cultures use a base-10 system. Some people say that this base is not the best one in terms of mathematics, but according to Ifrah (1994), this base has probably been selected because we have ten fingers and can count on them. In most of the Asian languages, the base-10 structure is very transparent. For instance, 12 is literally said 'ten two', 97 is literally said 'nine ten seven', and 253 is 'two hundred, five tens and three'. In many Western languages such as English, Dutch, French, German, and so on, besides words for units from 'one' to 'nine', and words expressing the powers of ten (ten, hundred, thousand …), there are also specific words for the 'teens' (from eleven to nineteen) and for the 'tens' (from 'ten' to 'ninety'). This renders the base-10 system less transparent. Indeed, it is not obvious that 'eleven' actually means 'ten plus one' or that 'twenty' refers to 'two times ten'. In French from France, they are traces of a vigesimal structure (base-20) with 80 being said 'quatre-vingt', literally 'four twenty', and 73 said 'soixante-treize', literally 'sixty-thirteen', and 97 said 'quatre-vingt dix-sept', literally 'four-twenty-ten-seven'. In all of these languages, spoken number words first express the bigger power of ten and then the lower power of ten. Yet, as regards the two lower powers of ten (the tens and the units), some languages such as German and Dutch invert the verbal structure. For instance, in Dutch or German, 534 is literally pronounced as 'five hundreds four and thirty'. We will see how these differences in the structure of the verbal number system may impact children's development of the base-10 representation or the mastery of number transcoding (number reading or writing under dictation).

Thus, typically, the spoken number systems are defined by a lexicon that always includes unit words and, in most Western languages, teens and tens

DOI: 10.4324/b22795-3

words. There are also specific words for expressing different powers of ten: 'ten, hundred, thousand ...'. Typically, to express the infinite variety of number magnitude, these words are combined with additive relations (e.g., *twenty-three* means *twenty* plus *three*) and multiplicative relations (*three hundred* means *three* times *hundred*). So, any verbal number can be represented as a series of imbedded additive and multiplicative relations between the basic quantities expressed by each word. For instance, *three thousand two hundred and four* actually means (*three* × *a thousand*) + (*two* × *a hundred*) + *four*.

In the written modality, the Arabic code is composed of ten symbols, the digits (from 0 to 9) which are written in sequences with the first one starting from the left being associated with the larger power of ten and the last one (for the whole numbers), at the right, being associated with the zero power of ten which equals the unit (1). So, for instance, 204 actually means 2×10^2 plus 0×10^1 plus 4×10^0. So this is a base-10 positional system. This system is widely used in our modern society, although we also use occasionally other written systems such as the Roman code for instance.

3.1.2 Magnitude representation

Animal studies and infant studies have led to the assumption that we are born with an approximate number system (ANS) that is an analogue and approximate representation of numerical magnitude (see Chapter 2). For instance, when comparing two quantities, a distance effect is typically observed, meaning that performance decreases as the two quantities involved are closer to one another, thus reflecting the analogue character of the magnitude representation. The other effect observed is a size effect, indicating that performance decreases as the two quantities involved increase in size, thus supporting the idea that the precision of the ANS decreases with magnitude. These effects are typically found for the comparison of collections (e.g., in animal and human studies) but, interestingly, the same effects are also reported in the comparison of two Arabic digits, which led to the assumption that these symbolic numbers are mapped onto the ANS to get their magnitude meaning.

Regarding larger numbers, Dehaene, Dupoux, and Mehler (1990) but also Restle (1970) assume that the magnitude of a two-digit number would similarly be processed, that is, large numbers would activate the corresponding magnitude representation on the ANS or be mapped holistically on the mental number line. Thus, the numbers would be processed as an integrated entity. This refers to the holistic view as the magnitudes of the numbers are represented as integrated quantities. According to this view, comparison time should only be a function of the numerical distance between the two numbers to compare. However, in the case of two-digit numbers, Nuerk, Weger, and Willmes (2001) have found that adult participants are significantly slower in comparing pairs such as 37_52 than pairs such as 42_57, although they both present a numerical distance of 15 between the two numbers. Why is it the case? In the first one (37_52), comparing the units (i.e., 7, 2) would lead to a reverse decision to the one for comparing the tens (i.e., 3, 5); these pairs are thus called 'incompatible'. On the other hand, in the latter pair (42_57), the results of both comparisons would bias the decision in the same direction; they are thus called 'compatible pairs'. The observation of this decade-unit compatibility effect cannot be accounted for by a pure analogue (holistic) model. Rather, these results speak in favour of a model where the individual digits of a number are processed in a decomposed fashion. Some have hypothesized that this processing would be in a sequential, digit-by-digit fashion starting at the leftmost digit pair until the first pair of corresponding digits differing from each other is encountered (Poltrock & Schwartz, 1984). Others have proposed that the digits are processed in parallel (Nuerk & Willmes, 2005), which could explain why the response is slower in the case of incompatible pairs because of the interference caused by the parallel comparisons of tens and units. This view of a decomposed parallel processing is supported by evidence using eye tracking techniques (Moeller, Fischer, Nuerk & Willmes, 2009).

So, this compatibility effect argues against the idea that we only develop an ANS. Other magnitude representations of numbers should thus be assumed and have been actually proposed. In particular, McCloskey, Caramazza, and Basili (1985) assume that our magnitude representation is precise and reflects the base-10 system (for instance, *three thousand and fifty* would activate the following semantic representation: $[3] \times 10^3$, $[5] \times 10^1$). Instead, Power and Dal Martello (1990) assume that our magnitude representation reflects the additive and multiplicative structure of the verbal system (for instance, *three thousand and fifty* would activate the following semantic representation $(C1000 \times C3) + (C10 \times C5)$, where Ci represents the semantic concept referring to i).

Currently, there is no clear scientific evidence in support of one of these conceptions. Yet, any teachers or math coaches know that at one point or another, the child has to understand the base-10 representation of the number, i.e., understand not only that thirty is larger than twenty-nine and is bigger by one unit but also that thirty actually refers to three tens whereas twenty-nine refers to two tens plus nine units. So, we could imagine that the child starts with an ANS and then develops later a precise unitary representation of numbers (based on the succession function, see Chapter 2), and then, a base-10 representation of symbolic numbers.

Given the rather arbitrary nature of the number system, children need to be taught explicitly about this structure. This understanding is crucial for the child's further mathematical development, and merely encountering the decimal structure does not seem to be sufficient to produce an understanding of it. Indeed, even in the case of the very transparent languages, the simple use of large numbers does not mean that the base-10 underlying structure is understood. For instance, Ho and Fuson (1998) showed that 4-year-old Chinese children could correctly say 'ten two' for the number 12 but could not say that 10 items plus 2 items resulted in a total of 12 items without counting.

3.1.3 The development of base-10 representation

According to Kreps, Squire, and Bryant (2003), children's understanding of the decimal structure requires the understanding of two underlying mathematical principles: (1) that any positive integer 'n' can be decomposed into two or more other numbers that precede it in the ordinal list of numbers (i.e., additive composition) and (2) that units can be of different sizes, for example ones, tens, hundreds, etc. Yet, in their study, Kreps et al. actually found that children first learn that numbers greater than ten can be composed of tens and ones, and only after, this understanding leads them to realize the more general principle of additive composition. So how does the child develop this understanding that numbers greater than ten can be decomposed into tens and units?

Fuson, Wearne, Hiebert, Murray, Human, Olivier, Carpenter, and Fennema (1997) and Fuson (1998) describe five different conceptual structures that the child can have with respect to two-digit numbers: 'unitary', 'X-ty group and ones', 'count-by-tens and ones', 'place value tens and ones', and 'integrated tens and ones'. According to these authors, these are not strictly speaking developmental stages, in the sense that each child does not necessarily go through each of these stages. Figure 3.1 provides a description of each of these five conceptions.

3.1.3.1 'Unitary' conception of two-digit numbers

Generally, two-digit numbers are encountered after the one-digit numbers. The latter correspond to an arbitrary (but conventional) sequence, and so

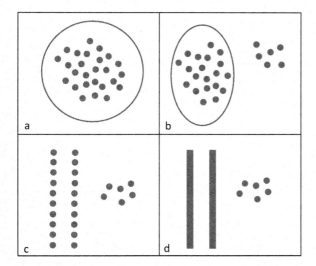

Figure 3.1 The different conceptions of two-digit numbers: (a) unitary; (b) X-ty group and ones; (c) count-by-tens and ones; (d) place value tens and ones (according to Fuson et al., 1997).

children need to learn them by simple memorization of the number words and of their association with the corresponding numerosities. This first approach to the numbers induces in the child a unitary conception (see Figure 3.1a). This same conception is then extended to two-digit numbers for which the child connects a verbal number to an inseparable two-digit number and the corresponding quantity (of units). This unitary conception of two-digit numbers is also favoured by the linguistic systems in which 'teen' words (eleven, twelve … sixteen) do not indicate a clear break after the unit names.

3.1.3.2 'X-ty group and ones' conception based on verbal counting

Gradually, especially through the increase of the verbal numerical chain, children begin to separate the two spoken number words, the tens word (seen as a cluster of ones) and the units word, and connect these two parts to separate quantities. So, for instance, the child understands that twenty-six is made of twenty 'ones' and six 'ones' (see Figure 3.1b). This same separation may operate in the Arabic code, but their writing may give rise to errors of concatenation (for example, 'twenty-six' transcoded as 'twenty' on the one hand, and 'six' on the other hand, i.e., 206).

3.1.3.3 'Count-by-tens and ones' conceptual structure

Here, the child conceives the tens as groups of ten, although the opacity of certain words ('twenty' or in French, 'quatre-vingt' or 'quatre-vingt-dix' …) makes this understanding difficult (see Figure 3.1c). So, for instance, twenty-six is conceived as two groups of ten 'ones' and one group of six 'ones'.

3.1.3.4 'Place-value tens and ones' conceptual structure

At this level, the child is capable of a higher level of abstraction: 'twenty' is not seen as two groups of ten units, but as two entities of a higher order, two 'tens' (or decades), see Figure 3.1d.

3.1.3.5 'Integrated tens and ones' conceptual structure

Finally, when the child can move from one of the two previous conceptions to the other – the ten can be seen sometimes as a group of 10 units, sometimes as a unit of higher order (ten or decade) – Fuson et al. (1997) speak of a conceptual structure of integrated tens and ones allowing a flexible representation that adapts to the needs of the situation. Koppel (1999) insists on this ability to adopt different points of view to move from 'thirty is thirty units' to 'thirty is three groups of ten units'. The child should be able to mentally switch from one point of view to the other, without the help of any external element (such as a string around 10 sticks to make a bundle of ten) to modify what is observed. Indeed, some children are convinced that forming a decade involves at least one spatial grouping of the elements. According to this author, the child at this stage must have understood three things: (1) the possibility of counting elements and groups, (2) the identity between ten units and a ten, and (3) the possibility of and the reason for the differences of point of view. The same reasoning will also be necessary when acquiring the measurement systems and more particularly the conversions between different units (for example, 1 dm = 10 cm) since here, too, it is not a question of modifying the value but of adopting different points of view on the same reality.

3.1.4 The positional system

According to Becker and Varelas (1993), the mastery of the positional system of the Arabic code requires more than the understanding of the base-10 representation of the numbers. Indeed, some children understand the amount to which a number refers and are able to decompose the number into a base-10 representation but are in trouble when it comes to integrating this information into a positional system. Arabic numeration requires a 'semiotic reversibility' since the same sign (the Arabic digit) corresponds to different referents according to its position in the number. The child thus has to learn the difference between the face value of the digit (i.e., the face value of 5 is the same in 53 and in 35 and corresponds to the quantity five) and the place value (i.e., the face value of the digit multiplied by 10^0, 10^1, 10^2 ... according to its position in the number starting from the right-hand side digit, e.g., the place value of 5 is five in the number 35 but fifty in 53).

Interestingly, Gervasconi and Sullivan (2007) reported that in first and second grade about a quarter of children exhibited problems in understanding the place-value structure of the Arabic number system. Yet, this is crucial for number magnitude comparison for instance. For example, when comparing 42 and 57, tens and units need to be put in the correct bins (e.g., Nuerk, Weger & Willmes, 2001). This means that one has to segregate which digits represent the to-be-compared decades (i.e., 4 < 5) and which the units (i.e., 2 < 7). Such unit-decade identification within the place-value system is especially important when the presented number pair is unit-decade incompatible (e.g., 47_62, 4 < 6, but 7 > 2). Above chance performance in incompatible trials requires necessarily, at least implicitly, place-value understanding.

Some children develop misconceptions of two-digit numbers. They rely on the unitary conception of single-digit numbers and use it to construct a two-digit conception of numbers, such as concatenated or assembled single units. In this view, the value of each digit is independent of its position in the number (for example, 45 and 54 refer to the same amount).

An informative test to diagnose the understanding of the decimal and positional system of Arabic numbers has been used by Sinclair, Garin, and Tièche-Christinat (1992). These authors presented multi-digit Arabic numbers to children between five and nine years old and asked them to select the number of tokens corresponding to each digit of the number. Most 6-year-olds selected the number of tokens for each digit regardless of its position in the number (for example, 2 and 3 tokens for the number 23). Towards 7 or 8 years old, globally correct answers appeared (the number of tokens corresponds to the quantity represented by the number), but the distribution of tokens between each digit composing the number was incorrect (for example, 24 tokens for the number 24 but 12 tokens allocated to each of the 2 digits). Finally, one last group showed perfect control of the positional system, and the decompositions were explained in terms of tens and units. Note that there is an overlap between these strategies: the same child may be at different 'stages' between items in the same task.

3.1.5 Influences of the language on the development of the base-10 system

As reported above, languages differ in their degree of transparency to the base-10 structure. Several studies have tried to see to what extent these differences impact children's ease in understanding the base-10 structure of numbers.

In particular, Miura et al. (Miura, Kim, Chang & Okamoto, 1988; Miura & Okamoto, 1989; Miura, Okamoto, Kim, Steere & Fayol, 1993; Miura, Okamoto, Kim, Chang, Steere & Fayol, 1994) used a simple task: they showed first-grade children an Arabic number and asked them to read it aloud and to show that number using blocks of ones and tens. Asian children (e.g., Chinese, Japanese, and Korean children) who had not yet been taught about the base-10 structure showed a preference for using a construction of tens and ones to show numbers (e.g., selecting 2 ten-blocks and 8 one-blocks to represent 28), whereas Western children (e.g., French, Swedish, and US children) showed a preference for using a collection of ones (i.e., selecting 28 one-blocks). Although these results were obtained in several studies and across different samples coming from different Asian and Western cultures, Laski, Ermakova, and Vasilyeva (2014) and Vasilyeva, Laski, Ermakova, Lai, Jeong, and Hachigian (2015) failed to replicate them with children speaking Korean, Mandarin, English, and Russian. They found that, no matter the country of origin, kindergartners used base-10 representations with the blocks in more than half of the trials. This difference is particularly unexpected as Miura et al. tested first graders whereas those later studies tested kindergarten.

3.1.6 Transcoding

3.1.6.1 Definition and models

Transcoding literally means going from one code (the input code) to another one (the output code). Number transcoding is a very common activity. Indeed, at a young age, the child already learns different codes to express numbers, the most widely used being the spoken verbal code and then the written Arabic code. Reading aloud Arabic numbers or writing them to dictation are the more frequent transcoding processes. In the former, the input code is the

Arabic code and the output code is the spoken verbal code, whereas it is the reverse for the other transcoding.

Some transcoding models, such as that of Deloche and Seron (1987) or of Barrouillet, Camos, Perruchet, and Seron (2004), assume that one could transcode numbers by directly applying rules to the input number to produce the output number. For instance, according to the model of Barrouillet et al. (2004), in the case of Arabic number dictation, the verbal string is encoded and a parsing process segments this string into units that can be processed sequentially from the start of the string to the end by means of a production system. This production system consists of condition and action procedures. At the start of learning, each unit resulting from the parsing process contains a single word. Yet, progressively, groups of words that are frequently perceived in direct temporal succession (e.g., decade-unit structures, such as twenty-three) would result in the formation of new representational units, and their transcoding would then simply require the retrieval from long-term memory of the corresponding digital form instead of the application of the rules.

Other models, by contrast, assume that these transcoding processes require understanding of the input number, i.e., the elaboration of a semantic representation of its magnitude, before being able to produce the output number. These models are called semantic transcoding models. This is the case for the model of McCloskey, Caramazza, and Basili (1985) which assumes that the semantic representation reflects the base-10 system (e.g., *three thousand and fifty* would activate the following semantic representation: $[3] \times 10^3$, $[5] \times 10^1$), and for the model of Power and Dal Martello (1990) which assumes that the semantic representation reflects the additive and multiplicative structure of the verbal system (e.g., *three thousand and fifty* would activate the following semantic representation: $(C1000 \times C3) + (C10 \times C5)$, where Ci corresponds to the semantic concept of i).

Finally, the triple-code model integrates the possibility of using both asemantic and semantic routes for transcoding (Dehaene, 1992).

At least under the assumption of semantic transcoding processes, one expects an association between base-10 understanding and transcoding abilities. Indeed, under these theoretical models, it is assumed that reading an Arabic number requires the understanding of the Arabic number and the ability to produce the corresponding verbal number. Similarly, writing a number to dictation requires understanding the spoken numbers and being able to produce the corresponding Arabic number.

3.1.6.2 Development of transcoding and type of errors

Using samples of about 50 children from different age groups, Noël (see Noël & Turconi, 1999) tested the reading and writing skills of French-speaking Belgian children from 6 to 8 years old. Performance in the two tasks was quite similar and increased with the child's development. At six years of age, children were nearly perfect in transcoding one-digit numbers and their accuracy

80 *Base-10 representation*

was about 50% for two-digit numbers. At seven years old, performance was nearly perfect for two-digit numbers and was around 80% correct for three-digit numbers. Similar results were found by Power and Dal Martello (1990) with Italian children: 7-year-olds were able to write Arabic numbers under dictation up to 100, but errors appeared for larger numbers. Finally, Noël found that eight-year-olds could transcode nearly perfectly all numbers up to four digits and were around 80% accurate for five-digit numbers.

Seron and Fayol (1994) used the model of McCloskey et al. (1985) to identify the locus of the errors produced by second-grade children in writing Arabic numbers to dictation by testing separately their comprehension of spoken numbers and their ability to produce Arabic numbers. They found that children's difficulties lay mainly in the production of Arabic numbers. Seron, Noël, and Van der Elst (1997) used a similar approach to understand first graders' errors in reading Arabic numbers. They found that even though some reading errors could be explained by children's difficulties in producing spoken numbers, the comprehension of Arabic numbers was even more problematic and thus played a larger role in explaining the children's reading difficulties.

In examining the nature of the errors produced, one could distinguish lexical and syntactic errors. Lexical errors correspond to the wrong selection of a word or a digit. For instance, Paul, an 11-year-old child, showed severe problems in reading and writing Arabic numbers (40–50% errors), and his errors were mostly of the lexical type (Temple, 1989; see Table 3.1a). Whereas CM (a 13-year-old teenager) was also performing very poorly in transcoding tasks (e.g., writing Arabic numbers to dictation led to 46% errors) but his errors were of a different type: the non-zero digits were correctly produced but the numbers were incorrectly formed (Sullivan, Macaruso & Sokol, 1996; see Table 3.1b). These are called syntactic errors, i.e., errors that concern the way the different words or digits are combined in the number.

In general, when children have to transcode verbal numbers into Arabic numbers or vice versa, their errors are almost exclusively related to managing the syntactic aspects of the number (Barrouillet et al., 2004; Camos, 2008;

Table 3.1 Examples of transcoding errors produced by Paul (a) and by CM (b)

(a) Errors of Paul (Temple, 1989)	(b) Errors of CM (Sullivan et al., 1996)
Arabic number reading	Three thousand five hundred two => 3.0520
1 => nine	
85 => eighty-two	Nine hundred two thousand seventy => 100.305
34 => seventy-six	
153 => a hundred and twenty-three	Sixty-six thousand one hundred and five => 66.15
Dictation of Arabic numbers	Five hundred six thousand one => 5.061
Two => 3	
Nine => 8	
Ninety-nine => 91	
Seven hundred and eleven => 511	

Power & Dal Martello, 1990, 1997; Seron & Fayol, 1994; Zuber, Pixner, Moeller & Nuerk, 2009). Power and Dal Martello (1990) analysed the errors produced by seven-year-old Italian children: most of them were syntactic errors, mainly consisting in the production of extra zeros (three hundred and sixty-five => 30065 or 3065). This was also the observation of Seron, Deloche, and Noël (1991). These authors tested second and third graders three times in the school year to examine precisely the evolution of their transcoding skills. They found that when children are confronted with numerals they cannot write, such as three-digit numbers, they first transcode each word to the Arabic counterpart (e.g., three hundred and twelve => 310012); this is called 'lexicalization'. Progressively, children master the multiplicative relationship between 'hundred' and the unit (e.g., they can master structures like 'three hundred' and would thus transcode 'three hundred and twelve' to 30012). Then, these children are able to master the additive relation with units. And this point, they can correctly transcode hundred + unit structures (such as 'one hundred and three' by 103) but they would typically make errors for other additive relations with hundred (e.g., they would transcode 'three hundred and twelve' to 3012, erroneously generalizing what they have learned on hundred + unit structures to hundred + teens or to hundred + tens structures). Then, finally, they become able to master all the additive relations with hundred. The same developmental path is also observed for thousand with the mastery of multiplicative relations preceding the mastery of additive relations.

3.1.6.3 Influence of the language structure on transcoding

Several studies have shown that writing Arabic numbers is largely influenced by the syntactic structure of the spoken language used to dictate the numbers. For instance, Miura, Okamoto, Kim, Steere, and Fayol (1993, 1994) compared the transcoding abilities of first graders from Asia (from China, Korea, and Japan) to those of Western children (from America, France, and Sweden). Let us remember that Asian language systems are much more transparent to the base-10 system than Western languages. They found that Asian children were better able to write Arabic numbers than Western children. A similar advantage for Asian children was observed in first grade (Lê & Noël, 2022) and third to sixth-grade children (Nguyen & Grégoire, 2014) when comparing Vietnamese- and French-speaking children. Two other systems that are worth comparing are English and Welsh, the latter being a very regular and base-10 transparent number system. Dowker, Bala, and Lloyd (2008) found that six- and eight-year-old children who spoke Welsh read and compared two-digit numbers more accurately than same-age children who only spoke English.

Other research examined the impact of more subtle differences between languages. For instance, Seron and Fayol (1994) compared French-speaking children from France and from Belgium as the French use vigesimal number names above 60, while the Belgians use decimal structures for all numbers but 80 (namely 'four- twenty'). They found that French children made more errors than Belgians when writing numbers above 60 to dictation, except for numbers containing 80.

Van Rinsveld and Schiltz (2016) reported a similar difference when comparing French and English (English numbers follow the decimal structure). They tested fifth graders (ten years old) and found that English-speaking children significantly outperformed French-speaking children for numbers following a vigesimal structure in French compared to a decimal structure in English (i.e., numbers >60).

Other studies examined the impact of languages where the pronunciation of two-digit numbers is inversed (e.g., 64 is pronounced as 'four-and-sixty'), such as Dutch and German. Krinzinger et al. (2011) showed that Dutch- and German-speaking children made more transcoding errors than did French-speaking children. Pixner et al. (2011) showed that seven-year-old children speaking Czech (which has an inverted and a non-inverted number language) made 49% errors when numbers were dictated in the inverted number language, of which about half were inversion-related, whereas errors dropped down to 37% when numbers were dictated in the non-inverted number language. Imbo, Vanden Bulcke, De Brauwer, and Fias (2014) also examined the impact of the inverted system by comparing second graders speaking Dutch (an inversed number language) and French (a non-inversed number language) in a task of Arabic digits writing to dictation. They found that, although globally the two groups had similar rates of transcoding errors, inversion errors (e.g., hearing 'zesenveertig', literally 'six and forty, wrote 64 instead of 46) were significantly more frequent in Dutch-speaking than in French-speaking children. Using regression analyses, they found that working-memory capacities were the only significant predictors of transcoding errors but language was the only significant predictor of inversion errors.

In summary, there is much evidence showing that transcoding is easier when the verbal system is more transparent to the base-10 system and the pronunciation order of the word is similar to the order of the digits.

3.1.7 Base-10 and calculations

Understanding the base-10 and positional system of the Arabic code also has repercussions for calculations. Indeed, understanding of the positional base-10 system is crucial for mental calculations involving multi-digit numbers. According to Fuson et al. (1997), children who have not acquired an appropriate representation of the base-10 positional system of a number can only resort to counting unit by unit from one of the operands (53 + 14 = 53, 54, 55, 56 ... 67). On the other hand, several methods are available for those who master the base-10 logic. They can decompose the second operand into tens and units and add it to the first operand (for example, 53 + 14 = 53 + 10 + 4), or separate the units and the tens in the two numbers, add them separately, and then add the two subtotals (for example, 53 + 14 = (50 + 10) + (3 + 4) = 60 + 7), or finally, mix these two strategies (for example, 53 + 14 = (50 + 10) = 60, plus 3 = 63, plus 4 = 67).

These operations are even more demanding when intermediate sums are above 10 and thus require a carry procedure, such as in 58 + 14. In this case, indeed, the intermediate result has to be integrated into one coherent number according to the place-value structure of the Arabic number system, and dealing correctly with this carry procedure requires an understanding of the place value. Let us take an example. Consider the problem 436 + 59. The child has to be able to realize the additions between the same position digits (not 4 + 5, but 3 + 5 and 6 + 9), and also integrate their sum into a coherent number with 4 in the hundred position, 8 in the decade position, and then consider the 15 units as 1 ten, that should be added to the other 8 tens, leaving 5 units, for a total of 495. Thus, multi-digit addition as well as subtraction involve a profound knowledge of the place-value structure of the Arabic number system, especially when carrying or borrowing procedures are involved.

Generally, the school teaches one strategy to the child to deal with multi-digit calculation. Those who do not understand the principle underlying the construction of the Arabic numerical system can only apply these rules in the manner of an arbitrary algorithm. In this case, there is a high risk of procedural errors. On the other hand, children who have an adequate understanding of the positional base-10 system will develop, besides the learned strategy, other personal methods of calculation. These children understand the meaning of the decompositions required by the calculation, and their risk of procedural errors is very low (Carpenter, Franke, Jacobs, Fennema & Empson, 1997).

There is some empirical evidence of a link between base-10 mastery and calculation abilities. For instance, Laski, Ermakova, and Vasilyeva (2014) and Vasilyeva, Laski, Ermakova, Lai, Jeong, and Hachigian (2015) tested base-10 representation in kindergarten by asking the children to read aloud a two-digit Arabic number and then select blocks of ones or tens to show the number. Interestingly, they found that the percentage of trials on which children used a base-10 block selection predicted the percentage of addition problems (such as 5 + 22 or 18 + 3) on which they used a base-10 decomposition strategy (i.e., to solve 18 + 3, add 18 + 2 which makes 20 and add 1).

This link between base-10 understating and calculation was also measured longitudinally. Moeller, Pixner, Zubern, Kaufmann, and Nuerk (2011) measured place-value understanding in first grade and examined whether it predicted calculation abilities when the kids were in third grade. In first grade, they used two tasks to measure base-10 understanding: transcoding and, in particular, inversion errors, as these children spoke German (a language with a decade-unit inversion), and two-digit number magnitude comparison with compatible and incompatible pairs. They found that performance in these tasks significantly predicted children's multi-digit addition performance when they were in third grade. More precisely, they found that pure inversion errors in transcoding and a larger compatibility effect in the comparison task (indicating difficulty in assigning the place-value of each digit) predicted a higher error rate in third-grade arithmetic performance.

Finally, Ho and Cheng (1997) tested the causality of this link. These authors provided specific training (for two months) on the decimal position system to Chinese first-grade children with arithmetic difficulties. At the end of this programme, the authors noted an improvement in the understanding of the decimal system, but also in multi-digit computation, in particular, as regards addition and subtraction. On the other hand, no improvement (neither in terms of the understanding of the decimal system nor in arithmetic) was visible at the end of these two months in a control group of children equally weak in mathematics who did not receive any intervention.

3.2 Difficulties in children with dyscalculia

A few studies have investigated the understanding of the base-10 system in children with math learning difficulties. In particular, Russell and Ginsburg (1984) compared the profile of fourth graders with math learning difficulties with two groups of children with no such learning difficulties: one of the same age and the other, one year younger (third-grade children). They used several tasks to assess children's understanding of the base-10 system. The tasks involved activities such as counting by tens, counting involving large numbers, decomposing numbers, and understanding the written convention designating place value.

In the counting-by-ten task, children were presented cards with dots arranged in horizontal rows of ten, in alternating rows of red and blue dots. They had to count the dots and say how many there were. All three groups were very accurate in this task and similarly used the counting by tens strategy.

In the counting-large-numbers task, children were given piles of play money and asked to say how much money there was (e.g., 4-$100, 3-$10, so $430). The math learning difficulty group performed less well than the fourth-grade control group but equally as well as the third-grade control group. In all cases, the errors were mainly 'place value' errors in which the child reported, for instance, thousands instead of hundreds.

In the decomposing-number task, children were asked 'How many Xs (a smaller number) are in Y (a larger number)?' For instance, how many 10s are in 100, or how many 20s are in 100. Here again, the math learning difficulty group performed less well than the fourth-grade control group but similarly to third-grade control group.

In the large written numbers task, children were presented with two large numbers with an equal number of digits and had to select the bigger one (e.g., 799999 versus 811111, or 833333 versus 177777). The performance of children with math learning difficulties did not significantly differ from that of control children.

Finally, in the representation-of-place-value task, children were asked to read a written number (in that case, 25 and 34) and take as many poker chips as the number. Then, they had to split the pile of poker chips so that the first pile represented the value of the decade digit and the second one the value of the unit digit. There was no difference between children with math learning difficulties and the other groups.

In summary, fourth-grade children with math learning difficulties showed a one-year delay in two of these tasks: the counting-large-numbers task and the decomposing-number task. Yet, some of these tasks led to near ceiling performance (e.g., the count by ten task) and were thus too easy for the age of the children tested. It would be interesting to use the same tasks but with a younger population to see the extent to which children with math learning difficulties are impaired relative to control peers.

Two other studies investigated the transcoding abilities of children with and without math learning difficulties. Moura, Wood, Pinheiro-Chagas, Lonnemann, Krinzinger, Willmes, and Haase (2013) assessed Arabic number reading and writing under dictation in children with and without math learning difficulties. They found that, both in early (first and second grade) and middle (third and fourth grade) elementary school, children with math learning difficulties performed more poorly in these transcoding tasks than control children. In the younger groups, errors were both lexical and syntactic whereas in older children, difficulties mainly concerned the acquisition of transcoding rules. According to the authors, children with math learning difficulties would fall behind their typical peers because they required more time to comprehend and master the complex transcoding rules.

Van Loosbroek, Dirkx, Hulstijn, and Janssen (2009) examined Arabic number dictation in nine-year-olds with and without arithmetical disabilities. They found that children with arithmetical disabilities were overall slower in planning Arabic digit writing than control children and also had a larger size effect. Indeed, for single-digit numbers, they needed more time to plan writing large digits (e.g., 8) than small digits (e.g., 3) while this was not the case for control children. According to the authors, this means that control children were using a direct asemantic route while children with arithmetical disabilities used a semantic transcoding route. For two- and three-digit numbers, the two groups of children showed a number size effect but the effect was larger for children with arithmetical disabilities than for control children. According to the authors, this stronger size effect reflects a delay in the development of quick and direct (or asemantic) transcoding.

In summary, children with math learning disabilities have been shown to have difficulties in understanding the base-10 system and in transcoding processes (mainly as regards the mastery of the syntactic rules). These difficulties will often lead to errors in calculation with large numbers.

3.3 Training studies

3.3.1 Encoding 10ness to better understand number magnitude

Zhang and Okamoto (2017) tested the idea that the encoding of '10ness' by manipulating the way two-digit numbers are counted is crucial to improve

86 Base-10 representation

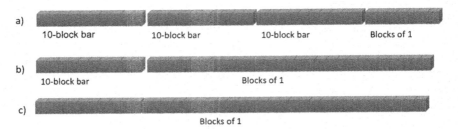

Figure 3.2 Illustration of the blocks used in (a) the Multiple 10, (b) Single 10, and (c) Multiple 1 conditions, in Zhang and Okamoto (2017), page 194 (with permission).

children's estimation of two-digit number magnitudes. In their study, first graders were randomly assigned to three training conditions. The training sessions (2 sessions of 15 minutes only) were conducted in small groups of 3 students. The experimental training was the 'Multiple 10 condition'. In this condition, children were provided with multiple 10-blocks and multiple 1-blocks (see Figure 3.2a). The experimenter first demonstrated how to 'show' (construct) 37 using base-10 blocks. He/she lay down three 10-blocks and seven 1-blocks horizontally and counted 'one ten, two tens, three tens, one, two, three ... seven [pause], thirty-seven'. Then children saw a card with 44 and were asked to say how many tens and ones are in 44. If they were correct, they were then asked to select the correct number of 10- and 1-blocks and place them horizontally. This Multiple 10 condition was compared to two other conditions: the Single 10 condition and the Multiple 1 condition. In the Single 10 condition (see Figure 3.2b), children were provided with a single 10-block and multiple 1-blocks. The demonstration and training were identical to the Multiple 10 condition, except that only one 10-block and multiple 1-blocks were used. Thus, for the demonstration of constructing 37, the experimenter first placed one 10-block and then 27 1-blocks horizontally as s/he counted 'ten (pause), one, two, three ... twenty-seven, (pause), thirty-seven'. In the Multiple 1 condition (see Figure 3.2c), 1-blocks only were provided.

The improvement in the two-digit number magnitude was assessed through the positioning of numbers onto a number line marked 0–100 at the extremities. The authors predicted that the Multiple 10 condition, not the Multiple 1 condition, would show improved representations on the number line.

As expected, the Multiple 1 condition did not lead to any significant change in number representation. The two other conditions led to significant changes but the gains made by children in the Multiple 10 condition were significantly greater than those in the Single 10 block (or Multiple 1 condition), and only the Multiple 10 condition led to a change from a logarithmic to a linear representation on the number line task. So, only 2 sessions of 15 minutes where children learned to show numbers using 10- and 1-blocks horizontally changed their estimation on the number line.

3.3.2 Training the decimal position system

Ho and Chen (1997) provided specific training of the decimal position system to Chinese (first-grade) children with arithmetic difficulties. To measure the impact of the training on the place-value understanding, the authors developed a test in which children were asked (1) to write numerals to represent the quantity of different combinations of ten and unit boxes and to indicate which numeral should be at the unit position and which at the ten position, (2) to rewrite addition formulae from horizontal to vertical format, (3) to draw ten and/or unit boxes to represent written numerals, (4), to complete addition formulae which required understanding that X-ten-Y equals X-ten plus Y (e.g., 92 = _ + 2), and (5) to increase some three- and four-digit numbers by one.

The training consisted of five weekly one-hour sessions given after school hours. Each training session involved direct instructions, demonstrations, games, classwork, and homework. Session 1 focused on refreshing and consolidating the children's oral and object counting skills through simple counting exercises (e.g., counting and reporting the quantity of a set of blocks). In Session 2, children were asked to count and tie ten straws into a bundle, and to put ten bundles of straws into a glass. When counting the straws in bundles, they counted in tens, and when counting the straws in glasses, they counted in hundreds. Then, they were asked to add or subtract some straws. In this process, the children needed to regroup the additional straws and the existing straws into bundles and glasses, or to untie an existing bundle in order to have enough single straws to give away. These activities of grouping, regrouping, and trading aimed at helping children understand that 10 units of 1 can be exchanged for 1 unit of 10 and vice versa. In Session 3, children were asked to use written numerals to indicate the quantity of objects counted. Straws and number cards with a decade number (e.g., '30') or unit number (e.g., '3') were used. For instance, when presented with two bundles of straws and three single straws, children were asked to use the number cards to show the quantity of the straws they had in bundles (i.e., the card with '20') and in single units (i.e., the card with '3'). The trainers then demonstrated that when we put the '3' card over the '20' card at the unit position, we got a new number, '23' (see Figure 3.3). With explanation, this activity helped the children to understand that '23' was twenty and three. The positional value of numbers was further elaborated by other games and activities. This positional value concept was

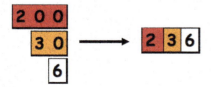

Figure 3.3 Use of Montessori cards where the different parts of the numbers are selected and then superposed to see the full number.

88 *Base-10 representation*

extended to three-digit numbers in Session 4. Session 5 mainly involved revision and consolidation of the place-value concepts learned in previous sessions.

A significant improvement in place-value understanding was observed in the group who received the training but not in the control group who did not receive it.

Mix, Smith, Stockton, Cheng, and Barterian (2017) contrasted two training programmes: one using only symbols and another using both symbols and base-10 blocks. Indeed, while some studies have shown improved mathematical performance for children taught using concrete models and manipulatives such as base-10 blocks (Fuson & Briars, 1990; Peterson, Mercer & O'Shea, 1988), others have argued that concrete models are detrimental because they themselves are symbolic, introduce extraneous, distracting details, and may lead to context-specific learning and thus weaker transfer (Goldstone & Sakamoto, 2003; Kaminski, Sloutsky & Heckler, 2008; McNeil et al., 2009; Uttal, Scudder & DeLoache, 1997). Mix et al. randomly assigned seven-year-old children to one of the three conditions: block training, symbol-only training, and no training conditions.

Children in the blocks condition used sets of base-10 blocks: ones, tens, hundreds, and thousands blocks. They also used mats that showed how written numerals, place value names, and blocks aligned (see Figure 3.4). In the symbols-only condition children completed the same activities either in writing or using a set of plain white note cards with hand-written single-digit numerals on them (range = 0–9). Children in the no-training group completed the pre-tests and post-tests at a four-week interval without any intervening training.

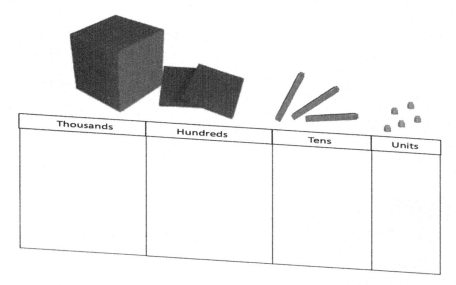

Figure 3.4 Base-10 blocks and mat with the different positions, similar to those used by Mix, Smith, Stockton, Cheng, and Barterian (2017).

The training sessions took place over four to six weeks and focused on six content lessons that introduced children to multi-digit number meanings and calculation. The first session aimed at understanding the meaning of multi-digit numbers, for example, by selecting blocks and arranging them in the right column of the positional table (block condition) or number cards (symbol condition) corresponding to Arabic or oral numbers. Session 2 dealt with the procedures for solving the addition of multi-digit numbers without carryover and Session 3 with carryover. For example, students were taught how to write addition problems using representations of blocks, how to realize that different combinations of blocks can be used to represent the same number (e.g., a stick of 10 = 10 blocks of 1), how to solve the addition problem with the help of these blocks and then write the answer using number cards (block conditions), or how to learn written notation of addition problems and practice solving addition problems with or without carryover (symbol conditions). Sessions 4 and 5 focused on learning the procedures for solving number subtractions without (Session 4) and with (Session 5) borrowing, and Session 6 was a review session.

The learning effect was assessed with three written measures: a place value test, the school sale problem, and a number line (0–1,000) estimation task. The place-value test involved different types of items: (1) numeral ordering (select the larger or smaller of two Arabic numbers (e.g., 567 vs. 439), order three three-digit numerals, look at two three-digit numbers with a gap in between and fill in the gap with the appropriate numbers), (2) numeral interpretation (identify among several numerals the one named by the experimenter or the one with a specific place value meaning (e.g., 'a 7 in the hundreds place?'), which of four expanded notations match a multi-digit numeral (e.g., 152 = 100 + 50 + 2)), and (3) vertically oriented multi-digit additions. The school sale problem assessed children's understanding of the hierarchical relations underlying place value, but these problems did not involve base-10 structures. Here is an example: 'Pretend you are packing erasers in bags and boxes. You have 38 erasers. You can fit 5 erasers in each bag. You can fit 5 bags in each box. How many full boxes can you make with the 38 erasers you have?'

Overall, children improved in both training conditions while there was no difference between pre- and post-test in the no-training group. More precisely, children who received blocks training demonstrated an advantage on measures that required understanding of base-10 structure – namely, numeral interpretation items and the school sale problem – but this advantage was not evident on other place value tasks, such as number ordering and multi-digit addition. One possible explanation for multi-digit calculations is that they can be solved through the use of procedures learned by rote so that improvement on these tasks can be shown without necessarily understanding base-10 structure. By contrast, symbols-only children improved on number line estimation, but this effect was small.

Interestingly, the authors also considered separately the high- and low-ability children based on their initial level. They found that high-ability children

90 *Base-10 representation*

had greater gains from symbols-only training while low-ability children benefitted more from the blocks training. Thus, using appropriate materials can be useful for understanding the base-10 system, especially with low-ability children.

3.3.3 Remediation programmes of transcoding

Sullivan et al. (1996) reported the case of a 13-year-old boy who had very poor transcoding skills and the intervention strategy they used. In writing Arabic numerals under dictation the teenage boy was only 54% correct, and 45% correct in writing Arabic numerals from written verbal numbers. His performance was better in reading aloud Arabic numbers (79% correct) or written verbal numbers (89% correct). As he was quite good at comparing the magnitude of two written verbal numbers (20/21 correct) or two spoken numbers (18/20 correct), the authors concluded that his errors in writing Arabic numbers from written or spoken verbal numbers were due to a difficulty in producing Arabic numbers rather than in the comprehension of verbal numbers (in reference to the model of McCloskey et al. (1985), see Section 3.1.6.1 of this chapter). His errors on these tasks were most often syntactic (see Table 3.1b page 80) revealing a difficulty in mastering the positional system of the Arabic code. On the basis of this analysis, the authors implemented a training programme designed to overcome CM's syntactic impairment.

In the training, they used a syntactic frame marking the positions of the ones, the tens, and the hundreds (see Figure 3.5a) to help CM in the production of Arabic numbers from one to three digits. CM was shown how to use the frame to write Arabic numbers corresponding to given written verbal numbers. In case CM was producing an error, he was directly corrected and an explanation was given to him. Then, CM was presented with an extended frame going from the ones to the hundred thousands (see Figure 3.5b) and practiced with 15 items corresponding to 3- to 6-digit numbers and then with 75 items corresponding to 1- to 6-digit numbers. Pre-training/post-training comparisons revealed significant improvement on the trained written-verbal-to-Arabic task (from 44% correct to 75% correct) as well as on an untrained

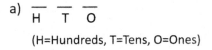

Figure 3.5 The frame used by Sullivan et al. (1996) to help the production of Arabic numbers.

spoken-verbal-to-Arabic task (from 55% to 79% correct) presumed to share the same Arabic numeral production process, whereas the performance in the other transcoding tasks did not change.

Another interesting intervention for transcoding difficulties was carried out by Fraitteur (2013). She worked with an adult presenting a developmental dyscalculia, Marie, a 34-year-old woman. Her difficulties in mathematics were quite global, but here we will present the work done with her regarding transcoding. In writing Arabic numbers under dictation, she was 44/60 correct, which is clearly abnormal for an adult. Her errors were quite similar to those produced by CM, e.g., /forty thousand and three/ was written 40.03, /two hundred and six/ was written 200.06 and /forty thousand twenty-five/ was written 40.23). To better understand the origin of these difficulties, a pre-test was created with nine tasks: two transcoding tasks, four tasks tapping her ability to understand numbers, and three tasks assessing her ability to produce numbers. All the tasks used a set of 30 large numbers including internal zeros (e.g., 2,004 or 516,004), as our first observation showed that numbers like these often led to transcoding errors by the patient. In writing Arabic numbers under dictation, she was only 53% correct (see Table 3.2). In reading Arabic numbers aloud, she was 70% correct. In tasks assessing her comprehension of Arabic or spoken numbers, such as comparing the magnitude of two Arabic or two spoken numbers, or selecting the bills (of ones, tens, hundreds, thousands …) corresponding to Arabic or spoken numbers, she was very good (performance between 93 and 100% correct). By contrast, in tasks tapping her number production abilities, she showed a clear dissociation between the verbal and the Arabic format. In particular, she was given several bills (e.g., two bills of a hundred and six bills of one) and asked to produce the corresponding number. If she was requested to produce

Table 3.2 Performance of Marie before, just after, and one year after the intervention

	Before the intervention	Just after the intervention	One year after
Transcoding			
Write Arabic numbers under dictation	53%	100%	100%
Read Arabic numbers aloud	70%	100%	100%
Number comprehension			
Compare two Arabic numbers	100%	97%	100%
Compare two spoken numbers	100%	100%	100%
Select bills corresponding to Arabic numbers	93%	97%	100%
Select bills corresponding to spoken numbers	100%	100%	100%
Number production			
Produce Arabic numbers corresponding to bills	30%	100%	100%
Produce spoken numbers corresponding to bills	97%	100%	100%
Base-10 comprehension			
A product cost this much, you only have 100$ bills, how many bills do you have to give?	51%	100%	97%

92 Base-10 representation

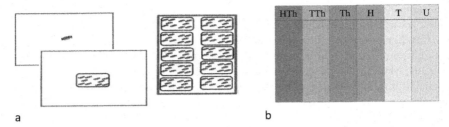

Figure 3.6 (a) Candy cards and (b) the positional chart (HTh = hundreds of thousands, TTh = tens of thousands, Th = thousands, H = hundreds, T = tens, and U = units).

the numbers in the verbal format (spoken numbers), her performance was really good (97%) but if she was requested to write Arabic numbers, her performance was really low (30%). Interestingly, in that latter case, her errors were of the same type as in the transcoding task of writing Arabic numbers under dictation, suggesting that her errors in these transcoding tasks were mainly due to difficulties in producing Arabic numbers whereas her number comprehension was preserved. Accordingly, the author decided to work on the positional system of the Arabic code using a chart with the different decimal positions (see Figure 3.6) in association with manipulatives representing the base-10 system. Seven training sessions were provided. In the first three sessions, the author worked with the Dienes material (as in Figure 3.4), but Marie did not seem to understand and no progress was noticed. At the fourth session, another material was used with cards with 1 candy, cards with bags of 10 candies, cards with boxes containing 10 bags (100 candies), pallets of 10 boxes (1,000 candies), and trucks transporting 10 pallets (10,000 candies); see Figure 3.6. This material was much more meaningful to the patient who showed rapid progress.

The intervention included exercises in representing a number (written verbal number) with the material (Dienes cubes or candy cards). For instance, 'imagine you go to the candy store and you want to buy 310 candies. You can buy them by pieces, by bags of ten, by boxes of a hundred. So, what can you do?' The patient was asked to think about different possibilities (e.g., buying 310 pieces or 31 bags of 10, or 3 boxes and 1 bag). The therapist started with units, decades, and decade-unit number structures, and then with three-digit numbers. Then, the positional chart was introduced with the idea of placing the selected material in the right position on the chart (e.g., the candies in the unit column, the bags in the decade column, …). Exercises were also proposed in which the patient was presented with two cards (e.g., one card with 3 bags and 5 candies and another card with 27 candies) and asked to decide which has more or discover equivalence (e.g., 16 boxes are the same as 160 bags). Then, numbers with thousands were introduced. After seven sessions, the performance of Marie was close to ceiling, and her progress remained stable one year later (see Table 3.2).

3.3.4 *In summary*

A few broad guidelines can be drawn from the literature presented above. For example, Zhang and Okamoto (2017) showed that it was important to help children develop a strategy of counting by ten in order to improve the representation of the magnitude of two-digit numbers. Mix et al. (2017) also showed that the use of blocks representing the powers of ten, in addition to symbolic numbers, was beneficial especially for children who are weaker in their mathematical learning. However, this material may be too abstract for some (e.g., Marie, in Fraitteur et al., 2013). In this case, more personally meaningful base-10 material should be used. Ho and Chen (1997), for example, worked with students to construct a material representing the powers of ten (ten straws to form a bundle, ten bundles in a glass, etc.) and helped them count this material in the corresponding base-10; count the bundles by tens, the glasses of straws by hundreds. They also used exchange games to improve the child's understanding of the equivalence between different ways of expressing quantity. To switch from this material in base-10 to Arabic numbers, they used Montessori cards which show how the different quantities can be integrated to form a new number. The production of Arabic numbers can also be facilitated by using a framework to guide the child's response (e.g., Sullivan et al., 1996) or by using a positioning table (see Fraitteur et al., unpublished).

In addition, Mix et al. (2017) use some arithmetic exercises in which addition and subtraction (without carry-over or borrowing) are first performed using the material expressing the powers of ten and the positioning table. Then, when the child is able to master the equivalence between different ways of decomposing the number, more complex calculations with carry-over and borrowing can be proposed, again with the support of the material expressing the powers of ten and the positioning table.

3.4 From research to practice: how to assess these competences?

Assessment of base-10 understanding can be found in some standardized assessment batteries. For instance, both the Tedi-Math (Van Niewenhoven, Grégoire & Noël, 2002) and the Tedimath Grands (Noël & Grégoire, 2015) have specific subtests to assess base-10 understanding. Some items of the Numeration subtest of the KeyMath-3 (Connolly, 2007) are also interesting for that purpose. Finally, the Multi-Digit Number Comparison and the Number Line subtests of the MathPro test (Karagiannakis & Noël, 2020) assess children's understanding of larger numbers' magnitude. This list is of course not exhaustive.

Other assessment tasks have been used in research papers. Here is a list of propositions.

(1) Task tapping the presence of counting by tens: give a material such as cubes and bars of ten cubes or dots arranged in rows of ten. Ask the

child to count them and record whether they use a count-by-ten strategy (Russell & Ginsburg, 1984).

(2) From symbolic numbers to the base-10 material or the reverse: give the child piles of play money (e.g., 4-$100s, 3-$10s) and ask him/her to say how much money there is, or to write this amount in Arabic digits (Russell & Ginsburg, 1984). This will allow you to see the child's understanding of the base-10 system and his/her ability to produce verbal or Arabic numbers. You may also explore the reverse task, i.e., asking the child to select the correct amount of play money (bills of ones, tens, hundreds, thousands …) corresponding to a spoken number or to a written Arabic number (this will allow you to assess the child's understanding of the base-10 structure underlying verbal or Arabic numbers).

(3) Number transcoding: ask the child to read aloud Arabic numbers or to write Arabic numbers upon dictation.

(4) Positional system: give the child pairs of Arabic numbers of the same length, including incompatible pairs, and ask him/her to select the bigger one (e.g., 42 – 39, 799999 – 811111, 833333 – 177777, Russell & Ginsburg, 1984). You can also present an Arabic number to the child (e.g., 25) and ask him/her to take as many poker chips as the number and then, to split the pile of poker chips so that the first pile represents the value of the first digit and the second one the value of the second digit (see Sinclair et al., 1992 or Russell & Ginsburg, 1984). Present different Arabic numbers and ask the child to select the one with a specific value at a specific position (e.g., select the one with 7 in the hundreds place among 1742, 2172, 3247, 7124, see Mix, Smith, Stockon, Cheng & Barterian, 2017). You can also ask the child to solve calculations that refer to the base-10 decomposition of numbers (e.g., 92 = _ + 2, or 152 = 100 + _ + 2, see Ho & Chen, 1997).

3.5 From research to practice: intervention

Based on this literature, in this section, we propose a series of five steps to constitute an intervention on the representation of multi-digit numbers, and in particular, on the understanding of the base-10 and the positional system of Arabic numbers. The first step aims at understanding the base-10 system of verbal numbers with the help of materials to be manipulated. The goal is to help the child understand, for example, that 'two hundred and fifty' actually means two times one hundred plus five times ten. In a second step, we work on exchange, equivalence, composition, and decomposition. For example, in this step, the child learns that 'two hundred and fifty' also means twenty-five tens. In the third stage, the child is introduced to the positional system in base-10 using positional tables, in association with the corresponding Arabic numbers. The fourth step is centred on the transcoding of verbal numbers to Arabic numbers and vice versa, with numbers of up to three digits. In the fifth step, the child discovers that everything he or she has learned can very easily be extended to handle very large numbers up to millions.

3.5.1 From verbal numbers to base-10 material and vice versa

For this first step, use materials that represent base-10 in a very transparent way. These may be Dienes blocks (Figure 3.7a represents the number 327), but for some children this material is abstract. It is best to use a material that you create with the child, such as straws, bundles of 10 straws, and glasses containing 10 bundles (Figure 3.7b represents the number 124), or candy and bags of 10 candies. With this type of material, the child sees the ten straws in the bundle, or the ten candies in the bag.

With this material, begin to develop the base-10 representation. For example, if I want 26 candies, I can take 26 but I can also take 2 bags (of 10) and 6 candies. Help the child discover that it is much faster and easier to take groups of ten directly. Explain to the child that these are 'tens' because each of them contains ten items. You can also do the opposite: give a set of items (*x* tens and *y* ones) and ask the child to say how many there are. Model the ten-count strategy first and encourage children to do so. Experiment with the child through both types of exercises, inviting them to talk aloud about what they are doing and explain how to do it. For example, 'To take 56 straws, I take five bundles of ten straws because five bundles is fifty and then I take six more to make fifty-six' or 'To take 56 straws, I take ten (taking one bundle), twenty (taking the second) ... fifty (taking the fifth bundle), and one, two ... six (taking the six straws alone)'.

After that, you can also introduce a more meaningful, but less transparent material, by using one-euro coins and ten-euro bills, or by using one- and ten-cent coins. Using this type of material can increase children's motivation as they experience that mathematics is relevant to their daily lives. However, this material should only be introduced at the end because it is not transparent at the base-10. Indeed, if you could see the ten candies in the bag or the ten straws in the bundle, here you do not see the ten euros in the ten-euro banknote, or the ten one-cent coins in the ten-cent coin.

You can also play comparison (or battle) games. For example, you can present two bundles and three straws on one side and three bundles and two straws on the other side and ask where are there the most?

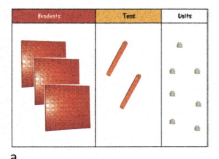
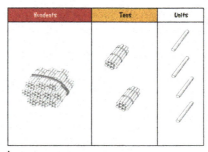

a   b

Figure 3.7 Base-10 material: base-10 (a) Dienes blocks or (b) straws.

96 *Base-10 representation*

In all these exercises, start with numbers less than a hundred; then you can introduce the hundreds and move on to the larger numbers (but less than a thousand).

3.5.2 Exchange, equivalence, composition, decomposition

With exercises such as the store, help the child discover that a 'ten' (or a decade) can be exchanged for ten 'ones' (or units) and vice versa. You can explain that there is a 'number machine' that exchanges (composes) every ten objects for one equivalent object of another type (larger, longer, or, etc.). In the case of 13 blocks, for example (Figure 3.8a), 10 of them can be exchanged for 1 bar of the same length as the 10 blocks. It then appears that a set of 13 blocks is equivalent (in length here) to the set of 1 bar and 3 blocks (Figure 3.8b). Use the base-10 materials you have selected for this child and show them how materials representing a decade equal ten units. Finally, you can also use euro coins as a more authentic way of explaining the concepts of exchange and equivalence. For example, it is important for the child to understand that ten one-euro coins are worth the same as a ten-euro bill, or that a dime is worth the same as ten one-cent coins.

You may want to explain to the child that this number machine is necessary because when we select Arabic numbers, only ten symbols (0, 1, 2, 3, 4, 5, 6, 7, 8, 9) are available to represent quantities from zero (nothing) to nine. So when you have ten objects, how do you represent them with Arabic symbols? You have to use the number machine and exchange ten objects for another one, of a different kind, but worth the same value.

The decimal 'number machine' functions inversely as well, that is exchanges one object for ten of equal value in total (decomposition). For example, suppose that you hold three ten-cent coins and four one-cent coins If you exchange one ten-cent coin with ten one-cent coins you still hold in total an equal amount of money (Figure 3.9). In general, stimulate different decompositions of the number: a canonical base-10 (54 = 5 tens + 4 ones) or non-canonical

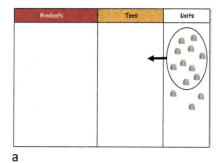 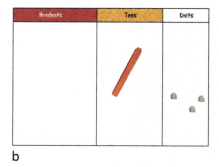

a   b

Figure 3.8 Exchange ten 'units' (a) for one 'ten' (b).

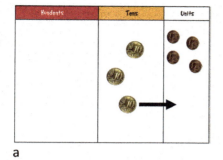 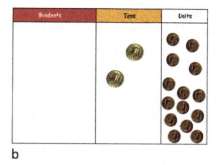

Figure 3.9 Exchange of one ten-cent coin (a) for ten one-cent coins (b).

ones (54 = 4 tens + 14 ones or 3 tens and 24 ones...), and write them down along with the drawing of the material.

3.5.3 Base-10 positional system, positional chart, and Arabic code

To go from the base-10 material and verbal numbers to the Arabic code, you can use Montessori cards (as in Ho & Chen, 1997) or similar cards but that would be transparent with a vertical line at the right. Begin by guiding the child in selecting the right card for a single type of item, for example, only units, or only tens, or only hundreds. For example, get 5 rods of 10 or 5 bundles of 10 straws and invite the child to select the corresponding '50' card. Next, you can use numbers with different types of base-10 units. For example, arrange two rods of ten and five cubes and ask the child to say aloud the corresponding number ('twenty-five'); then ask the child to take the corresponding cards (card '20' for the 2 rods and card '5' for the cubes) and place the smaller card (card '5') on top of the larger one (card '20'), as shown in Figure 3.10. Indeed, if the cards are superimposed and aligned on the right (as indicated by the line drawn on the right of each card), a new number '25' is obtained which corresponds to the whole. Use different materials (straws, candy, money) to train him/her to use different units of concrete measures (one straw, one candy, one cent) to facilitate long-term understanding of the different basic units (units, tens, hundreds, etc.). Finally, you can leave the concrete material behind and simply use a positional chart in which the columns are named by both the corresponding decimal rank (units, tens, hundreds, etc.) and the number of units (1, 10, 100, etc., Figures 3.11 and 3.12).

Do many exercises in which a verbal number is presented to the child who must produce the corresponding Arabic number using the Montessori cards and write the number on the positional chart or, when the child is comfortable, without further assistance.

You can also play a comparison game (or battle). Give two Arabic numbers (compatible and incompatible tens-unit structures) and ask the child to judge

98 *Base-10 representation*

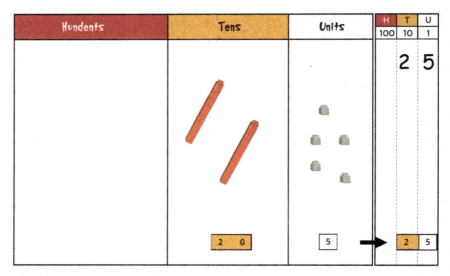

Figure 3.10 Montessori cards and positional charts with cubes and rods.

which one is the larger. Then you give two cards with only one Arabic digit written on them. Each player organizes his or her two cards to make a two-digit number (for example, with the cards '2' and '4', I can create the number '24' or '42'); then the battle begins and you find out who created the larger number. You can play this game by using playing cards as well.

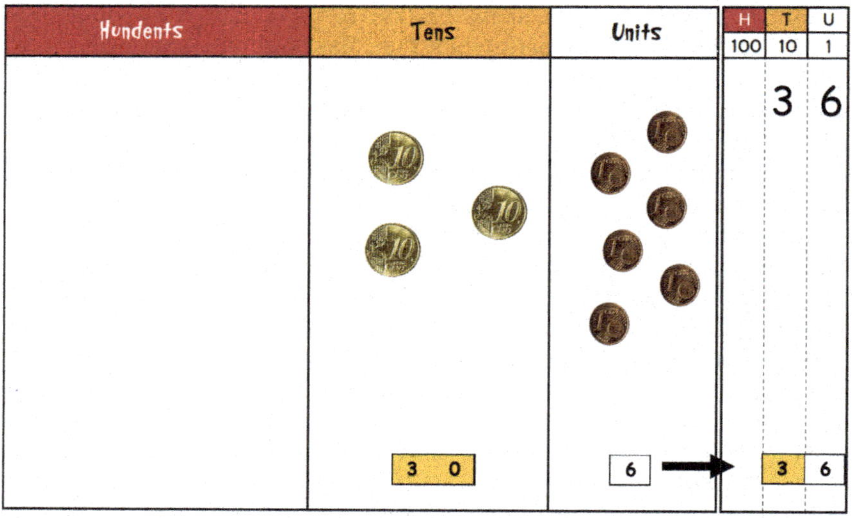

Figure 3.11 Montessori cards and positional charts with euro coins.

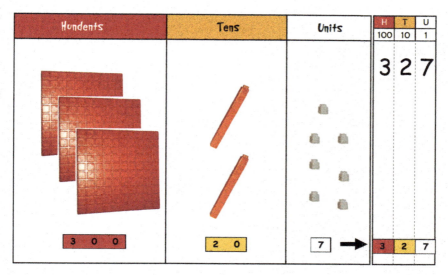

Figure 3.12 Montessori cards and positional charts with Dienes blocks.

3.5.4 From verbal numbers to Arabic numbers

In the course of learning how to transcode numbers, the errors that are produced by children are mostly syntactic errors, and most of the time, mastering additive relationships is more difficult than mastering multiplicative relationships. Montessori cards, as presented above, are a very useful tool: they help the child to combine the subparts of the numbers entering into additive relations with each other, to form the global number, by superimposing them with respect to the alignment on the line. An interesting representation showing number structure is the *Clever chart* (Cooreman, 2015). It is essentially the *Gattegno chart* presented vertically (starting from zero at the bottom) rather than horizontally, supporting the innate idea that the higher the position, the bigger the number (Figure 3.13). The Gattegno chart focuses on the way bigger numbers are constructed by identifying their constituent parts (Faux, 1998). Using the images presented in such a chart, the number symbols and the words to identify them can be brought together, making this transcoding transparent. Undue emphasis on the place value structure may invite a *digitwise* approach, which will generate many errors, both in transcoding but also in calculating later on. Gattegno charts presented either horizontally or vertically (Clever chart) can be used to practice naming and representing numbers with whole classes.

Faux (1998) suggests using the Gattegno chart in exercises such as the following: point to the '800' box and ask the child to say 'eight hundred', then point to the '50' box when the child says 'fifty' out loud and finally point to

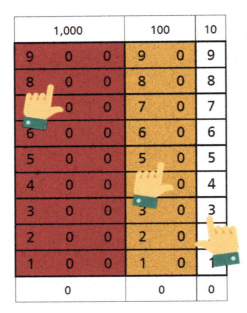

Figure 3.13 Clever chart (Cooreman, 2015).

the '3' box when the child says 'three' (see Figure 3.13). In this way, the oral verbal number 'eight hundred and fifty-three' is associated with the values that make it up, '800' and '50' and '3', and then the children write the corresponding Arabic number '853'. In this way, the children better understand the positional values of each digit composing the number. This understanding will be important when performing calculations on multi-digit numbers.

Do exercises in which you present a number orally and ask the child to first point to the boxes corresponding to the components of the number and then to write the corresponding Arabic number. Use two-digit numbers first, and then three-digit numbers later. Consider using numbers in which some zeros are present (for example, 'two hundred and three').

3.5.5 Generalization to big numbers up to millions

Once the child has understood the concept of the unit, the ten (or decade), the hundred, and their relationships through a series of exercises including transcoding exercises, you can introduce the larger numbers (containing four or more digits). In fact, the triptych hundred-tens-unit is the cornerstone for constructing all larger numbers because when it is repeated, it expresses thousands, millions, billions, etc. Use images to illustrate this in a simple way so that the student realizes the repetitive structure (Figure 3.14).

Base-10 representation 101

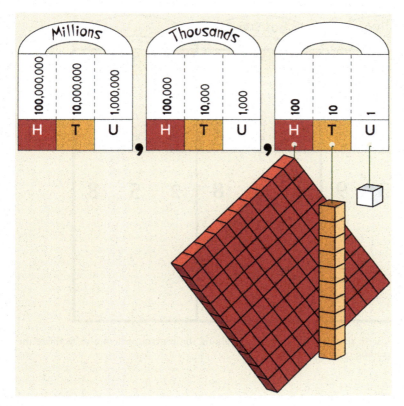

Figure 3.14 Visual representation of the triptych hundred-tens-unit (adapted from Karagiannakis, 2015).

Multi-digit numbers are read based on this triptych. First, you can present a large number directly in the positional chart (see Figure 3.15). Have the child read it out loud, starting with the first triplet followed by the word 'million' ('six hundred and thirty-nine million'), then the second triplet followed by the word 'thousand' ('four hundred and eight thousand'), and finally the last triplet ('two hundred and fifty-eight').

Afterwards, the child will be able to gradually free himself from the help of the chart and, when faced with a large number, first identify the triplet consisting of the last three numbers on the right, then identify the previous triplets. To help him/her, he/she can make a small mark between the triplets and, if necessary, indicate the multiplier to be used (thousand or million).

Finally, assess regularly the progress of the child and start the next level of the intervention only when the child is at ease with the current step you are practising.

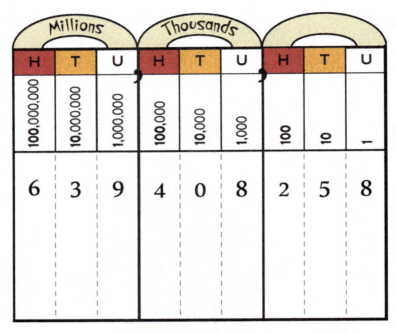

Figure 3.15 Use of the positional chart highlighting the triptych structure to facilitate the reading of large numbers.

References

Barrouillet, P., Camos, V., Perruchet, P., & Seron, X. (2004). ADAPT: A developmental, asemantic, and procedural model for transcoding from verbal to Arabic numerals. *Psychological Review, 111*(2), 368–394.

Becker, J., & Varelas, M. (1993). Semiotic aspects of cognitive development: Illustrations from early mathematical cognition. *Psychological Review, 100*(3), 420–431.

Camos, V. (2008). Low working memory capacity impedes both efficiency and learning of number transcoding in children. *Journal of Experimental Child Psychology, 99*(1), 37–57.

Carpenter, T. P., Franke, M. L., Jacobs, V. R., Fennema, E., & Empson, S. B. (1997). A longitudinal study of invention and understanding in children's multidigit addition and subtraction. *Journal for Research in Mathematics Education, 29*(1), 3–20.

Connolly, A. J. (2007). *KeyMath-3 diagnostic assessment: Manual forms A and B*. Minneapolis, MN: Pearson.

Cooreman, A. (2015), Rekentrappers 3HR module 2 Getalkaarten, buren en strategisch rekenen tot 1000, Leuven: Eureka ed.

Dehaene, S. (1992). Varieties of numerical abilities. *Cognition, 44*(1–2), 1–42.

Dehaene, S., Dupoux, E., & Mehler, J. (1990). Is numerical comparison digital? Analogical and symbolic effects in two-digit number comparison. *Journal of Experimental Psychology: Human Perception and Performance, 16*(3), 626–641.

Deloche, G., & Seron, X. (1987). Numerical transcoding: A general production model. In G. Deloche & X. Seron (Eds.), *Mathematical disabilities: A cognitive neuropsychological perspective* (pp. 137–170). Hillsdale, NJ: Lawrence Erlbaum.

Dowker, A., Bala, S., & Lloyd, D. (2008). Linguistic influences on mathematical development: How important is the transparency of the counting system? *Philosophical Psychology, 21*(4), 523–538. doi: 10.1080/09515080802285511

Faux, G. (1998). Using Gattegno charts. *Mathematics Teaching*, MT 163 June.

Fraiteur, S. (2013). *Rééducation d'une adulte dyscalculique par modules: Étude de cas*. Unpublished Thesis under the superviosn of MP Noël & A. DeVisscher. Faculté de psychologie et des sciences de l'éducation, Université catholique de Louvain.

Fuson, K. C. (1998). Pedagogical, mathematical, and real-world conceptual-support nets: A model for building children's multidigit domain knowledge. *Mathematical Cognition, 4*(2), 147–186.

Fuson, K. C., & Briars, D. J. (1990). Using a base-ten blocks learning/teaching approach for first- and second-grade place-value and multidigit addition and subtraction. *Journal for Research in Mathematics Education, 21*, 180–206.

Fuson, K. C., Wearne, D., Hiebert, J., Murray, H. G., Human, P. G., Olivier, A. I., ... Fennema, E. (1997). Children's conceptual structures for multidigit numbers and methods of multidigit addition and subtraction. *Journal of Research in Mathematics Education, 28*(2), 130–162.

Gervasconi, A., & Sullivan, P. (2007). Assessing and teaching children who have difficulty learning arithmetic. *Educational and Child Psychology, 24*, 40–53.

Goldstone, R. L., & Sakamoto, Y. (2003). The transfer of abstract principles governing complex adaptive systems. *Cognitive Psychology, 46*(4), 414–466.

Ho, C. S. H., & Cheng, F. S. F. (1997). Training in place-value concepts improves children's addition skills. *Contemporary Educational Psychology, 22*(4), 495–506.

Ho, C. S. H., & Fuson, K. C. (1998). Children's knowledge of teen quantities as tens and ones: Comparison of Chinese, British and American kindergartners. *Journal of Educational Psychology, 90*(3), 536–544.

Ifrah, G. (1994). *Histoire universelle des chiffres. L'intelligence des hommes racontée par les nombres et le calcul*. Paris: Robert Laffont.

Imbo, I., Vanden Bulcke, C., De Brauwer, J., & Fias, W. (2014). Sixty-four or four-and-sixty? The influence of language and working memory on children's number transcoding. *Frontiers of Psychology, 5*, 313. doi: 10.3389/fpsyg.2014.00313

Kaminski, J. A., Sloutsky, V. M., & Heckler, A. F. (2008). Learning theory: The advantage of abstract examples in learning math. *Science, 320*(5875), 454–455.

Karagiannakis, G. (2015). *Οι αριθμοί πέρα απ' τους κανόνες. Αθήνα: Διερευνητική μάθηση*.

Karagiannakis, G., & Noël, M.-P. (2020). Mathematical profile test: A preliminary evaluation of an online assessment for mathematics skills of children in grades 1–6. *Behavioral Sciences (Basel, Switzerland), 10* (8), 126.

Koppel, H. (1999). Bases nécessaires pour l'acquisition sereine du système décimal. In S. Vinter & A. Ménessier (Eds.), *Les activités numériques, opérations logiques et formulations langagières*. Pp. 175-188. Besançon: Presses Universitaires Franc-Comtoises.

Kreps, G., Squire, S., & Bryant, P. (2003). Children's understanding of the additive composition of number and of the decimal structure: What is the relationship? *International Journal of Educational Research, 39*(7), 677–694.

Krinzinger, H., Gregoire, J., Desoete, A., Kaufmann, L., Nuerk, H. C., & Willmes, K. (2011). Differential language effects on numerical skills in second grade. *Journal of Cross-Cultural Psychology, 42*(4), 614–629.

Lafay, A., & Helloin, M.-C. (2016). *Examath 8-15*. Editions Happy Neuron (sur internet).
Laski, E. V., Ermakova, A., & Vasilyeva, M. (2014). Early use of decomposition for addition and its relation to base-10 knowledge. *Journal of Applied Developmental Psychology, 35*(5), 444–454.
Lê, M.-L. T., & Noël, M.-P. (2022). Transparent Vietnamese number-naming system facilitates first graders transcoding—A cross-linguistic study with French. *Cognitive Development, 61*, 101145.
McCloskey, M., Caramazza, A., & Basili, A. (1985). Cognitive mechanisms in number processing and calculation: Evidence from dyscalculia. *Brain and Cognition, 4*(2), 171–196.
McNeil, N. M., Uttal, D. H., Jarvin, L., & Sternberg, R. J. (2009). Should you show me the money? Concrete objects both hurt and help performance on mathematics problems. *Learning and Instruction, 19*(2), 171–184.
Miura, I. T., Kim, C. C., Chang, C., & Okamoto, Y. (1988). Effects of language characteristics on children's cognitive representation of number: Cross-national comparisons. *Child Development, 59*(6), 1445–1450.
Miura, I. T., & Okamoto, Y. (1989). Comparisons of U.S. and Japanese first graders cognitive representation of number and understanding of place value. *Journal of Educational Psychology, 81*(1), 109–114.
Miura, I. T., Okamoto, Y., Kim, C. C., Chang, C. M., Steere, M., & Fayol, M. (1994). Comparisons of children's cognitive representation of number: China, France, Japan, Korean, Sweden and the United States. *International Journal of Behavioral Development, 17*(3), 401–411.
Miura, I. T., Okamoto, Y., Kim, C. C., Steere, M., & Fayol, M. (1993). First graders' cognitive representations of number and understanding of place value: Cross-national comparisons. *Journal of Educational Psychology, 85*(1), 24–30.
Mix, K. S., Smith, L. B., Stockton, J. D., Cheng, Y. L., & Barterian, J. A. (2017). Grounding the symbols for place-value: Evidence from training and long-term exposure to base-10 models. *Journal of Cognition and Development, 18*(1), 129–151.
Moeller, K., Fischer, M. H., Nuerk, H. C., & Willmes, K. (2009). Sequential or parallel decomposed processing of two-digit numbers? Evidence from eye-tracking. *Quarterly Journal of Experimental Psychology, 62*(2), 323–334.
Moeller, K., Pixner, S., Zubern, J., Kaufmann, L., & Nuerk, H. C. (2011). Early place-value understanding as a precursor for later arithmetic performance - A longitudinal study on numerical development. *Research in Developmental Disabilities, 32*(5), 1837–1851.
Moura, R., Wood, G., Pinheiro-Chagas, P., Lonnemann, J., Krinzinger, H., Willmes, K., & Geraldi Haase, V. (2013). Transcoding abilities in typical and atypical mathematics achievers: The role of working memory and procedural and lexical competencies. *Journal of Experimental Child Psychology, 116*(3), 707–727.
Nguyen, H. T.-T., & Grégoire, J. (2014). When 5004 is said. 'five thousand zero hundred remainder four': The influence of language on natural number transcoding: Cross-national comparison. *Research in Mathematical Education, 18*(2), 149–170.
Noël, M. P., & Grégoire, J. (2015). *TediMath Grands, Test diagnostique des compétences de base en mathématiques du CE2 à la 5ème*. Montreuil, France: ECPA.
Noël, M. P., & Turconi, E. (1999). Assessing number transcoding in children. *European Review of Applied Psychology, 49*(4), 295–302.
Nuerk, H. C., Weger, U., & Willmes, K. (2001). Decade breaks in the mental number line? Putting the tens and units back into different bins. *Cognition, 82*(1), B25–B33.
Nuerk, H. C., & Willmes, K. (2005). On the magnitude representations of two-digit numbers. *Psychology Science, 47*, 52–72.
Peterson, S. K., Mercer, C. D., & O'Shea, L. (1988). Teaching learning disabled students place value using the concrete to abstract sequence. *Learning Disabilities Research, 4*, 52–56.

Pixner, S., Zuber, J., Hermanova, V., Kaufmann, L., Nuerk, H. C., & Moeller, K. (2011). One language, two number-word systems and many problems: Numerical cognition in the Czech language. *Research in Developmental Disability, 32*(6), 2683–2689.

Poltrock, S. E., & Schwartz, D. R. (1984). Comparative judgement of multi-digit numbers. *Journal of Experimental Psychology: Learning, Memory, and Cognition, 10*, 32–45.

Power, R. J. D., & Dal Martello, M. F. (1990). The dictation of Italian numerals. *Language and Cognitive Processes, 5*(3), 237–254.

Power, R. J. D., & Dal Martello, M. F. (1997). From 834 to eighty thirty four: The reading of Arabic numerals by seven-year-old children. *Mathematical Cognition, 3*(1), 63–85.

Restle, F. (1970). Speed of adding and comparing numbers. *Journal of Experimental Psychology, 83*(1), 32–45.

Russell, R. L., & Ginsburg, H. P. (1984). Cognitive analysis of children's mathematics difficulties. *Cognition and Instruction, 1*(2), 217–244.

Seron, X., Deloche, G., & Noël, M. P. (1991). Number transcoding by children: Writing Arabic numbers under dictation. In J. Bideaud, C. Meljac & J. P. Fisher (Eds.), *Pathways to number* (pp. 245–264). Hillsdale, NJ: Lawrence Erlbaum Associates.

Seron, X., & Fayol, M. (1994). Number transcoding in children: A functional analysis. *British Journal of Developmental Psychology, 12*(3), 281–300.

Seron, X., Noël, M. P., & Van der Elst, G. (1997, 3–6 September). Where do Arabic number reading errors come from? Paper presented at the *8th European Conference on Developmental Psychology*, Rennes (France).

Sinclair, A., Garin, A., & Tièche-Christinat, C. (1992). Constructing and understanding of place value in numerical notation. *European Journal of Psychology of Education, 7*(3), 191–207.

Sullivan, K. S., Macaruso, P., & Sokol, S. M. (1996). Remediation of arabic numeral processing in a case of developmental dyscalculia. *Neuropsychological Rehabilitation, 6*(1), 27–53.

Temple, C. M. (1989). Digit dyslexia: A Category-specific disorder in development dyscalculia. *Cognitive Neuropsychology, 6*(1), 93–116.

Uttal, D. H., Scudder, K. V., & DeLoache, J. S. (1997). Manipulatives as symbols: A new perspective on the use of concrete objects to teach mathematics. *Journal of Applied Developmental Psychology, 18*(1), 37–54.

Van Loosbroek, E., Dirkx, G. S. M. A., Hulstijn, W., & Janssen, F. (2009). When the number line involves a delay: The writing of numbers by children of different arithmetical abilities. *Journal of Experimental Child Psychology, 102*(1), 26–39.

Van Niewenhoven, C., Grégoire, J., & Noël, M. P. (2002). *Tedi-math: Test diagnostique des compétences de base en mathématiques*. Paris: ECPA.

Van Rinsveld, A., & Schiltz, C. (2016). Sixty-twelve = seventy-two? A cross-linguistic comparison of children's number transcoding. *British Journal of Developmental Psychology, 34*(3), 461–468.

Vasilyeva, M., Laski, E. V., Ermakova, A., Lai, W. F., Jeong, Y., & Hachigian, A. (2015). Reexamining the language account of cross-national differences in base-10 number representations. *Journal of Experimental Child Psychology, 129*, 12–25.

Zhang, Y., & Okamoto, Y. (2017). Encoding '10ness' improves first-graders' estimation of numerical magnitudes. *Journal of Numerical Cognition, 2*(3), 190–201.

Zuber, J., Pixner, S., Moeller, K., & Nuerk, H. C. (2009). On the language-specificity of basic number processing: Transcoding in a language with inversion and its relation to working memory capacity. *Journal of Experimental Child Psychology, 102*(1), 60–77.

4 Arithmetic[1]

4.1 Introduction

Arithmetic skill is the ability to correctly solve arithmetic problems in a fluent way. It depends on the ability to understand the concept of the operation, the ability to develop and select effective resolution strategies (faster and less error-prone), and the ability to increase the fluidity (or speed) in the resolution of calculations.

In this chapter, we will see that arithmetic performance is modulated by factors related to the calculation itself and others related to the individual. At the level of the individual, difficulties in arithmetic may stem from a deficit in general cognitive processes or in specific numerical processes.

We will consider here the four basic arithmetic operations: addition, subtraction, multiplication, and division. These operations can be carried out on single-digit numbers (such as 4 + 5), which is generally called simple arithmetic, or on multi-digit numbers (such as 15 + 99), which is called complex arithmetic. In complex addition and subtraction, carry-overs and borrowings may be required. Carry-over occurs when, in addition problems, the sum of the digits of a specific position value (for example, units) exceeds 10, which requires adding the value of tens corresponding to this sum to the next position value (for example, in the addition 15 + 27, the sum of units is 12, so one must carry over '1' to the position on the left, i.e., to the tens in this case). In subtraction, when the term being subtracted includes a number in a particular position value that is greater than the number of the same position value in the first term, the units must be borrowed at the position value on the left (for example, 25 − 18 = 7); this is called borrowing.

As development progresses, the child's strategies for solving calculations evolve. Two main types of strategies are distinguished: procedural strategies and retrieval strategies. Procedural strategies require several steps to obtain the solution. They therefore involve knowing specific procedures, selecting the most appropriate procedure for the problem, and executing it correctly. The retrieval strategy consists in recovering the response to a calculation from

---

1 This chapter has been written by Marie-Pascale Noël, Alice DeVisscher and Giannis Karagiannakis.

DOI: 10.4324/b22795-4

long-term memory. We then speak of 'arithmetic fact' to refer to the association in long-term memory between a calculation and its response. This retrieval strategy is often faster than procedural strategies since it involves only one stage of cognitive processing. During development, more and more multiplication and simple addition problems are solved by the retrieval strategy. Procedural strategies, on the other hand, remain important for simple subtractions and divisions and for all complex operations.

Other parameters must also be taken into account, such as the modality and the way arithmetic problems are presented. Thus, arithmetic problems can be presented visually (with Arabic numbers) in a horizontal (initiating a mental procedure) or a vertical way (initiating a procedure known as written calculation or columnar calculation), or they can be presented orally (which will of course load the short-term memory system).

In the next section of this chapter, we will describe the development of the child's arithmetic skills. In the third section, we will examine the difficulties experienced by virtually all individuals with developmental dyscalculia or mathematics learning disabilities at this level, although these difficulties may differ from one individual to another. In the fourth section, we will review the published research on arithmetic training or remediation. This will allow us to identify practices that work. The last two sections will focus on clinical practice with, on the one hand, tools concerning the assessment of the child's arithmetic skills and, on the other hand, the presentation of concrete ways to accompany pupils with difficulties in arithmetic.

4.2 The development of arithmetic

Early in life, primitive approximate arithmetic abilities seem to be present in humans and animals. Wynn (1992) conducted the first study attesting to such capabilities. The paradigm is as follows: babies of about four months are seated in front of a puppet theatre, the experimenter introduces a puppet into the theatre and then closes the curtains. Visibly, s/he then introduces a second puppet behind the curtain, then opens the curtain. In half of the cases, two puppets are present on the scene of the puppet theatre ($1 + 1 \rightarrow 2$), which corresponds to the expected outcome. In the other cases, only one puppet is present; this is what the experimenters call the unexpected situation ($1 + 1 \rightarrow 1$). The gaze time of the child is measured and indicates that four-month-old babies look longer (and therefore seem surprised) when the result is unexpected (Wynn, 1992). This experiment has been replicated several times with other impossible outcomes (such as $1 + 1 \rightarrow 3$) or with subtraction (such as $2 - 1 \rightarrow 1$ or 2).

By two and a half years of age, young children are able to solve small addition or subtraction problems presented non-verbally (for example, Huttenlocher, Jordan & Levine, 1994; Jordan, Huttenlocher & Levine, 1994), whereas they are unable to solve these same calculations if presented verbally. The non-verbal condition is presented as follows: the child is shown an initial collection of objects (e.g., two tokens) that is then hidden under a scarf. Then another collection is added to the first collection (for example, three more tokens are slipped under the scarf). The child is then asked to put the same number of objects in front of him or her as there are under the scarf (and therefore not visible).

At the age of three, children can solve small calculations using objects. For example, when faced with the question, 'How much are three cars and two cars?', the child will typically count a first collection of three cars, then a second collection of two, and then count again (Fuson, 1982). By the age of four and five, children typically move on to finger counting, having realized that a finger can represent any object (Siegler & Shrager, 1984).

At the age of five, children who did not receive formal training can already perform approximate arithmetic (Barth et al., 2006). In this experiment, children observed on one side of the computer screen one array of blue dots being hidden behind an occluder, and successively a second array of blue dots being added to it (behind the occluder). Then an array of red dots appeared on the other side of the screen, and the children had to choose the larger array of dots between the hidden blue dots and the visible red dots. The quantities and settings in this experiment did not allow the children to count but forced them to use approximation (i.e., to use their ANS, see Chapter 2). In this task, children performed above chance, attesting to some approximate arithmetic abilities. Similar arithmetic approximation abilities have also been observed with 5-year-old children using symbolic arithmetic with large numbers, such as $64-13$ to be compared with 34 (Gilmore, McCarthy & Spelke, 2007).

With formal instruction, children are introduced to exact symbolic arithmetic, starting in the last of the preschool year and more formally and systematically in the first year of primary school. The arithmetical operations encountered by children start with addition, followed closely by subtraction, and later on by multiplication and division.

4.2.1 Simple addition and subtraction

At the onset of the arithmetic abilities, children rely on their counting abilities to solve arithmetical operations. Groen and Parkman (1972) suggested five counting strategies for simple addition in first-grade children. These will be presented along with their degree of maturity:

The first strategy is the *counting-all strategy*. The child counts from 1 and increments his or her count in steps of 1 for the value of the first term (or augend), then the second term (or addend), and then recounts all to find the sum (for example, $2+3$ is equal to 1, 2 and 1, 2, 3 so, 1, 2, 3, 4, 5). Very often, the child counts the objects referred to in the calculation or counts on his or her fingers. Thus, for the calculation $m+n$, he will count m fingers, then count n fingers, and recount the whole to obtain the sum. Using this strategy, the speed of resolution is highly correlated with the sum of the addition.

The next counting strategy consists in starting the count from the first term of the calculation and incrementing it by a number of steps equal to the value of the second term (for example, 2 + 3 is equal to 2 and 3, 4, 5). The opposite strategy is to start with the last term on the right and increment it a number of times corresponding to the first term. This is called the *counting-on strategy*. In order to use this strategy, the child must master one of the highest levels of the verbal numerical chain elaboration: the numerable chain. Indeed, he must be able to start counting from a number other than 1 while counting the number of counting steps he performs.

Finally, in the *counting-min strategy*, which is the most mature and fastest counting-based strategy, the child selects the largest of the terms and increments by a number of counting steps equal to the smallest term (for example, 2 + 5, 5 is the largest, therefore 5 and 6, 7). The response time is then a function of the size of the smallest term, which is why it is called the counting-min strategy. This strategy also requires a level of elaboration of the verbal numerical sequence corresponding to the numerable chain (see Chapter 2), but also, the ability to identify the larger of the two terms and therefore to have a good understanding of the magnitude of the numbers. Finally, an implicit understanding of the mathematical conceptual knowledge of commutativity may underlie the use of this strategy (knowing that 2 + 5 = 5 + 2) (see Baroody & Gannon, 1984).

In addition to these counting-based strategies, children also use the *retrieval strategy*. This is the most interesting strategy because it requires the least cognitive resources and is the fastest. Additions with small operands (e.g., 2 + 3) or two identical terms (also called 'ties', such as 3 + 3 or 5 + 5) are usually the first to be memorized. However, the retrieval of additive facts is currently the subject of discussion in the literature; some hypothesize that the very fast responses to these calculations come from a very fast and automated counting procedure (Thevenot, Barrouillet, Castel & Uittenhove, 2016).

Siegler's (1988) association distribution model suggests that each time the child uses a strategy to solve a calculation, the response thus obtained is associated with the problem in long-term memory. If the calculation is represented to the child and the same answer is obtained, the association between that answer and the problem becomes stronger. If, on the other hand, another answer is produced by the child, then another association is established between this new answer and the problem. Thus, both correct and incorrect answers could possibly be associated, in long-term memory, with the problem, to a greater or lesser extent depending on the frequency with which these answers are produced. Children who perform procedural strategies correctly will frequently find the correct answer, and will then be more likely to create a strong association between the problem and the correct answer. Conversely, children with weak procedural counting skills are likely to produce more errors and thus, on the one hand, develop weak associations between the problem and the correct answer and, on the other hand, create associations between the problem and incorrect answers. According to this model, the retrieval strategy can be implemented when the problem has a sufficiently strong association with a given response relative to other responses.

Finally, a last procedural strategy includes a retrieval step. This is the so-called *decomposition strategy*. In this strategy, the child is decomposing one of the addends to make the arithmetic problem easier. For example, a child who knows the answer to the calculation 5 + 5 but not the answer to the calculation 5 + 6 can solve the calculation 5 + 6 by transforming it into 5 + 5 + 1, which allows him or her to retrieve in memory the answer of 5 + 5, i.e., 10, and to add 1. This strategy is often used by modifying one of the terms to find a double (or tie) problem (for example, 7 + 8 modified into 7 + 7 + 1), or a sum equal to 10 (for example, 7 + 4 modified into 7 + 3 + 1).

At all ages, it appears that children use multiple strategies. However, over the course of development, the frequency of use of the less mature strategies decreases in favour of more mature strategies (see Siegler, 1996). Thus, in children aged four to five, we already observe the presence of various strategies such as counting all, counting min on fingers or verbally, decomposition, and retrieval (Siegler, 1987; Siegler & Robinson, 1982). In first-grade children, the predominant strategy observed is the counting-min strategy (Groen & Parkman, 1972). In subsequent years, a decrease in the use of the counting-min strategy and an increase in the decomposition and retrieval strategy are observed. It is a question of choosing the best strategy to use to solve a given calculation (Gandini & Lemaire, 2005). For example, retrieval will be more frequent for solving a small calculation (such as 3 + 3) than for solving a calculation with larger terms (such as 7 + 5), which may require a procedural strategy based on counting with perhaps the help of fingers. Arithmetic performance will also depend on the quality of execution of the strategy, that is, the speed and accuracy with which the child implements the strategy. The speed of execution varies according to the strategy (for example, the counting min is necessarily faster than the counting all) and its degree of automaticity. Indeed, the more automatic a strategy becomes, the faster it is executed.

Finally, it should be noted that some problems have a specific status. Thus, problems with the operand 0 are based on the knowledge of a rule, in this case, $n + 0 = n$ and $0 + n = n$. Thus, it is not necessary to retain the solution of 2 + 0, 3 + 0, 4 + 0, etc., but only this general rule to quickly solve all calculations of this type (see Campbell & Xue, 2001).

It is also important to note that the child has also to acquire some conceptual knowledge about addition, in particular, that it is a commutative operation and that it is the inverse of subtraction (i.e., if $A + B = C$, then $C - A = B$ and $C - B = A$).

With respect to the subtraction operation, Siegler and Jenkens (1989) describe different strategies used for children in second and fourth grades. The *counting-down* strategy consists in counting back from the minuend as many steps as the subtrahend (for example, to solve, 12 − 9 =, count backwards 9 steps from 12, i.e., 11, 10, 9, 8, 7, 6, 5, 4, 3, the answer is 3). Alternatively, in the *counting-up strategy*, the child adds up from the subtrahend to the minuend, and the number of counting steps made corresponds to the difference (for example, to solve 12 − 9 =, count forward from 9 up to 12, i.e., 10, 11, 12, the answer is 3 as you needed 3 counting steps). Retrieving the answer from long-term memory is another possible strategy for small subtractions. Another observed strategy is to recognize the inverse relationship between subtraction and addition and retrieve the answer from the addition to solve a subtraction (for example, to solve $8-3$, I remember that $3+5=8$, so the answer is 5).

The resolution of some subtractions seems to rely on the knowledge of rules and in particular, that $n-0=n$, and that $n-n=0$. Another important piece of mathematical conceptual knowledge is that subtraction is the inverse of addition.

4.2.2 Simple multiplication and division

The child's first approach to the concept of multiplication of $A \times B$ is usually to use an external support (tokens, for example) and to take A times the quantity B of tokens. This strategy is based on multiplication seen as repeated additions ($3 \times 4 = 4 + 4 + 4$). Other strategies will correspond to the enunciation of a numerical chain in steps. For example, to answer 6×2, the child can recite the counting by two sequence (2, 4, 6, ...) six times to find the number 12 corresponding to the product. Very quickly, the emphasis will be put on memorizing the multiplicative facts, thus favouring the retrieval strategy. Numerous research studies have examined the associative network of arithmetic facts for multiplications (e.g., Campbell & Xue, 2001; Roussel, Fayol & Barrouillet, 2002). In adults, the retrieval strategy is predominant (about 80% in simple multiplications), but other strategies are also used (LeFevre, Sadesky & Bisanz, 1996) such as repeated additions, number series (recitation of a table, e.g., for $7 \times 4 = 7, 14, 21, 28$), and derived facts (e.g., $6 \times 7 = (6 \times 6) + 6$, or $8 \times 9 = (8 \times 10) - 8$).

Problems with a factor of 0 or 1 are considered to be based on knowledge of a rule (e.g., $n \times 0 = 0$; $n \times 1 = n$).

The composition of the arithmetic fact network is unique to each individual and varies according to the frequency of problems encountered by the individual (Ashcraft & Christy, 1995) and his or her cognitive predisposition to memorizing arithmetic facts. However, in general, it is observed that multiplications with smaller factors (e.g., 2×4) are better memorized than those with larger factors (e.g., 7×8) and therefore result in more correct and quicker responses (see De Brauwer, Verguts & Fias, 2006; Zbrodoff & Logan, 2005). In addition, doubles or ties, i.e., calculations where the two factors are identical (e.g., 6×6), are also stored more easily. Another factor influencing performance in single multiplication problems is the similarity that each calculation has to other problems learned previously (De Visscher & Noël, 2014a and 2014b). Indeed, the more a new calculation to be memorized resembles the others already learned (i.e., sharing digits in common), the more there is interference in long-term memory and difficulty in creating a distinct trace for this precise arithmetic fact. Let's imagine that the child first learns the table of 2, then the table of 3, and by the time he has to learn the fact $3 \times 9 = 27$, he has already stored other facts in his memory that share two, three, or more digits in common with this new association. In particular, the digits 3 and 2 of this fact (i.e., $\underline{3} \times 9 = \underline{2}7$) are also found in $3 \times 2 = 6$, $4 \times 3 = 12$, $8 \times 3 = 24$, the digits 2 and 7 (i.e., $3 \times 9 = \underline{27}$) were already associated in $2 \times 7 = 14$, the digits 2 and 9 were already found in $9 \times 2 = 18$, and 3 and 9 in $3 \times 3 = 9$, and finally, the digits 3, 7, and 2 were already associated in $3 \times 7 = 21$. All this creates confusion and makes it more difficult to create a separate memory trace for this arithmetic fact.

Once these arithmetic facts have been memorized, interference phenomena will occur when solving the calculations (Campbell, 1987, 1995; Graham & Campbell, 1992). For example, in front of the 4×6 calculation, most of us will activate the answer 24 in long-term memory, but other answers may also be activated because they share one of the operands of the calculation (such as 16, 18, 12, etc.). This explains why many of the errors produced when someone tries to solve multiplications by retrieving the answer in memory correspond to so-called 'operand errors', i.e., they belong to the table of one of the operands of the calculation (for example, $4 \times 6 = 18$).

Finally, different conceptual knowledge is related to multiplication. In particular, the child must understand the property of commutativity ($A \times B = B \times A$), that it corresponds to a repeated addition ($3 \times 4 = 4 + 4 + 4$), and that it is the inverse of a division operation (which means that if $A \times B = C$ then C: $A = B$ and C: $B = A$).

Division has been much less studied than multiplication. It is thought that division problems are usually solved using associated multiplication facts rather than a direct retrieval strategy (Robinson et al., 2006, Campbell, 1997), based on the mathematical conceptual knowledge that division is the inverse operation of multiplication (i.e., to solve 64:8, the multiplicative fact $8 \times 8 = 64$ is activated in long-term memory and allows the answer to the calculation, '8', to be found).

Division problems with the terms 0 or 1 are also considered to be solved using rule-based knowledge (e.g., 0: $n = 0$, n: $n = 1$; n: $1 = n$).

4.2.3 Complex calculations

In complex calculations, i.e., involving multi-digit numbers, several strategies have been described. These are almost always procedural strategies since retrieval is almost never possible (except in the case of expert calculators or prodigies).

For complex additions, Lemaire et al. (Lemaire & Arnaud, 2008; Lemaire & Brun, 2018) reported nine different solving strategies (see Table 4.1) for problems with two two-digit operands, half of which required a carry-over. The proportion of use of each strategy changes with age. Third-grade children used mainly (83% of the time) the so-called columnar calculation strategy (see strategy 4 in Table 4.1). Fifth graders also used the written calculation strategy, but to a lesser extent (46%). The second strategy used by both groups was rounding both terms (strategy 3 in the table) and was used in 8.5% of problems in third

Table 4.1 Nine strategies for solving complex additions

	Strategies	Example (12 + 46)
1	Round the first operand to the nearest lower ten.	(10 + 46) + 2
2	Round the second operand to the nearest lower ten.	(12 + 40) + 6
3	Round the two operands to the nearest lower tens.	(10 + 40) + (2 + 6)
4	Retrieve the sums in columns (as a written calculation).	(2 + 6) + (10 + 40)
5	Round the first operand to the nearest upper tenth operand.	(20 + 46) − 8
6	Round the second operand to the nearest upper tenth operand.	(12 + 50) − 4
7	Round the two operands to the nearest upper tens.	(20 + 50) − 8 − 4
8	Group units on an operand.	18 + 40
9	Retrieve the answer in memory.	58

Source: Lemaire & Brun, 2018, page 587.

grade and 30% of problems in fifth grade. The strategies used by adults were similar to those used by fifth graders: the written calculation strategy in 44% of cases and the rounding strategy in 25% of cases.

In complex subtraction, using two-digit operands, Geary, Frensch, and Wiley (1993) observed that adults use four different strategies: the counting strategy (e.g., 32 − 6= is solved by doing 32 − 2 − 2 − 2 = 26), the decomposition strategy (32 − 3 is solved by doing 32 − 2 = 30 − 1 = 29), the rule strategy (32 − 9= is solved by doing 32 − 10 = 22 + 1 = 23), and the written calculation strategy (73 − 42= is solved by doing 3 − 2 = 1 and 7 − 4 = 3, so the answer is 31). The latter strategy is used by adults in 67% of the problems and the decomposition strategy in 18% of cases; the other two strategies are used in about 6% of cases. Another strategy was also reported by Peters, De Smedt, Torbeyns, Ghesquière, and Verschaffel (2013). This consists of counting from the second term (or subtrahend) to the first term (or minuend) to find the solution (e.g., solving 65 − 58 by calculating how much I need to add to 58 to arrive at 65, in this case 7), as in the counting-up strategy described above for simple subtractions. This strategy is particularly effective when the second term is much larger than the difference. It appears that this strategy is already frequently adopted by children in fourth to sixth grade.

In complex multiplication that includes one single-digit operand and one double-digit operand, Tronsky (2005) reported five main strategies used in adults: the written calculation algorithm strategy executed mentally (e.g., to solve 3 × 18, doing 3 × 8 = 24 and 3 × 1 = 3, so the answer is 54), decomposition (e.g., to solve 2 × 19, doing 2 × 16 = 32 and 2 × 3 = 6, so the answer is 38), the tens strategy (which is the same as the written calculation algorithm strategy except that the subject starts with solving the tens before the units), the repeated addition strategy (to solve 3 × 16, do 16 + 16 + 16 = 48), and the retrieval strategy (knowing the answer from long-term memory). Results showed that the participants mainly used the written calculation algorithm strategy (or the tens strategy).

Recently, Hickendorff, Torbeyns, and Verschaffel (2019) presented a synthesis of the work on the resolution of complex calculations. These authors propose distinguishing between resolution strategies along two global axes: the operation underlying the resolution process and the way in which numbers are processed. According to this first axis, they consider different cases depending on the initial calculation. Indeed, addition can only be solved by direct addition. Subtraction, on the other hand, can be solved by direct subtraction (i.e., the second term is subtracted from the first), indirect addition (one adds to the second term until the first term is obtained), or indirect subtraction (one determines how much must be subtracted from the first term to obtain the second term, see Table 4.2). Similarly, while the multiplication of multi-digit numbers can only be solved by direct multiplication, divisions can be solved by direct division or indirect multiplication (by determining how many times the divisor must be multiplied to reach the dividend).

Regarding the second axis, i.e., the way numbers are processed, they distinguish between the *digit-based strategies*, in which the place value of the digits is ignored (as in written algorithms where operations are calculated on the digits themselves) and *number-based* strategies in which the positional value of the digits in the number is respected (for example, the number 83 is decomposed into

Table 4.2 Complex addition and subtraction strategies

		Number-based strategies			Column-based	Digit-based strategies
		Sequential	Decomposition	Varying		
Addition (e.g.: 37 + 25)	Direct addition	37 + 20 = 57 57 + 5 = **62**	30 + 20 = 50 7 + 5 = 12 50 + 12 = **62**	40 + 25 = 65 65 − 3 = **62**	37 25 + 50 12 + **62**	1 37 25 + **62**
Subtraction (e.g.: 73 − 19)	Direct subtraction	73 − 10 = 63 63 − 9 = **54**	70 − 10 = 60 3 − 9 = −6 60 − 6 = **54**	e.g., compensation 73 − 20 = 53 53 + 1 = **54**	73 19 − 60 6 − **54**	6 13 73 19 − **54**
	Indirect addition	19 + 4 = 23 23 + 50 = 73 4 + 50 = **54**	9 + 4 = 13 10 + 50 = 60 4 + 50 = **54**	19 + 1 = 20 20 + 53 = 73 1 + 53 = **54**		
	Indirect subtraction	73 − 50 = 23 23 − 4 = 19 50 + 4 = **54**	70 − 50 = 20 3 − 4 = −1 50 + 4 = **54**	73 − 60 = 13 13 + 6 = 19 60 − 6 = **54**		

Source: inspired by Hickendorff et al., 2019.

80 and 3). In number-based strategies, Hickendorff et al. (2019) distinguish between four addition or subtraction strategies (see Table 4.2): (1) sequential (or jump) strategies in which numbers are considered as positions on the mental number line and operations are considered as forward or backward movements along this number line, (2) decomposition strategies in which numbers are considered in their decimal structure and operations involve partitioning or splitting numbers, (3) varying strategies which involve adapting numbers and/or operations to the problem, as in the compensation strategy where one of the operands is rounded to a close round number (e.g., subtract 70 instead of 69, then add the 1 that was over-subtracted), and (4) the strategy they call 'column-based strategy', which is taught in some countries with algorithms for calculation written in columns but which operates from left to right on whole numbers rather than digits (in the practice part of this chapter we will speak instead of an expanded written calculation method).

Cross-referencing these two axes, the authors propose a table (see Table 4.2) describing the different strategies used to solve complex additions or subtractions.

Typically, children begin by solving these operations using number-based strategies. These strategies are often influenced by the type of instruction received. For example, instruction that emphasizes mastery of the decomposition strategy, or the sequential number-based strategy, will encourage students to use this type of strategy. The only exception to this general trend is the use of indirect addition to solve subtractions. Indeed, research has shown that even when children are not taught this strategy, or are taught it only to a limited extent, they tend to use it often and effectively. This observation has been made in typical children aged 9 to 12 years (Peltenburg, van den Heuvel-Panhuizen & Robitzsch, 2012), but also in children with a math learning disability (Peltenburg et al., 2012; Peters, De Smedt, Torbeyns, Verschaffel & Ghesquière, 2014). On the other hand, children who have been taught focusing on strategy variety use more variable strategies. Then when the standard digit-based strategies are taught, the number-based strategies are typically abandoned in favour of the digit-based strategies.

For multiplication and division, Hickendorff et al. (2019) also distinguish between strategies based on the digits and those based on the numbers with, in the latter case, sequential, decomposition, and varying strategies. In sequential strategies, multiplication and division are solved by repeated addition or subtraction strategies (e.g., 437:23 can be solved by subtracting 23 from 437 several times until one reaches 0, and then considering the number of times this subtraction has been repeated). Division can also be solved by indirect multiplication using repeated additions. In decomposition strategies, numbers are decomposed (e.g., solving 23 × 19 by adding the results of 20 × 19 and 3 × 19). Finally, in varying strategies, the number and/or the operations are adapted, as for example in the compensation strategy (e.g., 23 × 19 = (23 × 20) − 23). Finally, there is also the column-based strategy based on the written calculation algorithm but based on numbers. This one uses the strategy of decomposition

116 *Arithmetic*

in multiplication and the strategy of repeated subtraction in division. On the other hand, the strategies based on digits operate on the digits ignoring their positional value and correspond to the classical algorithms of written calculations. We will however note the particularity of division, which is the only algorithm that proceeds from left to right and does not work with only one digit at a time.

Crossing the two axes of the type of operation used to solve a problem and the number or digit-based strategies, the authors draw a table (see Table 4.3) similar to the one in Table 4.2.

In multiplication, children first use sequential strategies, then decomposition strategies, and finally use the written calculation algorithm once it has been learned. In division, children use mostly sequential strategies, then use the written algorithm.

To solve multi-digit calculations effectively, it is important to have a good conceptual understanding of numbers (including the positional system), especially when dealing with number-based strategies, and a good arithmetic facts network (see, for example, Linsen, Torbeyns, Verschaffel, Reynvoet & De Smedt, 2016). Another important dimension is the understanding of arithmetic operations and corresponding symbols (see Robinson, 2017 and Selter, Prediger, Nührenbörger & Hußmann, 2012). For example, the use of indirect addition to solve a subtraction is based on a broader understanding of the minus sign, which indicates not only 'taking away' (resulting in direct subtraction: taking away the smaller from the larger number) but also 'bridging the difference' (which allows resolution by indirect addition). Similarly, this strategy also requires an understanding of the complementary relationship between the addition and the subtraction operation (i.e., understanding that $a - b = ?$ can be solved by $b + ? = a$). Baroody, Torbeyns, and Verschaffel (2009) and Robinson (2017) discuss in detail the research that has focused on the role of understanding addition and subtraction operations and their various arithmetic principles.

Some typical errors are observed in the resolution of complex calculations. For number-based strategies, incorrect factoring is a common cause of errors (e.g., $23 \times 19 = (20 \times 10) + (3 \times 9)$). Other errors arise from the fact that some children, both typical children and those with learning difficulties in mathematics, solve multiplication and/or division problems without writing anything down. However, these purely mental strategies lead more often to calculation errors than written strategies (Fagginger Auer, Hickendorff & van Putten, 2016; Hickendorff, Heiser, Van Putten & Verhelst, 2009). Yet, simply asking children to write the intermediate results while solving the calculation increases the performance in all children (Hickendorff, van Putten, Verhelst & Heiser, 2010) or in those with a math learning disability (Fagginger Auer et al., 2016).

As for strategies based on the digits (written calculation algorithms), systematic errors are regularly observed, so-called 'bugs' in certain procedures. These bugs correspond to the fact that certain steps of the procedure are neglected or incorrectly executed. For example, a common bug in subtraction is to

Table 4.3 Complex multiplication and division strategies

		Number-based strategies			Digit-based strategies
		Sequential	Decomposition	Varying	Column-based
Multiplication (e.g.: 43 × 19)	Direct multiplication	43 + 43 + 43 + … = **817** or 5 × 43 = 215 4 × 43 = 172 215 + 215 + 215 + 172 = **817**	43 × 10 = 430 43 × 9 = 387 430 + 387 = 817 or 40 × 10 = 400 3 × 10 = 30 40 × 9 = 360 3 × 9 = 27 400 + 30 + 360 + 27 = **817**	e.g., compensation 43 × 20 = 860 860 − 43 = **817**	43 19 × ―――― 400 (10 × 40) 30 (10 × 3) 360 (9 × 40) 27 + (9 × 3) ―――― **817**	43 19 × ―― 387 43 + ―― **817**
Division (e.g.: 182 : 13)	Direct division	182 − 13 = 169 169 − 13 = 156 (subtracting 13, *n* times up to reach 0, which is 14 times, thus the answer is **14**) or 182 − 130 (10 times) = 52; 52 − 52 (which is 4 times) = 0; 10 + 4 = **14**	130 : 13 = 10 52 : 13 = 4 10 + 4 = **14**	e.g., compensation 260 : 13 = 20 (260 − 182 = 78) 78 : 13 = 6 20 − 6 = **14**	182 : 13 = 130 − (10 times) 52 52 − (4 times) 0 10 + 4 = **14**	182 : 13 = **14** 130 − 52 52 − 0
	Indirect multiplication	13 + 13 = 26 26 + 13 = 39; 39 + 13 = … up to reach 182 13 must be added 14 times, thus the answer is **14**	13 × 10 = 130 13 × 4 = 52 10 + 4 = **14**	20 × 13 = 260 (260 − 182 = 78) 6 × 13 = 78 20 − 6 = **14**		

Source: inspired by Hickendorff et al., 2019.

always subtract the smallest digit from the largest one (leading to errors such as 258 − 179 = 121) or, in multiplication, to 'forget' to write zeros.

Overall, children with a good level of mathematics use a wide variety of strategies effectively and adaptively (Torbeyns, Hickendorff & Verschaffel, 2017). Yet, even children with math learning disabilities are also able to use a variety of number-based strategies adaptively (Peltenburg et al., 2012, Peters et al., 2013, 2014).

4.2.4 The role of estimation in arithmetic

Arithmetic estimation is the ability to estimate the result of a calculation without having carried out the calculation exactly. For example, the answer to 59 − 26 can be estimated to be necessarily less than 59 and around 20, or the sum of 47 + 39 must be more than 50, less than 100 and probably around 80. This estimation capacity is important for two reasons. First, it can allow the child to detect possible mistakes. Let's imagine a child who has not correctly mastered the carry-over procedure and who, in order to solve the calculation 47 + 39, first adds up the digits in the tens, 4 + 3 = 7, then those in the units, 7 + 9 = 16, and then writes the following solution 716. A rough estimate of the result will allow this pupil to see that something is wrong. Similarly, in the calculation verification tasks (34 + 79 = 143?), these estimation skills make it possible to quickly reject errors that are far from the correct result without having to calculate the correct answer (Ashcraft, Fierman & Bartolotta, 1984; Campbell & Graham, 1985).

Secondly, the estimation also helps to select the best resolution procedure. For example, when faced with subtraction, the choice between counting up or counting down depends on the difference between the two terms. If this difference is small, as in 9 − 7, the counting-up strategy is the most efficient (i.e., counting from 7 to 9, that is two counting steps). On the other hand, if the difference between the two terms is large, as in 9 − 2, the counting-down strategy will be more efficient (i.e., counting from 9, two steps, thus 8, 7). For most children beyond first grade, this selection of the strategy according to the difference in the size of the terms is automated. In more complex subtractions, with two-digit terms, children in fourth to sixth grades will use the counting-up strategy (indirect addition) when the subtrahend is much larger than the difference (e.g., 65 − 58=; Peters et al., 2013).

4.3 Difficulties observed in dyscalculia

Dyscalculia is a heterogeneous learning difficulty (Geary, 2004; Henik, Rubinsten & Ashkenazi, 2014; Rubinsten & Henik, 2009; Karagiannakis, Roussos & Baccaglini-Frank, 2017), and among the different profiles, several types of difficulties have been reported in arithmetic such as difficulties in mastering calculation procedures, use of immature strategies, and difficulty in storing or retrieving arithmetic facts in long-term memory.

For some, these difficulties would be related to basic numerical difficulties. For instance, some argue that the approximate number representation (the ANS) would support further mathematical development (Dehaene, Piazza, Pinel & Cohen, 2003; Halberda & Feigenson, 2008; Piazza et al., 2010; Wilson & Dehaene, 2007). Although some studies have observed correlations between the acuity of this ANS and mathematical performance, many other studies have not observed such results. On the other hand, symbolic number magnitude processing is strongly correlated with mathematical performance (see De Smedt, Noël, Gilmore & Ansari, 2013 for a review) with simple calculations capabilities (De Visscher, Noël & De Smedt, 2016; Vanbinst, Ghesquière & De Smedt, 2015), as well as with performance in solving complex subtractions (Linsen et al., 2016). Other views consider that the arithmetic difficulties could also stem from weaknesses in more general cognitive processes such as in memory for instance.

Several types of arithmetic difficulties have been described. A first subtype, called 'procedural dyscalculia' by Geary (2004), corresponds to children who tend to use immature strategies (e.g., counting-all strategy) and external support (e.g., counting on fingers) for longer than others. According to Geary (1990), the need to count on the fingers would reduce the working memory load. This author then hypothesizes that these children suffer from memory weakness and that this would explain why they make many mistakes when executing procedural strategies based on counting by counting too far or not enough (Hanich, Jordan, Kaplan & Dick, 2001). The use of immature counting procedures would also have a negative impact on the constitution of the arithmetic facts network in long-term memory. Indeed, these immature counting procedures take time, which would result in a long delay between the presentation or encoding of the problem and the obtaining of the answer, i.e., unfavourable conditions for memorizing an association between the problem and the answer (Geary & Brown, 1991; Geary, 2004). Furthermore, as we explained with Siegler's (1988) distribution model of associations (see Section 4.2.1 of this chapter), children who produce many errors in calculating answers will make connections in memory between problems and these incorrect answers, which will reduce the likelihood of retrieving the correct answer from memory. These hypotheses are supported by the observation of less frequent use of the retrieval strategy when performing simple additions in children with low working memory capacity compared to those with good working memory capacity (Barrouillet & Lépine, 2005, Kaufmann, 2002; Noël, Seron & Trovarelli, 2004).

In addition to working memory problems, immaturity of computational strategies could be explained by a lack of conceptual knowledge in mathematics (Geary, 2004). For example, children need to understand that it is not mandatory to start the counting sequence from one in order to apply a counting strategy (this is related to understanding the cardinal value of number words). In addition, more mature counting strategies require some level of development of the verbal number chain, especially in terms of its elaboration (see Chapter 2). In this respect, it is interesting to note that at the age of four to five years, children with lower verbal working memory skills have a lower level of development of the verbal numerical chain than others, both in terms of acquisition (length of the chain) and elaboration (Noël, 2009).

Furthermore, the transition from procedural counting strategies to memory retrieval strategies does not seem to occur in these children (De Smedt, Holloway & Ansari, 2011; Garnett & Fleischner, 1983; Geary, Brown & Samaranayake, 1991; Jordan & Montani, 1997). Several studies report significant difficulties in children with developmental dyscalculia or with math learning disabilities in solving simple calculations by retrieving the response from memory (Geary, Hoard, Byrd-Craven, Nugent & Numtee, 2007; Jordan, Hanich & Kaplan, 2003; Jordan & Montani, 1997; Slade & Russell, 1971). Some of these difficulties may stem from difficulties in calculation procedures, as explained above. However, some children are proficient in calculation procedures but have difficulty retrieving arithmetic facts from their long-term memory. According to Geary (2004), these difficulties fall under the subtype 'semantic memory type dyscalculia'.

According to Rourke and Strang (1983), this specific difficulty in memorizing arithmetic facts is linked to a more general problem of verbal memory. A similar hypothesis is also suggested by the Triple Code model of Dehaene, Piazza, Pinel, and Cohen (2003). It is true that difficulties in memorizing arithmetic facts are regularly observed in people with dyslexia (e.g., De Smedt & Boets, 2010; Geary, Hoard & Hamson, 1999; Kaufmann, 2002; Temple, 1991), but not always (e.g., Geary, Hoard & Bailey, 2012; Jordan et al., 2003; Landerl, Bevan & Butterworth, 2004). Some studies have more directly measured long-term verbal memory skills related to the acquisition of arithmetic facts. Again, the data are quite contradictory, with some results reporting a link between the two (De Smedt, Taylor, Archibald & Ansari, 2009; Simmons & Singleton, 2008) and others not (De Visscher & Noël, 2013; Mussolin & Noël, 2008).

In these difficulties relating to arithmetic facts, it seems important to us to distinguish between two processes: storage (i.e., encoding information into memory) and retrieval (i.e., recalling information that is in memory).

Recently, De Visscher and Noël have been interested in the difficulties concerning the storage of arithmetic facts. They reported results showing that hypersensitivity to similarity interference in memory may account for specific difficulties in memorizing arithmetic facts (De Visscher & Noël, 2013, 2014a and b; De Visscher, Berens, Keidel, Noël & Bird, 2015; De Visscher, Szmalec, Van Der Linden & Noël, 2015; De Visscher et al., 2018). Indeed, arithmetic facts such as multiplication tables are very similar since they share many identical characteristics (the digits). For example, $3 \times 8 = 24$ and $4 \times 8 = 32$ have 100% element overlap since they both include the digits 2, 3, 4, and 8. In cases of high similarity, memory models have shown that sharing common traits creates interferences that undermine the ability to store information correctly and distinctly in memory (Lewandowsky, Geiger & Oberauer, 2008; Nairne, 1990; Oberauer & Lange, 2008). Data from behavioural and neuroimaging studies of children and adults support this hypothesis and show an increased sensitivity to memory interference in individuals who have not been able to establish a sufficient network of arithmetic facts.

With regard to the retrieval process, several studies have highlighted difficulties for some people in inhibiting irrelevant information. For example, children with this type of difficulty produce a significant number of intrusive errors compared to control children. For example, in a multiplication task, they produce many so-called operand errors (e.g., $3 \times 4 = 16$ [4×4]), suggesting that they have difficulty inhibiting false but associated responses in long-term memory (Barrouillet, Fayol & Lathuliere, 1997). Similarly, in an arithmetic verification task, these children more frequently choose false answers corresponding to a multiple of one of the factors than other errors suggested (e.g., for $6 \times 4 =$, choose the wrong answer 18 rather than 15). Furthermore, in a verbal working memory task (the 'sentence span' in which the last word of each sentence heard is recalled), fifth graders with mathematical learning difficulties produce more intrusive errors (i.e., recall a word in the sentence that is not the last one) than the control group (Passolunghi & Siegel, 2004). Finally, this weak inhibition of irrelevant information would also explain why children with poor knowledge of arithmetic facts produce more association errors related to the counting chain (e.g., $3 + 5 = 6$, because 6 follows 5; Geary et al., 2012).

Finally, it goes without saying that difficulties already observed in performing simple calculations also have repercussions when performing complex calculations. However, dissociations can be observed. Thus, Temple (1991) reported two cases of children with dyscalculia with different arithmetic difficulties. SW had developed a normal arithmetic fact network but had selective difficulties with written calculation algorithms while the reverse profile was observed in HM, who had a normal mastery of written calculation algorithms but a very poor network of arithmetic facts. According to Temple, these two case studies thus show that arithmetic facts and calculation algorithms can evolve in a semi-independent way.

Similarly, Peters et al. (2014) observed, in 12-year-olds with mathematical learning difficulties, abilities to use different strategies to solve complex subtractions. They were also able to switch from a classical subtraction strategy to a resolution strategy based on addition according to the relative size of the second term and the difference, just like the children with no learning disabilities.

Finally, Rousselle and Noël (2008) studied the ability of children with mathematical learning difficulties to use their estimation skills in a simple or complex addition-verification task. In the case of children in second and third grades with no learning disability, when the proposed answer was far from the correct answer, they quickly rejected it, showing that they did not need to calculate the correct answer to compare it to the proposed one but that they based their judgement on their approximate calculation abilities. On the other hand, children with mathematical learning difficulties were not affected by the plausibility of the answers, showing that they were not using their approximate calculation skills.

4.4 Training and intervention studies

4.4.1 Trainings based on the ANS or magnitude representation

Considering the hypothesis that the ANS would be the basis for all subsequent numerical development, including arithmetic, several research have sought to improve the ANS and then measure the impact of this training on arithmetic capabilities. For example, Park, Bermudez, Roberts, and Brannon (2016) showed that training young children aged three to five in the ability to add or subtract approximately from collections increased their overall numerical abilities (for other research of this type, see Chapter 2).

Based on similar reasoning, some researchers have hypothesized that it is important to help children connect calculations with the magnitude representation of the operands and/or the answer. With this in mind, Vilette, Mawart, and Rusinek (2010) developed a software package called the Estimator. Several types of exercises are included in this software, including one on addition and another on subtraction. In these arithmetic exercises, the child sees a two-digit number calculation appearing on the computer screen above an ungraded line marked 0 and 100 at the ends. The child has to position the cursor to where he or she thinks the answer to the calculation is. If the child's estimate is broadly incorrect, the number corresponding to the cursor position is displayed in red and the child is prompted to make a new estimate. If the child's estimate is close to the target location, the number corresponding to the correct answer to the calculation is displayed in green (see Figure 4.1). These authors tested this game with 10 children with dyscalculia during 7 sessions of 30 minutes, while another group of children with dyscalculia practiced the same calculations but with a more conventional computer device where they had to

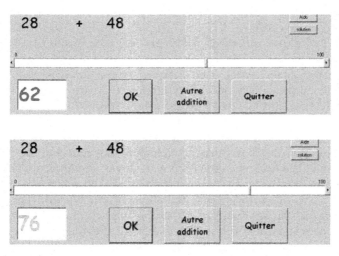

Figure 4.1 Illustration of the game 'The Estimator' developed by Vilette et al., 2010.

precisely calculate the answer. The authors noted a greater increase in calculation performance for the children who played the Estimator. Similar results were observed by Kucian et al. (2011) with a similar game. Positive results on arithmetic skills were also found in first graders receiving arithmetic training on the 0–100 number line, when the computer directly provided children with the correct position of the sum on the number line (Booth & Siegler, 2017).

4.4.2 Training in simple arithmetic

Codding, Burns, and Lukito (2011) examined (using a meta-analysis) 17 single-case studies in which an intervention was proposed to increase basic arithmetical-fact fluency. These studies involved 55 elementary-school children identified as performing below expectations for mathematics (or having mathematical learning difficulties). These authors found that drill (i.e., repeated practice of individual items or incremental rehearsal) and practice with modelling produce the largest treatment effects whereas intensive practice without modelling has negligible effects. This conclusion is also in line with the observations of two group studies, that of Codding et al. (2007) and that of Tournaki (2003), which show that adding demonstration to standard drill led to better outcomes.

For instance, in the study by Tournaki (2003), second-grade children, with or without mathematical learning difficulties, are divided into three groups: (1) the 'exercise' condition, in which they have to solve single-digit sums (for example, 5 + 3=), (2) the 'exercise plus model' condition, in which they also have to solve sums but are shown beforehand how to use the counting-min strategy, and finally, (3) the 'control' condition, in which there is neither instruction nor exercises. In conditions (1) and (2), children are given lists of sums to solve, presented in increasing order of difficulty. They are asked to work as quickly as possible. In the 'exercise' condition, the facilitators point out the children's mistakes at the end of each session and ask the pupils to recalculate the sums. If an error is made again, the facilitators give the children the correct answer. In the 'exercise plus model' condition, each session begins with a demonstration of the counting-min strategy in which the facilitator explains to the children that they have to select the smaller addend of the problem (e.g., 3 for 5 + 3), count that number on their fingers and raise the corresponding fingers (so that now they have three fingers raised), and then count from the larger number (in the example, that is counting from 5), this amount of steps shown on the fingers (so, count starting at 'five', three steps as indicated by their fingers 'six, seven, eight'). After this demonstration, the pupils are asked to solve the calculations of the session. Each time a mistake is made, the facilitator interrupts the child and explains the strategy again.

The children without mathematical learning difficulties improved significantly in the 'exercises' and 'exercises plus model' conditions. On the other hand, children with mathematical learning difficulties only improved in the 'exercise plus model' condition, which proves that these children need to be shown how to solve calculations in order to progress and that simple practice is not enough for them. Note that this difference could also be explained, in part, by the difference in the feedback given to the children between these two conditions. Indeed, this feedback was given directly after the production of an error in the 'exercises plus model' condition but only at the end of the session in the 'exercise' condition.

Koponen et al. (2018) tested the implementation of an intervention aimed at teaching another strategy, the derived fact strategy. In this intervention, children are helped to discover more efficient calculation strategies using their existing knowledge of number sequences, number concepts, and arithmetical facts (conceptual knowledge) (e.g., solve $5 + 6$ from its proximity to the nearby calculation, $5 + 5$). Their experimental intervention was intensive; it lasted 12 weeks with 4 sessions per week including 2 strategy training sessions and 2 short practice sessions. During the strategy instruction, the teacher modelled and discussed with the students the relationships between numbers. For example, he/she pointed out the relationship between counting further, addition, and magnitude; if I count two steps further than the number n, it is like adding two to n and the new number is larger than the original number (it is equal to $n + 2$). He/she also asked the children to focus their attention on the arithmetic facts and see how they are more or less close to each other in terms of numerical magnitude. For example, $(5 + 5)$ and $(6 + 5)$ are calculations that differ only in the first term and six is 'one more' than five; therefore, $(6 + 5)$ is also 'one more' than $(5 + 5)$. Children were encouraged to verbalize their thinking and strategies. Teachers emphasized that more than one strategy could be used; each student had to find the fastest and most effective strategies for him or her. These phases of strategy instruction and discussion with students were followed by games and exercises in which students practiced the strategies they had learned. The experimental intervention was thus based on a framework integrating factual, conceptual, and procedural arithmetic knowledge. It was compared with both a control reading intervention and regular school instruction.

The participants in the study were children in second to fourth grades with mathematical learning difficulties (69 participants) who were still using a counting strategy to solve addition problems. The authors found a significantly better improvement in arithmetic fluency after the experimental intervention than under the other two conditions. In particular, they observed a decrease in the frequency of use of counting-based strategies in favour of retrieval and decomposition strategies. These effects were sustained over a period of at least five months.

Fuchs, Fuchs, Powell, Seethaler, Cirino, and Fletcher (2008) developed another intervention programme integrating conceptual and strategic aspects to increase the simple addition and subtraction fluency of primary school students. This programme, called the Math Flash, runs for 16 weeks with 3 sessions per week.

During the first two sessions, the children learned the principle of commutativity of addition (but not for subtraction). These sessions included $n + 1$ and $n - 1$ problems, using manipulatives and number lines. In sessions 3 and 4, the same material was used and problems with $n+0$ and $n-0$ were introduced. In sessions 5 and 6, the children reviewed the problems seen previously, i.e., problems $n\pm 1$ and $n\pm 0$. In session 7, doubles from 0 to 6 (i.e., 0 ± 0, 1 ± 1 etc., up to 6 ± 6) were introduced in addition and subtraction with, again, the use of manipulatives and drill exercises. Subsequent sessions included problems of increasing difficulty ($+\,2, -2$), retrieval and counting-on strategies, and instructions on families of problems (for example, family 5 contains all problems with a 5).

Each session included five activities. Firstly, to 'warm up', the children used 'flash cards' with additions and subtractions (operands from 0 to 9) and tried to respond correctly to as many cards as possible for two minutes. The number of cards that the child answered correctly was indicated on a graph representing the child's personal performance. Then there was a phase of conceptual and strategic instruction with manipulatives. In particular, the retrieval strategy ('I know the answer') and the counting strategy were explained for addition and subtraction problems. The specific problems of the session were then introduced with the support of manipulatives and number lines. The third part of the session consisted of practicing the new problems learned using the corresponding flash cards for one minute. Then the children practiced on the computer with the ten new problems mixed with five previously seen ones. During this practice, the problem and its answer were presented on the screen for 1.3 seconds. The child had to repeat the calculation and then retype the calculation and its answer. If the production was correct, he/she was awarded points. If it was wrong, he/she was given a second try. This training stopped when the student had correctly answered the 10 newly learned problems twice or after 7.5 minutes. When the pass criterion was reached, the problems of the next level were introduced during the next session (with a maximum of four sessions on a given set). Finally, the children were given a paper-and-pencil test with 15 newly learned facts and 15 previously seen facts to be completed at home. A reinforcement programme was used to motivate the children; they were given golden stars and when they had accumulated a certain number, they could exchange them for a gift hidden in the treasure box.

This programme thus followed six important principles for effective practice (see Chapter 1): (1) the use of explicit instructions, (2) clear and well-integrated instructions, (3) the use of manipulatives (blocks, tokens, fingers) and number lines to reinforce the conceptual basis of arithmetic, (4) the use of drills and practice necessary for automation, (5) the cumulative review in each session of problems already learned and newly learned problems, and (6) the use of motivators (stars, gifts) to support and encourage children's motivation. This intervention showed a positive improvement in the mathematical abilities of the third-grade children with mathematical learning difficulties who followed it.

A very similar intervention was used by Iuculano et al. (2015). It consisted of 22 individual sessions of 40–50 minutes over an 8-week period. In the first four sessions, very small additions and subtractions (± 0, 1, 2) and doubles (from

1 to 6) were worked on using the number line, manipulatives (blocks), and clear instruction on the commutativity of addition but not of subtraction. In the fifth and sixth sessions, the children learned the counting-min strategy in addition and the counting-up strategy in subtraction. The children used these strategies to solve small problems and then progressively more complex problems up to 18. Each session began with a review of the problems previously worked on and the strategies to be used. Then, new problems were presented. The session continued with games mixing the problems of the current session with old problems. At the end of the session, the children received a summary of the new problems taught.

The games used were 'bingo', 'math war', and 'treasure hunt'. In the bingo game, a problem card (e.g., $3+8$) is picked. Each participant has to find the solution to the problem as quickly as possible and check whether it is part of his or her bingo card. If it is, he or she places a pawn on the square corresponding to the solution on his or her bingo card. The first person to fill out his or her bingo card is the winner. In the math war, each participant turns over two cards from his/her deck. The winner is the one with the higher sum of the two cards. Finally, in the treasure hunt, each time a child correctly solves a problem card (for example, $3+5$), he or she can fill in one of the stones on the treasure card with the problem and the correct answer. When all the stones are filled in, the treasure is found.

This intervention was given to 15 children with mathematical learning difficulties and compared to 15 children of the same age without difficulty. At baseline, the group of children with mathematical learning difficulties showed significantly lower mathematical performance than the group of children without difficulty. After only eight weeks of intervention, the performance in addition resolution (sums < 25) of the children with mathematical learning difficulties reached the level of that of the control children. In addition, the brain activity of these children was recorded in a functional magnetic resonance imaging machine while they were checking the accuracy of additions. Initially, higher activation in the prefrontal and parietal areas was observed in the children with mathematical learning difficulties than in the control children, i.e., brain areas that are typically involved when doing calculations. After the intervention, all difference between the two groups of children in terms of brain activity had disappeared, showing a normalization of both arithmetic performance and brain activation.

This same training was then used with two groups of third-grade children (Supekar, Iuculano, Chen & Menon, 2015) who had equivalent levels of arithmetic performance but differed in their level of mathematical anxiety; half had a normal level and the other half a high level, showing significant anxiety about situations involving calculation or number processing. Initially, these two groups showed differences in the brain activations recorded in an addition-verification task; children with high mathematical anxiety had higher activation of the parietal and prefrontal regions and of the right amygdala, the latter being a brain region involved in emotional regulation, including fear. Following this programme, which to some extent corresponds to exposure therapy, any difference in brain activation between the two groups disappeared.

This research provides encouraging results and shows that effective interventions can have an observable impact right down to the level of brain activity.

Beyond these interventions including a strategic dimension, we would like to mention two interventions dealing with simple multiplications and favouring their memorization by adding perceptual clues. These interventions were carried out in adult patients with acquired acalculia following brain damage. To our knowledge, they have not been the subject of experimental trials in children, yet they deserve our interest. In the first study, Domahs, Lochy, Eibl, and Delazer (2004) associated a specific colour with each problem according to the identity of the digit corresponding to the unit position of the response. For example, problems 4×3, 6×2, 8×4, 7×6, and 9×8 were all presented in yellow since their solutions, 12, 12, 32, 42, and 72 respectively, had the number 2 in the position of the units. These colours were used for the first ten teaching sessions, and then the calculations were presented in black for the last ten sessions. A table showing the numbers in their colour code was displayed in front of the patient during the first five sessions. In the intervention, a problem was presented on the screen and the patient was asked to type in the answer using the keyboard. If the written number did not correspond to the correct answer, it did not appear on the screen and the correct answer was displayed instead. The problem was then directly represented again. The idea was therefore to promote a virtually error-free learning process. After the first ten sessions, the authors observed that the patient solved the trained calculations better if they were presented in the colour code than if they were presented in black, which shows that the colour code helped the patient. At the end of the 20 sessions, the patient's performance had improved significantly, and he was equally successful with calculations presented in colour or black. Similarly, in another brain-damaged patient, Domahs, Zamarian, and Delazer (2008) used auditory cues this time. A particular sound was associated with each unit of the response, and this sound was played before the appearance of each calculation. Once again, these authors observed that these sound cues helped the patient to relearn multiplications.

4.4.3 *Complex calculations*

Very few studies have focused on complex arithmetic intervention. That of Caviola, Gerotto, and Mammarella (2016) shows that, as in simple arithmetic, it is important to give concrete instructions on the strategies to be implemented.

In this study, third and fifth graders participated in three intervention sessions in which they were asked to solve complex sums (with a term corresponding to a number of two or more digits). For half of them, the decomposition strategy (e.g., $85 + 13 = 85 + 10 = 95$; $95 + 3 = 98$) was explained during the intervention, while for the others no instruction was given on how to solve the problems. In both cases, children had a maximum of three attempts to solve the problem and received feedback after each attempt. The results of this study showed a positive effect of the two trainings on the performance of the pupils in addition. However, in third grade, the students showed a greater increase in the accuracy of their responses with the training including strategy instruction, while in fifth grade, the students showed a greater increase in their speed of calculation after the intervention without strategy instruction. These results show that at the beginning of learning, including instruction on the strategies to be used is important. Later (in the fifth grade in this case), this instruction is no longer useful since the students are already familiar with the strategy in question.

With regard to complex multiplication, Grabner and De Smedt (2012) offered to about 20 adults of all ages the opportunity to participate in 2 30-minute sessions (over 2 days), during which 10 complex multiplication problems were repeatedly presented. They were asked to solve them as quickly and accurately as possible. Feedback was given after each answer and the correct answer was presented to the participants. It was therefore a pure drill. The authors observed an increase in performance (greater accuracy and speed) and in the use of the retrieval strategy.

In summary, these studies show that (1) it is important to encourage students to estimate the results of the operation, such as by using a number line to position the estimated result (Vilette et al., 2010), (2) modelling the strategies you teach to the pupils leads to better improvement (Codding et al., 2011; Tournaki, 2003), (3) interventions mixing conceptual and strategic aspects are important (Fuchs et al., 2008; Koponen et al., 2018), (4) using perceptual cues might help in memorizing the arithmetical facts (Domahs et al., 2004, 2008), and finally (5) effective intervention can impact right down to the level of brain activity (Iuculano et al., 2015; Supekar et al., 2015).

4.5 From research to practice: the assessment of arithmetic skills

The evaluation of arithmetic skills will focus on (1) the conceptual aspects of arithmetic operations (i.e., understanding the meaning of the operations, their properties, their relations), (2) the memorization of the answers (i.e., the arithmetic facts network), and (3) the strategic aspects, i.e., the procedures implemented to solve the calculations and the mastery of the calculation algorithms written in columns.

At the conceptual level, assessment can begin with understanding the meaning of operations by asking the child to show with manipulatives (e.g., tokens) what calculations such as '3+4', '6−2', '3×4' or '8: 2' mean, for example. In response to this request, some children will be able to select the number of tokens corresponding to each term but will have difficulty representing the meaning of the operation itself. For example, to represent '6−2', the idea is to select 6 tokens and then remove 2 of those 6 and not to select 2 more. Similarly, '3×4' does not require a first selection of 3 and then of 4 tokens, but rather selecting 4 tokens once, then a second time, then a third time (or to take 4 triplets of tokens). Some items of this type can be found in the Key-Math 3 (Connolly, 2007) in the subtests Addition, Subtraction, Multiplication, and Division.

In older children, conceptual knowledge of operations can also be measured by assessing their knowledge of commutativity for addition and multiplication (but not of the other two operations) and the relationships between them (e.g., the relationships between addition and subtraction, multiplication and division, and repeated addition and multiplication). In the Tedimath (Van Niewenhoven, Grégoire & Noël, 2002) and the TediMath Grands (Noël & Grégoire, 2015), this knowledge is tested by presenting two complex calculations to the child; the response to the second may, possibly, be easily obtained from the response to the first, without the need for the calculation process. The questions are asked as true/false (e.g., 'if $38 + 28 = 76$, then $28 + 38 = 76$?') or by producing the answer to the second calculation from the first (e.g., 'if $38 + 28 = 76$, then $28 + 38 = ?$'). The same principle is used in the MathPro Test (Karagiannakis & Noël, 2020): items are of the type 'if $35 + 47 = 82$, what is $35 + 48 = \_$', and the child is requested to type in the answer.

Secondly, we will evaluate the child's performance in calculation. Depending on the educational level of the child, this performance will be assessed on simple (one-digit) calculations or on simple and complex calculations. This performance will be measured in terms of the answers' accuracy and speed. The first objective is, of course, that the child obtains the correct answer, thereby showing that he or she is using appropriate processes. However, speed is also important because it is an indirect measure of the degree of maturity of the strategies used. Indeed, the more immature the strategies are, the longer they take to execute, and the more mature and automated they are, the shorter the time needed to respond. A large number of tests offer lists of calculations of various complexities to measure children's arithmetic abilities. A smaller number of them allow a measure of speed. Speed can be assessed in three different ways. Either the measurement is taken on a set of calculations, or a time limit is given during which the child tries to solve as many calculations in a list as possible (as in arithmetic fluency tests such as the Tempotest Rekenen (TTR, De Vos, 1992) or the Tempo-Test-Automatiseren (TTA, De Vos, 2010)), or finally, the time is measured for each calculation. The first two methods are easy to implement as they usually only require paper and a stopwatch. The limitation of this type of test is that if the child is distracted at any time during the test or if he or she gets stuck on a calculation for a long time, the overall time measurement is affected. The purest measure is therefore that derived from the third method, but this requires the use of a computerized test. Timed and computerized calculation tests can be found in the TediMath Grands (Noël & Grégoire, 2015), in the Examath 8-15 (Lafay & Helloin, 2016), and in the MathPro test (Karagiannakis & Noël, 2020) in the Addition Fact Retrieval and Multiplication Fact Retrieval subtests.

While these time measures provide an overall assessment of the degree of maturity of the strategies and the ease with which they can be executed, this type of test generally does not allow for a precise determination of the type of strategies used by the child. From this perspective, direct observation of the child, his/her verbalizations, finger use, or use of objects, will be essential. When no behaviour can be observed but the answer is not given quickly, it is important to ask the child how he or she arrived at the answer. The goal will then be to be able to estimate the strategies repertoire of the child and the frequency of use of each of them.

Among these strategies, it should be remembered that the retrieval strategy is considered to be the most mature and that building up a good network of arithmetic facts (for addition undoubtedly and certainly for multiplication) is one of the objectives of elementary school. Calculations which are solved quickly, without the use of counting and for which the child answers the question 'how did you find the answer?' with 'I know it, I have it in my head', testify to the existence of a corresponding arithmetic fact or, in the case of particular calculations, such as $n \times 0$, $n + 0$, etc., to the use of a rule. When very few calculations are solved by retrieving the answer from memory, a problem with storing arithmetic facts may be suspected. On the other hand, if the child solves some calculations by retrieval but produces errors in the retrieved answer (for example, operand errors where the incorrect answer belongs to the table of one of the factors) or hesitates between two answers, a difficulty in retrieving the facts may be suspected. In order to distinguish between these two profiles, two other tasks may be used: table membership judgement and calculation verification. In the first, numbers are presented to the child who must judge whether or not they correspond to answers from the multiplication tables (for example, 36, 32, 49 are part of the multiplication tables while 51, 17, 23 are not). This task will be extremely difficult, if not impossible, for a person with a storage problem but easier for a person with a retrieval problem. In the calculation verification task, the calculations are presented sometimes with the correct answer (e.g., $7 \times 6 = 42$), sometimes with a wrong answer belonging to the table of one of the factors ($7 \times 6 = 48$) or with a wrong answer that does not belong to any table but is numerically close to the correct answer ($7 \times 6 = 43$). For people with a storage problem, the rejection of the two incorrect answers will take equivalent times, while for people with a retrieval problem, the answers that do not belong to the tables will be rejected more quickly than those that belong to the tables.

For young children (first, second grades), single-digit calculations will be used. However, the complexity of the calculations may increase for pupils in more advanced classes. In particular, it is important to propose calculations that may or may not involve the processes of borrowing or carrying and calculations that give the possibility of using clever strategies, such as rounding, for example, $230 + 999$ (which can be solved by $(230 + 1000) - 1$) or 324×50 (which can be solved by $(324 \times 100) : 2$) or $456 - 449$ (which can be easily solved by counting up from 449 or by $(456 - 450 + 1)$, etc.). The assessment of more complex mental calculations can be found in the Mental Calculation subtest of the MathPro test (Karagiannakis & Noël, 2020).

Finally, among pupils in higher classes, the mastery of columnar calculation algorithms can also be assessed. The TediMath Grands battery (Noël & Grégoire, 2015) includes a test of this type. Interestingly, the proposed test separately evaluates two processes: the positioning of numbers in space and performing the calculation procedures. Thus the calculation is dictated to the child who must write the numbers in space. In particular, we can observe the alignment of the numbers according to the positional ranks of the digits. Difficulties at this level have indeed been observed, in particular in children with visual-spatial difficulties (Mammarella, Lucangeli & Cornoldi, 2010; Venneri, Cornoldi & Garuti, 2003). If the positioning is not correct, the examiner places the calculation correctly and then asks the child to solve it. The child's performance of this algorithm is thus scored separately from the number positioning aspect.

Global measures of arithmetic skills can also be found in the Key-Math 3 (Connolly, 2007) in the subtests Addition, Subtraction, Multiplication, and Division and in the subtest Mental Computation in which calculations from the different operations are mixed. Yet, these subtests do not provide distinct assessments of the conceptual knowledge of the operations, the fluency in arithmetic retrieval, or the mastery of calculation procedures, as these are all integrated in the same subtest for each arithmetical operation in which items are presented according to increasing difficulty, starting from calculations on objects represented in pictures up to calculation on multi-digit numbers and then with rational numbers.

4.6 From research to practice: rehabilitation and teaching

In this section, we distinguish between working on addition and subtraction operations on the one hand and working on multiplication and division operations on the other. In these two cases, we work on the conceptual aspect, the resolution of simple calculations (relating to one-digit numbers), the resolution of complex calculations (relating to multi-digit numbers), and finally, the mastery of the written algorithm of calculation known as column calculation.

At the conceptual aspect level, it is a question of being able to represent the meaning of these operations with concrete objects. For addition and subtraction, it is also a question of understanding the link between the sequential aspect of counting, or the forward or backward movements on the number line, and addition and subtraction, and finally, approaching the inverse relationship that exists between addition and subtraction and the principle of commutativity which is valid for addition but not for subtraction. For multiplication and division, other aspects are discussed, such as the relationship between multiplication and repeated addition or step counting, the inverse relationship between multiplication and division, and the principle of commutativity, which applies to multiplication but not to division. The other major component of these interventions concerns the strategic aspect. This involves teaching the child the mastery of different strategies for solving calculations and the conceptual understanding of these strategies (why I can do this to solve this calculation) and also to reflect on the choice of the most effective strategy in relation to the problem presented. The different stages of intervention described below are presented in a hierarchical manner, i.e., each stage assuming the success and mastery of the exercises proposed in the previous stages. However, the math coach will need to adapt the proposals presented here to suit the child he or she is tutoring. For example, let us imagine a child in third grade for whom the very basics of addition need to be reworked. This work will of course begin with the simple calculations of single-digit numbers. Once these have been mastered, the coach will be able to progress in two different ways: either by moving towards more complex strategies, or by always working on the same strategies but applied this time to larger numbers (for example, I work on small doubles such as $3+3$, $4+4$, $5+5$, etc., and then I work on doubles such as $300+300$, $400+400$, etc.). This last type of approach can often be very rewarding for the child with a big delay who suddenly realizes that he or she can also do 'big calculations'.

In any case, it is important to bear in mind the main principles of rehabilitation discussed in Chapter 1 and reiterated by Fuchs et al. (2008) in their Math Flash programme. In particular, it is important to provide explicit, clear instructions that follow an integrated and coherent programme. It is essential to work on the conceptual aspects and to support this understanding through the use of manipulatives (such as blocks, card games, fingers, or number lines). As emphasized by the meta-analysis of Codding et al. (2011), repeated practice of exercises is important but is only really effective if accompanied by modelling. It is therefore always a matter of explaining and showing the child what to do and how to do it. Once the child is able to carry out the task using the strategy taught, it is important to present him/her with numerous exercises to repeat the practice and that this drill gradually leads to the automation of the procedure in question. Revisions of what has just been seen in the session should be planned and should be complemented by the inclusion of revisions of what has been seen previously. Without this regular 'refreshment' of what has already been learned, the child risks forgetting what has been learned previously. Finally, put in place factors that help motivate the child: measure with the child how well he or she performs on a given task at each session and monitor progress by graphing it on a chart, create games in which you practice the knowledge or strategies learned, and give positive feedback on a regular basis.

4.6.1 Addition and subtraction

4.6.1.1 Conceptual aspects

4.6.1.1.1 ADDITION

To work on the sense of operation, we can use concrete material such as marbles or card games or even drawings (we prefer manipulable material at the outset).

Exercise with boxes and handling of objects:

> 'We are going to solve an addition problem together. I put two marbles in this box and now I put three more/add three more. So we have $2+3$. How many marbles are there now? 1, 2, 3, 4, 5. There are 5 marbles: $2+3=5$'.

Arithmetic 133

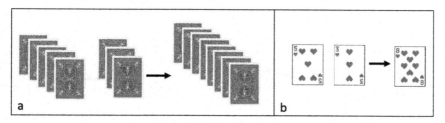

Figure 4.2 Explanation of the concept of addition with cards used face down (a) or face up (b).

Exercise with a deck of cards:

Ask the child to show you, for example, the calculation '5 + 3 = ?' using the playing cards (Cooreman & Bringmans, 2004). It is preferable to use the cards face down, considering them as countable material (Figure 4.2a). The child represents each term, puts the two groups of cards together, and counts them to find the sum. Explain that addition is the joining together of two or more groups.

In the next step, use the face-up cards (Figure 4.2b) to help link symbolic representations (Arabic numbers, verbal numbers) to non-symbolic quantities (the heart, pick, shamrock, tile icons on the card) in the addition.

It is important to also consider additions with zero. For example, ask the child: 'What is four plus zero?' using playing cards. The child will realize that if you do not add anything to 4 cards, you still have 4 cards, so 4 + 0 = 4. After providing several examples, provide written addition problems and ask the child to solve them by verbalizing them as shown in Table 4.4. Such activities help children conceptualize the role of zero in addition.

Table 4.4 Verbalizing the role of zero in addition and subtraction

Written form in digits	Verbal form
5 + 0 = 5	Five plus nothing equals/is five
0 + 3 = 3	Nothing plus three equals/is three
0 + 0 = 0	Nothing plus nothing equals/is nothing
5 − 0 = 5	Five minus nothing equals/is five
0 − 5 = ?	Nothing minus five equals/is impossible
0 − 0 = 0	Nothing minus nothing equals/is nothing

4.6.1.1.2 SUBTRACTION

Exercise with boxes and handling of objects:

"We're going to do a subtraction together. In this box I put 6 marbles, and now you are going to take 4 out. There are 2 left. So, 6 − 4 = 2.' Let the child practise.

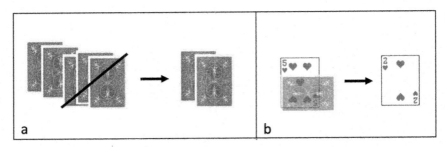

Figure 4.3 Explanation of the concept of subtraction with cards (a) face down or (b) face up.

Exercise with a deck of cards:

> The concept of subtraction can also be explained using playing cards. In contrast to addition, only the first term (or the minuend) has to be represented. So when a child is asked to show '5 − 3 = ?' s/he should take 5 cards face down and then, from those, take 3 cards (or the subtrahend) and then look at how many cards are left to find the result of the subtraction or the difference (Figure 4.3a). Alternatively, he/she can represent the first term with the corresponding card face up and then hide the quantity of objects represented by the second term (Figure 4.3b). Repeat the same for subtraction 3 − 5. The child will realize that it is not possible to remove five cards from the three cards s/he holds simply because s/he does not have enough cards or because he/she is missing two cards. Apply many examples to make them aware that subtraction is not commutative.
>
> Just as you did with addition, also explore subtraction with zero using playing cards (e.g., '5 − 0 = ?'; out of 5 cards, subtract 0, you still have 5), and then verbalizing the differences (Table 4.4).

4.6.1.2 Simple calculations

As in the article by Fuchs et al. (2008), the proposed intervention starts with the teaching of plus or minus one and plus or minus two calculations, then the counting strategies (counting on and then, counting min, see Tournaki, 2003), working with doubles, and then decomposition strategies based on known facts (such as Koponen et al., 2018).

4.6.1.2.1 N ± 1 AND N ± 2 CALCULATIONS

The activity 'Representing Numbers on a Real Staircase' (see Chapter 2) actually conceptualizes the $n \pm 1$ calculations. By finding the number just after a number n (one step up), or the number just before it (one step down), the student adds or subtracts one unit to the starting number. The aim is therefore to help the child understand the link between the serial aspect of the sequence of numbers and addition (going further in the numerical chain) or subtraction (going backwards in the numerical sequence) as in the study by Koponen et al. (2018). Afterwards, you can ask the child to find the neighbour of a single-digit number (Cooreman & Bringmans, 2004) by using the Clever chart with the number cards (see Chapter 3, on base-10). You can then extend the exercise to calculations $n \pm 2$. You can also (if the child is older) explore larger numbers using the tape measure and so easily solve 'big calculations' such as $67 + 2$ or $74 - 1$. Once the child has understood, it is important to automate the process. For example, you can use a deck of cards and ask the child to quickly give the answer of the value of that card plus one, or minus one, or plus two, or minus two. Also discuss with the child why it is impossible to solve a calculation such as $1 - 2 =$.

Note that this type of exercise requires a certain level of elaboration of the counting chain. For addition, the level of the breakable chain must be reached. For subtraction, the child must be able to count backwards and give the number that comes before another. Practice exercises at this level if this is not yet automated (see Chapter 2).

4.6.1.2.2 COUNTING STRATEGIES

Use again the representation of addition with the playing cards face up. You can teach the child to use the counting-on strategy. To motivate the child to use this strategy, you can put the first card (for example, card 5 for counting $5 + 3$) face down after seeing it for a short time and the second (card 3) face up, so that the child cannot count the icons on the first card. Make sure that the child has reached the level of the numerable chain (see Chapter 2) or else work on the counting chain before continuing. Next, consider calculations where the difference between the two terms is large (for example, $2 + 7$). Experience several times with the child the fact that the solution is the same depending on whether the counting starts with the first or the second term (principle of commutativity). Then see which strategy is the fastest and discuss with the child which is the best option: start counting with the smallest or the largest number? Next, provide them with lists of calculations and ask them to show which term is best to start counting and why, before implementing the counting strategy in question. Practise this strategy until the child has mastered it (correctly and quickly).

Proceed in the same way for subtraction. At this stage, the child should be able to solve small subtractions with a subtrahend of 1 or 2. Now you can practice exercises in which the subtrahend is slightly larger (for example, $6 - 3$, $8 - 5$, etc.). In this case, the child must keep track of the counting steps he or she performs. If this is not the case, show him/her how to use his/her fingers to help him/herself. A common mistake in this counting strategy (or counting-down strategy) is to start counting the counting steps with the minuend ($6 - 3 =$, that's 6, 5, 4, the wrong answer is 4). Rather, one should pronounce the name of the minuend and then only after, count the counting steps (6, (− 1)

5, (− 1) 4, (− 1), 3: the answer is 3). Start practicing this strategy with a medium such as a number line or a tape measure to track the counting steps. When the child feels more comfortable, gradually invite him/her to count without the support of the number line or tape measure (possibly using the fingers).

When the minuend and the subtrahend are close numbers (e.g., 9 − 8 =) or when the subtrahend is large enough (e.g., 4 or more), the counting strategy can be very laborious and error-prone. In these cases, the strategy of counting up is to be preferred (i.e., counting from 8 to 9, the answer is equal to the number of steps of over-counting, i.e., 1). As mentioned above, the use of this indirect addition strategy to solve a subtraction is based on a broader understanding of the minus sign, which indicates not only 'remove' but also 'find the difference'. This approach can be taught to children who have good reasoning skills. Show, for example, with coins that the calculation 5 − 4 can be solved by counting backwards 4 steps from 5, but also by counting the difference between 4 and 5. When I have 4 coins, how many would I need to get to 5? The result is identical in both methods (see Figure 4.4).

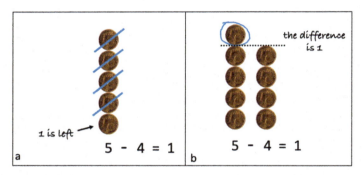

Figure 4.4 Subtraction solved by the counting-down (a) or counting-up strategy (b).

4.6.1.2.3 DOUBLES AND NEAR DOUBLES

Ties additions or doubles are those where the two terms are equal (e.g., 2 + 2, 3 + 3, 4 + 4, 5 + 5, etc.). In typical development, the responses to ties or double additions are usually memorized fairly quickly by children and will allow them to solve other close calculations that we have called the *near doubles*, such as 5 + 6, for example. To represent ties or doubles, you can ask the child to show each term on each hand as many African tribes apply (see Keshwani, 2010; Cooreman, 2014). If he joins his raised fingertips together, he can easily see that it is the same amount on both sides (Figure 4.5a). For numbers over five, the child can work with a partner, each representing one of the terms on his or her hands (Figure 4.5b). Help the child discover that once a term beyond five is present and both hands are to be used, the connection of the two complete hands is always equal to ten. Then simply add the sum of the other fingers (for

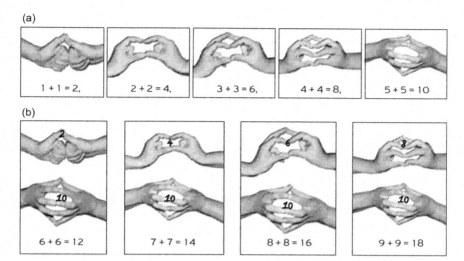

Figure 4.5 Representation of doubles with the fingers (Karagiannakis, 2015).

example, 7 + 7 corresponds to one hand plus one hand, so 10, plus 2 fingers plus 2 fingers, so 4, for a total of 14). The same thinking can be extended to the calculations themselves as shown in Table 4.5, where it can be seen that some doubles end with the same number as others, for example, 3 + 3 and 8 + 8.

Table 4.5 Commonalities between the doubles

1 + 1 = 2	2 + 2 = 4	3 + 3 = 6	4 + 4 = 8	5 + 5 = 10
6 + 6 = 12	7 + 7 = 14	8 + 8 = 16	9 + 9 = 18	10 + 10 = 20

Stimulate the retrieval of ties with playing cards. Shuffle the 40 playing cards ranging from 1 to 10 from a standard 52-card deck, give them to the child, and ask him/her to give the double of the number indicated on each card as quickly as possible (for example, in response to the '3' card, say '6'). If an error is made on one of the cards, give the child the correct answer and put the card back a little further into the deck for another try. Calculate how much time it takes to go through the entire deck. Repeat this exercise at other times and see (maybe with a chart) how the child's speed progresses (to motivate them).

Once the child has mastered doubles, enter calculations that are close, by 1 or 2 units, to doubles (for example, 5 + 4 =, 9 + 8 = or 7 + 5 =). Use fingers or other concrete materials (for example, real coins) to explain that this type of calculation can be broken down as a calculation of doubles, plus one (for example, 5 + 6 = (5 + 5) + 1, see Figure 4.6a) or plus two (for example, 5 + 7 = (5 + 5) + 2, see Figure 4.6b).

Finally, highlight (again with the help of concrete material, such as coins for example, and corresponding calculations written in digits) the inverse

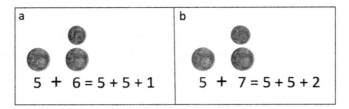

Figure 4.6 Representation of 'near-double' type calculations with coins.

relationship between addition and subtraction. In this way, the child will be able to solve the subtractions on the basis of the corresponding additive facts. For example, if the child knows the additive fact '4 + 4 = 8', then he or she will be able to deduce that 8 − 4 = 4. Next, practise a number of exercises involving double, near-double, and corresponding subtractions (Table 4.6), stimulating both retrieval and reasoning skills.

Table 4.6 Drill exercises on double, near-double additions, and corresponding subtractions

2+2=☐	3+3=☐	4+4=☐	5+5=☐	6+6=☐	7+7=☐	8+8=☐	9+9=☐
4−2=☐	6−3=☐	8−4=☐	10−5=☐	12−6=☐	14−6=☐	16−6=☐	18−6=☐
2+3=☐	4+3=☐	4+5=☐	5+7=☐	6+7=☐	7+8=☐	8+9=☐	9+8=☐

4.6.1.2.4 BONDS OF TEN FACTS

It is very important to automate the bonds of ten facts (10 = 1 + 9, 2 + 8, 3 + 7, 4 + 6, 5 + 5) since they are prerequisite for mental addition and subtraction with multi-digit numbers. Once you have conceptualized the decomposition aspect of the number ten (see Chapter 2), you will be able to discover the additions whose sum is ten. Invite the child to practice these calculations repeatedly and intensively. Using coin-like materials or a playing card of ten or the fingers of the hand, you and the child can complete a table of tens additions like the one shown in Figure 4.7a. Offer the child the table with the column on the left blank so that he or she can complete this column himself or herself. Then, hide the column on the left (with a playing card) and ask the child to say the hidden number (for example, say '8' in response to the number 2), then slide the playing card down to check the accuracy of his or her answer before giving the answer for the next number. Each time the child produces an error, he or she must start over from the beginning see Cooreman, 2014a). You can then invite the child to go faster and faster in this type of exercise without making mistakes. Then enter the corresponding subtractions by asking 'how much is ten minus one?' (Figure 4.7b). It is important that these exercises are repeated several times in a session and

a

10	
8 +	2
5 +	5
3 +	7
6 +	4
1 +	9
0 +	10
2 +	8
7 +	3
4 +	6
9 +	1

b

10	- 2	8
	- 5	5
	- 7	3
	- 4	6
	- 9	1
	- 10	0
	- 8	2
	- 3	7
	- 6	4
	- 1	9

Figure 4.7 Drill and practice on number bonds of ten for (a) addition and (b) subtraction.

over several sessions. Also ask the child to repeat these activities every day at home. These repetitions should continue until the child is able to respond correctly and quickly to all the calculations (one to two seconds per calculation). Set up a system where you record the speed of response to these lists of calculations and track the child's progress. Take the time to build different lists of calculations in which the presentation order changes each time.

4.6.1.2.5 CROSSING THE DECADE

Many students have difficulty with sums greater than 10 (e.g., 8 + 5, 9 + 6) because, on the one hand, the strategy taught for going beyond 10 involves different steps and requires good working memory resources to retain all the intermediate results (e.g., 8 + 5 = 8 + (2 + 3) = (8 + 2) + 3 = 10 + 3 = 13) and, on the other hand, they cannot compensate by representing the two operands on their fingers and therefore feel deprived. In Africa there are tribes that have adopted base 20. Perhaps this is owing to the fact that a barefoot lifestyle makes the toes available for use too (for more see Zaslavsky, 1970; Zaslavsky, 1999), letting children commonly use their toes, in addition to their fingers, to represent both terms for overcoming 10 (this is also common practice in Vietnam; for a similar idea see Cooreman, 2015b, 2015e). Similarly, to calculate 8 + 5 for example, suggest that the child think of 8 toes and show 5 fingers (see the first row of the Figure 4.8), then lower as many fingers as necessary to arrive at 10 toes (i.e., 2). The answer is 10 toes and 3 fingers raised, for a total of 13. Next, have him/her practice automating the 'fingers and toes' addition strategy to solve problems like those presented in Figure 4.8.

140 *Arithmetic*

8	+	5	=	10	+	3	=	13
9	+	6	=	10	+	4	=	14
8	+	4	=	10	+	2	=	12
9	+	6	=	10	+	5	=	15
8	+	7	=	10	+	5	=	15
9	+	5	=	10	+	4	=	14
9	+	8	=	10	+	7	=	17
8	+	6	=	10	+	4	=	14
9	+	7	=	10	+	6	=	16

Figure 4.8 Crossing the decade in addition using fingers and toes. (Cooreman, 2015b & e)

Then develop the exercises and the practice of addition with a term equal to 9 (e.g., 9 + 8 =). For example, you can use playing cards. Place a 9 card face up on the table and next to it a pile of shuffled cards from 1 to 9. Turn over the first card of the deck, say card 6 (Figure 4.9a). To obtain the sum of 9 + 6, consider that 9 is 1 unit less than 10. So, if you take a unit from the other card

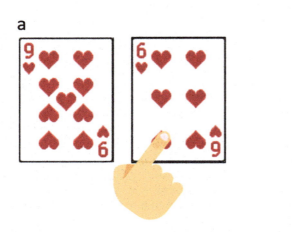

Figure 4.9 Work and automatise the addition facts with a term equal to nine.

Arithmetic 141

(the 6 card) and add it to 9, you will have 10 on one side, and 5 remaining (6 − 1) on the other. So, instead of calculating 9 + 6, the child can consider this to be 10 plus 5, which is quite easy. To make this procedure easier, ask the child to hide an icon on the second playing card with a finger to remind him/her that one unit has been subtracted. Once he/she proceeds without error, repeat the activity by measuring the time to automate the corresponding facts. You can then leave the concrete material (the playing cards) and work with the symbolic calculations as shown in the table in Figure 4.9b. Ask the child to hide the right-hand column with cardboard and to retrieve the hidden numbers as quickly as they can from top to bottom. You may have tables where you ask how much is 9 + n (e.g., 9 + 7), and then others where it is the reversed addition (7 + 9) without making mistakes.

The 'fingers and toes' strategy can also be applied for subtractions with a number greater than 10 given that there are 20 fingers available! For example, to calculate 14 − 5, represent 14 using 10 toes and 4 fingers (Figure 4.10). You should subtract five fingers in total. So lower all 4 fingers (14 − 4 = 10), and then take away 1 more from the toes (10 − 1 = 9).

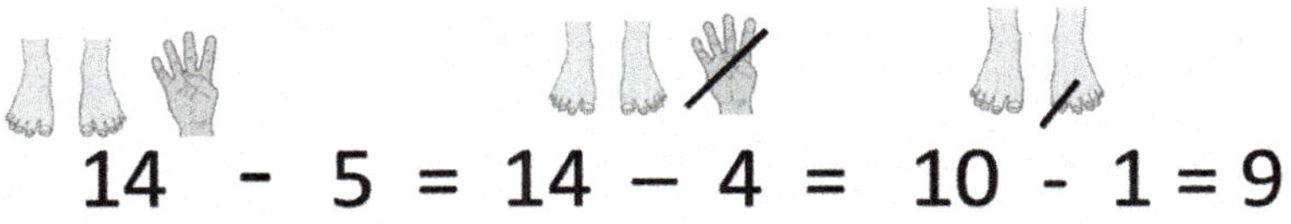

14 - 5 = 14 − 4 = 10 - 1 = 9

Figure 4.10 Borrowed subtraction, using fingers and toes.

4.6.1.2.6 RECAP OF SIMPLE ADDITION STRATEGIES

Figure 4.11 shows all small additions of two single-digit numbers. The facts above the diagonal are equal to those below the diagonal due to the

Figure 4.11 Addition facts between single-digit numbers.

commutativity of addition (e.g., 5 + 3 = 3 + 5). For this reason, the cells below the diagonal are empty. The strategies presented above were designed to help students become fluent in learning the addition facts as well as the corresponding subtractions. Each cell in the table shown in Figure 4.11 is coloured according to the strategy that seems to be the most effective for calculating the corresponding fact. Note that some facts can be derived from two strategies. For example, 8 + 7 = can be calculated using the 'fingers and toes' strategy or the 'near double' strategy. The only facts not covered by the above strategies are 5 + 3 and 6 + 3, which can be easily solved by the counting-min strategy. This table can be used by math coaches: after assessing the child's knowledge of each of these facts, the coach can select the most appropriate intervention strategy(ies) to teach the child.

4.6.1.2.7 BIG CALCULATIONS FOR BIG CHILDREN

For older children, stimulate mental arithmetic with larger numbers that can be derived from facts already known. Introducing a new group of facts each time, such as doubles or near doubles, bonds of ten or 9 + single-digit number, can be seen as horizontal progress, while increasing the numerical size within a particular group of facts is vertical progress (see Figure 4.12). The vertical approach can be conceptually facilitated by using the Clever chart (see Chapter 3) or parallel number lines (Figure 4.13).

	Bonds of ten	Doubles	Near doubles	Number + 9
↑ Vertical progress	6000+4000 = 10000	12000-6000 = 6000	6000+5000 =11000	9000+6000 = 15000
	600+400 =1 000	1200-600 = 600	600+500 = 1100	900+600 = 1500
	60+40 = 100	120-60 = 60	60+50 = 110	90+60 = 150
	6+4 = 10	12-6 = 6	6+5 = 11	9+6 = 15
Horizontal progress →				

Figure 4.12 Example of a horizontal or a vertical approach.

4.6.1.2.8 STIMULATING FLEXIBILITY

As we saw in the first chapter of this book, it is important to stimulate the child's flexibility, i.e., mastering several strategies and being able to choose the most effective one, especially when dealing with children with good reasoning skills but poor memory capacity. For example, in subtraction, when the distance between the two terms is small, it is easier to calculate the difference using counting up rather than counting down. It will therefore be a matter

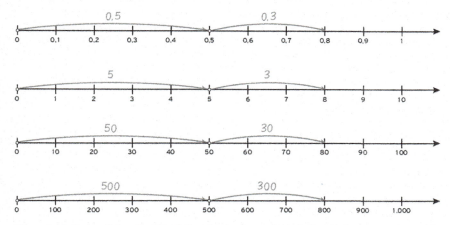

Figure 4.13 Generalizing the calculation 5 + 3 = 8 to calculations with larger numbers.

not only of teaching the child these two strategies, but also of training them to make the best choice based on the calculation presented. Thus, give them several calculations with small and large differences (between the minuend and the subtrahend) and ask them to decide which strategy is the most appropriate (Figure 4.14a). At this point, focus on making the decision and not on

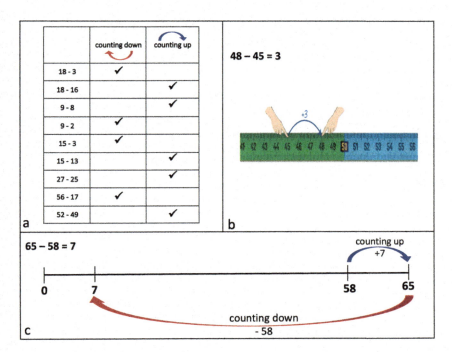

Figure 4.14 Stimulating flexibility in subtraction.

144 *Arithmetic*

calculating the final answer. For older children, you can also consider calculations with larger numbers (e.g., 65 − 58 or 48 − 45) and support the conceptual understanding of both strategies by representing the difference on a tape measure (Figure 4.14b) or visualize whether the subtrahend is much larger than the difference using a number line (Figure 4.14c).

4.6.1.3 Complex mental arithmetic

The purpose of this section is to provide strategies for children who have difficulty doing mental calculation with multi-digit numbers (e.g., 45 + 39 =_ or 84 − 37 =_) using traditional methods such as addition and subtraction bridging (Figure 4.15). These difficulties may be due to the fact that these sequential strategies (see Table 4.2) involve several steps, which increases the cognitive load, or they may be due to a problem with a more basic skill such as number composition-decomposition, probably related to a shallow understanding of the base-10 structure of numbers (see Chapter 3). As a result, these children use unproductive strategies such as counting from the first or largest term (e.g., 48 + 13 = 49, 50, 51, 52 ... 61).

Therefore, before introducing a child to a mental arithmetic strategy for multi-digit numbers, check that he or she is able to break down multi-digit numbers and, if necessary, return first to the number composition and decomposition activities presented in Chapter 3 (practice with Montessori cards in which the parts of the number overlap). The following strategies are presented in order of increasing difficulty. Wait until the child is comfortable with the

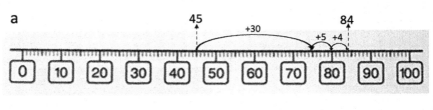

45+39 = 45 + (30 + 9) = (45+30) + 9 = 75 + (5 + 4) = (75 + 5) + 4 = 80 + 4 = 84

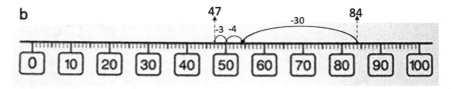

84−37 = 84 − (30 + 7) = (84−30) − 7 = 54 − (4 + 3) = (54 − 4) − 3 = 50 − 3 = 47

Figure 4.15 Bridging strategy in (a) addition and (b) subtraction.

number activities you suggest before moving on to the next step. Remember, however, that regular reviews of what is seen in the session and what has been seen and practiced in previous sessions should be part of your intervention programme.

4.6.1.3.1 ADDITION AND SUBTRACTION OF POWER OF TEN

You can repeat the activity 'Representing numbers on a real staircase' (see Chapter 2), this time extending it to numbers up to 100 (or use a number line on the floor). This time, place the label of the 10s on each step of the staircase (0, 10, 20 ... 100, see Figure 4.16). To represent the number 25, for example, stand on the second step labelled 20 and lift 5 fingers to make 25. The pupil therefore has the tens at foot level and the units at finger level. Ask the student to represent several two-digit numbers in this way. Then proceed by adding units such as 33 + 2, 65 + 4, 15 + 3 (using calculations that do not require carry-over). In this case, only the fingers change. Then add whole tens (for example, 25 + 20). In this case, only the feet change. Next, add tens-unit numbers that do not require carry-over (for example, 45 + 23). The feet should be changed first, then the fingers (Figure 4.16). You can then perform equivalent activities, but this time with subtraction (for example, 35 − 3, 76 − 5, 47 − 10, 58 − 20, 86 − 12, 27 − 13).

You can then use the same type of calculation but with the Clever chart (see Figure 4.17, Cooreman, 2015c). The child uses fingers or board game pieces to move up in addition or down in subtraction. These activities allow children to drill and practice composing, decomposing, adding, and subtracting between two- and three-digit numbers and to conceptualize addition as an upward movement ('I have more') and subtraction as a downward movement ('I have less').

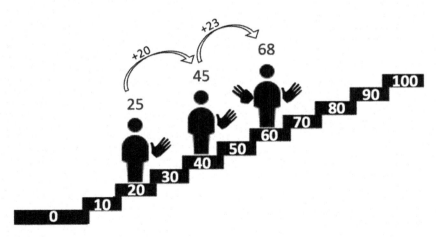

Figure 4.16 Addition and subtraction on the stairs.

146   Arithmetic

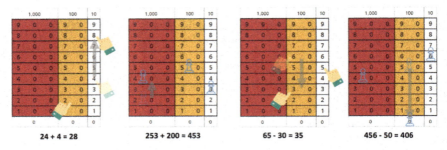

Figure 4.17 Addition and subtraction on the Clever chart (Cooreman, 2015c).

4.6.1.3.2 ADDITION AND SUBTRACTION WITH DECOMPOSITION USING THE BUBBLE STRUCTURE

Complex calculation requires the mastery of decomposition strategy which can be implemented in several ways (Beishuizen, 1993; Beishuizen & Anghileri, 1998; Selter, 2001; Hickendorff et al., 2019). An interesting way to do so is by using the bubble structure (Cooreman, 2004, 2018). In Table 4.7 we explain the decomposition strategy using the bubble structure for the calculation 45 + 23. It is transparent at four levels (we take the example 45 + 23):

Table 4.7 Example of the decomposition strategy for addition without carry-over using the bubble structure

Step	Bubble structure	Language	Mathematical expression
1	45 + 23 = ◯ ◯ =	Draw two bubbles because the greater number has two digits	45 + 23 =
2	45 + 23 = ◯ ◯ =	Decompose 45 into 40 and 5; decompose 23 into 20 and 3	45 + 23 = 40 + 5 + 20 + 3
3	45 + 23 = (60) ◯ =	Sum 40 and 20; write 60 in the first bubble	45 + 23 = 40 + 5 + 20 + 3 45 + 23 = 40 + 20 + 5 + 3 45 + 23 = (40 + 20) + 5 + 3 45 + 23 = 60 + 5 + 3
4	45 + 23 = (60) (+8) =	Sum 5 and 3; write +8 in the second bubble	45 + 23 = 60 + (5 + 3) 45 + 23 = 60 + 8
5	45 + 23 = (60) (+8) = 68	To find the result simply say the number word corresponding to each bubble starting from the left: 'sixty' 'eight', that is 'sixty-eight'	45 + 23 = 68

- *Base-10 decomposition transparency*: in the bubble strategy numbers are decomposed in terms of the multiples of powers of 10: $45 = 4 \times 10^1 + 5 \times 10^0 = 40 + 5$ (step 2) and not as '25 + 20' for example.
- *Unit transparency*: the decomposition proposed in the bubble strategy uses the same unit: 45 is 40 (units) and 5 (units) and not 4 tens and 5 units.
- *Base-10 composition transparency*: the four addends obtained from the decompositions (step 2) are composed or rearranged so that those with the same number of digits are added into the same bubble (step 3 and 4). So, in this particular example, the first bubble collects 40 and 20 and the second bubble collects 5 and 3. These steps in the bubble strategy correspond to the mathematical reorganization of the four addends through the commutative $(40 + 5 + 20 + 3 = 40 + 20 + 5 + 3)$ and the associative $[40 + 20 + 5 + 3 = (40 + 20) + 5 + 3]$ properties.
- *Language transparency*: the result of the addition can be found by simply reading aloud the number words corresponding to the number in each bubble from left to right (step 5).

The visual structure of the bubble (step 1) for addition provides very simple visual means for carrying out the procedure. This structure also provides support for recalling the next step to carry out: each bubble needs to be filled in, allowing the child to see in advance the steps of the procedure. Therefore, this structure avoids memory overload (which typically occurs with many other addition strategies), minimizing the chance of errors. For example, in addition problems with regrouping like $45 + 27 =$, a common incorrect answer is 612 ($4 + 2 = 6$ and $5 + 7 = 12$) or 62 (missing the carrying). Such mistakes are avoided using the bubble structure (see step 5, Table 4.8).

The decomposition strategy (see Table 4.2, Hickendorff et al., 2019) for subtraction (e.g., $75 - 32$) allows subtraction to be treated as addition, implicitly dealing with integers without formally introducing negative numbers (see how to introduce this in Chapter 1). Consequently, the four modes of transparency mentioned above also take place (Table 4.9).

When borrowing is necessary, not only is it postponed to the last stage of the procedure, but it is always applied in powers of ten to make it easier. For $75 - 38$, for example (see Table 4.10), borrowing is applied to the last step on the $40 - 3$ calculation, which is cognitively less expensive than doing the $15 - 8$ subtraction that would have been necessary at the beginning of other subtraction algorithms.

It should be noted that some children may have difficulty in performing $40 - 3$ subtractions since, in this case, both the unit and the ten will change. Using a table such as the one shown in the Figure 4.18 allows the child to work the change in the tens and units separately. First ask them to fill in the columns in the table (for example, $30 - 5$, $50 - 5$, $80 - 5$, etc.). When working vertically ($\downarrow$), the units digit obtained always remains the same (in the completed example, the units digit is always 1), only the tens digit changes, and this can be derived from the knowledge of the tens complements. Then continue horizontally ($\rightarrow$) by filling in the rows (e.g., $30 - 5$, $30 - 3$, $30 - 7$, etc.). Now the

148 *Arithmetic*

Table 4.8 Example of the decomposition strategy for addition with regrouping using the bubble structure

Step	Bubble structure	Language	Mathematical expression
1	45 + 27 = ◯ ◯ =	Draw two bubbles because the greater number has two digits	
2	45 + 27 = ◯ ◯ =	Decompose 45 into 40 and 5; decompose 27 into 20 and 7	45 + 27 = 40 + 5 + 20 + 7
3	45 + 27 = (60) ◯ =	Sum 40 and 20; write 60 in the first bubble	45 + 27 = 40 + 5 + 20 + 7 45 + 27 = 40 + 20 + 5 + 7 45 + 27 = (40 + 20) + 5 + 7 45 + 27 = 60 + 5 + 7
4	45 + 27 = (60)(+12) =	Sum 5 and 7; write +12 in the second bubble	45 + 27 = 60 + (5 + 7) 45 + 27 = 60 + 12
5	45 + 27 = (60)(+12) = 72	Since reading aloud 'Sixty' 'twelve' doesn't give a conventional number, to find the result decompose 12 into 10 and 2, and say 60 plus 10 is 'seventy', plus 2 is 'seventy-two'	60 + 12 = 60 + 10 + 2 60 + 12 = (60 + 10) + 2 60 + 12 = 70 + 2 60 + 12 = 72

change occurs on the units digit, while the tens digit remains the same (in the completed example, the tens unit is always 3). If a child has difficulty with this exercise, return to the 'Addition and subtraction with powers of ten' section above or use a tape measure or number line (Figure 4.18). Repeat the above activities until the child responds correctly and quickly. Then have the child fill in the boxes on the chart by randomly selecting the boxes to be filled in, which requires both vertical and horizontal procedures.

You can then increase the size of the numbers by subtracting whole tens from whole hundreds (for example, 300 − 40, see Table 4.11). Guide the child in comparing these two tables and how these calculations relate to the smaller ones seen earlier. In reality, only a zero at the end is added in all cases. Invite the child to practise with both small and larger numbers by masking any columns or rows in the tables and asking the child to retrieve the hidden answers repeatedly. Continue this practice until the child responds quickly and correctly. Using tables of this type with a cardboard strip to hide the answer actually allows you to practice a large number of calculations in a short period of time and to get direct feedback on the quality of the answer given and by comparing it to the correct answer.

Arithmetic 149

Table 4.9 Example of the decomposition strategy for subtraction without borrowing using the bubble structure

Steps	Bubble structure	Language	Mathematical expression
1	**75 - 32 =** ◯ ◯ **=**	Draw two bubbles because the first number has two digits	$75 - 32 =$
2	**75 - 32 =** ◯ ◯ **=**	Decompose 75 into 70 and 5; decompose 32 into 30 and 2	$75 - 32 = 70 + 5 - 30 - 2$
3	**75 - 32 =** (40) ◯ **=**	Take away 30 from 70, 40 is left, write 40 in the first bubble	$75 - 32 = 70 + 5 - 30 - 2$ $75 - 32 = 70 - 30 + 5 - 2$ $75 - 32 = (70 - 30) + 5 - 2$ $75 - 32 = 40 + 5 - 2$
4	**75 - 32 =** (40) (+3) **=**	Try to take away 2 from 5, 3 is left, so write +3 in the second bubble	$75 - 32 = 40 + (5 - 2)$ $75 - 32 = 40 + 3$
5	**75 - 32 =** (40) (+3) **= 43**	To find the result simply say the number word corresponding to each bubble starting from the left: 'forty' 'three', that is 'forty-three'	$40 + 3 = 43$

Table 4.10 Example of the bubble strategy for subtraction with borrowing using the bubble structure

Steps	Bubbles structure	Language	Mathematical expression
1	**75 - 38 =** ◯ ◯ **=**	Draw two bubble because the first number has two digits	$75 - 38 =$
2	**75 - 38 =** ◯ ◯ **=**	Decompose 75 into 70 and 5; decompose 38 into 30 and 8	$75 - 38 = 70 + 5 - 30 - 8$
3	**75 - 38 =** (40) ◯ **=**	Subtract 30 from 70; write 40 in the first bubble	$75 - 38 = 70 + 5 - 30 - 8$ $75 - 38 = 70 - 30 + 5 - 8$ $75 - 38 = (70 - 30) + 5 - 8$ $75 - 38 = 40 + 5 - 8$
4	**75 - 38 =** (40) (-3) **=**	Try to take away 8 from 5, 3 are missing, so write −3 in the second bubble	$75 - 38 = 40 + (5 - 8)$ $75 - 82 = 40 - 3$
5	**75 - 38 =** (40) (-3) **= 37**	To find the result, take away 3 from 40, which makes 'thirty-seven'	$40 - 3 = 37$

150   *Arithmetic*

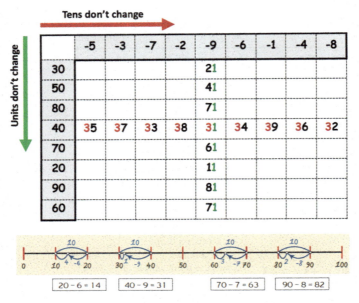

Figure 4.18 Subtracting single-digit numbers from whole tens.

Table 4.11 Subtracting whole tens from whole hundreds

	-50	-30	-70	-20	-90	-60	-10	-40
300					210			
500					410			
800					710			
400	350	370	330	380	310	340	390	360
700					610			
200					110			
900					810			

Hundreds don't change →
Tens don't change ↓

The decomposition strategy using bubbles for addition and subtraction can be extended to larger numbers and accompanied by concrete materials such as cards of superimposed numbers (Figure 4.19) or coins (see introductory chapter). Next, provide worksheets containing the bubble structure for drill and practice (Figure 4.20).

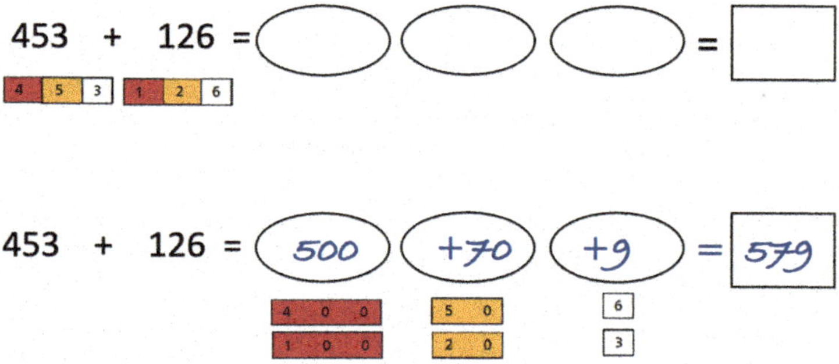

Arithmetic 151

453 + 126 = ◯ ◯ ◯ = ▢

453 + 126 = (500)(+70)(+9) = 579

Figure 4.19 Addition by the bubble structure along with Montessori cards.

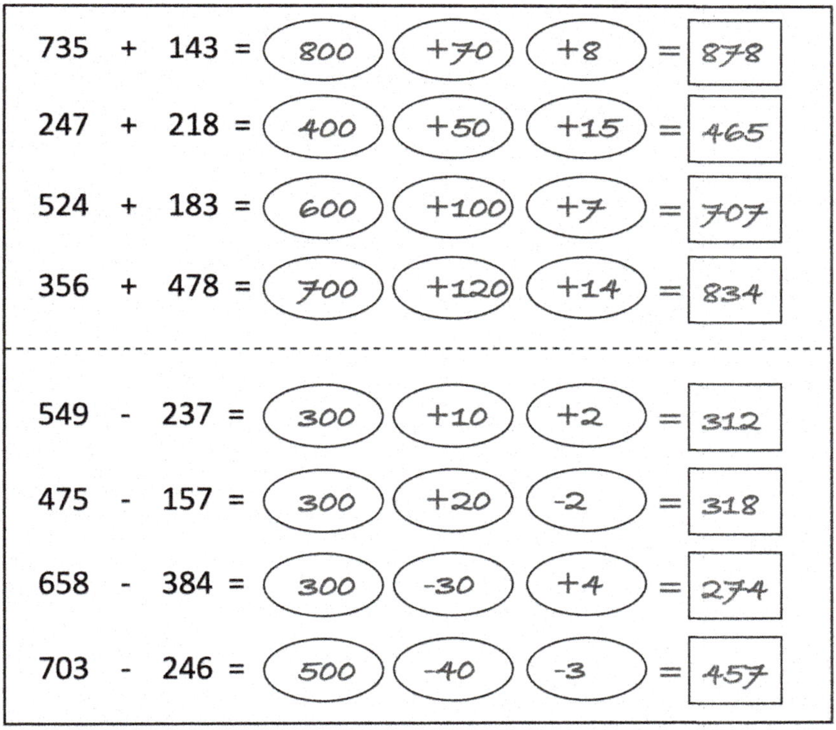

735 + 143 = (800)(+70)(+8) = 878
247 + 218 = (400)(+50)(+15) = 465
524 + 183 = (600)(+100)(+7) = 707
356 + 478 = (700)(+120)(+14) = 834
549 − 237 = (300)(+10)(+2) = 312
475 − 157 = (300)(+20)(−2) = 318
658 − 384 = (300)(−30)(+4) = 274
703 − 246 = (500)(−40)(−3) = 457

Figure 4.20 Addition and subtraction of three-digit numbers with decomposition using the bubble structure.

152 *Arithmetic*

Thompson (1997) argues that to reduce the gap between children's idiosyncratic mental arithmetic and traditional algorithms, we should opt for a holistic approach that more accurately reflects actual quantities (or number-based strategies in Hickendorf et al., 2019, see Section 4.2.3 of this chapter), rather than working with digits. Solving addition or subtraction problems using the decomposition strategy, starting with the numbers on the left, is a more natural approach as you start with the numbers that represent the largest quantities. The latter form the basis for making estimates of the outcome of the calculation and thus the ability to spot implausible answers when using a more formal digit-based method (Brown & Burton, 1978). Thus, for example, 258 + 465 should give an answer above 200 + 400, i.e., above 600, and 725 − 358 should give an answer in the 700 − 400 range, i.e., around 300.

The decomposition strategy using the bubble structure can also be integrated with the strategies seen above for solving simple addition problems; in particular, the strategy of doubles, near doubles, 9 + number, and bonds of 10 (see Figure 4.21).

For older children, stimulate the mental calculations with larger numbers that can be derived from already known facts. The introduction each time of a new group of facts like double or near-double calculations, bonds of tens, or 9 + number can be seen as horizontal progress whereas the increase of the numerical size within a particular group of facts is vertical progress (see Figure 4.12).

For calculations where one of the terms is close to a round number (tens, hundreds, or thousands, etc.), rounding this number makes addition and subtraction calculations much easier (see varying strategies on Table 4.2). For example, the addition problem 99 + 27 = can be solved more easily by

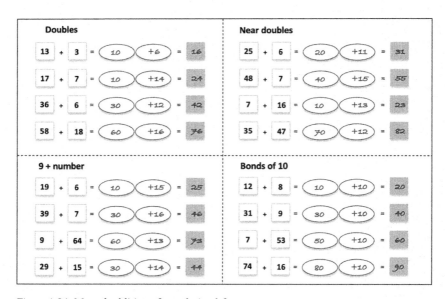

Figure 4.21 Mental additions from derived facts.

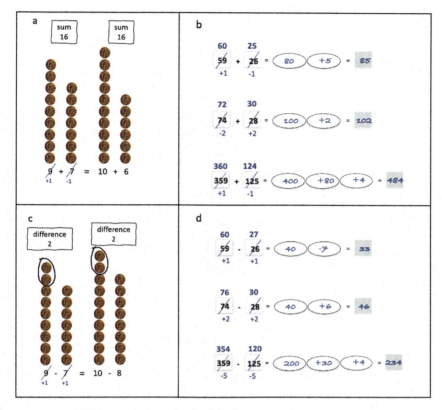

Figure 4.22 Addition and subtraction by rounding.

rounding the number 99 to the nearest hundred, or by transforming it into: $(100-1)+27=(100+27)-1=126$. An even quicker way is the 'counterbalanced' strategy; you add a quantity x to one term and subtract the same quantity from the second term so that the sum remains the same (Figure 4.22a). Thus, $99+27=$ can be treated as $(99+1)+(27-1)=100+26=126$. Both strategies are based on the associativity property of addition. The counterbalanced strategy for addition can be combined with the decomposition strategy using the bubble structure (Figure 4.22b). Rounding also works for subtraction (Figure 4.22d). But in this case, you must add (or subtract) the same number to both terms to keep the same difference (Figure 4.22c).

4.6.1.4 Written calculation

4.6.1.4.1 ADDITION

Written calculation is a tool that greatly facilitates multi-digit number calculations. The written calculation corresponds to algorithms containing several steps

154 *Arithmetic*

that must be applied precisely and in a fixed order. This process is difficult for children who have difficulty applying and memorizing procedures or who are unfamiliar with basic arithmetic facts. The problem is bigger when the algorithm is less transparent and children are unable to compensate conceptually. This is the case with the traditional method of 'columnar calculation' (Figure 4.23a),

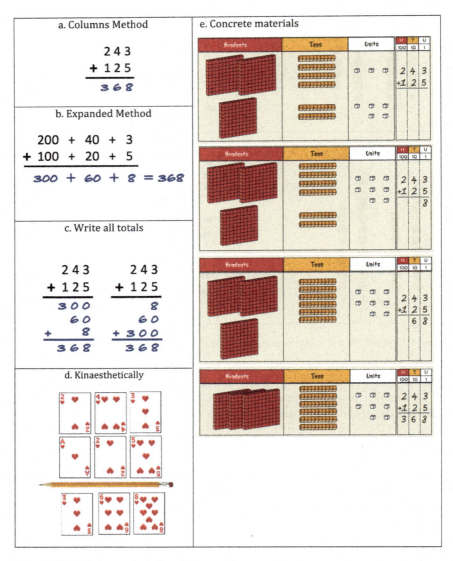

Figure 4.23 Written methods for addition without carrying.

Arithmetic 155

especially when carry-over is necessary (Figure 4.24a). For this reason, introduce written addition in a more transparent way.

Use concrete materials (blocks, straws, coins) to represent the terms (Figure 4.23e). Then you can easily explain that the principle of exchange takes place when the sum of a particular column exceeds ten (Figure 4.24d). Next, move

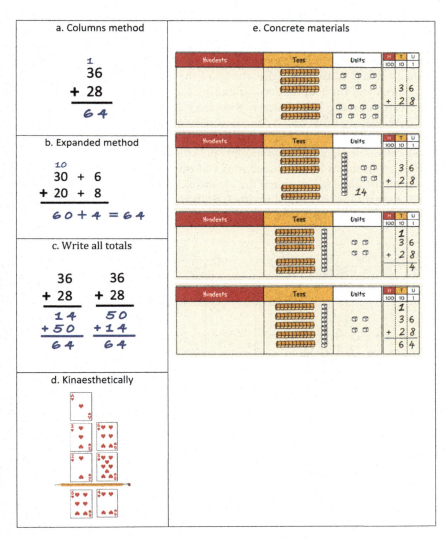

Figure 4.24 Methods for written additions with carry.

156 *Arithmetic*

on to the 'expanded method' (Figures 4.23b and 4.24b) or the 'write all totals method' (Fuson & Li, 2009) where the positional value of the terms is transparent (Figures 4.23b, 4.23c, 4.24c). The latter methods are in fact the same as the decomposition strategy (see Table 4.2) except that the numbers are placed vertically. Finally, introduce the 'column method' which, although the least transparent, is the fastest. If a child still has difficulty following the steps of the 'column method', represent the terms with playing cards (Figure 4.23d) by kinaesthetically applying the steps of the algorithm. This convenient method avoids possible carry-over errors. For example, in the problem 36 + 28 (Figure 4.24d), the sum of the units (6 + 8) equals 14 but the playing cards only go up to 10. This limit helps children realize that something different must be done (compared to adding without grouping) to 'solve' the problem. To deal with this, then explain to the child that the 4 (of the 14) should be placed in the units column and the 1 in the tens column. Using the 'column method' with playing cards can also help children who are still struggling with basic arithmetic facts. Playing cards have collections of symbols that the child can count to calculate sums.

In all cases, it is recommended to apply the columnar calculation method on structured worksheets in which columns and positional values appear (Figure 4.25a) until the child has mastered the algorithm. Zeros could be added to the addends so that they have equal numbers of digits (Figure 4.25b). These make the algorithm more transparent.

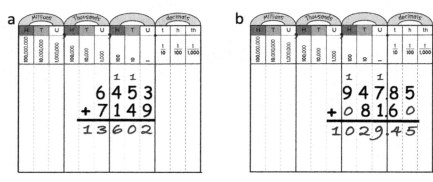

Figure 4.25 Columnar method for additions on structured worksheets with positional values.

4.6.1.4.2 SUBTRACTION

Introduce written calculations for subtraction following the same logic as for addition. Start with the most transparent method (Figure 4.26e), indicating that in subtraction, we represent with concrete materials only the first term (the minuend), taking off the amount the subtrahend represents. Also apply the column method using playing cards. In this case you can hide the number

Arithmetic 157

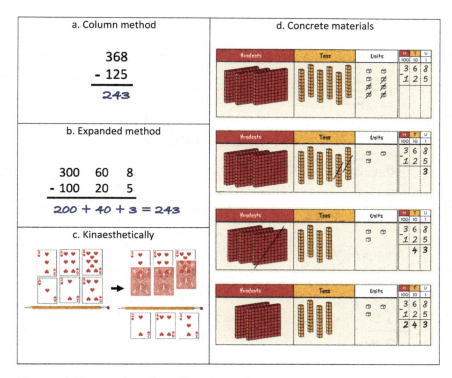

Figure 4.26 Written subtraction without borrowing.

of icons of the minuend indicated by each subtrahend playing card, turning them face down (Figure 4.26c). Then introduce the expanded method (Figure 4.26b) and then the classic column method (Figure 4.26a).

When the number I want to subtract (the subtrahend) is greater than the minuend number, the subtraction requires a borrowing procedure; this involves borrowing from the left-hand column (Figure 4.27) by applying the principle of exchange. Again, the borrowing technique needs to be explained starting from very transparent procedures using concrete materials such as blocks (Figure 4.27d), or playing cards (Figure 4.28), the expanded method (Figure 4.27b), and finally moving on to the traditional column method (Figure 4.27a). For children who find it difficult to cross down the decade (for example, 12 − 9) in the column method, suggest that they include the bonds of ten method. In the example shown in Figure 4.27c (1) a ten is exchanged for 10 units, (2) from these 10 units, the subtrahend (9) is subtracted, (3) the difference (1 unit) is added to the original number of units, i.e., 2.

In all cases, it is recommended to apply the columnar calculation method on structured worksheets in which columns and positional values appear (Figure 4.29)

158 *Arithmetic*

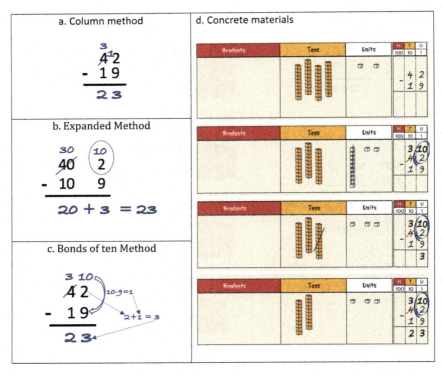

Figure 4.27 Written subtraction with borrowing.

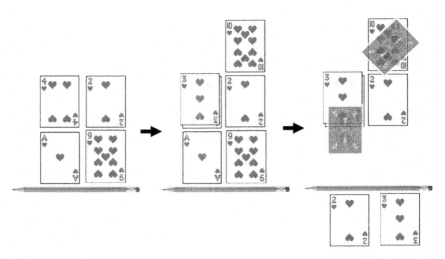

Figure 4.28 Column method for subtraction kinaesthetically using playing cards.

Arithmetic 159

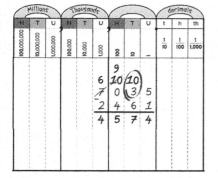 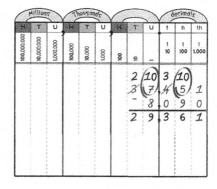

Figure 4.29 Columnar method for subtraction on structured worksheets with positional values.

until the child has mastered the algorithm. This makes the algorithm more transparent.

4.6.2 Multiplication and division

In this section we will discuss conceptual aspects and work on simple multiplications and divisions. For the sake of clarity, we have presented these two sections separately. Note, however, that it will be important to underline the link between the two operations. We then present strategies to help mental calculation and an approach to calculation algorithms written in columns for each of these two operations.

4.6.2.1 Simple multiplications

4.6.2.1.1 CONCEPTUAL ASPECT

Very often the concept of multiplication is learned in school without taking enough time to develop an informal understanding of it (which was the case for learning addition and subtraction). Therefore, it is important that the math coach first takes the time to explore with the child the very concept of multiplication and its importance in everyday situations. The simplest way to do this is to think of multiplication as repeated additions. For example, ask children, 'How many eyes or chair legs are there in the classroom?' Discuss that in real life, there are many equal groups (for example, all chairs have four legs, each child has two eyes) and that in these cases, adding the groups (or in this case, the four (legs) or pairs (of eyes)) is faster than counting the items (legs or eyes) one by one. Provide them with pictures and ask them to indicate both the number of groups and the size of each group (Figure 4.30).

160   *Arithmetic*

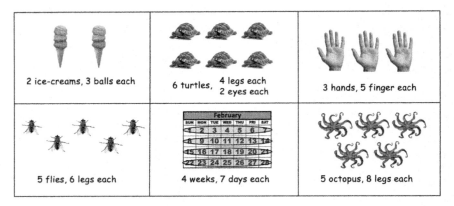

Figure 4.30 Examples of multiplication in everyday life.

Exercise with boxes and handling of objects

'We are going to do a multiplication together. In this box, I put two marbles, then, a second time, I put two marbles, then a third time, I put two marbles: so I put three times five marbles, that's 3 × 5. How many marbles are there now? 1, 2, 3, 4, 5, 6, 7, 8, 9, 10, 11, 12, 13, 14, 15 or 5 + 5 + 5, that makes 15 marbles'. Which way is easier? Let the child practise.

Exercise with a pack of cards

The way in which the factors are read is very important when introducing the concept of multiplication. For example, the product 3 × 2 can be read as: 'three times two' but also 'three twos'. At the beginning, it may be helpful to say 'three twos', as this indicates more transparently that one is referring to three groups of two objects each. Then ask the pupils to represent 'what is 2 × 3 (two threes)' (see Figure 4.31a) using playing cards.

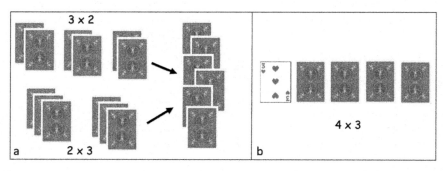

Figure 4.31 Explain the concept of multiplication with cards (a) face up or (b) face up and face down.

Arithmetic 161

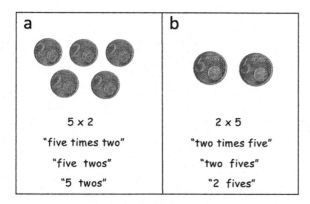

Figure 4.32 Commutativity property of multiplication.

Give the children many examples so that they can see for themselves the commutativity of multiplication.

Afterwards, ask them to show you with cards face up '5 × 3 =?' (five threes). As a deck of cards only has four threes, this is not possible. In this case, you can ask them to place one (3) card face up and any four other cards face down next to it (Figure 4.31b) as if these cards were also threes (Cooremans, 2015d). In this way, you can then represent larger products (such as 9 × 7, for example) and thus stimulate the understanding of multiplication as repeated additions.

Also use practical materials to introduce the commutativity property of multiplication. For example, ask the child to represent the product 5 × 2 using real coins (Figure 4.32a). Verbalize the task using more transparent words such as 'Show me five 2-cent coins'. Using such materials, the child needs to consider only the number of groups (5) and not the number of items each group includes (2). Then ask to represent the 2 × 5 product which is 'two 5-cent coins' (see Figure 4.32b). Explain why the result is the same although both the symbolic and non-symbolic representations are different. Check if this is the case by using different numbers as factors. It is very important to be aware of the commutativity property of multiplication as this reduces the number of multiplicative facts to be memorized.

Then work on the special cases where one of the factors is 1 or 0: 'Show me with the cards 1 × 3 (one three), 1 × 5 (one five) … or 3 × 1 (three ones), 5 × 1 (five ones)' and invite the child to discover the rule that $n \times 1$ or $1 \times n$ is always equal to n, that is one (1) is a neutral element of multiplication. Then move on to products with zeroes: 'Show me 0 × 3 (zero three) or 3 × 0 (three zeros)'. In this way children realize that there is nothing to take and that therefore the answer is either nothing or zero (zero (0) is the zero element in multiplication). Provide them with many products with 1 or 0 and ask them to solve them using meaningful verbalization (Table 4.12).

162 *Arithmetic*

Table 4.12 Verbalize the role of zero and one in multiplication and division

Numerical form	Verbal form
1 × 5 = 5	One five is five
5 × 1 = 5	Five ones is five
5 × 0 = 0	Five times nothing is nothing
0 × 5 = 0	None five is nothing
1 × 1 = 1	One one is one
0 × 0 = 0	Nothing times nothing is nothing
5:1 = 5	Five ones fit into five
0:5 = 0	Zero fives fits into zero

4.6.2.1.2 WORKING ON THE EASIEST TABLES

It is very important for the child to memorize the simplest tables, in particular, the tables of 2, 5, and 10, as these will serve as the basis for deriving the answer to other products from them. The table of 2 actually corresponds to the ties or double additions seen above. The table of 10 is generally not a problem and corresponds to counting in steps of 10, which should be mastered to allow for ease in reading two-digit Arabic numbers (see Chapter 2).

4.6.2.1.3 HOLISTIC AND CONCEPTUAL VISION OF MULTIPLICATION TABLES

For children who are unable to learn arithmetic facts, introduce them by adapting a more conceptual method that reveals the structure of multiplication tables in a holistic way rather than based exclusively on rote learning. Imagine that you want to introduce the table of 4s. Explain that this table corresponds to repeated additions of 4s. Take a tape measure (Figure 4.33) or a number line and start counting from the beginning in steps of 4s to 40 (or more) by reading aloud each time the number reached (1, 2, 3, 4, 'four'; 1, 2, 3, 4, 'eight'; 1, 2, 3, 4, 'twelve'; 1, 2, 3, 4, 'sixteen'; …).

Next, ask the child to get ten groups of four playing cards, arranged as shown in Figure 4.34. Work together to derive the most difficult products by manipulating the groups of four cards. Table 4.13 shows some examples.

For the larger number tables (6, 7, 8, 9), use one playing card for each group repeated. For example, to represent the table of 8, place one playing card of

Figure 4.33 Table of 4 using a tape measure.

Arithmetic 163

Figure 4.34 Representation of the table of 4 using playing cards.

Table 4.13 Deriving the most difficult facts

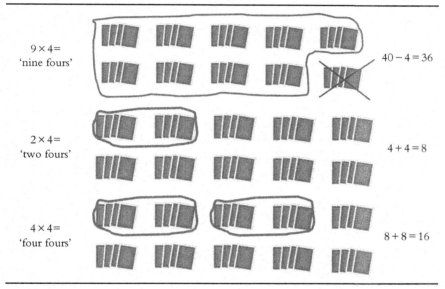

9 × 4 = 'nine fours'		40 − 4 = 36
2 × 4 = 'two fours'		4 + 4 = 8
4 × 4 = 'four fours'		8 + 8 = 16

8 face up and 9 other cards face down, imagining that they are also cards of 8 (Figure 4.35). Use simple facts (2 × 8 = 16, 5 × 8 = 40, 10 × 8 = 80) as well as commutativity to derive all the facts from the table of 8. Table 4.14 gives some ideas in this sense.

Use a number line like the one in Figure 4.36 to symbolically visualize the back and forth movement that the child can do to construct the answer to the difficult problems from the simpler facts from the table of 2, 5, or 10 (see also Figure 1.5 in Chapter 1).

Above, we have introduced strategies to derive all multiplicative facts from simpler facts from the ×1, ×2, ×5, ×10 tables. Apply the above activities for each multiplication table separately, starting with the easiest tables (×1, ×2, ×3, ×4, ×5, ×10). Figure 4.37a shows all the multiplication facts between

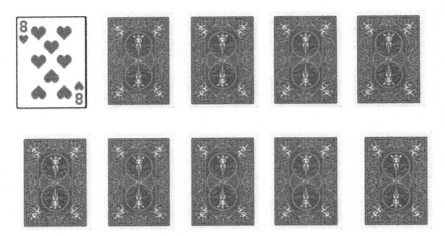

Figure 4.35 Representation of the table of 8 using playing cards.

two single-digit numbers. Facts that are above the diagonal of the graph are not included since they are identical to those below the diagonal, due to the commutativity of the multiplication (e.g., $5 \times 3 = 3 \times 5$). The cells highlighted in yellow are those corresponding to the simplest tables of ×1, ×2, ×3, ×4, ×5, ×10 that almost all students know or can easily find. This leaves only ten other facts (highlighted in blue). Then they can apply the strategies which were presented above to derive these more difficult facts. Use the multiplication table as an assessment tool to check facts already known, and then apply intervention strategies for particular facts that are not mastered.

4.6.2.1.4 RECITE THE SEQUENCES

Practice and drill will be very useful to automate the facts. Children with memory or language problems find it difficult to learn facts in a completely verbal routine ('one time six equals six', 'two times six equals twelve', 'three times six equals eighteen', etc.). You can decrease the short-term memory load by writing the results on the fingers (Figure 4.38, as for instance in Cooreman, 2015d) and suggesting that they recite only the results (6, 12, 18,) while pointing to the corresponding finger. After a few repetitions the child will be able to close the fist, give the first product, then open the corresponding finger to check the answer, then give the second and open the second finger, and so on. In this way s/he can get direct feedback on his/her production and correct himself/herself if necessary. When s/he is able to recite all the facts of the table in order, s/he can then have fun raising the fingers randomly to retrieve the facts in disorder (for example, raise the middle finger of the left hand, which corresponds to 'three times ...').

Arithmetic 165

Table 4.14 Derive the more difficult facts from the facts in the 2, 5, and 10 tables

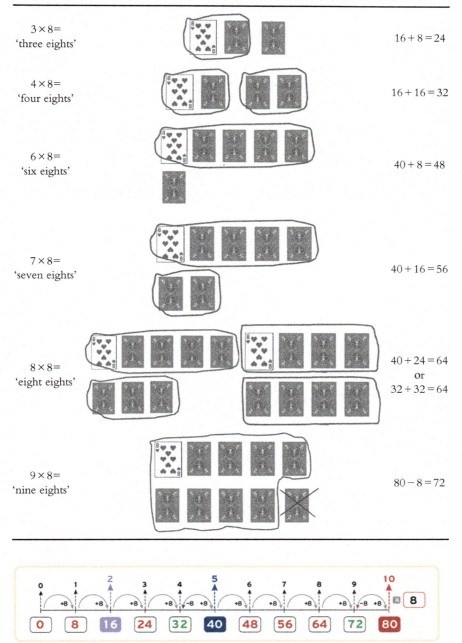

3 × 8 = 'three eights'		16 + 8 = 24
4 × 8 = 'four eights'		16 + 16 = 32
6 × 8 = 'six eights'		40 + 8 = 48
7 × 8 = 'seven eights'		40 + 16 = 56
8 × 8 = 'eight eights'		40 + 24 = 64 or 32 + 32 = 64
9 × 8 = 'nine eights'		80 − 8 = 72

Figure 4.36 The multiplication tables on a number line (Karagiannakis, 2015).

166   *Arithmetic*

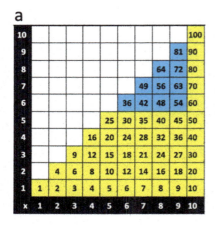

Figure 4.37 Multiplication chart.

Figure 4.38 Facilitate repetition of tables using fingers as in Cooreman, 2015d.

4.6.2.1.5 LIFEBUOYS FOR MEMORIZATION

For some children, memorizing multiplication tables is almost impossible. In these cases, the error rate is generally higher for multiplications of larger numbers (between 6 and 9) than of smaller ones (between 1 and 5). To quickly calculate the largest products of the multiplication tables (from 6×6 to 9×9), a finger algorithm can be used. Note that this algorithm can hardly be linked to a deep understanding of the underlying process. It is therefore a trick for children who are unable to memorize the results or to derive it from more familiar facts (as described above). It is, thus, a kind of 'last chance' strategy. In this calculation on the fingers, which only applies to products from 6 × 6 to 9 × 9, you will have to represent two numbers larger than 5 on the hands. Since you don't have enough hands, you will use your feet: the first operand will be represented by the toes of the left foot and the fingers of the left hand; the second operand will be represented by the toes and fingers of the right hand. Let's consider the calculation 7 × 8. The first operand, seven, is represented by the 5 toes of the left foot and two fingers of the left hand. The second operand, eight, is represented by the toes of the right foot and three fingers of the right hand (see Figure 4.39). The product 7 × 8 corresponds to the number which, for tens, is the sum of the raised fingers (here, 2 + 3 = 5) and for units, the product of the lowered fingers (here, 3 × 2 = 6). The answer is therefore 56.

Figure 4.39 Multiplication on the fingers.

4.6.2.1.6 RESISTING INTERFERENCE

Some children have difficulty retrieving a multiplicative fact from long-term memory due to hypersensitivity to interference. For example, for 3 × 8, they might give the answer 32 because 4 × 8 = 32. To improve their performance, provide them with tables such as those in Figure 4.40 and ask them to circle the results of the table with 8, for example. Ask them to start at the top left corner and circle the products in the table of 8 from the smallest to the largest (0, 8, 16 … 80). By doing this type of exercise, the child learns to resist interference. Then ask them to do the opposite, going from the largest to the smallest (80, 72, 64 … 0).

To help the child resist interference, it may also be helpful to provide him/her with charts (Figure 4.41) and flash cards (Figure 4.42) that include facts that strongly interfere with each other. Such activities attempt to prevent or somehow control hypersensitivity to interference.

168 *Arithmetic*

Figure 4.40 Find the multiples of 8 within miscellaneous numbers (inspired by Cooreman 2015d).

8	16	24	32	40
2 × _4_	4 × _4_	6 × _4_	4 × _8_	4 × _10_
8 × _1_	8 × _2_	8 × _3_	8 × _4_	10 × _4_
4 × _2_	2 × _8_	4 × _6_		8 × _5_
		3 × _8_		5 × _8_

Figure 4.41 Multiplications sharing the same products using charts.

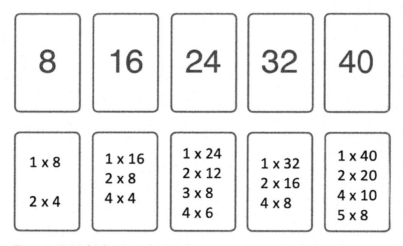

Figure 4.42 Multiplications sharing the same products using flash cards.

4.6.2.2 Simple divisions

4.6.2.2.1 CONCEPTUAL ASPECTS

Division can be approached in the form of sharing or grouping. In both cases, it is very important to stress that only the dividend is represented when one uses a concrete material. The model of sharing is often simpler for the child to understand, but the model of grouping will often be more effective in resolving divisions. Therefore, we propose to introduce the division with the sharing model, do some exercises using this model, and then present the grouping model and use it intensively.

4.6.2.2.1.1 The sharing model In this conception, which is often the most common, division is seen as a split in which you share the dividend equally.

Exercise with boxes and objects manipulation

> 'We are going to make a division together. I have three boxes and six marbles. I will distribute/share the marbles equally in each box: one, one, one, two, two, two. So there are two marbles in each box. So 6:3 = 2'. Then let the child practice.

Exercise with a deck of cards

> Using cards, ask the student to share 12 playing cards fairly (or equally) between 3 players (12:3=). For example, the players can be represented by the king, the queen, and the jack (Figure 4.43a). By sharing the 12 cards equally, s/he will find that each player receives 4 cards. This method of sharing can also be used to understand that the division is not commutative. For example, ask him/her to show 'what is 3:12', i.e., to share 3 cards between 12 players. This is not possible because there are not enough cards. The only way to divide them is to cut the cards into four equal parts, giving each player a quarter card (Figure 4.43b). Also explore the representation of problems with 1 or 0 ($n:1$ = and $0:n$ =) using meaningful verbal forms (see Table 4.13; for example, 'nothing divided into three means I have nothing to share between three people. How much will each have?').

The sharing method is considered easier when the divisor is 2 (then half is calculated) or 4 (then half of half is calculated). Present such division problems with playing cards. For younger children, offer only even numbers (Figure 4.44a). For older children who are already familiar with fractions, you can mix even and odd numbers (Figure 4.44b). Afterwards, offer many written exercises for repeated drill and practice. Ask the children to circle the first number (dividend) as a visual cue (Figure 4.44c) in order to remind them that this number always indicates, in division problems, the number of items they have to share.

170 Arithmetic

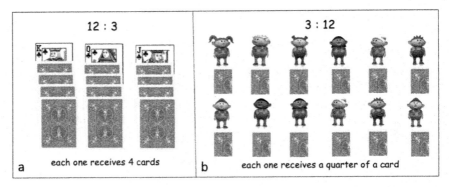

Figure 4.43 Division with the sharing method.

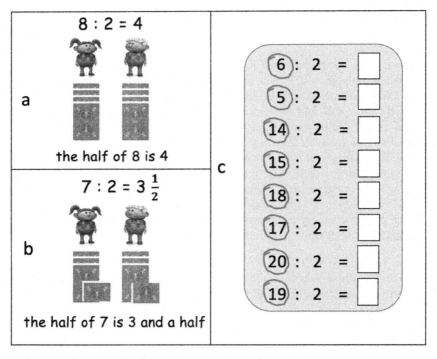

Figure 4.44 Find the half of a number using the sharing method.

4.6.2.2.1.2 The grouping model In the grouping model, the emphasis is on the inverse relationship between division and multiplication. For example, to represent with cards '6:3 =? ', the child has to place six cards face down and find the answer to the question 'how many threes make six or go into six'. The child must therefore start by making groups of three, until there are no more cards available and then count the groups: in this case, the child can make two groups of three, so the answer is two, 6:3 = 2 (Figure 4.45a). Alternatively, s/he can represent the dividend with a card of six, face up, to find out how many groups of three icons make up the card of six icons (Figure 4.45b).

The grouping model also makes it possible to experiment with the noncommutativity of division. Begin by representing a division problem with playing cards, for example, '12:4 =?'. The child should find 'how many groups of 4 (or 4s) are in 12?' (Figure 4.46a). To answer this question, therefore, he or she needs to pick up 12 cards and construct groups of 4 cards until no more cards are left. Then ask them to do the same to answer 4:12 =? So s/he has to take 4 cards (since the dividend is 4) and find out how many groups of 12 cards can be made by 4 cards. This problem is impossible (Figure 4.46b). Thus, the child is realizing the difference between these problems and understands that division is not commutative.

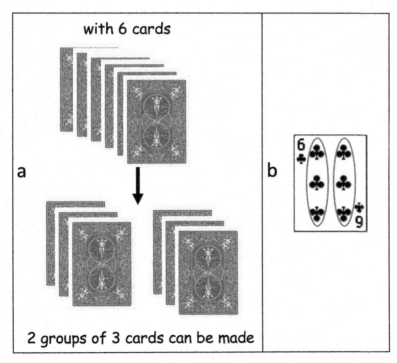

Figure 4.45 Division example with the grouping model.

172 *Arithmetic*

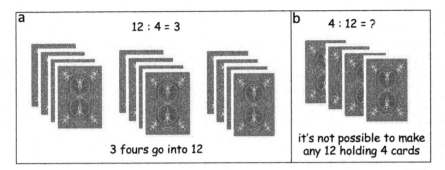

Figure 4.46 Explore the non-commutativity of division through the grouping model.

Based on this grouping model, you can also use your fingers to represent and solve a division problem. For example, to calculate '24:8 =?' or 'How many 8s go into 24?', imagine that each of your fingers counts as 8 (Figure 4.47); then start adding up the 8s until you reach 24 by lifting the corresponding fingers (8, 16, 24). Since you have raised 3 fingers, the answer is 3. This embodied strategy solves the division by repeated addition.

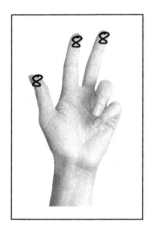

Figure 4.47 Division by repeated addition using the fingers.

4.6.2.3 *Stimulating the relationship between multiplication and division*

It is very important to underline the relationship between multiplication and division. For example, when a child is learning the multiplication table for a particular number (e.g., the table of 8), give them exercises on the corresponding divisions as well to practice on. You can provide them with written division exercises (Figure 4.48) and ask them to circle the dividend first to remind

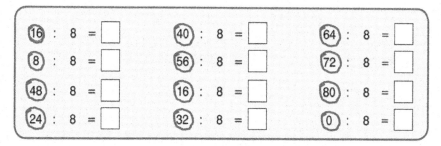

Figure 4.48 Exercise on the divisions corresponding to the table of 8 with a cue on the dividend.

them that this is the starting quantity they need to represent mentally in order to conduct the division. Repeat this for the tables of all other single-digit numbers to stimulate the relationship between multiplication and division.

Figure 4.49 presents a heuristic model of multiplication tables that attempts to represent multiplication as repeated addition and division as repeated subtraction and the interrelation between the two. The numbers below the number lines represent the results of multiplication (for example, the number 63 on the number line of the table of 7 is the result of 9×7) while the numbers above the number lines (0, 1, 2 …10) correspond to the results of division (9 is the quotient of 63:7). The simple multiplicative facts ($\times 2$, $\times 5$, $\times 10$) are highlighted with colours to encourage children to use them to infer more complex facts.

For children struggling with multiplicative facts, the table in Figure 4.37b (from the section on simple multiplication) can be used as a compensatory tool to resolve divisions. For example, to solve '32:8 =?', children should look at the column of 8 (the divisor) until they find the number 32 (the dividend). The result of the division is the number to the left of that line, which is 4.

As noted earlier, a major source of difficulty for many students is differentiating between the role of the number 0 and the number 1 in different arithmetic operations. To shed light on this subject, you can provide the child with a sheet as shown in Figure 4.50 which presents the problems containing 0 and 1 in the different operations. Do not vary the other number in the calculation (in this case, we have used the number 3 each time), since the aim of this card or exercise is not to retrieve arithmetical facts but to work on the 'rules' or the role of 0 and 1 in the different operations. Provide them with numerous worksheets changing the constant operand each time until the child completes these worksheets without any errors. Don't accept any mistakes! Of course, adjust the operations according to the child's age (only additions and subtractions for younger children; also include multiplications and divisions for more advanced students, and finally, fractions for even more advanced students).

174 *Arithmetic*

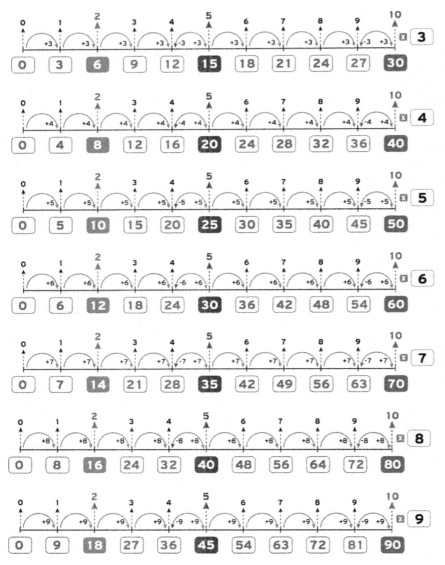

Figure 4.49 A heuristic model for times tables and the corresponding divisions (source: Karagiannakis, 2015).

4.6.2.4 Complex calculations on multi-digit numbers

4.6.2.4.1 MULTIPLICATION AND DIVISION BY POWERS OF TEN

Very often, to multiply or divide a number by a power of ten, children are given a rule of the following type: for multiplication: 'Add as many zeros as the power of ten considered' and for division: 'Remove as many zeros as the

3 : 3 =	3 x 3 =	3 + 0 =
3 − 0 =	1 : 3 =	3 + 3 =
0 − 3 =	3 : 1 =	0 : 3 =
3 x 1 =	3 x 0 =	3 − 3 =

Figure 4.50 Exercise on rules for solving small calculations.

power of ten considered'. However, these rules do not work for decimal numbers, whether multiplication (Figure 4.51b) or division, nor for the division of integers that do not end in zeros (Figure 4.51d). Choose an explanation based on positional ranks. In multiplication by a number corresponding to a power of ten (10, 100, 1000) the multiplied number will simply change positional ranks to the left (Figure 4.51a), as many ranks as indicated by the exponent of the power of ten (i.e., 1 for 10 (as it corresponds to 10^1), 2 for 100 (10^2), etc.) or the number of zeroes. Conversely, in dividing by powers of ten, the number changes positional rank to the right, or to a lower positional value (Figure 4.51c), as many ranks as indicated by the exponent of the power of ten of the divisor.

For older children who have already learned decimal numbers, use a more explicit approach. When multiplying, have children always move the decimal point that announces the decimal part (which is hidden to the right of the unit number in the case of whole numbers) to the right as many places as indicated by the exponent of the power of ten in question (Figure 4.52a). Similarly, for division, they must move the decimal point to the left (Figure 4.52b).

4.6.2.4.2 THE AREA MODEL

Multi-digit mental calculations are performed by applying the distributivity property: $a \times (b + c) = (a \times b) + (a \times c)$. This property of multiplication can be conceptualized by introducing the 'area model'. (Note that this model is not recommended for children with severe visual-spatial impairment.) To do this, provide the children with grid paper and ask them to represent the product

Arithmetic

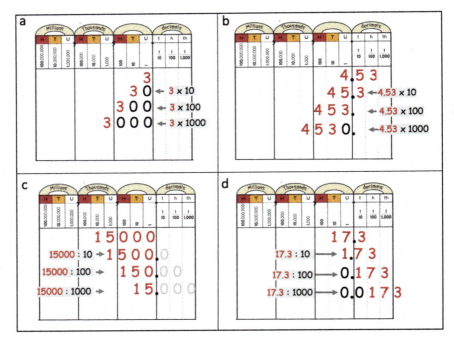

Figure 4.51 Multiply and divide numbers by powers of ten conceptually.

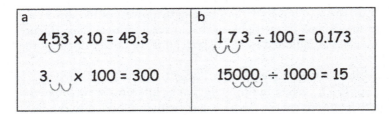

Figure 4.52 Multiply and divide numbers by powers of ten explicitly.

3 × 4 by drawing a rectangle. Discuss the two possible solutions (Figure 4.53a), re-emphasizing the commutativity property of multiplication ($a \times b = b \times a$). That is, the rectangle in Figure 5.53a can be seen horizontally as three fours or vertically as four threes. Then reverse the problem by asking them to draw all the possible rectangles that consist of 12 squares (Figure 53b). In this way, they realize that several multiplications can result in the same product 12, thus discovering the factors of 12. Stimulate this understanding by asking 'How many fours, threes, or sixes are there in the rectangle?', again promoting the link between multiplication and division.

Arithmetic 177

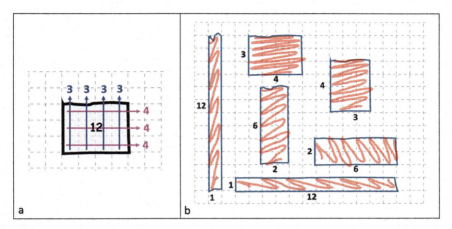

Figure 4.53 Area model to represent multiplication.

Many students confuse area and perimeter. For this reason, you can ask them to calculate the perimeter of these rectangles. They will discover that the perimeters are different even though the area is the same, which helps to differentiate them. The early introduction of the area model for multiplication is very important for representing and later understanding multiplication with multi-digit numbers, and even later multiplication in algebra.

The area model can also be used to find more complex multiplicative facts. Figure 4.54 shows different ways of deriving the 8 × 6 product by splitting the initial rectangle into pieces.

Then introduce multiplications between a one-digit and a two-digit number (e.g., 7 × 12 =). Ask the children to divide the two-digit number into smaller rectangles. Figure 4.55 shows two possible solutions: 12 broken down into 6 and 6 or 10 and 2.

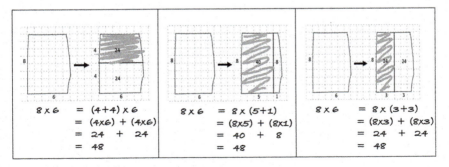

Figure 4.54 Deriving multiplication facts through the area model.

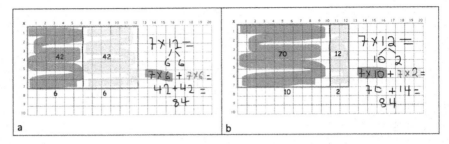

Figure 4.55 Explain distributivity through the area model.

4.6.2.4.3 MULTIPLICATION AND DIVISION THROUGH
    DECOMPOSITION USING THE BUBBLE STRUCTURE

The decomposition strategy for multiplication (Hickendorff et al., 2019; Ilukena, Utene & Kasandra, 2020) can also be applied for complex multiplications (see Table 4.15) using the bubble structure (Cooreman, 2018) if one of the factors is a single-digit number (when both factors are multi-digit numbers, it is preferable to use a written calculation). This is a transparent strategy that structures the surface model (see Figure 4.55) symbolically.

The decomposition method for division (Hickendorff et al., 2019) can be facilitated by using the bubble structure (Cooreman, 2018) as well but with a different decomposition of the dividend (Step 2, Table 4.16). Indeed, the

Table 4.15 Example of the bubble strategy for multiplication

Steps	Bubble structure	Language	Mathematical expression
1	27 × 3 = ◯ ◯	Draw two bubbles because the greater number has two digits	$27 \times 3 =$
2	27 × 3 = ◯ ◯ ╱╲ 20 7	Decompose 27 into 20 and 3	$27 \times 3 = (20 + 7) \times 3$
3	27 × 3 = (60) ◯ ╱╲ 20 7	Multiply 3 by 20; write 60 in the first bubble	$27 \times 3 = (20 \times 3) + 7 \times 3$ $27 \times 3 = 60 + 7 \times 3$
4	27 × 3 = (60)(+21) ╱╲ 20 7	Multiply 3 by 7; write +21 in the second bubble	$27 \times 3 = 60 + (7 \times 3)$ $27 \times 3 = 60 + 21$
5	27 × 3 = (60)(+21) = 81 ╱╲ 20 7	'Sixty' plus 'twenty-one' is 'eighty-one' following the addition bubble strategy steps	$27 \times 3 = 60 + 20 + 1$ $27 \times 3 = (60 + 20) + 1$ $27 \times 3 = 80 + 1$ $27 \times 3 = 81$

Table 4.16 Example of the decomposition strategy for dividing a two-digit number using the bubble strategy

Steps	Bubble structure	Language	Mathematical expression
1	72 ÷ 3 = ◯◯	Draw two bubbles because the dividend has two digits	72 ÷ 3 =
2	72 ÷ 3 = ◯◯ ／ 30 ⦅60⦆ 90	Find the greatest multiple of 30 (3 × 10) that doesn't exceed 72 (dividend). That is 60	1 × 30 = 30 2 × 30 = **60** 3 × 30 = 90
3	72 ÷ 3 = ◯◯ ／　＼ 30　　12 ⦅60⦆ 90	Decompose 72 into 60 and 12	72 ÷ 3 = (60 + 12) ÷ 3
4	72 ÷ 3 = ⦅20⦆◯ ／　＼ 30　　12 ⦅60⦆ 90	Divide 60 by 3; write 20 in the first bubble	72 ÷ 3 = (60 ÷ 3) + 12 ÷ 3 72 ÷ 3 = 20 + 12 ÷ 3
5	72 ÷ 3 = ⦅20⦆⦅+4⦆ ／　＼ 30　　12 ⦅60⦆ 90	Divide 12 by 3; write +4 in the second bubble	72 ÷ 3 = 20 + (12 ÷ 3) 72 ÷ 3 = 20 + 4
6	72 ÷ 3 = ⦅20⦆⦅+4⦆ = 24 ／　＼ 30　　12 ⦅60⦆ 90	To find the result simply say the number word corresponding to each bubble starting from the left: 'twenty' 'four' that is 'twenty-four'	72 ÷ 3 = 24

dividend is not decomposed in terms of decimal values (units, tens, hundreds) but in terms of numbers that are multiples of the divisor. See an example with a two-digit dividend (Table 4.16) and another where the dividend is a three-digit number (Table 4.17).

The implementation of the decomposition strategy for division as introduced both, in tables 4.16 and 4.17 explains in fact, in a transparent way, the steps taking place in long division algorithms.

4.6.2.4.4 STIMULATE FLEXIBILITY

Just as we have done for mental addition and subtraction, we would also like to introduce an efficient strategy for solving multiplication and division. These

180 *Arithmetic*

Table 4.17 Example of decomposition strategy for dividing a three-digit number using the bubble structure

Steps	Bubble structure	Language	Mathematical expression
1	972 ÷ 4 = ◯◯◯	Draw three bubbles because the dividend has three digits	972 ÷ 4 =
2	972 ÷ 4 = ◯◯◯ 　／ 　400 　⑧⓪⓪ 　1200	Find the greatest multiple of 400 (4 × 100) that doesn't exceed 972 (dividend). That is 800	1 × 400 = 400 2 × 400 = 800 3 × 400 = 1200
3	972 ÷ 4 = ◯◯◯ 　／＼ 　400　＼ 　⑧⓪⓪ 172 　1200	Decompose 972 into 800 and 172	972 ÷ 4 = (800 + 172) ÷ 4
4	972 ÷ 4 = ⑳⓪⓪ ◯◯ 　／＼ 　400　＼ 　⑧⓪⓪ 172 　1200	Divide 800 by 4; write 200 in the first bubble	972 ÷ 4 = (800 ÷ 4) + 172 ÷ 4 972 ÷ 4 = 200 + 172 ÷ 4
5	972 ÷ 4 = ⑳⓪⓪ ◯◯ 　／＼ 　400　＼ 　⑧⓪⓪ 172 　1200 ／＼ 　　40　＼ 　　80　＼ 　　120　＼ 　　⑯⓪ 12 　　200	Find the greatest multiple of 40 (4 × 10) that doesn't exceed 172 (dividend). That is 160. Decompose 172 into 160 and 12	972 ÷ 4 = 200 + (160 + 12) ÷ 4
6	972 ÷ 4 = ⑳⓪⓪ ⑭⓪ ◯ 　／＼ 　400　＼ 　⑧⓪⓪ 172 　1200 ／＼ 　　40　＼ 　　80　＼ 　　120　＼ 　　⑯⓪ 12 　　200	Divide 160 by 4; write +40 in the second bubble	972 ÷ 4 = 200 + (160 ÷ 4) + 12 ÷ 4 972 ÷ 4 = 200 + 40 + 12 ÷ 4
7	972 ÷ 4 = ⑳⓪⓪ ⑭⓪ ⑬ 　／＼ 　400　＼ 　⑧⓪⓪ 172 　1200 ／＼ 　　40　＼ 　　80　＼ 　　120　＼ 　　⑯⓪ 12 　　200	Divide 12 by 4; write +3 in the third bubble	972 ÷ 4 = 200 + 40 + (12 ÷ 4) 972 ÷ 4 = 200 + 40 − 3

(*Continued*)

Arithmetic   181

Table 4.17 (Continued)

Steps	Bubble structure	Language	Mathematical expression
8	972 ÷ 4 = ⟨200⟩⟨+40⟩⟨+3⟩ = 243 400 ⟨800⟩ 172 1200 40 80 120 ⟨160⟩ 12 200	To find the result simply say the number word corresponding to each bubble starting from the left: 'two-hundred', 'forty' 'three'	972 ÷ 4 = 243

strategies are recommended for children with good reasoning skills. In the case of multiplications, the first factor is divided by a number and the second factor is multiplied by the same number to obtain a simpler product. For example, let's imagine that we have to calculate 12 × 4 =. As these two numbers are even, we can divide the first factor by 2 (12:2 = 6) and multiply the second by 2 (4 × 2 = 8), which transforms the calculation into 6 × 8, a simpler calculation to solve. This strategy can be explained by using the area models of multiplication (Figure 4.56a) and showing that the two products (12 × 4 and 6 × 8) occupy the same area. Then provide appropriate examples to drill and practice this technique so that it becomes automatic (Figure 4.56b).

In division, the quotient remains the same if the two terms of the calculation, the dividend and the divisor, are both multiplied by the same number, or if they are both divided by the same number (whatever it is). For example, to solve for 12:4, you can divide each of the terms by two to obtain another equivalent ratio, 6:2, which will result in the same quotient, in this case 3. First, use concrete materials so that the child can experience the truthfulness and appropriateness of this procedure (Figure 4.57a), and then offer many such exercises that allow the child to drill and practice this strategy (Figure 4.57b).

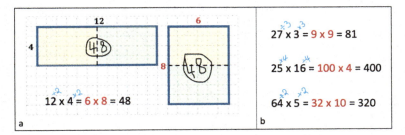

Figure 4.56 Counterbalance strategy for multiplication.

182 Arithmetic

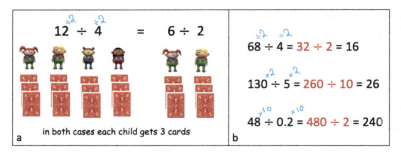

Figure 4.57 Equivalent ratio strategy for division.

4.6.2.5 Written calculation algorithms

In the previous section, we presented a variety of strategies for mentally resolving multiplication and division problems. Many children prefer to use written algorithms to solve these operations because their teachers guide them to use algorithms or they are not comfortable with mental arithmetic. The above strategies are also exemplified because they should make it easier for the child to understand the algorithms used in written calculation procedures. For this reason, when introducing a written algorithm, use methods that are as transparent as possible so that the child can understand the steps included in the algorithm. Figure 4.58 shows the multiplication 12×7 both through

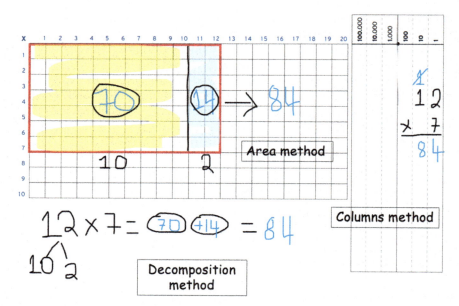

Figure 4.58 Different representation of multiplication.

Arithmetic 183

transparent methods (area and decomposition methods) and the less transparent traditional columns method.

4.6.2.5.1 WRITTEN MULTIPLICATION ALGORITHMS

Figure 4.59 shows multiplication between two multi-digit numbers, here 376 × 45, using different algorithms. In the classical method of written calculation 'in columns', we first multiply the units digit (5) of the lower number (45) by each digit of the upper number (376) from right to left and then write the by-products below (Figure 4.59a). If the by-products exceed 10 (e.g., 5 × 6 = 20), we write the units digit (0) in the units column and transfer or carry the tens digit to the next column to add it to the next by-product. The same procedure is followed with the tens digit (4), and we write the sum of the by-products on a line below. In this case, the units column is left blank or a zero is indicated because we multiply by the tens digit (4), i.e., with 40 units. Thus,

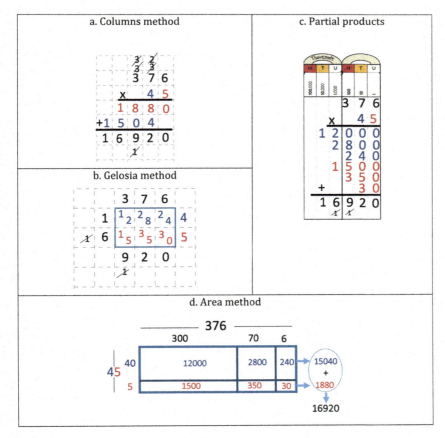

Figure 4.59 Written multiplication methods.

184 *Arithmetic*

the first product for the example (4 × 6) is 24 tens, i.e., 240 units. Finally, we add up the sub-products using the calculation method written in columns for addition. The 'column method' is considered the least transparent method. For this reason, introduce it with the area method to help the child understand the steps (see Figure 4.59d).

The Gelosia method is one of many methods that was used more than 800 years ago by Arab mathematicians. In this method, the factors (364 and 45) are placed along the length and width of a table, respectively (Figure 4.59b). Before starting, the diagonal of each cell in the table must be drawn. Next, the top number of the width (4) is multiplied by each digit of the number placed along the length by placing each sub-product in the corresponding cell. If the sub-product is a two-digit number, the tens digit is written above the diagonal and the units below, while when the sub-product is a one-digit number, a zero is placed above the diagonal of the cell in question. When all the cells are filled, the numbers of each diagonal must be added separately (the diagonal represents the positional ranks). This method has at least two advantages: (1) there is no need to manage carry-overs between sub-products and (2) the order of realization of the sub-products is not important.

The partial products method (Hickendorff et al., 2019, Ilukena, Utene & Kasandra, 2020) uses the same steps as the classic 'column method', but the advantage here is that the value of the partial products is transparent because they are written on separate lines. All partial products are aligned and do not need to be moved to the right. Finally, the order in which the partial products are obtained does not matter, it can be done from the highest place value digits (this is the case in the example shown in Figure 4.59c) or from the lowest. Here, we work directly with the positional values of the digits. For example, in the example shown, first multiply 40 by 300 (and write the complete answer, i.e., 12,000), then 40 by 70, and so on. This method is considered to be the most transparent written calculation method.

4.6.2.5.2 WRITTEN DIVISION ALGORITHM

The classical algorithm of written division is a difficult algorithm because, on the one hand, it contains many steps and, on the other hand, these steps are modified or added depending on the nature of the dividend and the divisor. To this end, we will first try to interpret the steps that take place in this complicated algorithm and then provide a heuristic model that is consistent with all division problems, whatever the nature of the terms of the calculation. Suppose we want to solve '276:12' or 'How many 12s fit into 276'. Figure 4.60 attempts to interpret the procedures involved in the written division algorithm both symbolically and non-symbolically.

Table 4.18 summarizes the steps of this algorithm (shown in Figure 4.60). It is a heuristic model for written divisions that helps children to understand, structure but also memorize the different steps included by simply following the mnemonic code: TAX- (Karagiannakis, 2015). Take into account that the

As we have already introduced in the decomposition strategy for division, the divisions start from the digit of the dividend that has the **largest place value** because if starts from the smallest it is possible the divisor not fit ever to the dividend (in the example above 12 doesn't fit into 6 but this doesn't mean that it doesn't fit in 276).	
So we will start from the digit of hundred (2) adding a sing above it (or a tag). The question is **how many whole Hundreds of 12 (100x12=1200) go to 2 H (200 U)**. The answer is no one so we write 0 at the place value of the Hundreds in the quotient.	
Then we recruit the next digit of Tens (adding a tag on it as well) composing the number 27 which stands for 27 Tens. The question now is **how many whole Tens of 12 go to 27 T (270 U)**. 2 Tens of 12 (2x12=24 T) can be constituted so we write 2 at the place of the Tens in the quotient. Now we have left 3 T.	
Finally, we tag the units (6) lowering it along with the remained tens and getting 36 U in total.	
The question now is **how many whole Units of 12 go to 36 U**. 3 units of 12 (3x12=36 U) can be constituted so we write 3 at the place of the units in the quotient. It is a perfect division since we don't have any units left. Therefore 23 whole 12 go into 276.	

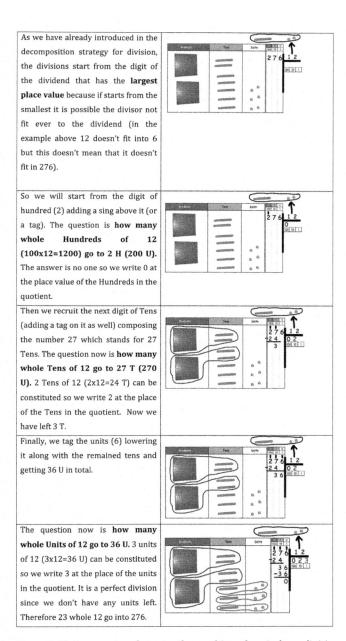

Figure 4.60 Interpreting the procedures taking place in long division.

186 Arithmetic

Table 4.18 A heuristic model for long division

T ↓	**T**agging and ↓lowering each digit starting from the right-hand side.
A	**A**nswer: divide, using the 'goes into' method, each digit by the divisor, and write down the answer in the predetermined place value of the quotient.
X	**Multiply** the quotient by the divisor.
−	**Subtract** the resultant product to find the remainder.

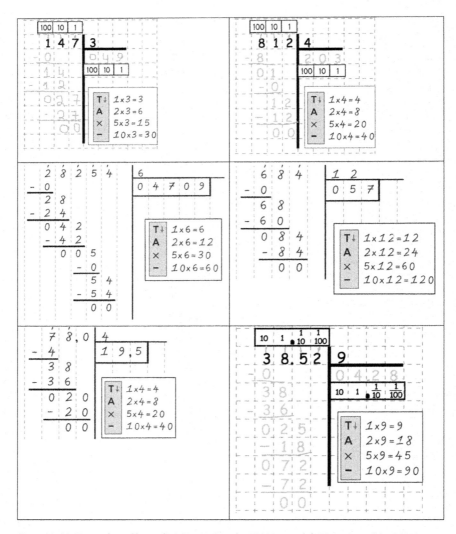

Figure 4.61 Examples of long divisions using the TAX- model (Karagiannakis, 2015).

number of digits for the quotient must always be equal to the number of digits for the dividend. Therefore, draw the boxes for the position values from the outset in order to avoid errors.

The TAX- strategy introduces a consistent way to approach division, since it can be applied to any division problem regardless of the nature of the divisor and the dividend. Figure 4.61 shows how different division problems can be solved using the TAX- strategy. Notice that beside each division problem we have added the simple multiples (×1, ×2, ×5, ×10) of the divisor which facilitates decision making among the several partial divisions that take place until the completion of the algorithm.

Finally, do not forget to motivate the child in the learning process by embedding the exercises into games and by establishing reward systems!

References

Ashcraft, M. H., & Christy, K. S. (1995). The frequency of arithmetic facts in elementary texts: Addition and multiplication in grades 1–6. *Journal for Research in Mathematics Education, 26*(5), 396–421.

Ashcraft, M. H., Fierman, B. A., & Bartolotta, R. (1984). The production and verification tasks in mental addition: An empirical comparison. *Developmental Review, 4*(2), 157–170.

Baroody, A. J., & Gannon, K. E. (1984). The development of the commutativity principle and economical addition strategies. *Cognition and Instruction, 1*(3), 321–339.

Baroody, A. J., Torbeyns, J., & Verschaffel, L. (2009). Young children's understanding and application of subtraction-related principles. *Mathematical Thinking and Learning, 11*(1–2), 2–9.

Barrouillet, P., Fayol, M., & Lathuliere, E. (1997). Selecting between competitors in multiplication tasks: An explanation of the errors produced by adolescents with learning difficulties. *International Journal of Behavioral Development, 21*(2), 253–275.

Barrouillet, P., & Lépine, R. (2005). Working memory and children's use of retrieval to solve addition problems. *Journal of Experimental Child Psychology, 91*(3), 183–204. doi: 10.1016/j.jecp.2005.03.002

Barth, H., La Mont, K., Lipton, J., Dehaene, S., Kanwisher, N., & Spelke, E. (2006). Non-symbolic arithmetic in adults and young children. *Cognition, 98*(3), 199–222.

Beishuizen, M. (1993). Mental strategies and materials or models for addition and subtraction up to 100 in Dutch second grades. *Journal for Research in Mathematics Education, 24*(4), 294–323.

Beishuizen, M., & Anghileri, J. (1998). Which mental strategies in the early number curriculum? A comparison of British ideas and Dutch views. *British Educational Research Journal, 24*(5), 519–538.

Booth, J. L., & Siegler, R. S. (2017). Numerical magnitude representations influence arithmetic learning. *Child Development, 79*(4), 1016–1031.

Brown, J. S., & Burton, R. R. (1978). Diagnostic models for procedural bugs in basic mathematical skills. *Cognitive Science, 2*(2), 155–192.

Campbell, J. I. D. (1987). Network interference and mental multiplication. *Journal of Experimental Psychology: Learning, Memory, and Cognition, 13*(1), 109–123.

Campbell, J. I. D. (1995). Mechanisms of simple addition and multiplication: A modified network-interference theory and simulation. *Mathematical Cognition, 1*(2), 121–164.

Campbell, J. I. D. (1997). On the relation between skilled performance of simple division and multiplication. *Journal of Experimental Psychology: Learning, Memory, and Cognition, 23*(5), 1140–1159.

Campbell, J. I. D., & Graham, D. J. (1985). Mental multiplication skill: Structure, process, and acquisition. *Canadian Journal of Psychology, 39*(2), 338–366.

Campbell, J. I. D., & Xue, Q. (2001). Cognitive arithmetic across cultures. *Journal of Experimental Psychology: General, 130*(2), 299–315.

Caviola, S., Gerotto, G., & Mammarella, I. C. (2016). Computer-based training for improving mental calculation in third- and fifth-graders. *Acta Psychologica, 171*, 118–127.

Codding, R. S., Burns, M. K., & Lukito, G. (2011). The division for learning disabilities of the council for exceptional children meta-analysis of mathematic basic-fact fluency interventions: A component analysis. *Learning Disabilities Research and Practice, 26*(1), 36–47.

Codding, R. S., Shiyko, M., Russo, M., Birch, S., Fanning, E., & Jaspen, D. (2007). Comparing mathematics interventions: Does initial level of fluency predict intervention effectiveness? *Journal of School Psychology, 45*(6), 603–617.

Connolly, A. J. (2007). *KeyMath-3 diagnostic assessment: Manual forms A and B*. Minneapolis, MN: Pearson.

Cooreman, A. (2014), *Rekentrappers 1HR module 4 basis Getalkaarten en tweelingen tot 20*. Leuven: Eureka Expert.

Cooreman, A. & Bringmans (2004). *Rekenen remediëren: Droom of haalbare kart?* Antwerp: De Boeck.

Cooreman, A. (2015a), *Rekentrappers 1HR module 6 Basis. Plusbrug*, Leuven: Eureka Expert.

Cooreman, A. (2015b), *Rekentrappers 1HR module 8 Basis. Plus en minbrug over 10. Strategisch rekenen en splitsingen automatiseren*, Leuven: Eureka Expert.

Cooreman, A. (2015), *Rekentrappers 2HR Module 13. Tafel van 4 en eerste breuken*, Leuven: Eureka Expert.

Cooreman, A. (2018), *Rekentrappers 4GDB Breuken 1. Inzicht en begrippen*, Leuven: Eureka Expert.

Cooreman, A. (2015c), *Rekentrappers 3HR module 2 Getalkaarten, buren en strategisch rekenen tot 1000*, Leuven: Eureka Expert.

De Brauwer, J., Verguts, T., & Fias, W. (2006). The representation of multiplication facts: Developmental changes in the problem size, five, and tie effects. *Journal of Experimental Child Psychology, 94*(1), 43–56.

De Smedt, B., & Boets, B. (2010). Phonological processing and arithmetic fact retrieval: Evidence from developmental dyslexia. *Neuropsychologia, 48*(14), 3973–3981.

De Smedt, B., Holloway, I. D., & Ansari, D. (2011). Effects of problem size and arithmetic operation on brain activation during calculation in children with varying levels of arithmetical fluency. *NeuroImage, 57*(3), 771–781.

De Smedt, B., Noël, M. P., Gilmore, C., & Ansari, D. (2013). How do symbolic and non-symbolic numerical magnitude processing skills relate to individual differences in children's mathematical skills? A review of evidence from brain and behavior. *Trends in Neuroscience and Education, 2*(2), 48–55.

De Smedt, B., Taylor, J., Archibald, L., & Ansari, D. (2009). How is phonological processing related to individual differences in children's arithmetic skills? *Developmental Science, 13*(3), 508–520.

De Visscher, A., Berens, S. C., Keidel, J. L., Noël, M. P., & Bird, C. M. (2015). The interference effect in arithmetic facts solving: An fMRI study. *NeuroImage, 1*(116), 92–101.

De Visscher, A., & Noël, M. P. (2013). A case study of arithmetic facts dyscalculia caused by a hypersensitivity-to-interference in memory. *Cortex, 49*(1), 50–70.

De Visscher, A., & Noël, M. P. (2014a). Arithmetic facts storage deficit: The hypersensitivity-to-interference in memory hypothesis. *Developmental Science*, *17*(3), 434–442.

De Visscher, A., & Noël, M. P. (2014b). The detrimental effect of interference in multiplication facts storing: Typical development and individual differences. *Journal of Experimental Psychology: General*, *143*(6), 2380–2400.

De Visscher, A., Noël, M. P., & De Smedt, B. (2016). The role of physical digit representation and numerical magnitude representation in children's multiplication fact retrieval. *Journal of Experimental Child Psychology*, *152*, 41–53.

De Visscher, A., Szmalec, A., Van Der Linden, L., & Noël, M. P. (2015). Serial-order learning impairment and hypersensitivity-to-interference in dyscalculia. *Cognition*, *144*, 38–48.

De Visscher, A., Vogel, S. E., Reishofer, G., Hassler, E., Koschutnig, K., De Smedt, B., & Grabner, R. H. (2018). Interference and problem size effect in multiplication fact solving: Individual differences in brain activations and arithmetic performance. *NeuroImage*, *172*, 718–727.

De Vos, T. (1992). *TTR. Tempotest rekenen [Arithmetic number fact test]*. Lisse, The Netherlands: Swets & Zeitlinger Publishers.

De Vos, T. (2010). *Tempo-test-automatiseren*. Amsterdam: Boom Test uitgevers.

Dehaene, S., Piazza, M., Pinel, P., & Cohen, L. (2003). Three parietal circuits for number processing. *Cognitive Neuropsychology*, *20*(3), 487–506.

Domahs, F., Lochy, A., Eibl, G., & Delazer, M. (2004). Adding colour to multiplication: Rehabilitation of arithmetic fact retrieval in a case of traumatic brain injury. *Neuropsychological Rehabilitation*, *14*(3), 303–328.

Domahs, F., Zamarian, L., & Delazer, M. (2008). Sound arithmetic: Auditory cues in the rehabilitation of impaired fact retrieval. *Neuropsychological Rehabilitation*, *18*(2), 160–181.

Fagginger Auer, M. F., Hickendorff, M., & van Putten, C. M. (2016). Solution strategies and adaptivity in multidigit division in a choice/no-choice experiment: Student and instructional factors. *Learning and Instruction*, *41*, 52–59.

Fuchs, L., Fuchs, D., Powell, S., Seethaler, P., Cirino, P., & Fletcher, J. (2008). Intensive intervention for students with mathematics disabilities: Seven principles of effective practice. *Learning Disability Quarterly*, *31*(2), 79–92.

Fuson, K. C. (1982). An analysis of the counting on solution procedure in addition. In T. P. Carpenter, J. M. Moser & T. A. Romberg (Eds.), *Addition and subtraction: A cognitive perspective* (pp. 67–81). Hillsdale, NJ: Lawrence Erlbaum.

Fuson, K. C., & Li, Y. (2009). Cross-cultural issues in linguistic, visual- quantitative, and written-numeric supports for mathematical thinking. *ZDM: The International Journal on Mathematics Education*, *41*(6), 793–808.

Gandini, D., & Lemaire, P. (2005). La résolution d'opérations arithmétiques au cours du développement. In M. P. Noël (Ed.), *La dyscalculie* (pp. 139–168). Marseille: Solal.

Garnett, K., & Fleischner, J. E. (1983). Automatization and basic fact performance of normal and learning disabled children. *Learning Disability Quarterly*, *6*(2), 223–230.

Geary, D. C. (1990). A componential analysis of an early learning deficit in mathematics. *Journal of Experimental Child Psychology*, *49*(3), 363–383.

Geary, D. C. (2004). Mathematics and learning disabilities. *Journal of Learning Disabilities*, *37*(1), 4–15.

Geary, D. C., & Brown, S. C. (1991). Cognitive addition: Strategy choice and speed-of-processing differences in gifted, normal, and mathematically disabled children. *Developmental Psychology*, *27*(3), 398–406.

Geary, D. C., Brown, S. C., & Samaranayake, V. A. (1991). Cognitive Addition: A short longitudinal-study of strategy choice and speed-of-processing differences in normal and mathematically disabled-children. *Developmental Psychology*, *27*(5), 787–797.

Geary, D. C., Frensch, P. A., & Wiley, J. G. (1993). Simple and complex mental subtraction: Strategy choice and speed-of-processing differences in younger and older adults. *Psychology and Aging, 8*(2), 242–256.

Geary, D. C., Hoard, M. K., & Bailey, D. H. (2012). Fact retrieval deficits in low achieving children and children with mathematical learning disability. *Journal of Learning Disabilities, 45*(4), 291–307.

Geary, D. C., Hoard, M. K., Byrd-Craven, J., Nugent, L., & Numtee, C. (2007). Cognitive mechanisms underlying achievement deficits in children with mathematical learning disability. *Child Development, 78*(4), 1343–1359.

Geary, D. C., Hoard, M. K., & Hamson, C. O. (1999). Numerical and arithmetical cognition: Patterns of functions and deficits in children at risk for a mathematical disability. *Journal of Experimental Child Psychology, 74*(3), 213–239.

Gilmore, C. K., McCarthy, S. E., & Spelke, E. S. (2007). Symbolic arithmetic knowledge without instruction. *Nature, 447*(7144), 589–591. doi: 10.1038/nature05850

Grabner, R. H., & De Smedt, B. (2012). Oscillatory EEG correlates of arithmetic strategies: A training study. *Frontiers in Psychology, 3*, 1–11.

Graham, D. J., & Campbell, J. I. D. (1992). Network interference and number-fact retrieval: Evidence from children's alphaplication. *Canadian Journal of Psychology/Revue Canadienne de Psychologie, 46*(1), 65–91.

Groen, G. J., & Parkman, J. M. (1972). A chronometric analysis of simple addition. *Psychological Review, 79*(4), 329–343.

Halberda, J., & Feigenson, L. (2008). Developmental change in the acuity of the 'Number sense': The approximate number system in 3-, 4-, 5-, and 6-year-olds and adults. *Developmental Psychology, 44*(5), 1457–1465.

Hanich, L. B., Jordan, N. C., Kaplan, D., & Dick, J. (2001). Performance across different areas of mathematical cognition in children with learning difficulties. *Journal of Educational Psychology, 93*(3), 615–626.

Henik, A., Rubinsten, O., & Ashkenazi, S. (2014). Developmental dyscalculia as a heterogeneous disability. In R. Cohen Kadosh & A. Dowker (Eds.), *The Oxford handbook of mathematical cognition* (pp. 662–677). Oxford: Oxford University Press.

Hickendorff, M., Heiser, W. J., Van Putten, C. M., & Verhelst, N. D. (2009). Solution strategies and achievement in dutch complex arithmetic: Latent variable modeling of change. *Psychometrika, 74*(2), 331–350.

Hickendorff, M., Torbeyns, J., & Verschaffel, L. (2019). Multi-digit addition, subtraction, multiplication, and division strategies. In A. Fritz, V. G. Haase & P. Räsänen (Eds.), *International handbook of mathematical learning difficulties* (pp. 543–560). Switzerland: Springer.

Hickendorff, M., van Putten, C. M., Verhelst, N. D., & Heiser, W. J. (2010). Individual differences in strategy use on division problems: Mental versus written computation. *Journal of Educational Psychology, 102*(2), 438–452.

Huttenlocher, J., Jordan, N. C., & Levine, S. C. (1994). A mental model for early arithmetic. *Journal of Experimental Psychology: General, 123*(3), 284–296.

Ilukena, A., Utene, C., & Kasandra, C. (2020). Strategies used by Grade 6 learners in the multiplication of whole numbers in five selected primary schools in the Kavango east and west regions. *International Education Studies, 13*(3), 3.

Iuculano, T., Rosenberg-Lee, M., Richardson, J., Tenison, C., Fuchs, L., Supekar, K., & Menon, V. (2015). Cognitive tutoring induces widespread neuroplasticity and remediates brain function in children with mathematical learning disabilities. *Nature Communication, 6*, 8453.

Jordan, N. C., Hanich, L. B., & Kaplan, D. (2003). Arithmetic fact mastery in young children: A longitudinal investigation. *Journal of Experimental Child Psychology, 85*(2), 103–119.
Jordan, N. C., Huttenlocher, J., & Levine, S. C. (1994). Assessing early arithmetic abilities: Effects of verbal and nonverbal response types on the calculation performance of middle- and low-income children. *Learning and Individual Differences, 6*(4), 413–432.
Jordan, N. C., & Montani, T. O. (1997). Cognitive arithmetic and problem solving: A comparison of children with specific and general mathematics difficulties. *Journal of Learning Disabilities, 30*(6), 624–634.
Karagiannakis, G. (2015). *Οι Αριθμοί πέρA Aπ' Τους κAνόνες. AθήνA: ΔιερευνηTική μάθηση.*
Karagiannakis, G., Baccaglini-Frank, A., & Roussos, P. (2017). Detecting strengths and weaknesses in learning mathematics through a model classifying mathematical skills, *Australian Journal of Learning Difficulties, 21*(2), 115–141.
Karagiannakis, G., & Noël, M.-P. (2020). Mathematical profile test: A preliminary evaluation of an online assessment for mathematics skills of children in grades 1–6. *Behavioral Sciences, 10*, 126.
Kaufmann, L. (2002). More evidence for the role of the central executive in retrieving arithmetic facts: A case study of severe developmental dyscalculia. *Journal of Clinical and Experimental Neuropsychology, 24*(3), 302–310.
Keshwani, S. (2010). Teaching mathematics using African cultural numerical history. Retrieved from https://uh.edu/honors/Programs-Minors/honors-and-the-schools/houston-teachers-institute/curriculum-units/pdfs/2008/african-history/keshwani-08-africa.pdf
Koponen, T. K., Sorvo, R., Dowker, A., Räikkönen, E., Viholainen, H., Aro, M., & Aro, T. (2018). Does multi-component strategy training improve calculation fluency among poor performing elementary school children? *Frontiers in Psychology, 9*, 1187. doi: 10.3389/fpsyg.2018.01187
Kucian, K., Grond, U., Rotzer, S., Henzi, B., Schönmann, C., Plangger, F., ... von Aster, M. (2011). Mental number line training in children with developmental dyscalculia. *NeuroImage, 57*(3), 782–795.
Lafay, A., & Helloin, M. C. (2016). *Examath 8–15 : Batterie informatisée d'examen des habilietés mathématiques.* Grenade, France: Happy Neuron.
Landerl, K., Bevan, A., & Butterworth, B. (2004). Developmental dyscalculia and basic numerical capacities: A study of 8–9-year-old students. *Cognition, 93*(2), 99–125.
LeFevre, J. A., Sadesky, G. S., & Bisanz, J. (1996). Selection of procedures in mental addition: Reassessing the problem size effect in adults. *Journal of Experimental Psychology: Learning, Memory, and Cognition, 22*(1), 216–230.
Lemaire, P., & Arnaud, L. (2008). Young and older adults' strategies in complex arithmetic. *American Journal of Psychology, 121*(1), 1–16.
Lemaire, P., & Brun, F. (2018). Age-related changes in children's strategies for solving two-digit addition problems. *Journal of Numerical Cognition, 3*(3), 582–597.
Lewandowsky, S., Geiger, S. M., & Oberauer, K. (2008). Interference-based forgetting in verbal short-term memory. *Journal of Memory and Language, 59*(2), 200–222.
Linsen, S., Torbeyns, J., Verschaffel, L., Reynvoet, B., & De Smedt, B. (2016). The association between symbolic and nonsymbolic numerical magnitude processing and mental versus algorithmic subtraction in adults. *Acta Psychologica, 165*, 34–42.
Mammarella, I. C., Lucangeli, D., & Cornoldi, C. (2010). Spatial working memory and arithmetic deficits in children with nonverbal learning difficulties (NLD). *Journal of Learning Disabilities, 43*(5), 455–468.

Mussolin, C., & Noël, M. (2008). Specific retrieval deficit from long-term memory in children with poor arithmetic facts abilities. *Open Psychology Journal, 1,* 26–34.

Nairne, J. S. (1990). A feature model of immediate memory. *Memory and Cognition, 18*(3), 251–269.

Noël, M. P. (2009). Counting on working memory when learning to count and to add: A preschool study. *Developmental Psychology, 45*(6), 1630–1643.

Noël, M. P., & Grégoire, J. (2015). *TediMath Grands, Test diagnostique des compétences de base en mathématiques du CE2 à la 5ᵉ.* Montreuil, France: ECPA.

Noël, M. P., Seron, X., & Trovarelli, F. (2004). Working memory as a predictor of addition skills and addition strategies in children. *Current Psychology of Cognition, 22*(1), 3–25.

Oberauer, K., & Lange, E. B. (2008). Interference in verbal working memory: Distinguishing similarity-based confusion, feature overwriting, and feature migration. *Journal of Memory and Language, 58*(3), 730–745.

Park, J., Bermudez, V., Roberts, R. C., & Brannon, E. M. (2016). Non-symbolic approximate arithmetic training improves math performance in preschoolers. *Journal of Experimental Child Psychology, 152,* 278–293.

Passolunghi, M. C., & Siegel, L. S. (2004). Working memory and access to numerical information in children with disability in mathematics. *Journal of Experimental Child Psychology, 88*(4), 348–367.

Peltenburg, M., van den Heuvel-Panhuizen, M., & Robitzsch, A. (2012). Special education students' use of indirect addition in solving subtraction problems up to 100—A proof of the didactical potential of an ignored procedure. *Educational Studies in Mathematics, 79*(3), 351–369.

Peters, G., De Smedt, B., Torbeyns, J., Ghesquière, P., & Verschaffel, L. (2013). Children's use of addition to solve two-digit subtraction problems. *British Journal of Psychology, 104*(4), 495–511.

Peters, G., De Smedt, B., Torbeyns, J., Verschaffel, L., & Ghesquière, P. (2014). Subtraction by addition in children with mathematical learning disabilities. *Learning and Instruction, 30,* 1–8.

Piazza, M., Facoetti, A., Trussardi, A. N., Berteletti, I., Conte, S., Lucangeli, D., ... Zorzi, M. (2010). Developmental trajectory of number acuity reveals a severe impairment in developmental dyscalculia. *Cognition, 116*(1), 33–41.

Robinson, K. M. (2017). The understanding of additive and multiplicative arithmetic concepts. In D. C. Geary, D. B. Berch, R. J. Ochsendorf & K. M. Koepke (Eds.), *Acquisition of complex arithmetic skills and higher-order mathematics concepts* (pp. 21–46). London: Academic Press, Elsevier Inc.

Robinson, K. M., Arbuthnott, K. D., Rose, D., McCarron, M. C., Globa, C. A., & Phonexay, S. D. (2006). Stability and change in children's division strategies. *Journal of Experimental Child Psychology, 93*(3), 224–238. doi: 10.1016/j.jecp.2005.09.002

Rourke, B. P., & Strang, J. D. (1983). Subtypes of reading and arithmetical disabilities: A neuropsychological analysis. In M. Rutter (Ed.), *Developmental neuropsychiatry* (pp. 473–488). New York: Guilford Press.

Roussel, J. L., Fayol, M., & Barrouillet, P. (2002). Procedural vs. direct retrieval strategies in arithmetic: A comparison between additive and multiplicative problem solving. *European Journal of Cognitive Psychology, 14*(1), 61–104.

Rousselle, L., & Noël, M. P. (2008). Mental arithmetic in children with mathematics learning disabilities: The adaptive use of approximate calculation in an addition verification task. *Journal of Learning Disabilities, 41*(6), 498–513.

Rubinsten, O., & Henik, A. (2009). Developmental dyscalculia: Heterogeneity might not mean different mechanisms. *Trends in Cognitive Sciences, 13*(2), 92–99.

Selter, C. (2001). Addition and subtraction of three-digit numbers: German elementary children's success, methods and strategies. *Educational Studies in Mathematics, 47*(2), 145–173.
Selter, C., Prediger, S., Nührenbörger, M., & Hubmann, S. (2012). Taking away and determining the difference–a longitudinal perspective on two models of subtraction and the inverse relation to addition. *Educational Studies in Mathematics, 79*(3), 389–408.
Siegler, R. S. (1987). The perils of averaging data over strategies: An example from children's addition. *Journal of Experimental Psychology: General, 116*(3), 250–264.
Siegler, R. S. (1988). Strategy choice procedures and the development of multiplication skill. *Journal of Experimental Psychology: General, 117*(3), 258–275.
Siegler, R. S. (1996). *Emerging minds: The process of change in children's thinking.* Oxford, UK: Oxford University Press.
Siegler, R. S., & Jenkins, E. (1989). *How children discover new strategies.* John M MacEachran memorial lecture series. Hillsdale, NJ: Lawrence Erlbaum.
Siegler, R. S., & Robinson, M. (1982). The development of numerical understandings. *Advances in Child Development and Behavior, 16*(C), 241–312.
Siegler, R. S., & Shrager, J. (1984). Strategy choices in addition and subtraction: How do children know what to do. In C. Sophian (Ed.), *Origins of cognitive skills* (pp. 229–293). Hillsdale, NJ: Lawrence Erlbaum.
Simmons, F. R., & Singleton, C. (2008). Do weak phonological representations impact on arithmetic development? A review of research into arithmetic and dyslexia. *Dyslexia, 14*(2), 77–94.
Slade, P. D., & Russel, G. F. M. (1971). Developmental dyscalculia: A brief report on four cases. *Psychological Medicine, 1*(4), 292–298.
Supekar, K., Iuculano, T., Chen, L., & Menon, V. (2015). Remediation of childhood math anxiety and associated neural circuits through cognitive tutoring. *Journal of Neuroscience, 35*(36), 12574–12583.
Temple, C. M. (1991). Procedural dyscalculia and number fact dyscalculia: Double dissociation in developmental dyscalculia. *Cognitive Neuropsychology, 8*(2), 155–176.
Thevenot, C., Barrouillet, P., Castel, C., & Uittenhove, K. (2016). Ten-year-old children strategies in mental addition: A counting model account. *Cognition, 146*, 48–57.
Tompson, I. (1997). *Teaching and learning early number.* Buckingham: Open University Press.
Torbeyns, J., Hickendorff, M., & Verschaffel, L. (2017). The use of number-based versus digit-based strategies on multi-digit subtractions: 9–12-year-olds' strategy use profiles and task performances. *Learning and Individual Differences, 58*, 64–74.
Tournaki, N. (2003). The differential effects of teaching addition through strategy instruction versus drill and practice to students with and without learning disabilities. *Journal of Learning Disability, 36*(5), 449–458.
Tronsky, L. N. (2005). Strategy use, the development of automaticity, and working memory involvement in complex multiplication. *Memory and Cognition, 33*(5), 927–940.
Van Niewenhoven, C., Grégoire, J., & Noël, M. P. (2002). *Tedi-math: Test diagnostique des compétences de base en mathématiques.* Paris: ECPA.
Vanbinst, K., Ghesquière, P., & De Smedt, B. (2015). Does numerical processing uniquely predict first graders' future development of single-digit arithmetic? *Learning and Individual Differences, 37*, 153–160.
Venneri, A., Cornoldi, C., & Garuti, M. (2003). Arithmetic difficulties in children with visuospatial learning disability (VLD). *Child Neuropsychology, 9*(3), 175–183.
Vilette, B., Mawart, C., & Rusinek, S. (2010). L'outil 'estimator', la ligne numérique mentale et les habiletés arithmétiques. *Pratiques Psychologiques, 26*(2), 203–244.

Wilson, A. J., & Dehaene, S. (2007). Number sense and developmental dyscalculia. In D. Coch, K. Fischer, & G. Dawson (Eds.), *Human behavior and the developing brain* (pp. 212–237). New York: Guilford Press.

Wynn, K. (1992). Addition and subtraction by human infants. *Nature, 358*(6389), 749–750.

Zaslavsky, C. (1970). Black African traditional mathematics. *The Mathematics Teacher, 63*(4), 345–356.

Zaslavsky, C. (1999). *Africa counts: Number and pattern in African culture.* Chicago Illinois: Lawrence Hill Books.

Zbrodoff, N. J., & Logan, G. D. (2005). What everyone finds: The problem-size effect. In J. I. D. Campbell (Ed.), *Handbook of mathematical cognition* (pp. 331–346). New York: Psychology Press.

5 Word problem solving

Problem solving is an important part of the school curriculum (Fayol, Thevenot & Devidal, 2005). Although some real-life situations are occasionally used to study arithmetic, academic arithmetic activities mostly use verbal problem statements. These describe situations in which the information provided is both incomplete and deductible. For instance, examine the word problem *'Paul had four marbles. Lucie gave him five. How many marbles does Paul have now?'* Some children can't understand the situation because they wonder how Lucie could give Paul marbles if it is not known whether she has marbles to start with.

Word problems are considered to be very important as they are supposed to be the bridge between arithmetic skills learning and solving problems in real-life situations, although most of the time, children are exposed to word problems that are not related to how they are living at the moment. However, children are often less proficient at solving a word problem than at solving the comparable arithmetic problem (Carpenter, Kepner, Corbitt, Lindquist & Reys, 1980), which means that other processing steps than just realizing an arithmetical operation are taking place when solving a word problem. This is what we will explain in the following section.

5.1 Why is it so hard to solve word problems?

When required to solve a word problem, the first step is to read and understand the sentences, which means understanding the meaning of each word and building a representation of their relations with one another so as to create a coherent network of their relations. Understanding the text is a key factor for problem solving (De Corte & Verschaffel 1985, Cummins et al., 1988). Indeed, it has been shown that the child's reading skills or reading comprehension is the best predictor of math problem solving, followed by their calculation capacities and then, and less consistently, by memory capacities (see Kail & Hall, 1999 in 8- to 12-year-olds and Swanson, Cooney & Brock, 1993, in 9-year-olds for reading and calculation skills and Swanson 1994, Passolunghi & Siegel, 2001 for the role of working memory capacities). Besides, children have to understand specific vocabulary such as 'gain', 'tare', 'cut off', 'remainder', 'altogether', 'more than', 'less than' … Even in adults, it has been shown

DOI: 10.4324/b22795-5

than the use of relational terms such as 'more than ' and 'less than' may lead to errors.

In addition, the statements sometimes describe situations in which the information provided is both incomplete and deducible such as in 'Paul had four marbles. Lucie gave him five. How many marbles does Paul now have?' where it is not specified that Lucy had marbles to begin with.

Moreover, the use of irrelevant information in the problem and the complexity of the semantic structure both increase the level of difficulty. A simple problem could be '*Sophie bought two rings. Each ring cost 5 euros. How much did she have to pay?*' A more complex problem would be '*Sophie washed the dishes and cleaned the floor of the old neighbour and received 12 euros for her help. With this money plus her saving, she has now 34 euros in her purse. She went to the shop and found two beautiful rings, one with a blue stone and one with a yellow stone. Each of the ring costs 5 euros. She really liked the two rings so she decided to buy both of them. How much did she have to pay?*' Russell and Ginsburg (1984) compared fourth graders with math learning disability to typical third and fourth graders on problems involving manipulating the complexity of the semantic structure and the inclusion of irrelevant information. They found no difference between the groups for simple addition problems involving two or three addends but when irrelevant information was included in three-addend problems, the performance of children with mathematical learning difficulties deteriorated more than that of typical children.

Beyond understanding all the words and each sentence, the real challenge will be for the child to reconstruct situations mentally, or analogically, and thus to establish links between the actions, objects, and relations mentioned in the verbal utterances in order to elaborate the corresponding mathematical symbolism to represent the arithmetical operations (Fagnant, 2005). This is called mathematical modelling (Verschaffel & de Corte, 2005). Several studies have shown that this modelling step is facilitated when the question is presented prior to the rest of the problem rather than at the end, like it is typically done in math classes. Indeed, several studies have shown that placing the question prior to the rest of the text actually increases children's performance and this is even more true for children with poorer mathematical skills, rather than typical mathematical skills, and when the problems are more difficult (Thevenot, Devidal, Barrouillet & Fayol, 2007). According to these authors, placing the question at the beginning of the word problem helps children to figure out the situation described by the text and allows the construction of a more appropriate representation or mental model of the situation.

Once this step is completed, the child will have to carry out the calculations to arrive at the final result and finally to evaluate this result with regard to the initial situation and the question asked, or even ideally, to verify this result, before communicating it. However, for some problems, the solution does not correspond directly to the result of the calculation. Indeed, some problems require a contextualization of the answer (Verschaffel & De Corte, 2005). For example, a problem like: '*An army bus can carry 36 soldiers. If 1,128 soldiers need to go to their training camp, how many buses will be needed?' (Carpenter, Lindquist, Matthews & Silvers, 1983) gives rise to the frequent response of 31.33 or of 31 with a remainder of 12, but the correct answer (32) is only very seldom produced. The students here clearly disregard the initial meaning of the utterance operation evoked is applied to the numbers presented in the statement and the result thus obtained is regarded as the final answer without verifying the plausibility of the answer given the context of the story. This lack of contextualization could come from a conception of the problems as being artificial without any real need for taking into account the concrete situation described (Verschaffel & De Corte, 2005).

Finally, sometimes a problem needs several solving steps because the problem actually can be decomposed into several problems embedded in one another. In this case, the students need to identify the main problem and the sub-problems and plan the different solving steps that are needed and execute them in the right order.

In conclusion, solving a word problem requires many different cognitive skills:

- language skills (including reading);
- the ability to detect relevant information and to resist the tendency to take into account all available numerical information;
- mathematical modelling skills;
- planning skills;
- computational skills;
- an ability to contextualize the response.

All these factors can account for difficulties in solving word problems.

Although all these are very important, research has shown that the major challenge in word problem solving is the mathematical modelling step. Indeed, different word problems solved using the exact same arithmetic operation may lead to dramatically different performance. For instance, Riley, Greeno, and Heller (1983) present to first-grade children word problems which can all be solved by doing the simple subtraction '8 − 5'.

a) 'John had eight marbles. He gives five marbles to Peter. How many marbles does John have now?'
b) 'John had five marbles; Peter gave him some more marbles. Now John has eight marbles. How many marbles did Peter give him?'
c) 'John and Peter have eight marbles altogether. John has five marbles. How many marbles does Peter have?'
d) 'John has eight marbles. He has five more marbles than Peter. How many marbles has Peter?'

All of the pupils succeed in solving the word problem (a). Only half of them succeed in solving problem (b), and the success rate drops to 39% with problem (c). Finally, the worst performance, 11% success, is observed with word problem (d). To account for these huge differences in performance, researchers have proposed word problem typologies that differentiate between the semantic structures of the problems.

5.2 Typologies of word problems

5.2.1 Additive and subtractive problems

Riley, Greeno, and Heller (1983) have proposed a typology of problems referring to addition and subtraction operations. They distinguish between four categories: change, combine, compare, and equalize problems.

In *change* type problems, an initial set is transformed either by adding (such as in problem (b) above) or removing items (such as in problem (a) above), which results in a final state. The question asked to the child either concerns the final state (such as in problem (a) above), the transformation (such as in problem (b) above), or the initial state (such as '*John had some marbles. He gave five marbles to Peter. Now, John has three marbles. How many marbles did John have at the beginning?*').

In *combine* problems, two separate subsets are considered, as well as their total quantity. They are also sometimes referred to as part-whole problems. The question addressed to the child can be about the cardinal of one of the subsets/parts or of the total/whole quantity. Although these problems are also solved by addition or subtraction, there is no action, no cardinality change. The situation is static. Problem (c) above is an example of such a combine problem with the unknown being the cardinal of one of the subsets.

In *compare* problems, two separate subsets are also considered in a static situation (as in the combine problems) but here, the quantity of one set is put into a comparison relationship with the other. These problems often include terms such as more/less. The child has either to determine the quantity of one set based on the other, taking into account their comparison relationship (such as in problem (d) above), or has to determine the comparison relationship between the two sets (e.g., '*John has eight marbles. Peter has five marbles. How many more marbles than Peter does John have?*').

Finally, in *equalize* problems, two distinct sets are considered and one of them has to be modified (either by addition or subtraction) so that both sets would be equal. The following word problems are example of this type: '*John has 8 marbles. Peter has 5 marbles. How many marbles does Peter have to buy to have as many marbles as John?*' or '*John has 8 marbles. If he eats 3 marbles he will have as many as Peter. How many marbles does Peter have?*'

Riley et al. (1983) observed that, globally, the change problems are those that lead to larger success whereas the compare problems are the worst. But, within each type of problem, performance depends on the place of the unknown. For instance, in change problems, performance in first grade goes from 100% correct for an additive or subtractive change with the unknown at the final stage, to around 65% when the unknown is the transformation, and to around 30% when the unknown is the initial state. Similarly, for combine problems, performance is much better when the unknown is the whole than when it is one of the parts. One possible explanation is that in young children, problems are solved by some sort of simulation of the situation such as counting the two parts and then the whole for combine problems or putting the two quantities in one-to-one correspondence for the compare problems. Yet, when the unknown is the initial state for a change problem, for instance, or when the action is difficult to simulate, children cannot use this kind of strategy. In compare problems, one of the difficulties lies in the understanding of the relational terms such as 'more than' or 'less than'. Typically, children activate an addition procedure when the problem involves the term 'more than' and a subtraction strategy when it involves the term 'less than' although this is not always appropriate. Even with adults, Lewis and Mayer (1987) found better success for problems such as *'Jim has three balls. Tom has five balls more than Jim. How many balls does Tom have?'*, than for *'Jim has three balls. He has five balls less than Tom. How many balls does Tom have?'* Indeed, the first problem involves the term 'more than' and should be solved with addition, while the second problem has the term 'less than' but should however be solved with addition and not with subtraction (see also Mayer & Hegardy, 1996).

5.2.2 Multiplicative problems

As regards multiplicative problems, Hardiman and Mestre (1989) introduced a distinction between extensive and intensive quantities. Extensive (E) quantities denote a set of objects or measurements (number of miles, of hours, of litres, etc.) while intensive (I) quantities refer to a map between two extensive quantities (such as the price per quantity, the number of miles per hour, etc.). Four types of problems are distinguished: compute, compare, combine, and change.

Both compute and compare problems are $E_1 \times I = E_2$ problems. In *compute* problems, one must determine the number of E_2 based on E_1 and on the I quantity relating E_1 and E_2. The following problem (Figure 5.1a) is an instance of a compute problem: *'John needs to buy 3 kilos of cherries. Cherries cost 8 euros*

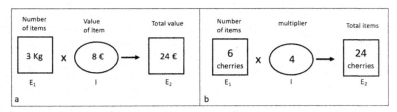

Figure 5.1 (a) Example of a compute multiplication problem; (b) example of a compare multiplication problem.

per kilo. How much will he have to pay?' In this case, E_1 refers to the 3 kilos of cherries, I to the price per kilo, and E_2 to the amount to pay.

Compare problems involve a size comparison between a start set (E_1) and a referent set (E_2). These start and referent sets can differ or they can refer to a single set that changes over time. The following problem (Figure 5.1b) is an example of a compare problem: *'John had six cherries. Peter has four times more cherries as John. How many cherries does Peter have?'* In this case, E_1 is the six cherries of John, E_2 is the cherries of Peter, and 'four times more' refers to the size comparison (or I) between E_1 and E_2.

Combine problems are of the type $E_1 \times E_2 = E_3$. They thus involve two extensive quantities, whose units are or are not the same and which are combined to give a third extensive quantity. Examples of combine problems are: *'John has four different pairs of shoes and five different caps. How many different combinations can he make with these clothing accessories?'* (Figure 5.2a) or *'This table is 4 metres long and 1.5 metres wide. What is the area of the table?'* (Figure 5.2b).

Finally, *convert* problems are of the type $I_1 \times I_2 = I_3$. For instance, *'The scooter was travelling 12 miles per hour. There are 1.6 kilometres in a mile. How many km per hour did the scooter travel?'* (Figure 5.3). It should be noted, however, that the latter two types of problems are generally introduced after sixth grade.

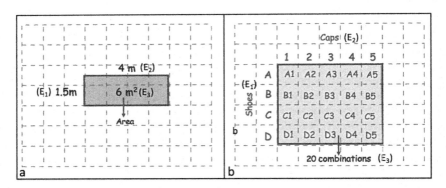

Figure 5.2 Examples of combine multiplication problems.

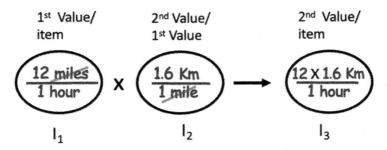

Figure 5.3 Example of a convert multiplication problem.

5.2.3 Proportional or ratio problems

Proportional or ratio problems are the most difficult ones. Indeed, the types of problems mentioned above usually link three data points. For example, additive problems involve the two sets and their sum, or multiplicative problems involve two types of units and their products. In the case of proportional problems, four items have to be integrated considering their relationships. Here is an example of a proportional problem: '*Every day Bob puts 3 euros in his piggy bank and Tim puts 5 euros in his wallet. When Bob has 12 euros, how many euros will be in Tim's wallet?*'

In this type of problem, the child must determine one term of a ratio so that it is equivalent to another. To solve such problems, children can develop a personal context-based strategy and informal representations of the problem (Hart, 1994). For example, a child could act by repeated additions: Bob will have 3 euros on the first day, 3 + 3 on the second day, 3 + 3 + 3 on the third day, and 3 + 3 + 3 + 3 on the four days, making a total of 12 euros, so that, in parallel, the child could also count 5 + 5 + 5 + 5 for the same four days for Tim. This strategy is not based on the multiplicative relation between the elements but leads to a correct answer. Very often, however, children will implement an incorrect additive strategy (Fuson & Abrahamson, 2005). For instance, they could calculate that to go from 3 to 12 euros, Bob's savings would increase by 9 euros and therefore that the money in Tim's wallet would also increase by 9 euros, for a total of 5 + 9 euros or 14 euros. Thus, one should help children ground these problems in a multiplicative context.

Typically, the four items involved in the ratio problems are actually of two types, entering into intra- and inter-relationships (Lamon, 1994). For instance, in the following problem '*4 balloons cost 9 euros, how much will 12 balloons cost?*', the 2 types of elements are the number of balloons and their price. The intra-relations are those that are established between elements of the same type: 4/12 balloons and 9/? Euros. The inter-relations are those that are established between the two different types of elements, the number of balloons and prices: 4/9 and 12/?. The resolution of the problem can be realized through a strategy based either on intra- or on inter-relationships. Depending on the problem, one of these strategies may be easier to implement. In the example above, working on the intra-relationship is preferable: the ratio of the balloons (4/12) is a ratio of 1 to 3, and I have to find x so that the ratio 9/? Would also be a 1:3 ratio, thus by computing 9 × 3 (Figure 5.4a).

Conversely, if the problem was '*3 balloons cost 9 euros, how much will it cost for 11 balloons?*', the intra-relationships would be 3/11 balloons and 9/? Euros and the inter-relationships, 3/9 and 11/?. In this case, working on inter-relationships seems more appropriate (Figure 5.4b). The child should thus be able to switch from one strategy to another, according to the problem that is presented.

Solving the problem can also imply using division. For instance, in the problem '*3 balloons cost 9 euros, how many balloons will cost 33 euros?*', it is easier to work with the inter-relationships 3/9 and ?/33 and thus divide 33 by 3 to get 11 (Figure 5.4c).

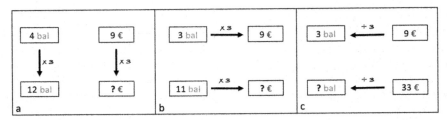

Figure 5.4 Different types of relations between items: (a) intra-relation ratio using multiplication; (b) inter-relation ratio using multiplication; (c) inter-relation ratio using division.

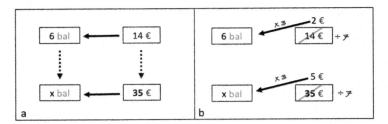

Figure 5.5 Example of a ratio problem where initially neither intra-relation nor inter-relation works (a), but after dividing the euros items by 7, the inter-relation ratio using multiplication works (b).

Finally, an additional difficulty factor concerns problems that involve ratios that do not constitute a multiple or a divisor of the other. For example, if the problem had been '*6 balloons cost 14 euros, how many balloons will cost 35 euros?*', then neither the intra-relationships (6/? And 14/35, see in Figure 5.5a the vertical arrows) nor the inter-relationships (6/14 and ?/35, see in Figure 5.5a the horizontal arrows) give an easy answer. In the first case, I have to find x so that $6/x = 14/35$. This can be done by simplifying the second fraction with 7, that is $6/x = 2/5$, so $x = 15$ (Figure 5.5b). The notion of fraction equivalence (including multiplication fact retrieval and fluency in fraction simplification) plays a very important role here.

5.3 Difficulties in word problem solving in dyscalculia

While a considerable amount of research has focused on arithmetic difficulties in dyscalculic children, very little research has been done on their mathematical problem-solving abilities. Here we present some of the most important studies on the subject.

Jiménez and Garcia (1999) compared the performance of two groups of children with math learning disability, one where math abilities were lower than expected on the basis of the child's intelligence, the other where poor math achievement was in accordance with the child's intellectual capacity. They found that both groups had difficulties in word problem solving and that they were equally affected by the semantic structure of the word problems and the position of the unknown quantity in the problem. In short, it is the level of the child's mathematical ability that determines his or her problem-solving skills.

Russell and Ginsburg (1984) compared the problem-solving performance of third- and fourth-grade pupils without learning difficulties (typical children) to fourth-grade pupils with a learning disability in mathematics. The authors had taken care to vary the complexity of the semantic structure of the problems and the inclusion or not of irrelevant information, and to use a scoring grid for problem solving that did not take into account calculation errors. They found no difference between groups for simple addition problems involving two or three numbers, but when irrelevant information was added to problems involving the addition of three numbers, the performance of children with mathematical learning difficulties deteriorated more than that of typical children.

It should be noted, however, that these two studies did not control for the existence of reading difficulties possibly associated with mathematical learning difficulties. Epidemiological studies indeed show that almost half of the children with mathematical learning difficulties have associated dyslexia (see Chapter 1). This factor was taken into account in the following three studies.

For example, Jordan and Oettinger (1997) assessed both computational and mathematical problem-solving skills in children with mathematical learning difficulties or with difficulties in both mathematics and reading. They found that the group with mathematical learning difficulties only showed particular difficulty in retrieving arithmetic facts from memory while the group with learning difficulties in both mathematics and reading showed difficulty conceptualizing and solving word problems. Similarly, Jordan and Hanich (2000) compared second-grade students showing learning difficulties in mathematics, in reading, or in both to typical students. They found that the mathematical learning difficulties group performed less well than the group with reading difficulties and the control group. However, these three groups performed better than the group with difficulties in both reading and mathematics, which showed greater difficulties.

Finally, Fuchs and Fuchs (2002) compared the mathematical problem-solving abilities of three groups of pupils in fourth grade: one group of children with mathematical learning difficulties, another with mathematical and reading learning difficulties and a control group. The authors used different types of problems. The simplest problems present a short text contiguous to the question and require a one-step solution. The most complex problems have a longer text, may include non-essential details or irrelevant numbers and require one to three stages of resolution. For these different types of problems, they calculated two scores: (1) the number of problems correctly solved, and (2) the number of problems for which students used the correct numbers, plus those for which they used the correct arithmetic operation. For simple problems, they observed that children with mathematical learning difficulties performed better than those with both reading and mathematical learning difficulties on both measures. For more complex problems, the two groups with mathematical learning difficulties, associated or not with reading difficulties, performed similarly but less well than the control group on measure (1), i.e., the number of problems solved correctly. For measure (2), i.e., the use of correct numbers and operations, the mathematical learning difficulties group scored higher than the group with both math and reading learning difficulties.

In summary, children with mathematical learning difficulties do have difficulties in word problem solving even when the calculation errors are not taken into account. However, when learning difficulties concern both math and reading, difficulties in word problem solving are even stronger.

5.4 Experimental intervention or instruction programmes

In this section, we will first present research in which the authors have developed intervention or instructional programmes aimed at improving students' problem-solving skills and tested their effectiveness. Next, we will present a didactic method developed in Singapore, which seems to yield very good results.

5.4.1 Research on intervention or instruction programmes

Fuchs, Powell, Seethaler, Cirino et al. (2009) created an intervention programme focused on word problem solving (WP programme) and compared it to a programme focused on number combination (NC programme) and to the classical mathematics programme (control condition). They conducted their study on third-grade students with learning difficulties in mathematics or with difficulties in both mathematics and reading.

The two experimental conditions (NC and WP) consisted of 48 20–30-minute sessions over 16 weeks. In the NC programme, the emphasis was on solving addition and subtraction problems. The programme included the use of manipulatives (tokens, etc.), fingers, and number lines. The children were taught the commutative property of addition but not of subtraction, and were taught two strategies for solving calculations: either retrieving the answer from memory or counting if they did not know the answer by heart. In the latter case, students were taught to start, in the case of addition, with the larger number and count a number of steps equivalent to the smaller number (e.g., for 4 + 7: start at 7 and count 4 steps: 8, 9, 10, 11); and in the case of subtraction, students start with the number just after the minus sign and count up to the first number in the equation (e.g., for 6 − 3: count from 3, up to 6).

Programme WP had the same duration and consisted of four parts. The first part consisted of six sessions and focused on calculations. Students learned counting strategies to solve addition and subtraction, reviewed doubles (in addition and subtraction), and learned how to solve a simple algebraic equation with the unknown in any position ($a + b = c$, $c - b = a$, with a, b, or c as the unknown).

In the other three parts, one word problem type was introduced and the previous ones were revised. Three problem types were considered: total (two or more amounts are combined), difference (two amounts are compared), and change (an initial amount increases or decreases). For each of these problem types, students learned a multi-step problem-solving methodology: the RUN strategy. This involved first reading (R) the problem, then underlining (U) the question, and then naming (N) the type of problem. Students were taught how to identify and label relevant information (see Box 5.1), solve the equation, and check the accuracy and plausibility of the answer. They also learned to identify and cross out irrelevant information, to recognize and solve problems with missing information in the first or second position, to solve problems with two-digit numbers, and to look for relevant information to solve problems in diagrams, pictures, and other types of materials.

BOX 5.1   Labels used to represent numerical information about the problem (Fuchs et al., 2009)

Problem type *total*: $\boldsymbol{P_1 + P_2 = T}$
   with P_1 for part 1, P_2 for part 2 and T for total.
Problem type *difference*: $\boldsymbol{B - s = D}$
   with B being the bigger amount, s the smaller, and D the difference.
Problem type *change*: $\boldsymbol{St \pm C = E}$
   with St being the starting amount, C the changed amount, and E the ending amount, using + or − according to whether there is an increase or decrease of the starting amount.

Each session of parts 2, 3, and 4 of the programme started with a few minutes warm-up where the child had to do some simple calculations. Then there was 15–20 minutes of conceptual and strategic instruction. The third activity was WP sorting: problems are read and children have to put them in the corresponding box: total, difference, change, or 'I don't know'. Different types of WP used similar cover stories to discourage children from using superficial features to categorize the WP (for instance, classifying WP of marbles on one side and WP on money on the other side). The session ended with a paper and pencil review that included a two-minute assessment of addition and subtraction solving and a two-minute assessment of WP solving.

Pre- and post-intervention measurements were taken for number combination, procedural calculation, and WP solving. As regards the number combination abilities, both tutoring groups similarly outperformed the control group, and there was no difference between them although the NC tutoring spent dramatically more time on number combination. Thus, at that age, teaching an efficient counting strategy and providing frequent and small practice moments have comparable effects to an extended tutorial programme. Furthermore, these effects were observed on both single-digit and double-digit calculations, whereas the WP and NC interventions only involved single-digit calculations. Thus, working on simple calculations allowed children to develop better strategies and even to store answers in memory and thus use fewer cognitive resources to solve them. Consequently, when faced with calculations with larger numbers, they were more capable of having the cognitive resources needed to perform sub-calculations and manage the calculation procedures (for example, for 52 + 37, the following sub-calculations must be solved: 5 + 3 and 2 + 7). The authors also observed that the children in the WP group were better than the control group at solving incomplete calculations (or algebraic equations of the type $a \pm b = c$ with the unknown in first, second, or third position), whereas the NC group did not differ from the other two groups. Finally, the WP group also performed better than the other two groups in solving verbal problems and in writing the algebraic equation corresponding to a verbal problem read aloud. In addition, the authors noted that the benefit of the interventions was equivalent in children with difficulties in mathematics alone and in those where these were associated with reading problems.

Thus, this study shows that word-problem tutoring can be effective with children with mathematical learning difficulties and that adding a small amount of instruction and practice on addition and subtraction solving strategies can lead to significant improvement in calculation abilities. In this study, children were taught a global heuristic to solve the problem, which they called RUN (read the problem, underline the question, and name the problem type) and they were explicitly taught the different types of problems (total, difference, and change) with the corresponding equations. This intervention proved to be efficient in increasing children's ability to write the algebraic equation corresponding to a problem and also to accurately solve word problems.

The study by Jitendra, Griffin, Haria, Leh, Adams, and Kaduvettoor (2007) goes further, comparing the effectiveness of two types of instruction programmes for problem solving: general instruction and instruction based on the use of specific schema for each type of problem. Indeed, according to the schema theory, learning to solve word problems means developing schemas for grouping problems into types that require the same solving strategy (Gick & Holyoack, 1980). The broader the schemas, the higher the chance for the student to see a connection between the problem that s/he is solving and old ones that s/he has learned to solve. This is called transfer. However, often, children base their categorization on shared surface features, like the cover story of the word problem rather than the deeper structure of the problems, and this is even more the case for children with mathematical learning difficulties (e.g., see Novick, 1988). To help children build a higher-order relational structure, introducing schema and varying the cover stories can be beneficial. Building a higher-order representation is key if one wants the child to transfer what s/he has learned when solving some problems to other new ones.

In this study, Jitendra et al. (2007) worked with third-grade children who were randomly assigned to two strategy instructions for addition and subtraction word problem solving: general strategy instruction (GDI) and schema-based instruction (SBI). Both programmes included 32 sessions and worked on 1- and 2-steps problems of the change, combine, or compare types. Children were tested before and after the instruction and again six weeks later.

In GDI, children were instructed to follow a four-step word problem solving procedure:

(1) *Read and understand the problem*: both the teacher and the students read the problem, and the teacher asks facilitative questions.
(2) *Plan to solve the problem*: the students are prompted to use manipulatives such as counters to represent the problem, then implement the stituation or drawing pictures representing the problem, then choosing an operation or writing a number sentence.
(3) *Solve the problem* by applying the strategy or operation chosen in the previous step.
(4) *Look back* at the problem *and check*, to consider whether the answer makes sense.

In SBI, students were taught to construct a model to represent the situation in the text followed by solution planning based on the model. Instruction started with one-step problems. In the first phase for learning problem schema, students worked on story situations that did not contain any unknown information and were taught to identify the problem type (change, combine, compare) and represent the features of the story situation using the schematic diagrams (see Figure 5.6). For instance, children were told that in change problems, an initial quantity either increases or decreases due to a direct or implied action. When the change action causes an increase, then the ending quantity represents the bigger or the whole; when the change action involves a decrease, the beginning quantity is the big number or the whole. Then, during the problem solution instruction phase, they were shown problems with unknowns and were taught to follow a four-step strategy:

(1) find the problem type;
(2) organize the information using the diagram (which at the end were no longer presented but had to be drawn by the child);
(3) plan to solve the problem;
(4) solve the problem.

After having worked with one-step problems, two-step problems were presented. Children were taught to first identify the primary problem schema,

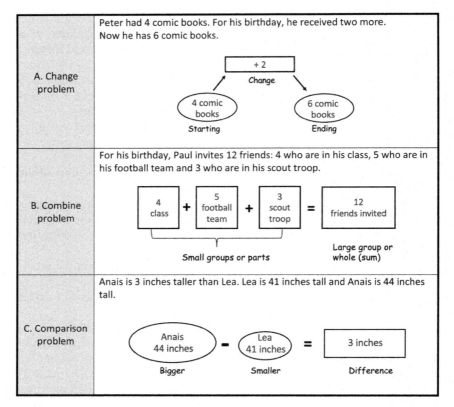

Figure 5.6 Schemas used for the change (a), combine (b), and compare (c) problems in Jitendra et al. (2007), page 119.

based on the question asked in the problem, and then to identify the secondary problem that must be solved to answer the primary problem. Accordingly, they had to write partial answers (PA) for the missing elements in the primary problem schema that had to be derived from the secondary problem.

Results showed that both directly after completion of the intervention, as well as six weeks later, the SBI group outperformed the GSI group. Furthermore, the SBI group also obtained better performance on a global math test. But no difference between groups was observed on computation performance, indicating the specificity of the training effect. This study thus shows the benefit of providing children schemas to help them build a correct representation of the problem.

One of the key issues in problem solving is to teach children to transfer what they have learned in solving word problems to other new problems. To deal with this, Fuchs, Fuchs, Prentice et al. (2003a) developed a type of instruction, which explicitly teaches this transfer competence. Twenty-four teachers were randomly assigned to 4 instruction conditions: the regular instruction (control condition) and

3 experimental conditions: (1) 20 sessions on solution instruction (20_Solution), (2) 20 sessions on solution instruction plus 10 sessions involving the transfer treatment (20_Solution_10_Transfer), and (3) 10 sessions on solution instruction plus 10 sessions involving the transfer treatment (10_Solution_10_Transfer).

In the solution instruction phase, students were taught rules to solve problems and ways to develop (narrow) schemas for sorting problems that require the same solution method. In the transfer instruction phase, teachers first explained the notion of transfer and gave examples of skills children had to transfer (e.g., the baby learns to drink from a toddler cup and then learns to drink using a real cup and then a glass). Second, students were taught that problems which differ in superficial features (see Box 5.2) might have the same underlying structure and require the same solution procedure. Finally, teachers alerted the students to the possibility that novel problems might incorporate changes in superficial problem features but involve an already familiar structure and thus a known solution procedure.

BOX 5.2   Same problem structure but different superficial features (Fuchs et al., 2003a, page 305)

Problem

'You want to buy some lemon drops. Lemon drops come in bags with ten lemon drops each. How many bags should you buy to get 32 lemon drops?'

Same problem but different words

'You want to buy some lemon drops. Lemon drops come in packages with ten lemon drops in each package. How many packages should you buy to get 32 lemon drops?'

Same problem but different format

- *You want to buy some lemon drops.*
- *The sign at the store looks like this : 'LEMON DROPS ON SALE!!! 10 IN EACH BAG!'*
- *How many should you buy to get 32 lemon drops? 3, 4, 2 or 5?*

Same problem with an additional question

'You want to buy some lemon drops. Lemon drops come in bags with ten lemon drops each. How many bags should you buy to get 32 lemon drops? If each bag costs $4, how much money will you spend?'

To see the differential effect of these four conditions, three types of problems were used to measure, respectively, the immediate-transfer (similar problems as those trained but using novel cover stories), near-transfer (problems with a novel cover story and a change in one superficial problem feature), and far-transfer (problems with different cover stories, changes in several superficial problem features, and additional elements of novelty).

On the immediate-transfer measure, all three experimental groups outperformed the control group. On the near-transfer measure, the three experimental groups outperformed the control group and the 20_Solution_10_Transfer group was better than the 10_Solution_10_Transfer group. Finally, for the far-transfer measure, only the two groups who received the transfer sessions outperformed the control group, but only the 20_Solution_10_Transfer group performed better than the 20_Solution group; this was not the case for the 10_Solution_10_Transfer group.

This study thus shows that explicitly teaching transfer facilitates mathematical problem solving. This can be done by explaining to students what transfer is, promoting a higher level of abstraction by broadening the categories by which students group the problems requiring the same solution, and prompting the students to find similarities between novel and old problems.

In the following study, the same research team (Fuchs, Fuchs, Prentice, Burch, Hamlett, Owen & Schroeter, 2003b) used the problem-solving transfer instruction as just reported here above, in association with instruction about self-regulated strategies. Self-regulated strategies (SRL) are a set of strategies that students can apply in order to become more metacognitively, motivationally, and behaviourally active in their learning. These promote goal setting to increase motivation and mobilize and sustain effort, combined with self-evaluation to monitor one's progress. So, besides the control condition (business as usual), 2 experimental conditions were compared (with 32 sessions): problem-solving transfer (PST) instruction and the PST plus self-regulated strategies (SRL) instruction. The SRL components were as follows:

(1) after working independently on a problem, students scored their work;
(2) they recorded their daily scores on an individual thermometer and examined their progression;
(3) each session started by examining their chart and a reminder to try to beat their previous score and set a goal to beat their highest score that day;
(4) students scored their homework before giving it to the teacher;
(5) students had to find and report to the class, examples of how they had transferred the type of problem they were working on, to another part of the school day or outside the school;
(6) a graph of the class recorded how much homework was submitted, and the number of children reporting a transfer event.

Measures to examine the immediate, near, and far transfer on WP solving were the same as those used by Fuchs et al. (2003a). There was also a four-question questionnaire about self-regulation strategies in which children were asked about their self-efficacy ('*I know how to transfer skills to new kinds of math problems*' and '*I learned a lot about math problem solving this year*'), their goal orientation and self-monitoring ('*When I do math, I think about whether my work is getting better*'), and their effort ('*I worked hard this year so that I could get better in math*').

As already reported by Fuchs et al. (2003a), the PST instruction showed larger improvement on both immediate- and near-transfer problem-solving measures relative to the control group, but not as regards the far-transfer WP. The PST + SRL group also showed greater improvement than the control group for immediate and near-transfer problem solving, but it also showed higher improvement for far-transfer WP solving. Finally, on the four SRL questions, children from the PST + SRL group scored higher than those of the PST group. These effects did not differ between low- and average-achieving children.

So, this study replicates the previous one showing that the PST instruction is efficient. Adding SRL instruction led to improvement even in the far-transfer WP and led children to feel more self-efficient, goal-oriented, and better at self-monitoring their effort.

In summary, these studies show that

(1) word-problem tutoring can be used efficiently even with children with mathematical learning difficulties (Fuchs, Powell, Seethaler et al., 2009);
(2) word-problem tutoring that includes schemas to help children build a correct representation of the problem are more beneficial than tutoring which only includes a multi-step solving procedure (Jitendra, Griffin, Haria et al., 2007);
(3) transfer can be improved by explicitly teaching this transfer competence (Fuchs, Fuchs, Prentice et al., 2003a and Fuchs, Fuchs, Prentice, Burch, Hamlett, Owen & Schroeter, 2003b);
(4) adding instruction about self-regulated strategies leads to better benefit from the training and led children to feel more self-efficient, goal-oriented, and better at self-monitoring their effort (Fuchs, Fuchs, Prentice, Burch, Hamlett, Owen & Schroeter, 2003b).

5.4.2 A successful didactical programme: the Singapore method

Beyond the results from these training studies, it is worth mentioning the Singapore method. This method was developed by the Ministry of Education in Singapore a few years ago. We are not aware of any studies that have compared the benefits of this method to others, but today it is used in all schools in Singapore and has led Singaporean students to the top rank in the international mathematics test organized by the OECD, the PISA assessment. For this reason, we will briefly describe the main features of this method with regard to verbal problem solving.

This method uses schematic representations for additive/subtractive problems but also for multiplicative or ratio problems. Ng and Lee (2009) present

212 Word problem solving

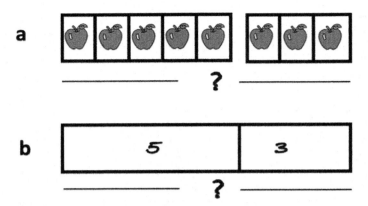

Figure 5.7 Representation of an additive problem using a picture (a) or rectangles (b).

the models used in this method. In the instructional process, children begin to solve very simple verbal problems using pictures of familiar objects to represent the problem (see Figure 5.7a), then learn to draw rectangles to represent quantities (see Figure 5.7b), and then write the arithmetic operation.

Children are taught to read the problem and represent each chunk of information using the schema, then return to the text, and process the following chunk. It is only when all the text chunks have been represented in the schema that the child moves onto the next phase: writing the symbolic equation, and then doing the computation. To build their schemas, children need to understand the part–part–whole relationship of numbers or their decomposition. They need to understand that rectangles stand for numbers or quantities and that a relatively longer rectangle is used for a bigger number and a shorter one for a smaller number, or that an arbitrary length is used to represent unknown. They also need to be taught how to represent comparative relations such as *more than, less than,* and *as many as, x many times more/less.* It is also sometimes more helpful for children to use dotted lines instead of plain lines to show the partition of a rectangle or quantity.

Let us consider the three main types of addition–subtraction problems: the combine, change, and compare problems. The combine word problem can refer to an arithmetic situation ($a + b = ?$) or an algebraic one ($? + a = b$), with the question mark standing for the unknown. These types of problems can be represented as two rectangles and their union, such as in Figure 5.8a and 5.8b. The *Swimming pool* problem (inspired by Ng & Lee, 2009) would correspond to the arithmetic situation ($a + b = ?$): '*On Saturday, 146 people went to the swimming pool. On Sunday, 125 people went to the swimming pool. How many people went to the swimming pool over the two days?*' (see Figure 5.8c); while the Museum problem would correspond to the algebraic situation: $a + ? = b$: '*There were 85 visitors at the museum, 36 of them were adults and the rest were children. How many children visited the museum?*' (see Figure 5.8d).

Word problem solving 213

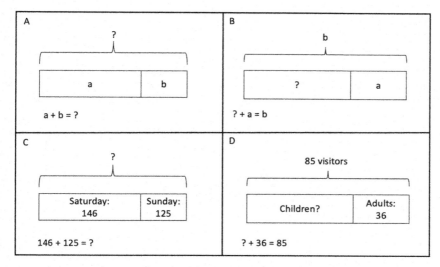

Figure 5.8 Representation of combine problems with algebraic equations (a, b) and the Swimming pool example (c) and the Museum problem example (d).

A similar schema can be used for the change problem. For instance, '*Mary had some stamps. She gave seven stamps to her younger brother. Mary then had 14 stamps. How many stamps did Mary have at first?*' The child will start to draw a rectangle corresponding to the stamps Mary had to start (Figure 5.9, left panel). This will be a rectangle with a question mark as we do not know how many stamps she had. Then, she gave seven stamps to her brother, so a part of that rectangle corresponds to the part she gave and should be noted as seven (Figure 5.9, right panel). Then we know that 14 stamps are left. Now, it is easy to see that the unknown actually corresponds to the sum of 7 and 14.

For the compare problem, the schema shows the relationship between different quantities that are compared. Figure 5.10 shows the types of schema that can be used to represent this type of problem with variations of the place of the unknown.

Let us take an example: '*Rosy has five friends. Pam has four friends more than Rosy. (a) How many friends has Rosy? Or (b) how many friends do they have*

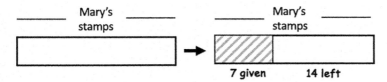

Figure 5.9 Representation of a change problem.

214 *Word problem solving*

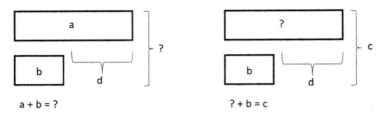

Figure 5.10 Schemas for the compare problems.

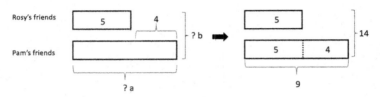

Figure 5.11 Schematic representation of a compare problem, the Friends problem.

altogether?' In the specific case of this problem, children can start by drawing a rectangle corresponding to Rosy's friends (Figure 5.11). Then, they should draw a larger rectangle for Pam's friends, nothing that she has four friends more. Finally, they should specify the unknown which is the number of friends of Pam (?a) or the number of friends in total (?b).

This same type of schema can be used to represent more complex comparison problems. For instance, '*A cow weighs 150 kg more than a dog. A goat weighs 130 kg less than the cow. Altogether, these three animals weigh 410 kg. What is the mass of the cow?*' (Ng & Lee, 2009, page 286). To represent this problem (see Figure 5.12), the child will start to draw a rectangle corresponding to the weight of the dog and then a larger rectangle for the cow's weight, noting that it is 150 kg more. Then, the student has to draw a rectangle for the goat's weight, noting that it is 130 kg less than the cow, or 20 kg more than the dog.

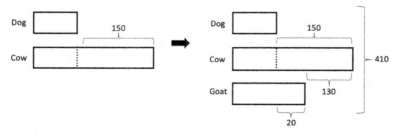

Figure 5.12 Schematic representation of a complex compare problem, the animal weight problem (Ng & Lee, 2009, page 287).

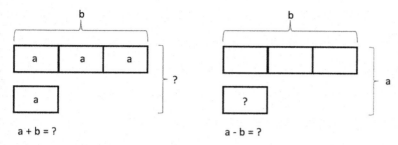

Figure 5.13 Schema for a multiplication problem.

Finally, the student notes that, altogether, the weight of these three animals is 410 kg. We thus have three times the dog's weight, plus 150, plus 20 equals 410. On this basis, we can calculate that the dog's weight is (410 − 170) ÷ 3 = 80 kg, and from that, that the cow's weight is 80 + 150 = 230 kg.

Let us see now how these schemas can be used to represent multiplicative or division problems. Let us take an example: '*Paula and Irma collect stamps. Paula has 230 stamps. Irma has three times as many stamps as Paula. How many stamps do they have altogether?*' Figure 5.13, left panel represents the schema for this problem. Paula's stamps are represented by a. Irma's stamps are represented by $3 \times a$ or b. And the question is about the total, so $a + b$. Figure 5.13, right panel represents another version of a similar problem: '*Paula and Irma collect stamps. Altogether, they have 468 stamps but Irma has 3 times more than Paula. How many stamps does Paula have?*' Now, 'a' corresponds to the 468 stamps they have altogether, and 'b' to Irma's stamps. This same schema could also be used to represent a problem with fractions such as this one: '*Paula and Irma collect stamps. Altogether, they have 468 stamps but the size of Paula's collection is only 1/3 of Irma's. How many stamps does Paula have?*'

Finally, this method can also represent ratio problems. For instance, '*The ratio of Sarah's pocket money to David's pocket money is 3:5. David has 75 dollars. How much money does Sarah have?*' The child should start drawing rectangles representing the pocket money of David and Sarah by expressing their ratio (see Figure 5.14): using identical small rectangles, he/she should take 3 to represent Sarah's money and 5 to represent David's money. Now we know that David has 75 dollars. Accordingly, each little rectangle represents 75 ÷ 5 = 15 dollars. So Sarah has 15 × 3 = 45 dollars

In summary, the Singapore method moves from representations using images of familiar objects to schematic representations using rectangles. This method offers schemas for all types of problems (many more than those presented here are available on the Internet). We are not aware of any studies that have compared the effectiveness of using this type of schema with other types of schema, such as those used by Jitendra et al. (2007) for example. However, it seems to us that these rectangle representations have several advantages.

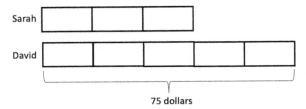

Figure 5.14 Schema for a ratio problem.

Firstly, they show the magnitude relationship between the numbers involved, with smaller numbers being represented by smaller rectangles than larger ones. Secondly, the representations more clearly evoke the type of arithmetic operation being involved (add, subtract, multiply, etc.). For example, for change type problems, the diagrams of Jitendra et al. (2007) start with a circle on the left representing the initial state, then an arrow moves up to a frame indicating addition or subtraction (marked by the plus or minus sign), and finally another arrow moves down from this frame to a circle on the right representing the final state (see Figure 5.6). In the Singapore method, on the other hand, a first rectangle represents the initial state. The change of type addition is represented by a new rectangle, which is juxtaposed to the first one, while the withdrawal is represented by a portion of the initial rectangle, which is hatched and therefore removed (see Figure 5.9). This representation of the addition and subtraction operations is therefore much more transparent.

5.5 From research to practice: assessing problem-solving skills and analysing the origin of difficulties

As we have seen throughout this chapter, problem solving generally includes solving a calculation but above all involves a mathematical modelling step in which sentences are transformed into a mathematical equation. Errors in problem solving can therefore arise from this mathematical modelling phase, or from the resolution of the calculation. Very often, the two components are confused in tests. It will therefore be left to the clinician, teacher, or math coach to make the distinction, for example, by comparing performance in the problem-solving task with that in a similar calculation-solving test. In the Tedi-Math (Van Niewenhoven, Grégoire & Noël, 2002), the problems used correspond to calculations presented in the arithmetic part of the test. The math coach can therefore easily compare the two performances. In the Tedimath Grands (Noël & Grégoire, 2015), for most of the problems posed, the child is simply asked to say the calculation that should be done to obtain the answer. It is only in more complex problems requiring more than one solving step that the calculations have to be performed. These two tests, Tedi-Math for the youngest pupils (first to third grades) and Tedimath Grands for the older pupils (from third grade), allow the evaluation of a large sample of different types of problems ranging from combination problems and comparison problems, to proportional problems, including irrelevant information or requiring the context to be taken into account in order to establish the final answer.

Similarly, in the Math Protest (Karagiannakis & Noël, 2020) a recent computerized battery, word problems are presented to the students, who are asked to specify the calculation they would do to solve them by typing on the computer screen calculator the way each problem should be solved (e.g., 28 + 17) and not the final solution. Furthermore, in order to reduce the possible impact of reading difficulties, the problems are one to three sentences long and they are both written on the computer screen and read aloud through the computer speaker. Eighteen problems are presented. Thirteen of these are addition-subtraction problems among which there are five compare, five change, two combine, and one equalize problems. The other five trials consist of multiplication-division problems.

A 'Problem Solving' subtest also exists in the KeyMath battery (Connolly, 2007).

In addition to measuring the child's abilities, it is also important to analyse the origin of any difficulties identified in problem solving. Indeed, solving a word problem requires many skills, and difficulties in any one of them could jeopardize the resolution of the problem. It is necessary for the child to be able to read and understand what he or she is reading and to have sufficient calculation skills. In the first case, speech therapists have specific assessment tools to detect difficulties or weaknesses in word decoding, vocabulary, or reading comprehension, although their tests do not usually include specific vocabulary related to the numerical domain. With regard to arithmetic skills, children should understand, at the level of addition and subtraction, the decomposition of numbers (e.g., 6 can be obtained by combining 4 and 2, or 1 and 5, etc.), the commutative principle of addition but not of subtraction, and the specific inverse relationship between addition and subtraction. Similarly, a clear understanding of multiplication and division is required for the other problems: the idea that numbers can be expressed as products (12 equals 3×4 or 2×6), that multiplication but not division is commutative, and that one is the inverse of the other. Finally, children should be able to solve a simple algebraic equation with the unknown in any position such as '$a + ? = c$' or '$? \times a = b$'. A review of all these concepts was included in the curriculum of Fuchs et al. (2009) and proved to be very beneficial for performance in calculation but also in problem solving. Checking these skills and, if necessary, working on them with the student should therefore be part of the preliminary or very early stages of the problem-solving intervention programme (see Chapter 4 on this topic).

If the child is able to produce the equation corresponding to the problem presented, it can be concluded that he or she is able to read, understand the problem, and pass the mathematical modelling stage. In this case, errors in problem solving should probably be attributed to the last step, i.e., the calculation or contextualization part of the answer. If, on the other hand, a child is

218 *Word problem solving*

able to solve a mathematical equation that corresponds to a verbal problem that he/she could not solve, this means that his/her difficulties lie in the reading, comprehension, or modelling stages (see Box 5.3).

BOX 5.3 Synthetic representation of the analysis of difficulties in word problem solving

- The child is able to write the calculation to solve the problem but gives an incorrect answer.
    - text comprehension is good
    - mathematical modelling is good
    - the difficulty lies in carrying out the calculations (see Chapter 4 on calculation) or possibly in contextualizing the answer
- The child is unable to write the calculation to solve the problem.
    - the child's difficulties concern the comprehension of the text and/or mathematical vocabulary => observe whether the same difficulties appear when you read the problem to the child; ask the child to tell you the story and mime it with materials, consult a speech therapist
    - and/or the child's difficulties concern mathematical modelling => see our proposals below

---

We will not consider reading problems here as they go beyond the purpose of this book, nor will we deal with problems of calculation as they have been discussed in the previous chapter. Our focus will be on how to help the student create the mathematical model of the problem, plan the different steps, and contextualize the answer.

5.6 From research to practice: helping the student to solve word problems

5.6.1 *Building a progression*

As in any intervention or teaching programme, it is important to follow a progression, starting with easy problems and gradually increasing the level of difficulty. So start with additive/subtractive problems before moving on to multiplicative problems and finish with proportional problems. In each of these categories, start with the one-step problems before moving on to the two- or multi-step problems. In each of these broad categories of problems, start with a specific problem of the simplest type, then another, then review both before introducing a third, and so on. For example, in the case of additive/subtractive problems, start with change type problems and finish with comparison type problems (see Box 5.4).

> **BOX 5.4 Suggested progression in the word problems worked on**
>
> **Additive/subtractive problems**
>
> A. Start with one step of resolution
>   - Change type
>
>   With unknown in the final state
>   With unknown in the transformation
>   With unknown in the initial state
>
>   - Combine type
>   - Equalize type
>   - Compare type
>
> B. Continue with two or more resolution steps
>
> **Multiplicative problems**
>
> A. Start one step of resolution
>   - Compute type
>   - Compare type
>   - Combine type
>   - Change type
>
> B. Continue with two or more resolution steps
>
> **Ratio or proportional problems**

Gradually introduce vocabulary specific to word problems and explain these concepts. Pay particular attention to keywords such as 'together' or 'in total' which usually refer to a combine problem, and 'more than/less than' which usually refer to compare problems. But also make sure to include problems that do not necessarily include these specific keywords and make it more difficult to identify the type of problem. For example, it is easier for students to recognize that the next problem is a combine problem (*'Paul has three cars. Jim has four cars. How many cars do they have in total?'*) than this one (*'Paul has three cars. Jim has four cars. How many cars do they have?'*), the solving performance being higher for the former.

Facilitate the transfer by using problems with very different stories and different modes of presentation (Fuchs et al., 2003a, see Box 5.2); this will make it easier to construct a more abstract schema. Explain the concept of transfer to students, discuss with them situations in which they have already used transfer, and draw their attention to the fact that new problems might in fact have a similar structure to already known problems and require the same solving procedure.

When dealing with more complex problems, such as two-step problems, help students to identify the outline of the main problem, based on the question posed in the problem, and then identify the secondary problem to be solved before solving the main problem.

Finally, you can also help students analyse charts, pictures, and other types of documents to find information relevant to solving the problems (Fuchs et al., 2009).

5.6.2 Supporting mathematical modelling

As noted at the beginning of this chapter, the mathematical modelling stage is usually the main challenge in solving word problems. The use of schemas has proven to be useful in helping children solve problems. Schemas were used by Jitendra et al. (2007) see Figure 5.6 and have been extensively developed in the Singapore method. To help children identify the type of problem, Jitendra et al. (2007) provide them with verbal clues. For example, in change type problems, an initial quantity increases or decreases due to direct or implicit action. When the action of change involves an increase, the final quantity is the largest number or the total; when the action of change involves a decrease, the initial quantity is the largest number or the total.

You can work on simple situations with no unknowns first; ask the child to explain the problem in their own words, use objects (tokens or other) to represent the problem, then draw pictures to represent the problem, and finally use schemas to represent the problem. Ideally, these schemas should be based on the representations created by the child and allow him or her to develop a more general model, independent of the surface characteristics of the problem (the type of objects exchanged, the context of the story (shop, marbles, etc.)). It is important for the math coach to be comfortable with different types of methods to guide the mathematical modelling of the pupils so that s/he can choose the one that is most appropriate for each child. For example, the use of rectangles, as in the Singapore method, is probably suitable for children with good visual-spatial skills, but perhaps less so for those with difficulties at this level. In the latter case, modelling using specific verbal labels such as those used by Fuchs et al. (2009) may be more appropriate (see Box 5.1). Finally, be aware of the possible confusion that can occur in the child's mind if the method you teach is very different from the one used in the classroom. It is therefore important to ask if the teacher is using a specific method and then either help the child to use that method if it suits him or her, or suggest another method that suits him or her better and then explain your practice to the teacher to ensure that the pupil will be allowed to use this new method in class. When more than one type of problem has been presented, you can use classification games in which you read a problem and ask the child to put it in the appropriate box for this type of problem (as in Fuchs et al., 2009).

5.6.3 Proposing a heuristic

As solving word problems requires different steps, it is important to introduce some heuristic to the child to guide his/her process. Fuchs et al. (2009) and Jitendra et al. (2007) have proposed guides in this respect. As you can see in Table 5.1, the steps proposed by these authors are very similar, except that Jitendra et al. do not specify the step of 'underlying the question'.

Table 5.1 Comparison of the heuristics proposed by Fuchs et al. (2009) and Jitendra et al. (2007)

Fuchs, Powell, Seethaler et al. (2009)	Jitendra et al. (2007)
(1) Read and understand the problem	(1) Read and understand the problem
(2) Underline the question	
(3) Name the problem type	(2) Find the problem type
(4) Identify the important information and label it	(3) Organize the information using the diagram/schema
(5) Solve the equation	(4) Solve the problem
(6) Check the answer and its plausibility	(5) Look back at the problem and check to see whether the answer makes sense

The first step, of course, is to read the problem and understand what is being described. It is important to accompany the student by giving him or her the opportunity to ask questions about possible words he or she may not understand and then ask the student to describe what is stated in the problem. Next, the question should be highlighted. It is from the identification of the question that the problem can be reread to identify the relevant information, i.e., the arithmetic quantities associated with the name of the object to which they relate and key words in the mathematical domain (plus, minus, profit, loss, three times, etc.). On the basis of the question and the identification of the relevant information, the pupil will be able to draw a schema representing the situation, incorporate the numerical data available to him/her, and then mark the unknown in the form of a question mark, for example. On the basis of this schema, the pupil is then asked to write the calculation or equation that will enable the problem to be solved, and then to solve it. Once the answer has been obtained, a final check is necessary. At that final stage, the pupil interprets the mathematical solution obtained by verifying that it is correct in terms of calculation but also that it is valid, i.e., that it makes sense in relation to the initial data (for example, more or less than something) and that it is plausible, especially in relation to the reality of the original situation of the problem (cf. contextualization, for more see Heylock and Manning, 2014).

In line with this view, Karagiannakis (2015) proposed the COSMOS heuristic that includes six steps: circle, organize, sketch, mind-guess, operate, and scan (see Figure 5.15). These six steps are described here.

Circle: after having read the problem and the question, the student is required to circle the important information of the problem. Important information

222 *Word problem solving*

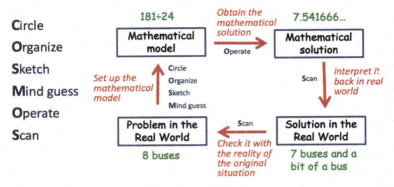

Figure 5.15 The COSMOS heuristic (Karagiannakis, 2015) along with a contextualization framework for word problems (Heylock & Manning, 2014).

includes the arithmetical quantities associated with the name of the object to which they refer and mathematical keywords (more, less, profit, loss, three times, …) which are crucial to understanding the problem. Having the question in mind will also help students to distinguish the relevant from the irrelevant information of the problem.

Organize: the student is required to separate the knowns from the unknowns. This can be achieved by underlining/highlighting the phrase/s that indicate the unknown. He/she has already circled the facts/knowns in the previous stage. The aim of this stage is to determine the unknowns (one or more) of the problem.

Sketch: the student is required to visualize the problem by drawing an image (sketch, diagram, or table), in relation to the type of the problem, in which the information that he/she has circled and underlined at the two previous stages is conveyed. The sketches can be rectangular frames such as in the Singapore method or diagrams or any type of schema.

Mind-guess: according to the image drawn, the student is required to invent a mathematical model that will include the appropriate operations in order to find the mathematical solution. This stage offers also a good opportunity (if possible) for an approximate estimation of the solution (for example, more or less than something). This will be a first and quick check of the validity of the final answer.

Operate: the student is required to execute the arithmetic operations included in his/her mathematical model.

Scan: the student checks the validity of the result, even comparing with the approximate estimation that he/she had done at the mind-guess step or/ and by judging if the result makes sense, reflecting on his/her drawn image.

5.6.4 Concrete examples

In this last section, we propose an example for each type of problem. In particular, we will present examples for additive/subtractive problems of different types (change, combine, compare, equalize), multiplication/division problems, ratio or proportional problems, and percentage problems. Each example is accompanied by two types of schematizations (schemas or the rectangles of the Singapore method) and sometimes model labels (equations with letters, Fuchs et al., 2009). This should enable the math coach to select or create the help that best suits the student he or she is coaching.

To the left of each problem, a vertical banner presents the key words that refer to the heuristic proposed to the pupil (see Figure 5.15). In this section, we will illustrate the use of the COSMOS heuristic (read the problem, identify the question and circle important information, sketch the problem, write the arithmetical operation, find the solution, and see whether this makes sense).

All this material aims to inspire the math coach and give him/her a basis for the creation of his/her rehabilitation material. The main thing is to propose a coherent progression to the student and to be vigilant in choosing the most appropriate help tools considering his/her specific profile.

5.6.4.1 Addition and subtraction word problems

5.6.4.1.1 CHANGE PROBLEMS

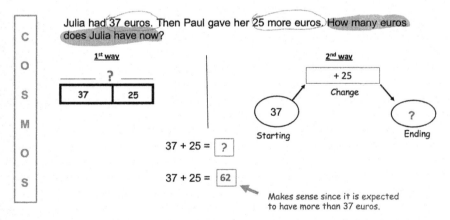

Figure 5.16 Example of an addition change problem where the unknwon concerns the **ending amount** ($St + C = ?$, with St being the starting amount and C the changed amount).

224 *Word problem solving*

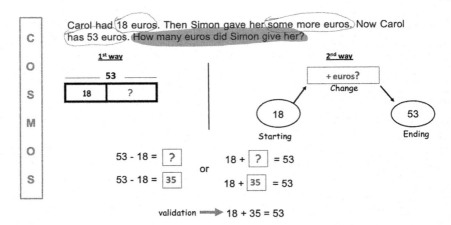

Figure 5.17 Example of an addition change problem where the unknwon concerns the **transformation** ($St + ? = E$, with St being the starting amount and E the ending amount).

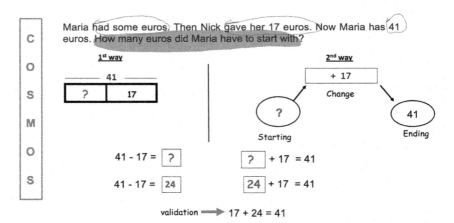

Figure 5.18 Example of an addition change problem where the unknwon concerns the **initial state** ($? + C = E$, with C the changed amount and E the ending amount).

Word problem solving 225

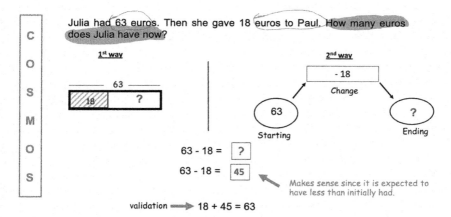

Figure 5.19 Example of a subtraction change problem where the unknwon concerns the **ending** ($St - C = ?$, with St the starting amount and C the change).

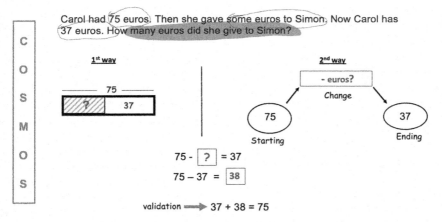

Figure 5.20 Example of a subtraction change problem where the unknwon concerns the **transformation** ($St - ? = E$, with St being the starting amount and E the ending amount).

226 Word problem solving

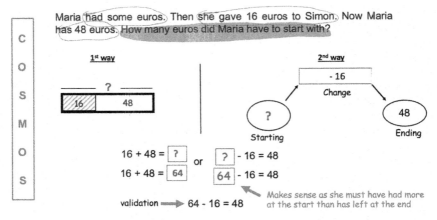

Figure 5.21 Example of a subtraction change problem where the unknwon concerns the **starting state** (? − C = E, with being C the changed amount and E the final amount).

5.6.4.1.2 COMBINE PROBLEMS

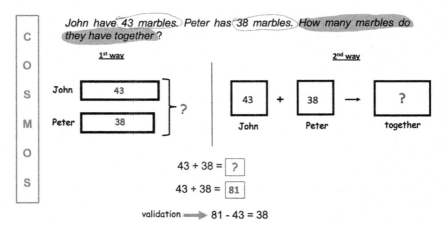

Figure 5.22 Example of a combine problem where the unknwon concerns the **total** ($P_1 + P_2 = ?$, with P_1 and P_2 being the parts).

Word problem solving 227

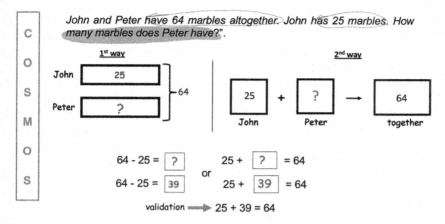

Figure 5.23 Example of a combine problem where the unknwon concerns the **subset** ($P_1 + ? = T$, with P_1 for the part and T the total).

5.6.4.1.3 EQUALIZE PROBLEMS

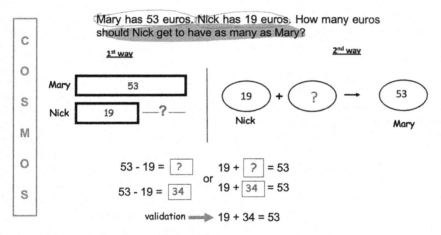

Figure 5.24 Example of an equalize problem.

5.6.4.1.4 COMPARE PROBLEMS

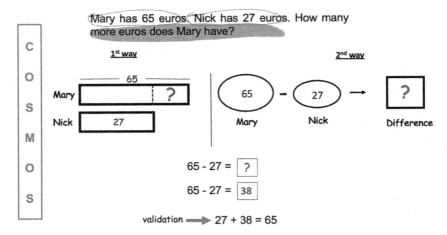

Figure 5.25 Example of a compare problem where the unknwon concerns the **difference** ($B - s = ?$, with B being the bigger amount, and s the smaller).

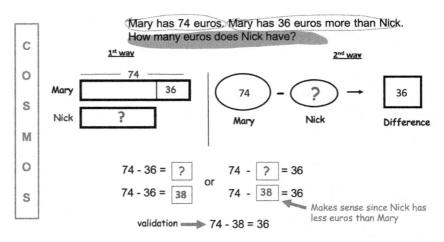

Figure 5.26 Example of a compare problem where the unknwon concerns the **smaller amount** ($B - ? = D$, with B being the bigger amount, and D, the difference).

Word problem solving 229

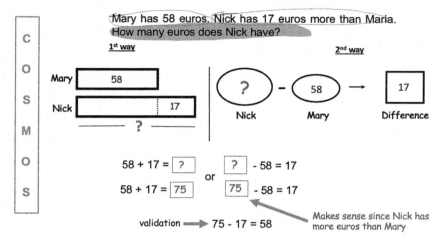

Figure 5.27 Example of a compare problem where the unknwon concerns the **bigger amount** (? − s = D, with s being the smaller amount and D, the difference).

5.6.4.2 Multiplication and division word problems

5.6.4.2.1 MULTIPLICATION COMPUTE PROBLEMS

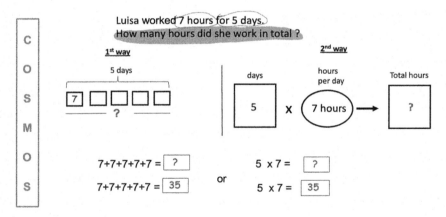

Figure 5.28 Example of a compute multiplication problem.

230 Word problem solving

5.6.4.2.2 MULTIPLICATION COMPARE PROBLEMS

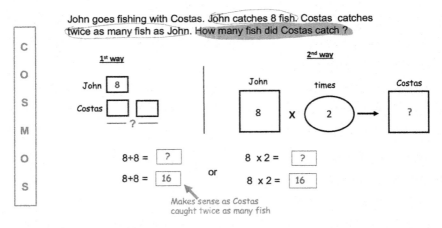

Figure 5.29 Example of a compare multiplication problem.

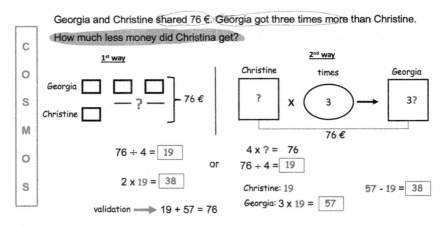

Figure 5.30 Example of a compare multiplication problem.

5.6.4.3 Proportional problems

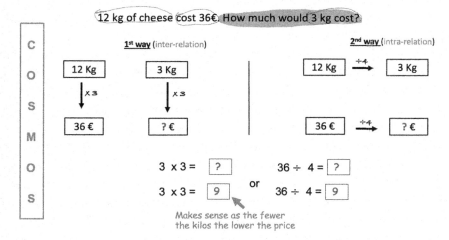

Figure 5.31 Example of a proportional problem solved by using the ratio between elements either of different types (inter-relation): kg/€ (first way) or of the same types (intra-relation) kg/kg (second way).

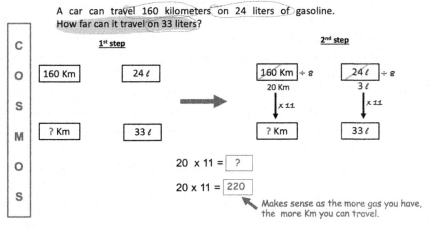

Figure 5.32 Example of a proportional problem involving ratios that do not initially constitute a multiple or a factor of the other. After simplifying the inter-relation ratio (km/L) it is solved by using the ratio of the same types (km/km).

232 Word problem solving

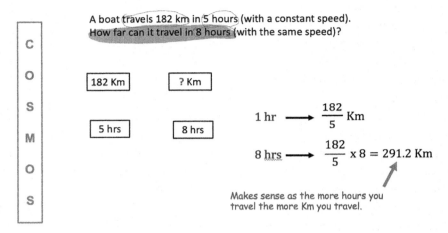

Figure 5.33 Example of a proportional problem involving ratios that do not constitute a multiple or a factor of the other, solved using an equation.

5.6.4.4 Problems of percentages

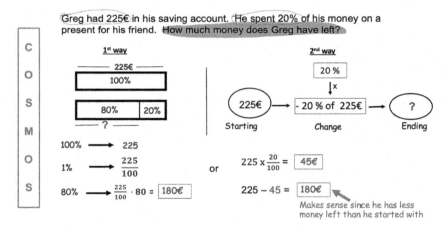

Figure 5.34 Example of an increase percentage problem.

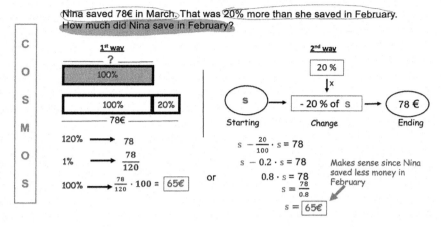

Figure 5.35 Example of a decrease percentage problem.

References

Carpenter, T. P., Kepner, H., Corbitt, M. k., Lindquist, M. M., & Reys, R. E. (1980). Solving verbal problems: Results and implications from national assessment. *Arithmetic Teacher, 28,* 10–12, 44–47.

Carpenter, T. P., Lindquist, M. M., Matthews, W., & Silver, E. A. (1983). Results of the third NAEP mathematics assessment: Secondary school. *Mathematics Teacher, 76*(9), 652–659.

Carpenter, T. P., & Moser, J. M. (1983). The acquisition of addition and subtraction concepts. In R. Lesh & M. Landau (Eds.), *Acquisition of mathematical concepts and processes* (pp. 7–44). New York: Academic Press.

Connolly, A. J. (2007). *KeyMath-3 diagnostic assessment: Manual forms A and B.* Minneapolis, MN: Pearson.

Cummins, D., Kintsch, W., Reusser, K., & Weimer, R. (1988). The role of understanding in solving word problems. *Cognitive Psychology, 20*(4), 405–438.

De Corte, E., & Verschaffel, L. (1985). Beginning first graders' initial representation of arithmetic word problems. *Journal of Mathematical Behavior, 4,* 3–21.

Fagnant, A. (2005). Résoudre et symboliser des problèmes additifs et soustractifs en début d'enseignement primaire. In M. Crahay, L. Verschaffel, E. de Corte & J. Grégoire (Eds.), *Enseignement et apprentissage des mathématiques: Que disent les recherches psychopédagogiques?* De Boeck: Bruxelles.

Fayol, M., Thevenot, C., &, Devidal, M. (2005). La résolution de problèmes. In M.-P. Noël (Ed.), *La dyscalculie, trouble du développement numérique de l'enfant.* Marseille: Solal.

Fuchs, L. S., & Fuchs, D. (2002). Mathematical problem-solving profiles of students with mathematics disabilities with and without comorbid reading disabilities. *Journal of Learning Disabilities, 35*(6), 564–574.

Fuchs, L. S., Fuchs, D., Prentice, K., Burch, M., Hamlett, C. L., Owen, R., ... Jancek, D. (2003a). Explicitly teaching for transfer: Effects in third-grade students' mathematical problem solving. *Journal of Educational Psychology, 95*(2), 293–305.

Fuchs, L. S., Fuchs, D., Prentice, K., Burch, M., Hamlett, C. L., Owen, R., & Schroeter, K. (2003b). Enhancing third-grade students' mathematical problem solving with self-regulated learning strategies. *Journal of Educational Psychology, 95*(2), 306–315.

Fuchs, L. S., Powell, S. R., Seethaler, P. M., Cirino, P. T., Fletcher, J. M., Fuchs, D., ... Zumeta, R. O. (2009). Remediating number combination and word problem deficits among students with mathematics difficulties: A randomized control trial. *Journal of Educational Psychology, 101*(3), 561–576.

Fuson, K. C., & Abrahamson, D. (2005). Understanding ratio and proportion as an example of the apprehending zone and conceptual-phase problem-solving models. In J. I. D. Campbell (Ed.), *Handbook of mathematical cognition* (pp. 213–234). New York: Psychology Press.

Gick, M. L., & Holyoack, K. J. (1980). Analogical problem solving. *Cognitive Psychologist, 12*(3), 306–355.

Hardiman, P. T., & Mestre, J. P. (1989). Understanding multiplicative contexts involving fractions. *Journal of Educational Psychology, 81*(4), 547–557.

Hart, K. M. (1994). *Ratios: Children's strategies and errors*. Windsor, UK: The NFER-Nelson Publishing Company.

Haylock, D., & Manning, R. (2014). *Student workbook for mathematics explained for primary teachers*. London: SAGE Publications Ltd.

Jiménez, J. E., & Garcia, A. I. (1999). Is IQ-achievement discrepancy relevant in the definition of arithmetic learning disabilities? *Learning Disability Quarterly, 22*(4), 291–301.

Jitendra, A. K., Griffin, C. C., Haria, P., Leh, J., Adams, A., & Kaduvettoor, A. (2007). A comparison of single and multiple strategy instruction on third-grade student's mathematical problem solving. *Journal of Educational Psychology, 99*(1), 115–127.

Jordan, N. C., & Hanich, L. B. (2000). Mathematical thinking in second-grade children with different forms of LD. *Journal of Learning Disabilities, 33*(6), 567–578.

Jordan, N. C., & Oettinger, T. (1997). Cognitive arithmetic and problem solving: A comparison of children with specific and general mathematics difficulties. *Journal of Learning Disabilities, 30*(6), 624–634.

Kail, R., & Hall, L. K. (1999). Sources of developmental change in children's word problem performance. *Journal of Educational Psychology, 91*(4), 660–668.

Karagiannakis, G. (2015). *Οι αριθμοί πέρα απ' τους κανόνες. Αθήνα: Διερευνητική μάθηση*.

Karagiannakis, G., & Noël, M.-P. (2020). Mathematical profile test: A preliminary evaluation of an online assessment for mathematics skills of children in grades 1–6. *Behavioral Sciences, 10*, 126.

Lamon, S. (1994). Ratio and proportion: Cognitive foundations in unitizing and norming. In G. Harel & J. Confrey (Eds.), *The development of multiplicative reasoning in the learning of mathematics* (pp. 89–119). Albany, NY: State University on New York Press.

Lewis, A., & Mayer, R. E. (1987). Students' miscomprehension of relational statements in arithmetic word problems. *Journal of Educational Psychology, 79*(4), 363–371.

Mayer, R. E., & Hegarty, M. (1996). The process of understanding mathematical problems. In R. S. sternberg & T. Ben Zee (Eds.), *The nature of mathematical thinking*. Mahwah, NJ: Lawrence Erlbaum Associates.

Ng, S. F., & Lee, K. (2009). The model method: Singapore children's tool for representing and solving algebraic word problems. *Journal for Research in Mathematics Education, 40*(3), 282–313.

Noël, M.-P., & Grégoire, J. (2015). *TediMath Grands, Test diagnostique des compétences de base en mathématiques du CE2 à la 5ᵉ*. Pearson France – ECPA, Montreuil.

Novick, L. R. (1988). Analogical transfer, problem similarity, and expertise. *Journal of Experimental Psychology: Learning, Memory and Cognition, 14*(3), 510–520.

Passolunghi, M. C., & Siegel, L. S. (2001). Short-term memory, working memory, and inhibitory control in children with difficulties in arithmetic problem solving. *Journal of Experimental Child Psychology, 80*(1), 44–57.

Riley, M. S., Greeno, J. G., & Heller, J. I. (1983). Development of children's problem solving hability in arithmetic. In H. P. Ginsburg (Ed.), *The development of mathematical thinking*. New York: Academic Press.

Russell, R. L., & Ginsburg, H. P. (1984). Cognitive analysis of children's mathematical difficulties. *Cognition and Instruction, 1*(2), 217–244.

Swanson, H. L. (1994). Short-term memory and working memory: Do both contribute to our understanding of academic achievement in children and adults with learning disabilities? *Journal of Learning Disabilities, 27*(1), 34–50.

Swanson, H. L., Cooney, J. B., & Brock, S. (1993). The influence of working memory and classification ability on children's word problem solution. *Journal of Experimental Child Psychology, 55*(3), 374–395.

Thevenot, C., Devidal, M., Barrouillet, P., & Fayol, M. (2007). Why does placing the question before an arithmetic word problem improve performance? A situation model account. *Quarterly Journal of Experimental Psychology, 60*(1), 43–56.

Van Niewenhoven, C., Grégoire, J. & Noël, M. P. (2002). *Tedi-math: test diagnostique des compétences de base en mathématiques.* Paris, France: ECPA.

Verschaffel, L., & De Corte, E. (2005). La modélisation et la résolution des problèmes d'application: De l'analyse à l'utilisation efficace. In M. Crahay, L. Verschaffel, E. de Corte & J. Grégoire (Eds.), *Enseignement et apprentissage des mathématiques: Que disent les recherches psychopédagogiques?* De Boeck: Bruxelles.

6 Rational numbers

A rational number is the quotient of two integers. Rational numbers are presented in three different notations: fractions (1/4), decimal numbers (0.25), and percentages (25%). During the last years of the primary school cycle (around fourth or fifth grade), the child is introduced to rational numbers. Mastering these rational numbers is important for school success already in primary schools, but also beyond. Thus, the knowledge of fractions is essential for more advanced mathematical achievement such as algebra, but is also a predictor of the ability to participate in the labour force in the United States (Geary, Hoard, Nugent & Bailey, 2012; Siegler & Pyke, 2013). Indeed, it has been observed that poor mastery of rational numbers prevents access to many middle- and high-income jobs (McCloskey, 2007). However, this learning is a problem for many students, including those in middle school or high school, mainly because they do not understand the meaning of these rational numbers.

6.1 Learning rational numbers: a challenge!

Learning rational numbers is a real challenge for children. According to a study carried out by the French Community of Belgium (1996, unpublished), major difficulties persist in this learning among students in seventh or eighth grades (around the age of 13). For example, about 1 out of 4 students is unable to find a number between 2 decimal numbers (e.g., between 72.4 and 72.5), and half of them are unable to calculate a percentage (e.g., 21% of 6,200). Similarly, among a large sample of college students in the United States, only 33% correctly identified the largest of four fractions (Stigler, Givin & Thompson, 2010). One of the main reasons for this challenge is that children are facing a real conceptual shift, and the mistakes they make reveal misconceptions about rational numbers. Indeed, in many cases, the errors can be explained by the fact that students tend to view fractions and decimals as whole numbers and to apply to them the rules previously used on natural numbers. The interference of prior knowledge when learning rational numbers seems to be one of the main sources of difficulties and has been identified in the literature as the *natural number bias* (Ni & Zhou, 2005). Indeed, many conceptions that children have

DOI: 10.4324/b22795-6

constructed on the basis of their natural number learning are questioned when learning rational numbers (Siegler & Lortie-Forgues, 2017).

A first difference between natural numbers and rational numbers lies in the notion of order. Natural numbers are classified according to the counting sequence (1, 2, 3, etc.) and each number has a well-defined predecessor and successor. This happens simply because integers have a well-defined unit of measurement, which is '1'. In contrast, an infinite number of units of measurement are used for rational numbers. In the case of fractions, this number of units is determined by the denominator (1/2, 1/3, 1/4, etc.). No rational number directly follows or precedes another, and no counting sequence is naturally imposed. Rational numbers are ordered continuously, unlike natural numbers, which are discrete. If counting is one of the bases for understanding the meaning of whole numbers, it cannot be of any help in understanding rational numbers. Where 'one' is the smallest natural number, it proves impossible to determine a single smaller rational number. Children are thus led to understand that there is an infinite number of rational numbers that can be interspersed between two rationals, which refers to the notion of density. Children, high school students, and even many adults have a poor understanding of this concept. For example, Tirosh, Fischbein, Graeber, and Wilson (1999) found that only 40% of school teachers knew that there was an infinite number of numbers between 0.23 and 0.24 and only 24% of them knew that there was an infinite number of numbers between 1/5 and 1/4.

Second, while each integer is represented by a unique string of symbols in the Arabic code (e.g., 'fifteen' is written as '15'), a numerical value can be written in different ways when considering a decimal number (0.15 = 0.50 = 0.150000, etc.) or a fraction (1/2 = 2/4 = 4/8 = 100/200, etc.). In addition, children need to understand that decimal numbers and fractions are alternative notations representing the same quantities (1/4 = 0.25). Hiebert and Wearne (1983) examined the ability of children (fifth, seventh, and ninth grades, i.e., 10, 12, and 14 years old) to translate fractions into decimal numbers or the reverse. For proper fractions (i.e., less than 1) with 10 or 100 as the denominator (e.g., 3/10), children in fifth grade had a rate of correct responses between 19% and 31% when writing the corresponding decimal numbers, whereas in the reverse translation, the percentage of correct responses did not exceed 10% for decimal numbers with one or two digits in the decimal part. About a quarter of these students kept the same digits, but changed the writing format (e.g., 0.37 = 3/7; 4/10 = 4.10). The accuracy of these translations increased for the higher grades with 70% correct answers for seventh graders and 85% correct answers for ninth graders. According to the 2004 National Assessment of Educational Progress in the United States, only 29% of 11th-grade students (about 16 years old) correctly translated 0.029 into 29/1000 (Kloosterman, 2010).

Third, unlike natural numbers, the size of a fraction does not automatically increase with the size of its components. Thus, although 7 is larger than 4, a fraction containing a 7 may be larger or smaller than a fraction containing a 4 (e.g., 4/8 < 7/8 but 8/4 > 8/7), and while the sequence 2, 3, 4, 5, etc., increases, the sequence 1/2, 1/3, 1/4, 1/5, etc., decreases. Similarly, in the case of decimal numbers, the longest number (in number of digits) does not necessarily correspond to the largest number (e.g., 0.500 is longer but not numerically larger than 0.5, and 0.123 is longer but numerically smaller than 0.3).

In summary, learning rational numbers poses major challenges because children, and even adults, continue to be influenced by their conception of natural numbers when dealing with rational numbers. This natural number bias is at play when processing fractions or decimal numbers, and this influence can be seen particularly in magnitude comparison tasks and in arithmetic. For example, if multiplying a natural number by another natural number (greater than 1) makes it systematically larger and dividing it by another natural number makes it smaller, this is not the case for rational numbers. Thus, multiplying a number by 1/4 decreases its magnitude but multiplying it by 8/7 increases it.

In the next section, we will look in more detail at the type of difficulties that children experience in numerical magnitude comparison tasks and calculation tasks with rational numbers.

6.1.1 Difficulties in comparing decimal numbers

For the comparison of decimal numbers, more than half of the errors produced by children in fourth grade correspond to errors related to the natural number bias, leading them, for example, to estimate that 0.345 is greater than 0.67 because 345 > 67 (Rittle-Johnson, Siegler & Alibani, 2001) or that 0.1814 is greater than 0.385 because 1814 > 385 (Hierbert & Wearne, 1986). Sackur-Grisvard and Leonard (1985) asked children in fourth to seventh grades (approximately 9 to 12 years old) to order 3 decimal numbers and showed that the errors were due to their use of two implicit but incorrect rules.

- The first is to select as the smallest number the one whose decimal part corresponds to the smallest whole number (e.g., 12.4 < 12.17 because 4 < 17). According to Resnick et al. (1989), this first 'incorrect rule' corresponds to an erroneous conception based on natural numbers, which is why it is sometimes referred to as the 'integer rule' (Tian & Siegler, 2018). A child using this rule would rightly consider 3.2 to be less than 3.47 but would wrongly consider 5.8 to be less than 5.63.
- The second is to select as the smallest number the one with the most digits in the decimal part. This second 'incorrect rule' comes from learning fractions with the idea that a tenth is greater than a hundredth and a hundredth is greater than a thousandth, etc. A student using this rule would correctly say that 5.63 is less than 5.8 but would incorrectly consider 3.47 to be less than 3.2 (Resnick et al., 1989).

Desmet, Grégoire, and Mussolin (2010) studied the comparison of decimal numbers among children in third to sixth grades (approximately 8 to 11 years old). They observed that children's decisions were based both on the value of the digits in the decimal part of the number and on the length of the number. In third and fourth grades, children tend to believe that the longest number is also the one with the greatest magnitude. This bias is reversed in fifth grade (which could correspond to an overcorrection of the bias) and finally disappears in sixth grade. The influence of the value of numbers in the decimal part is even more important. For third- and fourth-grade children, when the largest value does not correspond to the largest number, the percentage of correct answers is only 20% (e.g., 0.09 vs. 0.2: the value '9' is larger than the value '2' and yet 0.2 is the largest number). These authors also underline the role of zeros in the decimal parts. They distinguish between positional zeros (0.01) and leading zeros at the end of the number (0.10). The positional zero is not taken into account by third- or fourth-grade children who consider either that it plays no role (which leads them to consider that 0.1 and 0.01 are of equal magnitude), or that it contributes to the length of the decimal part; they therefore consider that the longer number is the greater in terms of magnitude. In both cases, the positional value is not taken into account. From fifth grade onwards, most children are able to understand the role of a zero placed just after the decimal point.

With regard to the zeros at the end, most pupils in third and fourth grades consider that they increase the size of the number (they therefore consider 0.20 to be greater than 0.2). The percentage of correct answers is significantly higher in fifth grade, although not all pupils still admit that a zero at the end of a decimal number actually plays no role. This type of zero no longer causes errors from sixth grade onwards.

6.1.2 Difficulties in the comparison of fractions

Difficulties related to the natural number bias are also observed in the processing of fractional numbers. At the beginning of learning, the elements constituting a fraction are often considered as two independent natural numbers (English & Halford, 1995). From this perspective, the larger fraction is the one composed of the larger numbers (for example, 3/8 is considered larger than 1/2 because 3 and 8 are larger than 1 and 2), while the magnitude of a fraction requires taking into account the relationship between the numerator and the denominator.

On the basis of the performance of 200 students aged 10 to 16 who had to compare the magnitude of fractions and justify their answers, Stafylidou and Vasniadou (2004) distinguished between three representations of the fraction:

- The first one stems directly from the initial theory that the child develops on the basis of natural numbers and considers the fraction as two independent natural numbers (as already reported by English & Halford, 1995).
- The second considers fractions as parts of a whole, taking into account the relationship between the numerator and the denominator. In this order

of ideas, the fraction expresses one or more parts of the same object (two or five parts of a pie chart) or a subset of a group of objects (two pizzas out of five); the numerator corresponds to the number of parts or objects taken and the denominator to the number of parts of the unit or set of objects. This representation comes mainly from all the exercises practised at school in which a portion of a shape (of a pie, for example) or a subset of objects in a collection is coloured. At this level, some children consider that a fraction is always less than one, but some students nonetheless develop techniques to deal with fractions greater than one. This representation can already be encountered at the preschool age (Mix, Levine & Huttenlocher, 1999).

- In the third representation, students are able to understand the relationship between the numerator and the denominator; they know that fractions can be smaller than, equal to, or even larger than the unit, depending on whether the numerator is smaller, larger, or equal to the denominator. They have reached the conception of 'fraction as a measure' and consider that the fraction refers to a number. At this level, some children have also acquired the notion of density (i.e., the number of fractions is infinite and it is impossible to determine the smallest or the largest fraction), while others have not yet mastered these notions. This representation of fraction as a measure is less intuitive than previous ones and depends much more on formal instructions explaining the conventions of symbolic notation of fractions. The development of this interpretation of fractions as a measure is considered an essential mechanism in the knowledge of fractions (Geary et al., 2008).

In adults, the comparison of fractions has been the subject of several studies. Research has attempted to determine whether participants base their decision on the overall magnitude of the whole fraction or, on the contrary, on the magnitude of the components of the fractions. Considering this question, they calculated whether the comparison times varied with the distance between the magnitude of the two fractions (for example, for the pair of fractions 2/5 and 7/8, the distance is equal to the absolute value of (2/5 − 7/8), i.e., 0.475) or with the distance between the numbers making up the fractions (the distance between the numerators (5) or between the denominators (3)). Bonato, Fabbri, Umiltà, and Zorzi (2007) conducted the first research of this type. These authors asked participants to compare fractions with numerators equal to 1 (1/1, 1/2, 1/3, 1/4, etc.) with the fraction 1/5. They found that the response time did not vary with the distance between the magnitude of the whole fractions but with the distance between the components of the fraction. They concluded that these results showed a more analytical than global approach to the fraction. However, other research has also shown that adults were able to base their judgement on the global magnitude of fractions. In particular, when, in the same experiment, pairs of fractions with the same denominator (e.g., 3/8 and 7/8) are used together with pairs of fractions with the same numerators (e.g., 2/7 and 2/3), adults base their judgement on the magnitude of the numerator in the first type of pair and on the magnitude of whole fractions in the second. Similarly, when they have to compare fractions without common components (e.g., 3/5 and 2/9), they also base their judgements on the magnitude of the whole fraction (Meert, Grégoire & Noël, 2010).

Meert, Grégoire, Seron, and Noël (2012) developed another task and showed that it favours the processing of the magnitude of the fraction as a whole. They asked participants to fill a virtual glass with the same proportion as that expressed by a symbolic fraction (e.g., 2/5) or by a non-symbolic ratio of orange dots among a set of dots (e.g., two orange dots in a collection of five dots). Participants proved to be able to perform this type of task since the glass filling increased with the magnitude of the ratio presented. Furthermore, adults' estimates were actually more accurate with fractions than with non-symbolic ratios (sets of dots). Finally, the estimates produced by the participants in this task were an excellent predictor of the time needed to compare fractions, suggesting that the same representation is used in both tasks.

Meert, Grégoire, Seron, and Noël (2013) also used the same task of filling a virtual glass with children and found that, by the age of 11, children were also more accurate with symbolic ratios than with non-symbolic ones.

A very similar task, the positioning of a fraction on a number line, was used by Siegler, Thompson, and Schneider (2011) with children aged 11 and 13. They used both ungraded lines with ends marked 0 on the left and 1 on the right to position proper fractions (such as 1/19, 1/7, 1/4, 3/8, etc.) and lines marked 0 on the left and 5 on the right, to position both proper (1/19, 4/7) and improper (7/5, 13/9, 8/3, etc.) fractions. The authors found that the children were more accurate with lines 0–1 than with lines 0–5 and that the accuracy of the estimates correlated significantly with the children's accuracy in comparing and calculating with fractions, as well as with their overall performance on a mathematical test. Based on these results, they concluded that, despite all the differences between natural numbers and fractions, in both cases it is essential to understand their numerical magnitude and to be able to place them on a number line.

Similarly, Bailey, Siegler, and Geary (2014) also showed that knowledge of the numerical magnitude of whole numbers measured at age 6 was a significant predictor of understanding of the magnitude of fractions at age 13, even after controlling for the influence of intelligence, working memory skills, and the socio-economic level of students. Jordan, Resnick, Rodrigues, Hansen, and Dyson (2017) followed children in third to sixth grades (approximately 8 to 11 years old) and found that the ability to place whole numbers on a number line in third grade was the best predictor of their subsequent knowledge of fractions. These results support the idea that an understanding of the magnitude of whole numbers is an essential basis for understanding other types of numbers, such as fractional numbers.

6.1.3 Which is the greater challenge: fractional or decimal numbers?

Some may find it more difficult to deal with fractional numbers than decimals because the meaning of the fraction is not based on the base-10 positional system and an infinite number of different fractions denote the same magnitude (e.g., 1/2, 2/4, 8/16, etc.). A few studies have compared the processing of the two types of rational numbers (see Tian & Siegler, 2018, for a review).

Using a number line marked 0 and 1 at the ends, Iuculano and Butterworth (2011) tested sixth-grade students (about 11 years old) and adults and asked them to position decimal numbers and fractions. They found that the positioning of decimals was more accurate than that of fractions and that the numerical estimates of children and adults indicated a linear relationship for decimals but not for fractions. Wang and Siegler (2013) also found greater accuracy in positioning decimal numbers on a number line than fractions in fourth and fifth grades (nine to ten years old). However, DeWolf, Bassok, and Holyoak (2015) found that in seventh grade (about 11 years old), the accuracy of positioning fractional numbers on a number line was identical to that of decimal numbers.

With the magnitude comparison task, Ganor-Stern (2013) also obtained results suggesting better mastery of decimal numbers than fractions. Similarly, Wang and Siegler (2013) found better performance among fourth and fifth graders (nine to ten years old) in comparing decimal numbers than fractions. Finally, among university students, Hurst and Cordes (2016) found that they were faster when comparing pairs of decimal numbers than pairs consisting of a decimal number and a fraction, and were slowest when comparing two fractions.

A majority of these studies therefore show better performance when dealing with decimal numbers rather than fractions. However, according to Tian and Siegler (2018), in almost all comparison experiments in which an advantage for decimal numbers was found, these were tasks in which the pairs consisted of numbers with the same number of digits in the decimal part. This may explain the advantage of decimal number comparisons, as it is well known that this comparison is easier when items have the same number of digits after the decimal point (Desmet et al., 2010). Similarly, in number line tasks, experiments where an advantage for decimal numbers was present all used decimal numbers with two digits after the decimal point (Iuculano & Butterworth 2011, Wang & Siegler 2013), whereas in the task using decimal numbers with varying lengths, the accuracy was identical for decimal numbers and fractions (DeWolf et al., 2015). In conclusion, it is not obvious that the processing of decimal numbers is really easier than that of fractions.

6.1.4 The challenge of arithmetic with decimal numbers

In calculations with decimal numbers, if the two addends have the same number of digits after the decimal point, addition and subtraction are quite similar to those with natural numbers (e.g., 1.42 + 5.23). Cases where the numbers of decimal digits differ are more challenging and lead to errors such as 0.42 + 0.5 = 0.47. Hiebert and Wearne (1985) found that only 48% of seventh graders correctly answered 0.86 − 0.3, whereas 84% correctly answered 0.60 − 0.36. When there are different numbers of digits in the decimal parts, incorrect alignment of the decimal operands is the most frequent source of errors (Hiebert & Wearne, 1985). Children indeed tend to align the rightmost digit of decimals, which is correct in whole number arithmetic and when adding or subtracting decimals with equal numbers of digits to the right of the decimal point, but such alignment is incorrect in decimal addition or subtraction with unequal numbers of digits to the right of the decimal point. For example, when adding 6 and 0.32, 43% of fifth graders answered 0.38 (Hiebert and Wearne, 1985).

On multiplication and division, sixth through ninth graders are able to correctly handle the calculation algorithm but then do not adjust the position of the decimal point. This accounted for 73% of middle school students' decimal multiplication errors (Lortie-Forgues & Siegler, 2017). According to Hiebert and Wearne (1985), 76% of sixth graders' multiplication answers could be accounted for by an incorrect generalization from addition to multiplication of the procedure for placing the decimal point. Indeed, if '0.3 + 0.6 = 0.9', '0.3 × 0.6' does not equal 1.8 (see Siegler & Lortie-Forgues, 2017).

6.1.5 The challenge of arithmetic with fractions

With regard to arithmetic with fractions, Siegler and Lortie-Forgues (2017) highlight the different challenges that children face. For addition and subtraction, the simplest case is when the denominators are equal. In this case, the numerators are added or subtracted as if they were whole numbers. However, the main thing is that the common denominator remains unchanged (3/5 + 4/5 = 7/5 and not 7/10). When the denominators are different, a common denominator must first be found and one or both fractions must be transformed into equivalent fractions with the same denominator. This notion of equivalence of fractions is a real challenge for many students. In their longitudinal study of students in third to sixth grades, Jordan et al. (2017) observed that good multiplication skills with natural numbers make it easier for children to recognize equivalent fractions (e.g., 1/2, 2/4, 8/16) and that good division skills with whole numbers make it easier to simplify fractions (e.g., simplifying a fraction such as 14/35 into 2/5).

If in the case of the addition or subtraction of fractions it is necessary to transform the terms of the problem into equivalent fractions with a common denominator and then add or subtract their numerators and retain the common denominator in the answer, the same is not true for multiplication. Indeed, it is not necessary to find a common denominator and transform the terms since the numerators and denominators will simply be multiplied (3/5 × 4/5 = 12/25). However, some children produce errors such as '3/5 × 4/5 = 12/5' (Siegler et al., 2011), interpreted by Siegler and Pyke (2013) as operation errors in which a procedural step in one arithmetic operation is mistakenly used for another operation. In the case of fraction multiplication, these 2 authors also observed such operation errors in sixth and eighth graders (11 and 13 years old) on 46% of the problems.

To divide one fraction by another, invert one of the fractions, then multiply the numerators together and the denominators together. This procedure remains very opaque for many students, probably in part, because it is also misunderstood by most teachers themselves (Ball, 1990). Siegler and Pyke (2013) found that sixth and eighth graders made operating errors on 55% of fraction division problems. These errors were also common among early primary teachers (Newton, 2008).

According to Siegler and Lortie-Forgues (2017), explaining the multiplication of whole numbers by repeated additions does not help to understand how it works for fractions. Instead, they propose to explain multiplication in the form of 'N of M' with whole numbers (e.g., 6 × 3 means 'six of the threes') but also with fractions (e.g., 1/3 × 1/2 means 1/3 of the 1/2). Similarly, they propose that the division should be explained by indicating how many times the divisor goes into the dividend (the grouping method of division, see Chapter 4). For example, 16 ÷ 4 can be explained as the number of times 4 is included in (or goes into) 16, and 1/2 ÷ 1/4, as the number of times 1/4 is included in (or goes into) 1/2. This might help children understand why multiplying one fraction by another (proper) fraction leads to a decrease in its magnitude, whereas dividing one fraction by another can lead to a larger number, which is the complete opposite of what the child has experienced with multiplying or dividing natural numbers.

6.2 Difficulties with rational numbers in children with dyscalculia

As mentioned above, understanding the magnitude of fractional or decimal numbers and operating on these magnitudes is a real challenge for many students. For children with learning difficulties in mathematics or dyscalculia, it is obviously the same. As noted above, understanding whole numbers provides a foundation from which children will build their understanding of rational numbers (see Bailey et al., 2014; Jordan et al., 2017). Given that access to the magnitude of natural numbers is already problematic for children with learning difficulties in mathematics (see Chapter 2), it is not surprising that they encounter difficulties in rational number comprehension. We will present here two studies that specifically studied the learning of fractions in children with mathematical learning difficulties.

In a longitudinal study of children in third to sixth grades, Jordan et al. (2017) found that children with learning disabilities showed almost no progression in their understanding of fractional numbers during these years and that some of them had, after several years of teaching, only a very rudimentary understanding of the meaning of a fraction. Pupils who, at the beginning of the study when they were in third grade, were not very accurate in positioning whole numbers on a number line and had not developed a good network of arithmetic facts, showed very little progress in the ability to position fractions on a number line. Students with persistent learning difficulties with respect to fractions showed difficulties at several levels, in particular, in placing fractions on a number line, determining equivalent fractions, comparing or ordering fractions, and estimating the sum of two fractions. They generally consider all fractions to be less than 1 and therefore inaccurately place improper fractions (such as 3/2) on a number line of 0–2. They tend to perform arithmetic operations directly on numerators and denominators as if they were four independent numbers (e.g., 1/5 + 1/5 = 2/10) even in sixth grade.

It is interesting to note, however, that some children, who had a poor understanding of the concepts of fractions, were nevertheless able to learn procedures for solving calculations with fractions; they gave the impression that they understood because they applied the calculation procedures correctly, but in reality this is not quite the case.

Mazzocco, Myers, Lewis, Hanich, and Murphy (2013) also conducted another longitudinal study. They followed students in fourth to eighth grades (approximately ages 9 to 13), distinguishing between those who performed normally in mathematics, those who performed poorly, and those who had mathematical learning difficulties (performance below the 10th percentile). They used a fraction comparison test containing pairs of fractions presented in Arabic form (e.g., 1/2 and 1/4) or in the form of surface models (e.g., ▆▫ and ▆▫▫▫). The pairs had either the same numerator (e.g., 1/16 and 1/10) or the same denominator (e.g., 4/10 and 3/10).

They found that the 'normal-performance' group had a success rate of over 90% by sixth grade, while the other two groups had persistent difficulties.

With regard to the format of stimuli, in young children, surface models led to better performance than the Arabic format. For typical children, this advantage for surface models disappeared from sixth grade onwards. For children with mathematical learning difficulties, on the other hand, this advantage of surface models persisted at least until the eighth grade. Furthermore, with these surface models, children with mathematical learning difficulties were more likely to compare the area of the shaded shapes than their proportions, which could lead to misjudgement (especially when the shaded area representing the largest fraction was physically smaller than the shaded area of the smallest fraction).

Another difference between typical and mathematical learning difficulties children was the role of the 1/2 fraction in learning. For the typical children, from the beginning of the study, when the children were in fourth grade, the pairs of numbers containing the 1/2 fraction (e.g., 1/2 and 1/4) were more easily compared than the others. Furthermore, children's progressions on pairs with 1/2 appeared to precede comparable progressions on other fraction pairs, suggesting that the 1/2 fraction plays a fundamental role in learning fractions.

In contrast, among children with mathematical learning difficulties, the advantage for items with 1/2 only appeared in seventh grade.

6.3 Intervention studies

6.3.1 Interventions on decimal numbers

Many errors in the processing of decimal numbers are due to misconceptions about the representation of their magnitude. For example, 0.25 is considered greater than 0.8 because 25 is greater than 8. As a result, Durkin and Rittle-Johnson (2012) have questioned whether showing children examples of both correct and incorrect answers could mitigate these misconceptions and help their learning of decimal numbers. In their study, children in fourth and fifth grades (nine to ten years old) who had just received an introduction to decimal numbers were first tested on their conceptual and procedural knowledge of decimal numbers and then randomly assigned to two groups. In these two groups, the children received a short introductory presentation on decimal numbers and were then asked to complete a series of six pages of exercises involving the placement of decimal numbers on a number line from 0 to 1. At the top of each of these pages, two examples of number placement by a fictitious child were provided with the procedure that this child had used. The difference between the two groups was that the 'correct group' only received examples of correct placement on the number line, whereas the 'correct-incorrect group' received examples of both correct and incorrect placements on each of the six pages. The correct and incorrect examples used were constructed on the basis of the solving procedures used by the students in previous studies (see Figure 6.1). The correct examples were constructed on the basis of three types of correct strategies:

> "1) focus on the number of tenths and place the value close to where that number of tenths would go, 2) imagine the line divided into the number of pieces specified by the smallest unit (tenths, hundredths, thousandths), and 3) estimate based on knowledge of the decimal's magnitude in relation to a benchmark number (0, 0.5, or 1) »..
> (Durkin and Rittle-Johnson, 2012, p. 208)

The incorrect examples used one of the three strategies previously observed in the students' responses;

> "1) treat decimals like whole numbers (e.g., thinking that 0.9 is like 9, a small number compared to other whole numbers like 743, and thus placing 0.9 close to 0 on the small end of the number line), 2) misunderstand the role of zero by ignoring zeros in the tenths place and adding magnitude for zeros on the end, and 3) place all decimals before zero ».
> (Durkin & Rittle-Johnson, 2012, p. 208)

Rational numbers 247

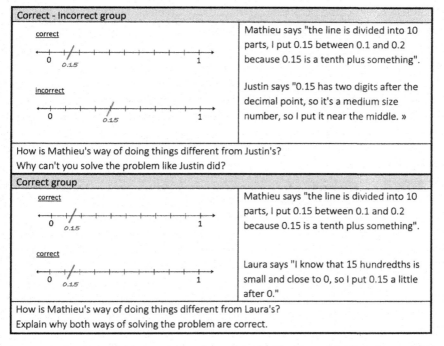

Figure 6.1 Correct and incorrect examples used in the Durkin and Rittle-Johnson (2012, page 208) study.

Children were asked to reflect on the two examples and complete the exercises. They were tested directly after the work session and again two weeks later.

While no major differences appeared between the two groups in the direct post-test, two weeks later, the students in the correct-incorrect group had significantly fewer errors than those in the correct group. These results indicate that it may be beneficial to explicitly address misunderstandings of decimal numbers with children.

Manalo, Bunnell, and Stillman (2000) investigated arithmetic operations with decimal numbers and tested the effectiveness of mnemonic processes in retaining procedures. To this end, the authors worked with 29 13-year-old students who performed poorly in mathematics because of their poor ability to perform arithmetic procedures rather than because of a weakness in arithmetic facts. These adolescents were randomly assigned to one of four conditions: mnemonic process, demonstration-imitation, and two control conditions, one promoting learning skills (instructions to improve reading, note-taking, mind-mapping, and concentration) and the other without any instruction. In the demonstration-imitation group, the instructors presented the steps to be followed to solve an operation and the students

248 *Rational numbers*

had to imitate it by carrying out the same steps on the same type of problem. In the mnemonic-process group, a story was used as a mnemonic for remembering the steps to perform each arithmetic operation. As an example, Box 6.1 illustrates the story proposed for subtraction. The four basic operations (addition, subtraction, multiplication, and division) were taught in the mnemonic-process and demonstration-imitation groups. The authors observed that the improvement was better after the interventions in the mnemonic-process and demonstration-imitation groups compared to the control condition groups, but the improvements associated with mnemonic-process instruction lasted longer than those with demonstration-imitation.

BOX 6.1   Example of a mnemonic procedure for subtraction steps used by Manalo et al., 2000

For subtraction:

"Imagine the two numbers as two groups of warriors fighting each other. Each warrior wears a number that indicates his strength. For example, a warrior with a 7 is stronger than a warrior with a 4 (all these elements were illustrated on the board with simple drawings). For each group of warriors, the comma separates the warriors who are classified and those who are not. The numbers to the left of the comma are the classified warriors, while those to the right of the comma are the unclassified warriors. In order to fight, warriors must line up correctly so that the classified warriors of one group are aligned with the warriors of the other group who are also classified. Likewise, those who are not classified align with the other unclassified ones. (The students were shown how to align the two numbers correctly using the comma as a reference).

For example, 75.6 − 43 would be aligned as follows:

75.6

−43.0

The top group (75.6) is the 'attackers' and the bottom group (43.0) is the 'defenders'. The defenders are easily recognizable because they have their knives drawn: the sign of subtraction '−'. The attackers try to overtake the defenders and go through the door behind the defenders (the line below the bottom numbers). But as they make their way past the defenders, they weaken. So, every time one of them passes through the opposite defender and through the door, his strength (the number he is carrying) decreases by the same amount as the strength of the defender he had to pass through. So, to know the

> strength of the attacker after passing a defender and going through the gate, we must subtract the strength of the attacker from the strength of the opposing defender. If the strength of the attacking warrior is less than the strength of the opposite defender warrior, it must first be increased by 10 points, otherwise the attacking warrior cannot overtake the defender warrior who is more powerful. But be aware, in such cases the strength of the next defender must be increased by 1".
>
> (Manalo, Bunnell et al., 2000, p. 142)

6.3.2 Interventions on fractions

Test and Ellis (2005) investigated the effects of a mnemonic to solve addition and subtraction with fractions. They worked with 6 eighth graders (13 years old) who had mathematical learning difficulties. The intervention was offered to the students in pairs but at different times, allowing the authors to see whether the performance of these students changed in parallel with the time of the intervention.

The mnemonic used was the acronym LAP for look, ask, pick, referring to the steps described in Box 6.2. These steps were taught to students who received a mnemonic strategy card and different games to help them memorize the meaning of the three letters LAP.

Next, they were taught how to determine whether the bigger denominator could be divided by the smaller denominator without a remainder (step 'A' or 'ask' of the LAP). This learning took place in a playful context (for example, students took a card from a game containing calculations of fractions; they divided the highest denominator by the lowest denominator. If their answer was correct, they received rewards for the game; if it was incorrect, they received penalties).

Finally, they were presented with a card with a fraction calculation, and they were asked to say which type of fraction problem it was, type 1, 2, or 3, as indicated in step 'P' or 'pick' of the LAP.

BOX 6.2 The LAP method of Test and Ellis (2005, inspired by table 1, page 14)

1. **L → look**: look at the sign (check if it is the sign of addition or subtraction) and the denominators (numbers at the bottom of the fraction); see if they are the same or different.

If they are the same, go to 'Pick the type of fraction' and select type 1.
If they are different, go to 'Ask'.

2. **A → ask**: ask yourself if the remainder of the division of the highest denominator by the lowest denominator is zero.

If yes, go to 'Pick the type of fraction' and select type 2.
If no, go to 'Pick the type of fraction' and select type 3.

3. **P → pick**: pick the type of fraction.

Type 1 (e.g., $\frac{1}{8} + \frac{3}{8} =$): the bottom numbers are the same.

Type 2 (e.g., $\frac{1}{4} + \frac{1}{12} =$): the bottom numbers are different, and if I divide the largest number by the smallest, the rest equals zero.

Type 3 (e.g., $\frac{2}{3} + \frac{3}{4} =$): the numbers at the bottom are different and if I divide the largest number by the smallest, the rest is not equal to zero.

As soon as pupils mastered the steps of the LAP strategy, they were taught to use this strategy to solve each type of fraction (see Box 6.3), starting with type 1 fractions, then type 2, then type 3. Once they had mastered these types of calculations, they were offered a mix of these three types of calculations.

Several times before, during, and up to six weeks after the interventions, students were tested both on their knowledge of the LAP strategy and on their ability to add and subtract fractions. The results showed a clear relationship between the timing of the intervention and the acquisition of the LAP strategy and their progress in their ability to apply the strategy to perform addition and subtraction of fractions. Five of the six students mastered both skills and maintained this learning over a six-week period.

BOX 6.3 Steps of the LAP intervention (Test & Ellis, inspired by table 2 p. 17)

Fraction of type 1 (e.g., $\frac{4}{7} + \frac{2}{75} =$)

- Add or subtract the top numbers. Bottom numbers remain the same.

$$\frac{4}{7}+\frac{2}{7}=\frac{6}{7}$$

Fraction of type 2 (e.g., $\frac{5}{12}+\frac{1}{6}=$)

- Place a box around the fraction with the lowest number at the bottom.
- Ask yourself 'how much is 12 divided by 6?'
- Write an '×' sign and the answer you found in the box.

$$\frac{5}{12}+\left(\frac{1}{6}\times\frac{2}{2}\right)=$$

- Write the fraction that has not been changed below the original problem.
- Write the sign of the operation and a new fraction next to it.
- Multiply the two numbers from above that are in the box. Write your answer at the top of the new fraction.
- -Multiply the bottom two numbers in the box. Write your answer at the bottom of the new fraction.

$$\frac{5}{12}+\frac{2}{12}=$$

- Add or subtract the top numbers. Bottom numbers remain the same.

$$\frac{5}{12}+\frac{2}{12}=\frac{7}{12}$$

Fraction of type 3 (e.g., $\frac{3}{5}+\frac{2}{7}=$)

- Draw two lines for new fractions below the problem presented.
- Multiply the two numbers from below (5 × 7). Write your answer at the bottom of the two new fractions.

$$\frac{3}{5}+\frac{2}{7}=$$

$$\frac{}{35}+\frac{}{35}=$$

- Take the number from the bottom of the right starting fraction (7) and multiply it by the number from the top of the left starting fraction (3). Write this answer (21) at the top of the new left-hand fraction.

$$\frac{21}{35}+\frac{}{35}=$$

- Take the number at the bottom of the left starting fraction (5) and multiply it by the number at the top of the right starting fraction (2). Write this answer (10) at the top of the new line fraction.

$$\frac{12}{35} + \frac{10}{35} =$$

- Add or subtract the top numbers. Bottom numbers remain the same.

$$\frac{21}{35} + \frac{10}{35} = \frac{31}{35}$$

Shin and Bryant (2015) reviewed 17 studies of fraction intervention for mathematical learning difficulties students. They pointed out several intervention components that led to higher benefits.

First, explicit rather than implicit instruction is more beneficial for students with difficulties in learning fractions (e.g., Misquitta, 2011).

Second, the use of concrete and visual representation is important, with the former adding to the efficacy of the instruction. For instance, Butler et al. (2003) compared two instructional sequences of equivalent fraction concepts and procedures in middle school students with mathematical disabilities: the concrete-representational-abstract (CRA) and the representational-abstract (RA) instructional sequence. The two treatment groups received carefully sequenced instruction over ten lessons with the only difference between the two being that the CRA group used concrete manipulative devices for the first three lessons while the RA group used representational drawings. Specifically, teachers used concrete objects such as fraction strips and folded construction paper to aid in students' understanding of equivalent fractions, and other commercial fraction circles and representational drawings in a sequential manner. Students also learned how to use those manipulatives and drawings while solving fraction problems. Results showed that students from the CRA condition performed better than the RA group, indicating the importance of the manipulation of physical object (e.g., pie pieces). For a similar conclusion, see Martin and Schwartz (2005).

Third, promoting mathematical verbalization with a 'think aloud' strategy leads to improvement. We will now present some of these interventions in more detail.

As we saw earlier, a key aspect is children's understanding of the representation of the magnitude of fractions and, in particular, of the understanding of the fraction as a number (or as a measure). Indeed, children generally begin with an understanding of fractions based on the experience of sharing (sharing a pie, a pizza, or a set of objects), but later they need to develop an understanding of the fraction as a number that can be interspersed between naturals. This is particularly important when approaching calculation with fractional numbers. This conception of fraction as a measure is less intuitive and depends much more on formal instruction explaining the conventions of symbolic notation. The development of this representation of fractions is considered essential (Geary et al., 2008) and, according to Siegler et al. (2011), placing fractions on a number line is an activity that favours this representation since this medium suggests continuity with other numbers (and natural numbers in particular) and also allows the representation of improper fractions.

Some interventions have tried to assess the efficiency of this type of representation tool. Saxe, Diakow, and Gearhart (2012) provided 19 intervention lessons to fourth and fifth graders who also followed the same curriculum as children in the comparison group for the rest of their classes. These children first received instruction on whole numbers with the number line and then learned fractions within the same number line context. Compared with children from the control group, those who benefitted from these number line sessions performed better directly after but also five months after the intervention on both knowledge of whole numbers and fractions. Even children with mathematical learning difficulties benefitted from these sessions and actually performed similarly to medium achievers (those in the middle one-third of the distribution) in the end-of-year tests.

Based on this idea, Fuchs, Schumacher, Long et al. (2013) compared the effectiveness of a control curricula, focusing more on the part-whole interpretation of fractions and on procedures *versus* an experimental intervention focusing more on the measurement interpretation of fractions by using number lines and focusing largely on conceptual skills before working on calculation procedures. Tutoring involved 36 sessions spread over 12 weeks (see in Box 6.4), and the participant sample was very large. They found better improvement after the experimental intervention than after the control one. Furthermore, the training also improved fraction arithmetic, and this gain was mediated by the improvement in measurement interpretation of fractions. Let us however note that both programmes involved both number line representation and objects with shaded regions (see Figure 6.2), but in different proportions. Furthermore, one big difference between the two conditions was the size of the groups during the teaching as the control programme was delivered in whole-class arrangement while the experimental intervention was given in small groups of three children. We can thus not exclude that this difference between the two conditions might, in part, explain their difference in efficiency.

254 *Rational numbers*

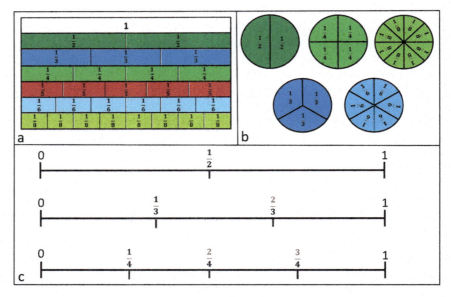

Figure 6.2 Representing fractions through rectangles (a), circles (b), and number lines (c).

BOX 6.4 The programme for the experimental intervention of Fuchs et al. (2013)

Thirty-six sessions of intervention (30 minutes each). Four types of activities are used in each session:

(1) the introduction of concepts or skills (8–12 min), using concrete manipulatives (e.g., fraction tiles, fraction circles), visual representations, and problem-solving strategies;
(2) group work (8–12 min): students take turns leading the group through problems, while all students show how they work for each problem;
(3) speed game: this is designed to build fluency. For instance, to build fluency on fractions equivalent to 1/2, tutors give each student a paper showing 25 fractions, and students have 1 min to circle fractions equivalent to 1/2;
(4) individual work (8 min): students independently complete a two-sided practice sheet. One side presents problems taught in the day's lesson; the other side is a cumulative review.

The programme was spread over 12 weeks in the following way:

- **Weeks 1 and 2 (Lessons 1–6)**, the focus is on the understanding of fraction magnitude, starting with the relevant vocabulary (e.g., *numerator, denominator, unit*), and relying on a combination of part/whole relations, measurement, and equal sharing to explain the fraction magnitudes. Instruction emphasizes the role of the numerator and denominator and how they work together to constitute the fraction, which is one number, even though it is comprised of two whole numerals.
- **Week 3 (Lessons 7–9)**, students practice what they had learned, i.e., naming fractions, reading fractions, and comparing two fractions when the denominators are the same or when the numerators are the same. Two types of flash cards were used to build fluency with the meaning of fractions. In the first one, students were presented with one fraction and had to read it and state the meaning of the fraction (e.g., for 1/4, 'one-fourth, one of four equal parts'). In the second one, two fractions are presented and students determine if the fraction pairs have the same numerators, same denominators, or different numerators and different denominators. For these two exercises, children try to be as fast as possible while being accurate. Finally, each student receives two fraction cards and places the greater than or less than sign between fractions and explains their rationale to the group.
- **Weeks 4 and 5 (Lessons 10–15)**, students learn about fractions equivalent to 1/2 (2/4, 3/6, 4/8, 5/10, 6/12). They also learn chunking and segmenting strategies for comparing two fractions differing both in terms of the numerators and denominators, using 1/2 as a benchmark for comparison and writing the greater than, less than, or equal sign between the fractions. Then, they are introduced to placing two fractions on the 0 to 1 number line, marked with 1/2, and ordering three fractions from smallest to largest.
- **Week 6 (Lessons 16–18)**, students continue to work on comparing two fractions, ordering three fractions, and placing fractions on the 0 to 1 number line, now without the 1/2 marker, though being encouraged to think about where 1/2 goes on the number line in relation to placing other fractions. They are also introduced to fractions representing a collection of items and fractions equivalent to one.
- **Week 7 (Lessons 19–21)** is a cumulative review on all concepts and skills.
- **Weeks 8 and 9 (Lessons 22–27)** focus on simple calculations: the addition of like fractions (i.e., with the same denominators) (Lesson 22), the subtraction of like fractions (Lesson 23), mixed addition and

> subtraction (Lesson 24), addition and then subtraction with unlike fractions (or different denominators), with in each case one fraction being equivalent to 1/2 or 1 so that students can use equivalent fractions they have already learned (Lessons 25 and 26). Lesson 27 reviews addition and subtraction with the same and different denominators.
> - **Weeks 10 to 12 (Lessons 28 to 36)** are a cumulative review.

Fuchs, Schumacher et al. (2014) tested the compensatory hypothesis that in the case of low cognitive resources, such as low working memory capacity for example, learning is poor, and building automation through fluency practice would improve performance since the limitations would be compensated for. To test this, they compared, in fourth-grade students with mathematical learning difficulties, a classical instruction programme (students are in class and follow the usual courses focusing mainly on the part/whole relationship) to two experimental instruction programmes aiming at learning fractions. The interventions were very similar to those of Fuchs et al. (2013) and consisted of a series of 36 30-minute sessions. The only difference between the two experimental programmes concerned five minutes of each of these sessions. Indeed, in one of the programmes, the five minutes were used to build fluency in learning, while in the other, the five minutes were used to continue with exercises aimed at the conceptual aspect (i.e., understanding fractions). In both cases, children had to decide whether a fraction was 1/2 or not, choose the larger of two fractions, and indicate whether the fractions were proper or not. In the first programme, students were encouraged to be accurate and to respond more and more quickly, while in the second, they were asked to represent fractions on circles or rectangles and then to respond and explain their reasoning to the group. The authors observed that both experimental programmes led to a better improvement in students' performance than the control programme. Again, it should be noted that the experimental programmes were delivered to small groups of students while the control programme was delivered to the whole class, which again may partly explain the differences in effectiveness. Interestingly, the authors observed that the difference between the two experimental programmes varied according to the working memory abilities of the children, but not in the sense foreseen by the compensatory hypothesis. Indeed, for students with low working memory capacities, additional conceptual exercises lead to better improvement than exercises aimed at fluency, in contrast to children with better working memory capacities.

Finally, Krowka and Fuchs (2017) examined the cognitive profiles of students who did not benefit from these fraction interventions using number lines to favour a representation in terms of 'fraction as a measure' (Fuchs et al., 2014; Fuchs, Schumaker et al., 2016; Fuchs, Malone et al., 2016).

They measured each student's processing speed, reasoning, working memory, attention, and auditory comprehension skills and found that those who did not actually improve their accuracy in positioning fractions on the number line after the instruction programme were generally characterized by relatively poor reasoning skills. According to these authors, positioning a fraction on a number line requires good reasoning skills. Indeed, it is necessary to interpret visual stimuli, and understand and compare the magnitude of the target fraction to that of strategically selected reference fractions according to their position on the number line (for example, 1/2 and 3/4 serve as reference points for the target fraction 5/8), while engaging in relational thinking to determine where the target fraction is located in relation to the reference fractions.

In all these studies, a better improvement was observed for the experimental instruction programme compared to the control programme, suggesting that the use of number lines brings real additional richness. However, as already mentioned, in each of these studies, the experimental programme was delivered to small groups of students, whereas the control programme was followed by the whole class. Hamden and Gunderson's (2017) study proceeded differently, but their intervention was extremely short (only 15 minutes) and involved a smaller sample of participants. They randomly assigned second- and third-grade participants to one of three conditions: a number line training, an area-model training, and a control cross-word puzzle condition. In the number line condition, students were presented with a tick line (or a rectangle) going from 0 to 1 and a fraction written on the top (i.e., 1/4). They were instructed first to look at the bottom number which shows how many equal parts they need to make on the number line, then to look at the top number which shows how many of these parts they need to colour in, starting from 0 and then placing a hatch mark at the end of the coloured part. In the area model, they were presented with a circle and were given nearly the same instruction: look at the bottom number which tells how many equal parts to draw, then look at the top number and colour this number of parts, and then write the fraction near the coloured parts. Before and after the intervention, children were presented with three tests: positioning a fraction on a number line, shading a fraction of a circle and comparing two fractions. As one could expect, children from the number line condition improved more than the others on positioning fractions on the number line and conversely, children from the area model were better, after the intervention, at colouring fractions on circles. More importantly, when the children were presented with fraction comparison, an exercise they were not trained on, children from the number line condition were better than the two other groups.

In summary, it is crucial to work on understanding the magnitude. We need to start with a part-whole conception and then help children develop a conception of fraction as a measure. The use of number lines seems to be important to meet the latter goal.

6.3.3 Conclusion

Intervention strategies on fractions and decimal numbers that appear to be effective according to the literature review presented above are summarized below.

In general terms

- First, develop a good understanding of whole numbers, as the accuracy of their positioning on a number line is a good predictor of understanding fractions and decimal numbers (Bailey et al., 2014; Jordan, Resnick et al., 2017).
- Use explicit rather than implicit instructions (Misquitta, 2011).
- Use concrete-representational-abstract sequence representations (CRA, Butler et al., 2003).
- Promote mathematical verbalization with a strategy of 'thinking aloud' (Shin & Bryant, 2015) by guiding children on how to do it, vocabulary to use, and appropriate explanations or reasoning to develop (Fuchs et al., 2016).
- Do not go too fast in fluency practice, especially with students with low working memory skills; in-depth conceptual intervention leads to better improvement for them (Fuchs et al., 2014).
- Explicitly address misconceptions, for example by presenting and discussing correct and incorrect examples (see Durkin and Rittle-Johnson, 2012).

For decimal numbers

- Work on the basis of a thorough understanding of the base-10 positional system.
- Resist the bias of natural numbers.
- Introduce arithmetic operations on these numbers, when the child appears to have a good understanding of the meaning of decimal numbers.
- Use mnemonics to help memorize the steps in the arithmetic process (Test & Ellis, 2005).

For fractions

- Begin with learning part-whole representation and then develop the interpretation of fractions as a measure using number lines (Fuchs et al., 2013; Hamden & Gunderson, 2017; Saxe et al., 2012; Siegler et al., 2011).
- Pay particular attention to the 'one-half' fraction as a reference around which the understanding of other fractions is built (Mazzocco et al., 2013).
- First use number lines from 0 to 1 to work on understanding proper fractions, then move to larger number lines (e.g., 0–2) to address improper fractions.

- Introduce arithmetic operations on fractions when the child seems to have a good understanding of the meaning of the fraction.
- Use mnemonic means to help memorize the steps in the arithmetic process (Manalo et al., 2000).

6.4 From research to practice: assessing the ability to process rational numbers

There are not many tests assessing children's understanding of rational numbers and their ability to operate on them. At the clinical test level, the Tedimath Grand battery (Noël & Grégoire, 2015) includes a subtest assessing the child's ability to process rational numbers, including matching a fraction to a part of a shape or collection or calculations on fractional or decimal numbers. The Examath 8-15 battery (Lafay & Halloin, 2016) also includes these types of items but in specific subtests each time: one subtest assessing the mapping between a fraction and a picture, another testing the comparison of fractions, or the positioning of a fraction on a number line. The KeyMath-3 (Connolly, 2007) has also a subtest assessing the processing of rational numbers.

Ideally, the assessment of decimal numbers and fractions should include tasks assessing the child's understanding of magnitude, equivalence, and density and their ability to use these rational numbers (see, for example, the test developed by Durkin and Rittle-Johnson, 2015, to assess children's conceptions of decimal numbers).

For fractions, understanding of magnitude can be measured using colouring tasks, comparison tasks, and tasks for positioning numbers on a number line. In colouring tasks, children are asked to colour or circle an area of a shape (e.g., a pizza) or a subset of objects in a collection according to the fraction presented (e.g., 2/5). This type of task measures the child's understanding of the fraction in its part-whole representation. Depending on the items, this task may also assess the child's ability to find equivalent fractions if, for example, the set is not the same size as the denominator of the fraction (e.g., circle 2/14 in a 7-point set). Magnitude comparison tasks are interesting because they show whether or not the child is resistant to the bias of natural numbers. It is therefore important to consider

- pairs with the same denominator (e.g., 2/8 and 5/8) in which the largest fraction has the largest numerator;
- pairs with common numerators in which this time the largest fraction has the smallest denominator (e.g., 2/9 and 2/7);
- pairs without common components, some of which can be transformed into equivalent fractions with a common denominator (e.g., 2/7 and 5/35), and others which cannot and where the largest fraction consists of the smallest components (e.g., 1/3 and 6/27).

Placing fractions on a number line also gives a lot of information about the child's interpretation of the fractions. In this case, and depending on the age of the child, we may consider placing proper fractions on a line from 0 to 1 (with items such as $\frac{1}{5}, \frac{13}{14}, \frac{2}{13}, \frac{3}{7}, \frac{5}{8}, \frac{1}{3}, \frac{1}{2}, \frac{1}{19}$ and $\frac{5}{6}$) or a mixture of proper and unproper fractions to be placed on lines from 0 to 2 (e.g., $\frac{1}{3}, \frac{7}{4}, \frac{12}{13}, 1\frac{11}{12}, \frac{3}{2}, \frac{5}{6}, \frac{5}{5}, \frac{1}{2}, \frac{7}{6}, 1\frac{2}{4}, 1, \frac{3}{8}, 1\frac{5}{8}, \frac{2}{3}, 1\frac{1}{5}, \frac{7}{9}, \frac{1}{19}, 1\frac{5}{6}, \frac{4}{3}$, items from Siegler et al., 2011). The notion of equivalence can be tested directly by asking the child, for example, to select among different possibilities the fractions equivalent to a target (e.g., 'could you circle all the fractions equivalent to 3/4 among 5/6, 13/14, 9/12, 18/24?'). To evaluate the density property, questions such as 'write a fractional number between 1/3 and 2/3' can be proposed, although some adults have not yet acquired this notion.

For decimal numbers, comparing numbers and placing numbers on a line are generally used (Durkin & Rittle-Johnson, 2015). Again, the numbers to be compared should vary in the length of their decimal portion to see how well the child is able to resist the bias of natural numbers or has a tendency to assume that the higher the number of decimal digits, the smaller the magnitude of the number (see Resnick et al., 1989). Therefore, items should involve pairs where the largest number has a smaller number of decimal digits (e.g., 0.7 and 0.68) and others where it does not (e.g., 0.45 and 0.3) and pairs where the largest number has a decimal part that corresponds to the largest natural number (0.68 and 0.4) and others where the largest number has a decimal part that corresponds to the smallest natural number (e.g., 0.8 and 0.35). The notion of equivalence can be evaluated by manipulating the position of zeros in numbers. For example, 'circle all numbers equal to 0.61 (0.6100, 0.061, 0.610, 601, 61)'. Questions can also be asked about the density property, such as 'write a decimal number between 0.6 and 0.7' (Durkin & Rittle-Johnson, 2015).

You can also ask questions assessing the child's ability to understand the equivalence between the two notations, asking them to translate fractions into corresponding decimal numbers (e.g., write the decimal number corresponding to 1/2, 3/4, 7/10, 6/100, etc.).

Finally, the arithmetic operations on these rational numbers must be measured. For Bailey, Hansen, and Jordan (2017), the following items were used to test children's ability to add and subtract fractional numbers (based on Hecht, 1998) : $\frac{2}{5}+\frac{1}{5}, \frac{3}{4}-\frac{1}{4}, \frac{3}{6}+\frac{1}{6}, \frac{5}{6}-\frac{2}{6}, 1\frac{3}{4}-\frac{1}{4}, \frac{3}{4}+\frac{2}{4}$, $\frac{5}{6}-\frac{2}{6}, 1\frac{3}{4}-\frac{1}{4}, \frac{3}{4}+\frac{2}{4}, 3\frac{3}{8}+1\frac{2}{8}, 2\frac{2}{3}-1\frac{1}{3}, \frac{5}{6}+\frac{2}{3}, \frac{7}{8}-\frac{1}{2}, 1\frac{1}{3}-\frac{4}{5}, \frac{3}{4}+\frac{2}{3}$.

For decimal numbers, be sure to use numbers with decimal parts of different sizes to see how well children master the positioning system (for example, 2.5 + 2.13). Problems should also vary depending on the absence or presence of carry-over operations (e.g., 2.5 + 2.82).

Multiplication and division can only be tested in older children or adolescents.

6.5 From research to practice: rehabilitation paths

6.5.1 Proposal of the different steps of intervention on fractions

In this section, we propose a series of steps constituting an intervention in the processing of fractions.

6.5.1.1 Fraction as part of a whole or of a single object

The first step is to guide the child in understanding the magnitude of fractions by explaining the relevant vocabulary (fraction, numerator, denominator) and how the two components of fractions fit together to form the meaning of the fraction: denominators refer to the number of equal parts and the numerator refers to the number of those parts to be selected. Also introduce specific fraction names (e.g., half, third, quarter, etc., Figure 6.3).

Fraction	$\frac{1}{1}$	$\frac{1}{2}$	$\frac{1}{4}$	$\frac{1}{5}$	$\frac{1}{10}$
Part-whole	1 piece out of 1	1 piece out of 2	1 piece out of 4	1 piece out of 5	1 piece out of 10
Visuals		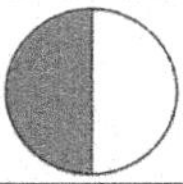	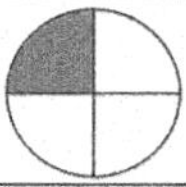	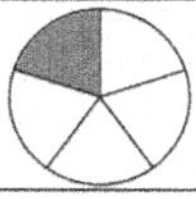	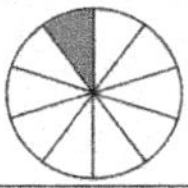
Verbal	whole	half	quarter	one fifth	one tenth
Manipulatives (Unit = 1€)					
Decimal	1	0.50	0.25	0.20	0.10
Percentage (%)	100 %	50 %	25 %	20 %	10 %

Figure 6.3 Represent the fraction as part of a whole or of a single object (a circle) and associate the corresponding verbal label with it, and then possibly use ecological material (inspired by Cooreman, 2017).

262 *Rational numbers*

> **EXERCISES**
>
> - Using items representing the whole (a pizza, a pie, a chocolate bar, a circle, a rectangle, etc.), ask the children to colour in a certain fraction of this 'whole' or 'unit' or 'one'. Teach them to focus first on the denominator (circle the denominator to make it more salient!) as it tells them how many equal parts the whole should be divided into, and then have them colour in the number of parts indicated by the numerator. Invite students to explain what they are doing.
> - Propose two fractions and ask the child to determine if they have the same denominator.
> - Give a fraction to the child who must 'name' it and explain what it means (for example, '3/4 is three-quarters, it means three parts out of four equal parts', that is ▌▌▌).
> - Give pictures with some parts of the whole coloured. Have the child say and write down the corresponding fraction and explain why.
> - Give two fractions of the same denominator (for example, $\frac{5}{6}$ and $\frac{2}{6}$) and ask the child to choose the larger one. To do so, in a first step, ask the child to use concrete materials or drawings to represent the fractions and help him/her in the comparison of their magnitude. When the child feels comfortable, use only symbolic fractions.

6.5.1.2 The fraction as a number (comparison and positioning on a number line)

By comparing the size of fractions, the child has already understood that fractions are numbers. However, using the placement task on a number line seems to further emphasize this conception of the fraction as a number or as designating a specific numerical magnitude. The following exercises are intended to deepen this understanding.

> **EXERCISES**
>
> - Have the child place natural numbers on a number line (first on a line from 0 to 10, then on a line from 0 to 100).
> - Have the child place proper fractions on a number line marked 0 and 1 at each end by:
>   (1) looking at the denominator that indicates the number of equal parts to be created on the number line.

(2) looking at the numerator that indicates the number of parts to be coloured, starting at 0.
(3) indicating the position of the fraction on the number line with a mark at the end of the coloured part (Hamden & Gunderson, 2017).

- Use number lines from 0 to 1 and have the child place two fractions with the same denominator on the line, and determine, based on this, which one is the larger.
- Use number lines from 0 to 1 on which you have placed $\frac{1}{2}$ in the middle. Choose a fraction and have the child place it on the line and determine if it is smaller or larger than $\frac{1}{2}$.
- Do the same, but this time the child must first position the $\frac{1}{2}$ fraction on the line.
- Use the number line and ask the child to position two fractions with different denominators and then determine which one is larger. Especially when one of the fractions is smaller and the other larger than $\frac{1}{2}$, ask them to use the $\frac{1}{2}$ criterion.

6.5.1.3 Proper, improper, and equal-to-one fractions

It would be efficient to introduce, at a very early stage, the notion of improper fractions and fractions that are equal to one, into the learning process. Indeed, if for a long time only proper fractions are proposed, the child risks confusing the denominator with the largest number, or believing that fractions are always less than one. To avoid these misconceptions, you can suggest the following situation: 'Your mummy is going to a pizzeria. She wants to buy 2/2 (◐, ◐) of a pizza (or two half pizzas), show me what she will get'. Reproduce the exercise with several fractions corresponding to one (3/3, 4/4, etc.) and then invite the child to determine what characterizes all these fractions (the denominator equals the numerator). Next, you can propose a slightly different situation such as: 'Your mommy goes to a pizzeria. She wants to buy 3/2 of a pizza'. Can you show me 3/2 of a pizza? Help the child to (1) check the denominator, (2) take the pizza cut in half as indicated by the denominator, (3) take the number of slices as indicated by the numerator (3 in this example), and (4) knowing that a pizza only allows you to take two halves and that the mum wants to buy three slices, you will have to take slices from another pizza to get the three halves. Invite the child to observe that a fraction like 3/2 of a pizza (◐, ◐, ◐) is actually more than 1 pizza. Continue to represent other improper fractions in this way using a variety of materials (e.g., a chocolate bar). Think with the child about what differentiates a fraction that is less than

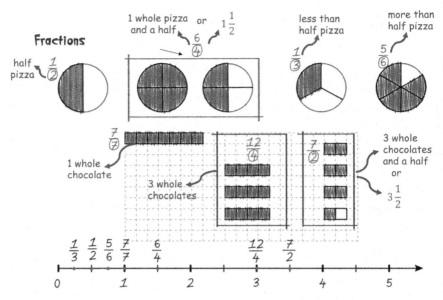

Figure 6.4 Representation of fractions as parts of a whole, using different materials, pizzas, chocolate bars, numerical line (adapted from Karagiannakis, 2015).

1, i.e., a proper fraction (e.g., 5/6), from a fraction that is greater than one or improper (e.g., 7/2). Discuss the relationship between the numerator and denominator in each case (Figure 6.4).

> **EXERCISES**
>
> - Show some fractions to the child who must determine whether they are larger or smaller than one (he/she can use drawings if necessary) and explain why. At the beginning, explain how he/she should formulate and justify the answer.

For example, '5/6 of a pizza is smaller than a pizza because the pizza has 6 slices and I take 5 slices (Figure 6.4), so there is still 1 slice left'; or 'it's less than a pizza as the number of slices I take (5) is less than the number of slices (6) of the whole pizza' or 'the numerator is smaller than the denominator, so the fraction is less than one'.

Or for 6/4 of a pizza, 'it is more than 1 pizza because I cut it into 4, I want to take 6 slices; as I don't have enough slices, I have to cut another pizza into

Rational numbers 265

4 and take 2 slices, to have 6 in total (Figure 6.4); it is then more than 1 pizza as the number of slices I take (6) is greater than the number of slices I cut from the pizza (4)'; or 'the numerator is greater than the denominator, so the fraction is greater than one'.

- Ask the child to classify the fractions into three categories: smaller, equal to, or greater than one.
- Use number lines from 0 to 2 or 0 to 3 and ask the child to place the natural numbers (1 and 2) and then place proper and improper fractions, and fractions corresponding to 1 or to 2, which are presented in a random order (Figure 6.4).

For example, to place 4/3, I divide the segments of 1 (the distance between 0 and 1, and the distance between 1 and 2) into 3 equal parts each; I colour 4 parts from the left and then mark the 4/3 position.

You can also ask the child to position fractions whose numerator and denominator are the same (for example, 4/4, 3/3, 5/5 …) and then ask them why these fractions occupy the same position on the number line.

6.5.1.4 Fractions as part or subset of a collection

Exercises similar to those performed with fractions using a single object can also be performed with sets of objects. Again, invite the child to focus first on the denominator (e.g., circle it!) to determine the number of equal parts. To take 1/4 of a set, first divide the set into 4 equal parts. If you have 12 cents, then in each of the 4 equal parts there are 3 cents. Then look at the numerator and take the number of shares it indicates. So, 1/4 of 12 cents is one share of the 4 equal parts of 3 cents, so 3 cents (Figure 6.5). On the other hand, 2/3 of 12 cents is 2 shares of the 3 equal parts of 4 cents, so 2 × 4 cents, or 8 cents in total.

Fraction	$\frac{1}{2}$	$\frac{1}{3}$	$\frac{2}{3}$	$\frac{1}{4}$	$\frac{3}{4}$
Manipulatives	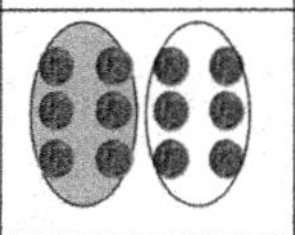	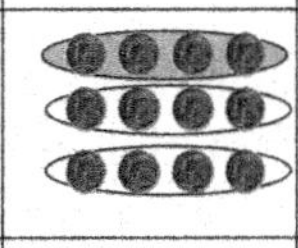	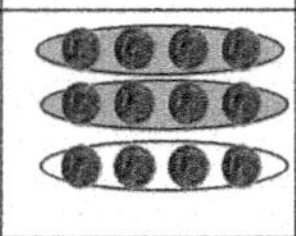	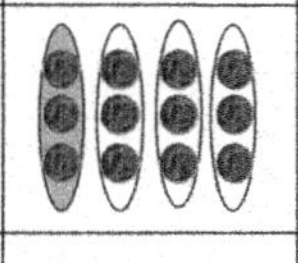	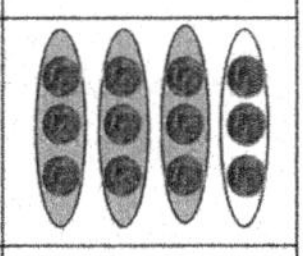
Verbal	a half of 12 cents is 6 cents	one third of 12 cents is 4 cents	two thirds of 12 cents are 8 cents	a quarter of 12 cents is 3 cents	three quarters of 12 cents are 9 cents
Symbolic	$\frac{1}{2}$ of 12 → 6	$\frac{1}{3}$ of 12 → 4	$\frac{2}{3}$ of 12 → 8	$\frac{1}{4}$ of 12 → 3	$\frac{3}{4}$ of 12 → 9

Figure 6.5 Fractions as part-whole of a group of objects (12 cents) using manipulatives, words, and symbolic writing.

266 *Rational numbers*

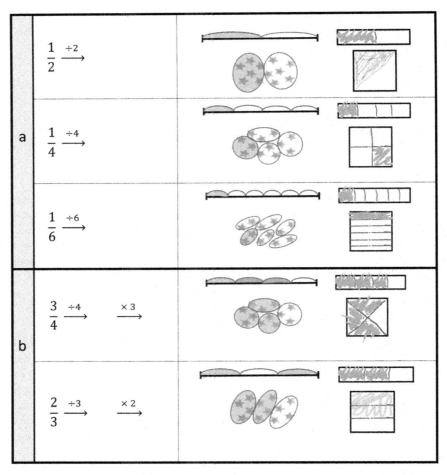

Figure 6.6 Representing fractions of a single object or a group of objects, underlining that in all cases first a division with the denominator is needed (a) and then a multiplication with the numerator if it is not 1 (b).

When using sets, you can refer to the operations of division and multiplication: dividing sets by the denominator and multiplying them by the numerator (Figure 6.6). To calculate 1/4 (a quarter) of 12 stars you only need to divide by 4 (12:4) which is 3 stars (Figure 6.6a). To calculate 3/4 of 12 stars, one more step is required. You should first divide 12 stars by 4 (12:4), which gives 3, and then get 3 such groups by multiplying the result by 3 (3 × 3), which gives 9 stars (Figure 6.6b).

After working with concrete material and drawn representations, it is time to evoke symbolic representations. This transfer will not be difficult, since

Rational numbers 267

Explicit procedure	Schema	Symbolic
$\frac{2}{3}$ of 12€ $\xrightarrow{\div 3}$ 4 $\xrightarrow{\times 2}$ 8€	Number of parts: $\frac{2}{3}$ × Value of whole: 12 € → Total value: 8 €	$\frac{2}{3} \times 12 = 8$
$\frac{3}{5}$ of 200m $\xrightarrow{\div 5}$ 40 $\xrightarrow{\times 3}$ 120m	Number of parts: $\frac{3}{5}$ × Value of whole: 200 m → Total value: 120 m (E_1, I, E_2)	$\frac{3}{5} \times 200 = 120$
$\frac{4}{9}$ of 108Kg $\xrightarrow{\div 9}$ 12 $\xrightarrow{\times 4}$ 48Kg	Number of parts: $\frac{4}{9}$ × Value of whole: 108 Kg → Total value: 48 Kg	$\frac{4}{9} \times 108 = 48$
$\frac{3}{2}$ of 50L $\xrightarrow{\div 2}$ 25 $\xrightarrow{\times 3}$ 75L	Number of parts: $\frac{3}{2}$ × Value of whole: 50 L → Total value: 75 L	$\frac{3}{2} \times 50 = 75$
$\frac{a}{b}$ of whole $\xrightarrow{\div b}$ __ $\xrightarrow{\times a}$ __	Number of parts: □ × Value of whole: ○ → Total value: □	$\frac{a}{b} \times$ whole =

Figure 6.7 Calculating the portion of a whole using the explicit method, schema, or symbolic form.

you have already explicitly introduced the required procedure in the previous activities. So, to calculate 2/3 of €12, the children must first divide by the denominator, 12 ÷ 3 = 4, and then multiply the quotient by the numerator (4 × 2 = €8). Initially you can implement such problems by using the explicit procedure presented in Figure 6.7. At this stage, you can also represent the problems using a multiplication problem schema (Figure 6.7), of the 'compute' type in particular (see Chapter 5). Finally, do a lot of exercises using the symbolic method (Figure 6.7). For this activity, it is important to also work on improper fractions (for example 3/2), in order to resist the misconception that fractions represent only a sub-part of the whole.

The main objective of the last three activities is to familiarize children with the idea that a fraction is not a specific number (such as whole numbers), but a relationship between two numbers (numerator and denominator), which can be applied in the same way to different quantities (the whole). The whole can be any quantity. Therefore, fractions acquire a substance when they refer to a specific whole. This differentiates their value each time, depending on the quantity.

268 *Rational numbers*

> **EXERCISES**
>
> • Use collections whose size is a multiple of the denominator of the fraction and have the child select the portion corresponding to the fraction (for example, 2/3 of 15 apples) or determine the fraction corresponding to a detectable portion of the collection. Start with manipulatives or drawings, then use only symbolic numbers.

6.5.1.5 Equivalent fractions

In the previous exercises, the child has found that some fractions (e.g., 2/2, 3/3, 4/4, ...) equal the whole or 1. The notion of equivalent fractions, which is a key notion, has thus already been evoked. Using concrete examples, ask children to colour parts of a whole using several fractions equivalent to half (colour 1/2, 2/4, 3/6, etc., Figure 6.8). Make them realize that the results obtained all correspond to the same coloured area. Similarly, you can also use the number line and ask them to place equivalent fractions on it, so that the child discovers that they are all in the same position.

Recall the notion that fractions have different units of measurement. In some cases they are halves, in others they are thirds, quarters, etc. Make a table

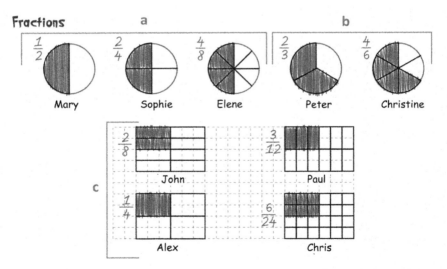

Figure 6.8 Images representing equivalent fractions of 1/2 (a), 2/3 (b), and 1/4 (c) (adapted from Karagiannakis, 2015).

Rational numbers 269

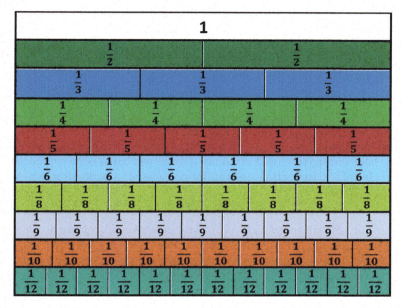

Figure 6.9 Table of possible partition of 1 with different units of measurement.

with the child as shown in Figure 6.9 where different units of measurement are used. You will see that with different units of measurement, the same quantity can be represented (1/2 = 2/4 because 2 quarters have the same value or length as a half).

Once children realize that the same quantity can be referred to by different fractions, introduce them to the arithmetic procedure used to produce equivalent fractions, i.e., multiplying or dividing the numerator and denominator by a non-zero number. Prerequisite skills for identifying or producing equivalent fractions are good knowledge of multiplication tables. Therefore, do not hesitate to pass on to the child a multiplication chart (see Chapter 4, Figure 4.37) of multiplication tables as an aid to these exercises if the child has difficulties in this area.

EXERCISES

- Ask the child to find fractions equivalent to a given fraction using any number to multiply or divide the numerator and denominator.
- Ask them to find a fraction equivalent to another fraction by giving them the numerator or denominator of the new fraction in advance (e.g., $\frac{3}{7} = \frac{}{21}$).

- Introduce a pair of fractions with different denominators, one of which is a multiple of the other (e.g., 3/7 and 4/21), and ask the child to choose the larger of the two, after turning one of them into an equivalent fraction with the same denominator (so in this example, it would be 9/21 and 4/21).

6.5.1.6 Fractions as a division

As suggested by Jordan et al. (2017), it is very important to help the child identify the link between fractions and divisions. This is another way to approach the fraction. Indeed, any fraction a/b can be considered as a division $a \div b$ where the dividend is the numerator and the divisor is the denominator. $\frac{a}{b}$ is the same as $a:b$ or 15:3 is equivalent to $\frac{15}{3}$. In fact, if I take 1:2 (a pizza divided by two), the solution is 1/2 (one-half). This conception of the fraction is very useful, especially when we consider an improper fraction (for example, 15/3 or 3/2).

This division may then be calculated using the grouping method or the sharing method (for more information, see Chapter 4). When a fraction is interpreted as a division, emphasis should be placed on the numerator, as this indicates the amount to be divided. Use everyday scenarios to encourage an intuitive approach to fractions as division. For example, if a pizza is divided equally between two children, how much does each child receive (Figure 6.10a)? Or, for the 18/3 fraction, if you have 18 playing cards, how many 3-card groups can be created (Figure 6.10d)? It is very important that children become familiar with both approaches to fractions, as part of a whole and as a division. The latter helps children to approach fractions as a measurement since after the division they get one single number or measure (e.g., $\frac{1}{2} = 0.5$ or $\frac{6}{2} = 3$). Some examples are best dealt with using the 'part of a whole' perspective (mainly for proper fractions), while others are best dealt with using division (mainly for improper fractions). The skills children acquire through the above activities help them to solve more complex exercises involving fractions, such as simplifying fractions, solving equations, and dealing with algebraic presentations that will be introduced around seventh grade.

6.5.1.7 Addition and subtraction of like fractions

The addition and subtraction of fractions should be introduced using first fractions with common denominators (or like fractions). In order to facilitate the child's understanding, use materials to manipulate and, in particular, materials that the child can remove (for subtraction). For example, you can use

Rational numbers 271

	Fraction	Scenario	Division method	Measure
a	$\frac{1}{2}$			$\frac{1}{2} = 0.5$
b	$\frac{5}{5}$			$\frac{5}{5} = 1$
c	$\frac{6}{3}$			$\frac{6}{3} = 2$
d	$\frac{18}{3}$	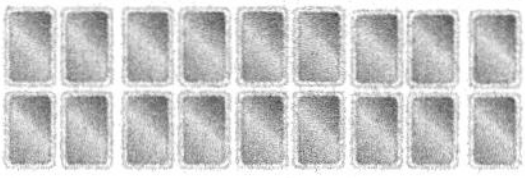		$\frac{18}{3} = 6$

Figure 6.10 Processing fractions as division using either the sharing method (a, b, c) or the grouping method (d).

cardboard pizzas that you and the child have cut into a number of equal parts (e.g., a pizza cut into thirds, another into quarters, another into fifths, etc., see Figure 6.11), but also rectangular materials such as chocolate bars. Some will represent the calculation $\frac{1}{4} + \frac{2}{4} =$ using the image of a pizza with one shaded quarter pizza, then the '+' sign, then the image of another pizza with 2/4

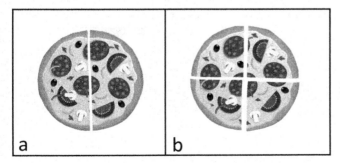

Figure 6.11 The pizza cut in halves (a) or in quarters (b).

272 *Rational numbers*

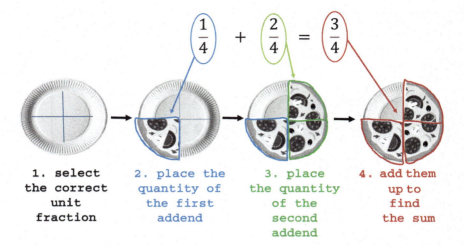

Figure 6.12 Using pizzas for doing addition (here, $\frac{1}{4}+\frac{2}{4}=$).

shaded. This visualization, whether proposed to the child or drawn by the child, is misleading and favours the wrong answer 3/8 since the child actually sees that the sum is 3 parts of a total of 8 parts drawn.

In the case of the addition, the child will have to: (1) find the pizza cut with the same number of equal parts as indicated by the denominators. For example, for '1/4 + 2/4 =', the child should select the pizza cut into quarters, (2) select the number of slices as indicated by the first fraction, (3) add the number of slices as indicated by the second fraction, and (4) find the fraction corresponding to all the slices (see Figure 6.12).

In the case of subtraction, start by recalling this operation with whole numbers (e.g., 5 – 2), stressing that this operation works in the same way with fractions. The first term of the subtraction should therefore be represented, the second being removed from the first. For fractions, teach the child to (1) use the pizza cut into the same number of equal parts as indicated by the denominators, (2) represent the first fraction, (3) remove the parts corresponding to the second fraction, and (4) determine the result (see Figure 6.13).

EXERCISES

- Use pizzas or rectangular constructions such as chocolate bars to solve additions, then subtractions, then a mixture of the two operations with fractions of the same denominator.
- Use only symbolic fractions and invite the child to solve additions and subtractions of fractions with the same denominator. If an error of the type '2/8 + 3/8 = 5/16' is produced, correct the error directly

Rational numbers 273

and return to manipulating the material so that the child can see that this answer is incorrect. Then explain very clearly that the denominators remain the same and explicitly ask the child to be aware of the trap and not to fall into it.

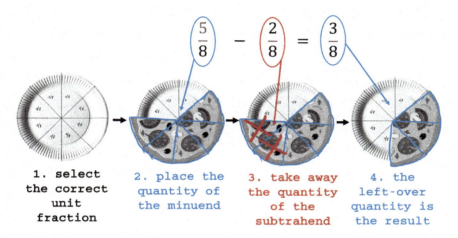

Figure 6.13 Using pizzas for doing subtraction (here, $\frac{5}{8} - \frac{2}{8} =$).

6.5.1.8 Adding or subtracting unlike fractions

You can now introduce additions of unlike fractions (i.e., with different denominators), with one denominator being a multiple of the other (Figure 6.14). Discuss the typical misconceptions of adding the two numerators and the two denominators separately and show them that this would lead to incorrect answers (see Figure 6.14c).

It is essential to ask children to simplify fractions as much as possible before adding up, as this can greatly simplify the problem (Figure 6.15).

Then follow the same steps for subtraction (Figure 6.16).

When the child understands that in order to add or subtract fractions, they must have the same denominator (or like fraction) and is able to produce equivalent fractions, you can add and subtract fractions with larger numbers (e.g., $\frac{7}{12} - \frac{5}{18}$) where children must find the least common multiple (LCM) of the denominators in order to determine the common denominator. Table 6.1A shows explicitly how to determine both the LCM and the greatest common factor (GCF) of two or more large numbers.

274   *Rational numbers*

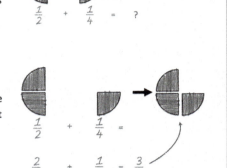

A. Same denominators Start with like fractions such as $\frac{2}{4}+\frac{1}{4}$ by visualizing the corresponding amounts. So adding 2 quarters to 1 quarter, I get 3 quarters	
B. Different denominators Then present additions of unlike fractions (i.e., with different denominators) such as $\frac{1}{2}+\frac{1}{4}$. It is apparent that it isn't possible to add **halves** with **quarters** since the shapes are different. Ask students what they can do to make shapes of equal size. It is easy to "cut" the half into 2 quarters. So now they see that there are 3 quarters in total. Ask finally the students to write symbolically the above procedure.	
C. Resist to misconception For students who apply the addition by adding separately the numerators and the denominators (e.g. $\frac{1}{2}+\frac{1}{4}=\frac{2}{6}$), visualize both the addends and the incorrect sum and point out the mismatch between them.	

Figure 6.14 Additions of fractions.

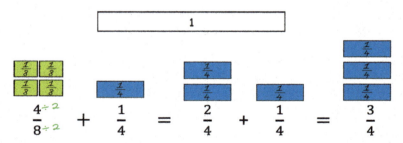

Figure 6.15 Example of addition problem presented both in visual and symbolic form in which simplification precedes addition.

Rational numbers 275

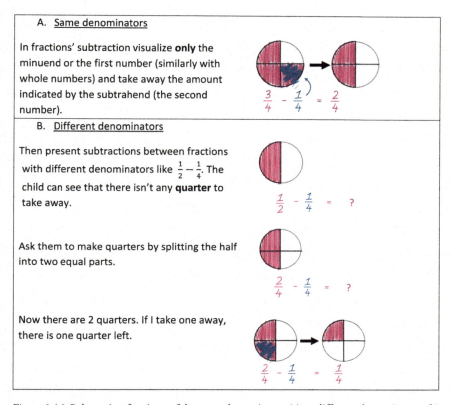

Figure 6.16 Subtracting fractions of the same denominator (a) or different denominators (b).

Table 6.1B presents the steps to do subtraction between two fractions. It introduces a flexible strategy to find out the factor by which each fraction should be multiplied in order to make their denominators equal, avoiding the division students typically are asked to perform (36 ÷ 12 = 3 and 36 ÷ 18 = 2 in the particular example). This is a compensatory method especially for students who struggle with mental multiplications (for calculating the LCM) and mental division. Table 6.1C provides an example of an addition between three fractions. As you can see the steps to find the factor by which each fraction should be multiplied to get equivalent fractions with the same denominator don't change. The strategy presented in Table 6.1C can be applied to addition and subtraction problems no matter the number of fractions.

Finally, if the child does not manage to master any of these procedures or if the denominators are prime numbers (that is GCF = 1), the butterfly method can be used. It is simple but can lead to fractions composed of very large numbers. For this technique (Figure 6.17), the child draws the wings

Table 6.1 Explicit instruction for adding or subtracting fractions with different denominators

A. Calculate both the *Least Common Multiple* & *Greatest Common Factor*	
Find the *Least Common Multiple* (LCM) by dividing consecutively both denominators (12 and 18) with the series of the prime numbers: 2, 3, 5, 7, 11, 13, ... until all quotients became 1. Cross out each time a number is divided. Circle the prime numbers who divide both partial quotients (the crossed lines help to indicate them). The product of the circled numbers is the *Greatest Common Factor* (GCF).	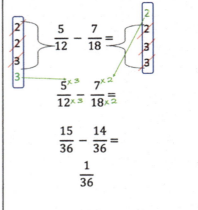 LCF (12, 18) = 2 · 2 · 3 · 3 = 36 GCF (12, 18) = ②·③ = 6
B. Example of two fractions subtraction	
-Once you find the LCM = 2 · 2 · 3 · 3, cross out the prime numbers whose product is equal with the first denominator (12= 2 · 2 · 3). -Multiply both numerator and denominator with the product of the prime numbers that are left (number 3 in this example). -Do the same for the second denominator (18= 2 · 3 · 3, so number 2 is left) -Proceed to the subtraction since the fractions have equal denominators	$$\frac{5}{12} - \frac{7}{18} =$$ $$\frac{5 \times 3}{12 \times 3} - \frac{7 \times 2}{18 \times 2} =$$ $$\frac{15}{36} - \frac{14}{36} =$$ $$\frac{1}{36}$$

of the butterfly and performs the cross multiplication thus drawn (numerator of the first fraction with the denominator of the second fraction: 5 × 18 = 90 and numerator of the second fraction with the denominator of the first fraction: 7 × 12 = 84), the numbers obtained will become the new numerators of the equivalent fractions. The denominator of these fractions will be the product of the original denominators (12 × 18 = 216). The result is a calculation with fractions of the same denominators, which is easily solved.

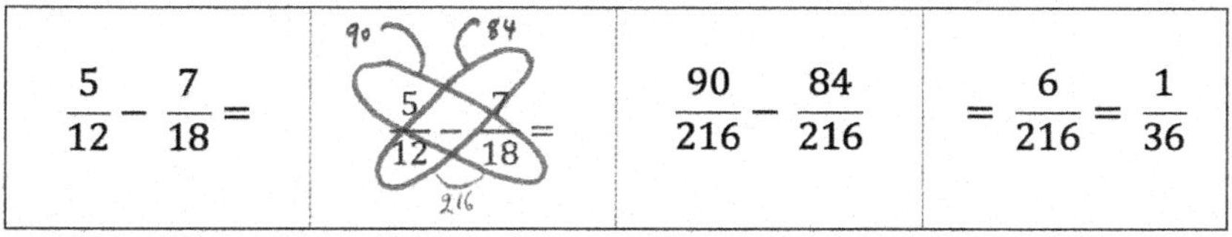

$$\frac{5}{12} - \frac{7}{18} = \qquad \frac{5}{12} \bowtie \frac{7}{18} = \qquad \frac{90}{216} - \frac{84}{216} = \frac{6}{216} = \frac{1}{36}$$

Figure 6.17 Butterfly strategy.

However, once the result is obtained, it will be important to simplify the fraction as much as possible. Notice that this method can be applied to no more than two fractions.

EXERCISES

- Ask the child to solve additions of fractions that do not have the same denominators, but one is a multiple of the other (e.g., 3/8 + 1/4). Start with sums that add up to less than one, and then you can use proper and improper fractions as terms or as a solution. Do the same type of exercises with subtractions.
- Introduce the child to the addition of fractions with different denominators, one being a multiple of the other only after simplifying one (e.g., 4/6 + 3/9) or both (e.g., 8/24 + 6/21). Do the same type of exercise with subtractions.
- Add and subtract fractions with larger numbers (for example, $\frac{13}{24} - \frac{5}{18}$) where children need to know the GCF to simplify any fraction as well as the LCM to determine the common denominator.

6.5.1.9 Multiplication with fractions

Multiplication between two integers can be seen as a repeated addition (e.g., 3 × 4 = 4 + 4 + 4). Similarly, multiplication of a fraction with an integer can be represented as a repeated addition of that fraction (e.g., 2 × 1/4 = 1/4 + 1/4) (Figure 6.18a). However, when a fraction is multiplied by another fraction, this explanation is less clear. Siegler and Lortie-Forgues (2017) propose to explain multiplications as N of M, so that 3 × 4 is three of four and 1/3 ×

278 Rational numbers

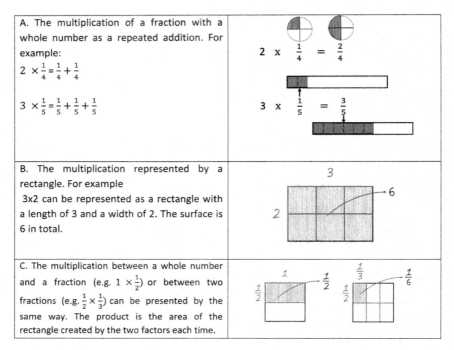

Figure 6.18 Multiplication with fractions.

1/2 is equal to 1/3 of 1/2. In this case, you take 1/2 and then, from this part, you take a third, which corresponds to 1/6. For those who are very visual, multiplication can be represented by a rectangle where the length and width correspond to the factors, and the area corresponds to the product (see Figure 6.18b for an example with whole numbers and Figure 6.18c for an example with fractions). This can be used for the product of two whole numbers, an integer and a fraction, or two fractions.

After applying the strategies 'N of M' or rectangles to solve multiple multiplications with fractions, it appears that the product is obtained by multiplying the numerators and denominators of each of the fractions separately $\frac{a}{b} \times \frac{m}{n} = \frac{a \times m}{b \times n}$). You can then present multiplications with larger numbers by applying the above procedure. At this stage, it is important to encourage children to simplify the fractions involved as much as possible, either vertically or crosswise, before proceeding with multiplication in order to keep the size of the numbers involved as small as possible (Figure 6.19). If students have difficulties finding the common factors to simplify the

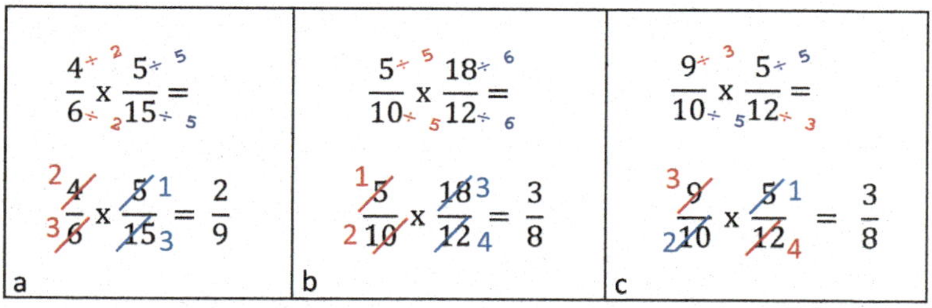

Figure 6.19 Vertical (a, b) or crosswise (c) simplification of fractions in multiplication.

numerator-denominator pairs (especially when the numbers are large, i.e., 18/12, see Figure 6.19b), ask them to find the GCF by using the strategy we presented in Table 6.1A.

EXERCISES

- Experiment with the child in multiplying a fraction with an integer using the M of Ns conception or rectangle visualization. Then, ask the child to solve the multiplication of a fraction with a whole number presented in symbolic form.
- Demonstrate to the child the multiplication of a fraction with another fraction using the M of Ns conception or rectangle visualization. Then, have the child solve a variety of multiplications of two fractions with small numbers as numerators and denominators.
- Ask the child to solve a variety of multiplications of two fractions, using large numbers as numerators or denominators, and encouraging them to simplify fractions as much as possible.

6.5.1.10 Division with fractions

Begin to explain the division of fractions using the simpler situation where a fraction is divided by an integer. In this case, the child can imagine the situation using the division analogy. For example, $\frac{4}{5} \div 2$ is like having 4/5 of a pizza to share between 2 children, it is easy to see (with drawings) that each child will have 2/5 (see Figure 6.20a).

However, this analogy is not very useful when one fraction is divided by another fraction. In this case, the grouping method, already used for division

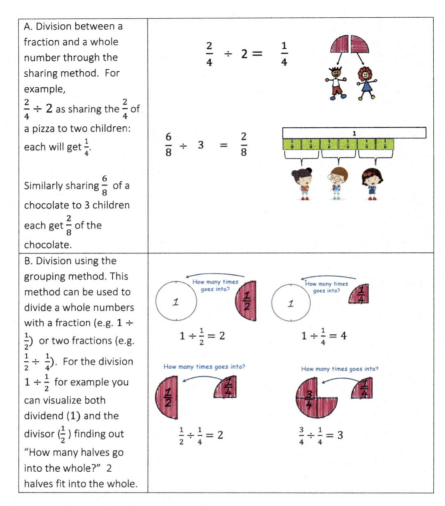

Figure 6.20 Division of fractions with the sharing method (a) and the grouping method (b).

between two whole numbers (see Chapter 4), can be applied. This is also the method recommended by Siegler and Lortie-Forgues (2017), who propose explaining division as the number of times the divisor enters the dividend, for example for 16:4 =, it is a question of determining how many times 4 enters/is included in 16. This approach can also be used with the division of a natural number by a fraction, for example, $3 \div \frac{1}{2}$ can be solved by answering the question how many times 1/2 (or one-half) is included in 3. The answer is 6. This can also be used with dividing a fraction by another fraction, for example,

$\frac{1}{2} \div \frac{1}{4}$ can be solved by examining how many times 1/4 (or a quarter) is included in 1/2 (Figure 6.20b).

This approach to the meaning of division helps the child understand that the meaning of the concept of division does not change when moving from whole numbers to fractions. However, this method does not work if one fraction is not a multiple of the other (e.g., $\frac{3}{5} \div \frac{6}{7}$). To deal with all cases, a very simple formula can be taught. It consists of multiplying the first fraction by the inverse of the second fraction (in this example, $\frac{3}{5} \times \frac{7}{6}$). You can explain this strange procedure by explaining that in reality it is exactly the same as in natural number divisions (for example, 6 ÷ 2, corresponds to how many times 2 is included in 6, and also to multiplying the first number by the inverse of the second number, i.e., 6 × 1/2).

EXERCISES

- Start with some examples of a fraction divided by a natural number using the drawings and the method of division. Then, the same type of exercise can be presented to the child, this time using symbolic writing only (for example, 6/8 ÷ 3=).
- Introduce the grouping method, first for divisions of natural numbers, then for fractions. Ask the child to practice different exercises containing a natural number divided by a fraction using the grouping method (for example, 4 ÷ 1/2).
- Then use the same method for dividing one fraction by another, presenting the child with multiple fractions of each other (for example, 2/3 ÷ 1/6).
- Explain the formulas: $\left(\frac{n}{m} : \frac{a}{b} = \frac{n \times b}{m \times a} \right)$ and check in all previous exercises that this formula leads to the correct answer.
- Give a series of divisions of one fraction by another, using any type of fraction. Ask the child to simplify the resulting solution (this can already be done in the formula, before obtaining the products $\left(\frac{n \times b}{m \times a} \right)$, see Figure 6.19).
- Present a mixture of division and multiplication exercises to solve.
- With the child, construct a worksheet that summarizes how to proceed for each of the four operations on fractions (you can draw on Tables 6.3 and 6.4 at the end of this chapter).

282 *Rational numbers*

- Use a combination of addition, subtraction, division, and multiplication exercises with the help of the worksheet.
- Use a mixture of all of the arithmetic operations without the card.

6.5.2 Working with decimal numbers

6.5.2.1 The understanding of decimal numbers

As the understanding of the decimal numbers is based on the base-10 positional system, it is very important to first make sure that the child is at ease with this system with natural numbers. It is only in a second step that this positional system will be extended to integrate the tenths, and then the hundredths, etc.

First, use manipulatives that make sense, like coins, or using different types of representations. Talking about 10-cent and 1-cent coins at first will make more sense than talking from the very beginning about 'tenths', 'hundredths'. Subsequently, connect these manipulatives to their decimal fractions $\frac{1}{10}, \frac{1}{100}$, which will help students to understand the origin of the corresponding number words 'tenth' and 'hundredth'. Help them to remember the words and avoid the confusion with those of 'tens' and 'hundreds' (Figure 6.21).

Then, the 'thousandth' can be introduced using a tape measure or Dienes blocks by considering the big cube as the unit. Subsequently, connect these decimal fractions to the decimals' notation 0.1, 0.01, 0.001. Explain that the unit of measurement of each decimal number is determined by the place value of the last number. At this point, you can use the same type of

Decimal	1	0.1	0.01
Fraction	$\frac{1}{1}$	$\frac{1}{10}$	$\frac{1}{100}$
Verbal	One unit	One tenth	One hundredth
Visuals			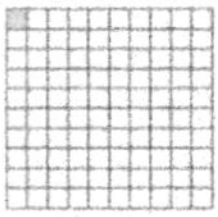
Manipulatives (Unit= 1€)			
Everyday words	1 euro	10-cent or one tenth of a euro	1 cent or one hundredth of a euro

Figure 6.21 Interrelation of decimal (up to hundredth place value) and fractions through different representations.

Rational numbers 283

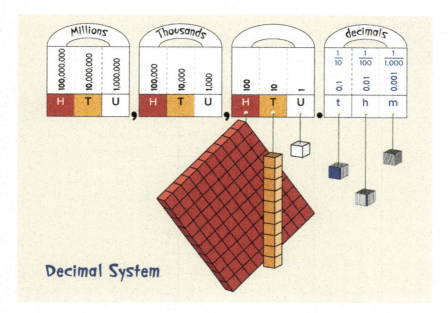

Figure 6.22 Visual representation of the decimal system (adapted from Karagiannakis, 2015).

table that you used for the positional system in whole numbers (see Chapter 3) but now extended on the right side to show all the decimals (see Figure 6.22). Explore the table so that they can discover that, like with the natural numbers, the digits after the decimal point (Figure 6.23) increase in value when they move to the left (0.003, 0.03, 0.3, 3) and decrease in value when they move to the right (2, 0.2, 0.02, 0.002, ...). However, make it clear that they should not fall into the trap of the words. Whereas hundreds are bigger than tens, hundredths are smaller than tenths! Teach the students to read decimal numbers analytically (e.g., 0.3 = '3 tenths', 0.27 = '27 hundredths') revealing the deep meaning of the number value rather than using labels such as 'zero point three' for 0.3. Using that type of labelling will ease the translation between the decimal number and the fraction form (e.g., $0.3 = \frac{3}{10}$ = '3 tenths', $0.27 = \frac{27}{100}$ = '27 hundredths'), since both forms are read exactly the same way.

You can then go back to the notion of equivalent fractions and the fact that 1/10 = 10/100 = 100/1000, etc., and connect this with the notion of equivalent decimal numbers as 0.1 = 0.10 = 0.100, etc. To do this, ask students to visualize equivalent decimals (e.g., 0.1 and 0.10) and compare each area occupied or use euro coins to represent their value. In both cases, it becomes clear that the numbers are equivalent (Figures 6.24 and 6.25).

284 *Rational numbers*

Decimal System

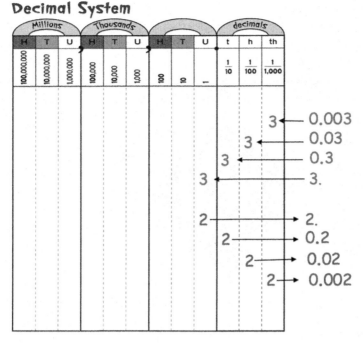

Figure 6.23 Presentation of how the numerical size of a decimal number changes when it moves left or right.

EXERCISES

- Use 1-cent and 10-cent coins, asking the child to make the correspondence between the value in cents (e.g., 7 cents), the value in terms of a fraction of one euro (e.g., 7/100 of a euro), and decimal notation (e.g., 0.07 euros).
- Use the table of the positional system. Put numbers in the table and ask the child to read them (e.g., 0.07 = '7 hundredths').
- Present decimal numbers on the positional system table and ask the child to read it by referring to the place value of the last number, e.g., 0.7= '7 tenths', 0.06 = '6 hundredths'.
- Work with different types of materials and ask the child to use them to represent decimal numbers (e.g., a square divided in 100).
- Work on the equivalence between different decimal numbers. First, give a decimal number to the child and ask him/her to produce an equivalent decimal number. Second, give two decimal numbers to

Rational numbers 285

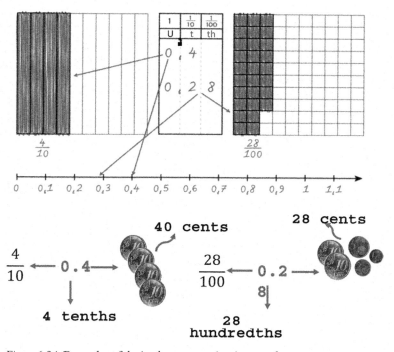

Figure 6.24 Examples of decimal representation in several ways.

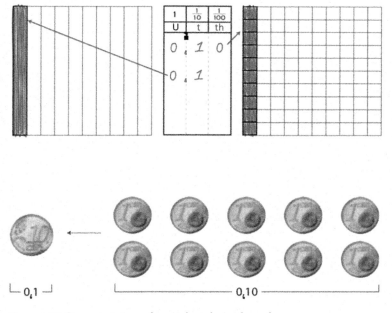

Figure 6.25 Representation of equivalent decimal numbers.

- the child who has to decide whether they are of the same value or not (e.g., 0.75 and 0.7500 but not 0.75 and 0.075).
- Work with number lines and ask children to posit decimal numbers on the line (0–1 lines to start).
- Give pairs of decimal numbers with decimal parts of different lengths and with the 'value of the whole numbers corresponding to the decimal part' being sometimes congruent (e.g., 0.2 and 0.37) and sometimes incongruent (0.7 and 0.63) with the value of the decimal number. Ask the child to first position each number on the number line, and then select the bigger one.
- Give pairs of decimal numbers with decimal parts of different lengths (e.g., 0.2 and 0.37); ask the child to transform one of them so that they have the same length (i.e., 0.20 and 0.37) and then to select the bigger one.
- Give pairs of decimal numbers with different lengths; ask the child to select the bigger one and justify his/her answer.
- Finally, to stimulate a deep understanding, provide students with several fractions and decimals (see an example at Figure 6.26) and ask them to order them on a number line, justifying their decision.

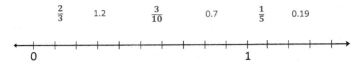

Figure 6.26 Stimulating the understanding of rational numbers.

6.5.2.2 Arithmetic operations on decimal numbers

Start by highlighting that each operation has the same meaning in decimals as it has in whole numbers or in fractions. You can do this by representing examples of each operation through number lines or money (Figure 6.27).

Like in natural numbers, in which units have to be added to units and tens added to tens, in decimals also, it is important to respect the positional rank of the digits.

Like in fractions, where you first convert each fraction into an equivalent one using a common denominator, the same process can be applied in decimals. For instance, before calculating 0.75 − 0.3, adjust numbers so that both have the same unit of measurement (or equal number of decimal digits), i.e., 0.75 − 0.30. This will decrease the number of errors due to the whole number bias (i.e., 0.75 − 0.3 leading to the incorrect answer 0.72).

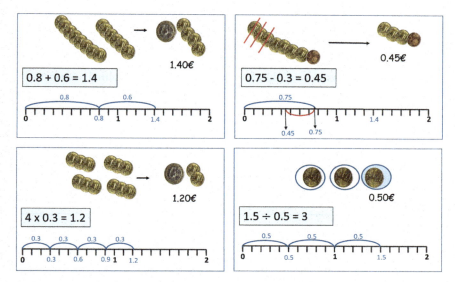

Figure 6.27 Conceptual approach to the four operations with decimals.

Another possibility is to convert the decimals into the corresponding fractions and use the procedure learned on fractions (Cooreman & Bringmans, 2016). Once the children have found the result in fraction form, they can easily convert it back to decimal notation. The efficacy of this explicit strategy is based on the fact that students finally apply calculations between whole numbers, as highlighted in red (Table 6.2). This technique of converting decimals into the corresponding fractions is also a very efficient way to deal with divisions and multiplications.

EXERCISES

- Propose additions of two decimal numbers with different lengths in the decimal portion. Ask the child to first convert the addends so that they have the same length in the decimal part and then to do the calculation. You can use coins or then after, the number line to check the validity of the obtained answer.
- Do similar exercises with subtractions.
- Propose using the conversion into fraction method. Here again, the first step will be to change the problem so that the two fractions have the same denominator and then do the calculation.
- Do the same with subtractions.

288 *Rational numbers*

> - Use the index card that you constructed with the child, which summarizes how to deal with the four arithmetical operations using fractions. Practice now multiplications and divisions of decimal numbers using the conversion to fraction procedures.
> - Propose a mixture of the four operations with decimal numbers using the technique of converting numbers into fractions.

Table 6.2 Calculations with decimal numbers by converting them into fractions

Convert decimals into fractions	Common mistake
Addition	
$0.3 + 0.9 = \dfrac{3}{10} + \dfrac{9}{10} = \dfrac{3+9}{10} = \dfrac{12}{10} = 1.2$	$0.3 + 0.9 = 0.12$
$0.32 + 0.6 = \dfrac{32}{100} + \dfrac{6}{10} = \dfrac{32}{100} + \dfrac{60}{100} = \dfrac{32+60}{100} = \dfrac{92}{100} = 0.92$	$0.32 + 0.6 = 0.38$
$1.8 + 0.4 = \dfrac{18}{10} + \dfrac{4}{10} = \dfrac{18+4}{10} = \dfrac{22}{10} = 2.2$	$1.8 + 0.4 = 1.12$
Subtraction	
$0.65 - 0.3 = \dfrac{65}{100} - \dfrac{3}{10} = \dfrac{65}{100} - \dfrac{30}{100} = \dfrac{65-35}{100} = \dfrac{35}{100} = 0.35$	$0.65 - 0.3 = 0.62$
$0.247 - 0.03 = \dfrac{247}{1000} - \dfrac{3}{100} = \dfrac{247}{1000} - \dfrac{30}{1000} = \dfrac{247-30}{1000} = \dfrac{217}{1000} = 0.217$	$0.247 - 0.03 = 0.244$
Multiplication	
$0.5 \times 3 = \dfrac{5}{10} \times \dfrac{3}{1} = \dfrac{5 \times 3}{10 \times 1} = \dfrac{15}{10} = 1.5$	$0.5 \times 3 = 0.15$
$0.7 \times 0.3 = \dfrac{7}{10} \times \dfrac{3}{10} = \dfrac{7 \times 3}{10 \times 10} = \dfrac{21}{100} = 0.21$	$0.7 \times 0.3 = 2.1$
Division	
$6 \div 0.3 = \dfrac{6}{1} \div \dfrac{3}{10} = \dfrac{6}{1} \times \dfrac{10}{3} = \dfrac{6 \times 10}{1 \times 3} = \dfrac{60}{3} = 20$	$6 \div 0.3 = 0.2$
$1.5 \div 0.5 = \dfrac{15}{10} \div \dfrac{5}{10} = \dfrac{15}{10} \times \dfrac{10}{5} = \dfrac{15 \times 10}{10 \times 5} = \dfrac{150}{50} = 3$	$1.5 \div 0.5 = 0.3$

Source: inspired by Cooreman & Bringmans, 2016.

Table 6.3 Verbal explanation of the heuristic model of operations on fractions

1. Check if it is possible to simplify any fraction before proceeding to any operation between them. It is important to keep the numerical size of both the numerators and the denominators as small as possible. Simplify with the proper numbers 2, 3, 5, 7, … or by calculating the greatest common factor for large numbers.

2. Transform any whole, decimal, or mixed numbers into fraction notation for example:
$2 \to \frac{2}{1}$, $0.3 \to \frac{3}{10}$, $1\frac{2}{3} \to \frac{5}{3}$. Revise this if needed.

3. Perform the arithmetic operations respecting the order of operations (as for whole numbers) by using the mnemonic **BEMDAS** (**b**rackets, **e**xponents, **m**ultiplication–**d**ivision, **a**ddition–**s**ubtraction).

4.

Addition	**Subtraction**	**Multiplication**	**Division**
Calculate the least common multiple so that the fractions have the same denominators.		Simplify any numerator with any denominator of the fractions.	Multiply the first fraction with the reciprocal of the second.
Add the numerators, keeping the same denominators.	Subtract the numerators, keeping the same denominators.	Multiply separately the numerators and the denominators.	Follow the steps of multiplication.

5. Simplify the result by dividing the numerator and the denominator with the prime numbers 2, 3, 5, 7, … or with the greatest common factor.

Source: adapted from Cooreman & Bringmans (2016).

290 *Rational numbers*

Table 6.4 Visual representation of the heuristic model of operations on fractions

1	**Simplify** by dividing by 2, 3, 4, 5, 7, or by the GCF*
2	Convert any: **whole, decimal, or mixed numbers** into fractions
3	B E M D A S

+	−	×	÷
Same denominator LCM*		Simplify	🙌 × 🙇
$\dfrac{\text{numer.} + \text{numer.}}{\text{denom.}}$	$\dfrac{\text{numer.} - \text{numer.}}{\text{denom.}}$	$\dfrac{\text{numer.} \times \text{numer.}}{\text{denom.} \times \text{denom.}}$	Follow the steps of ×

| 5 | **Simplify** by dividing by 2, 3, 5, 7, or by the GCF* |

Source: adapted from Cooreman & Bringmans, 2016.

(*GCF = greatest common factor; LCM = least common multiple.)

6.5.3 Working with fraction and decimal numbers together

At a higher level, students will be required to handle various arithmetic operations within the same calculation, that may involve a mixture of integers, decimals, and fractions (for example, $3 + 0.8 + \dfrac{3}{5} = ?$). The heuristic model presented in Tables 6.3 and 6.4 (adapted from Cooreman & Bringmans, 2016) allows the resolution steps of this type of calculation to be organized. This heuristic is proposed in both verbal and visual form with explicit instructions (see Tables 6.3 and 6.4).

This heuristic model will be particularly useful for students with memory problems (it works like a mnemonic sheet for memorizing all these procedures) and for those with weak mathematical reasoning skills (it gives them the most economical strategy and shows them fixed steps to follow). The model can be used to solve simple problems, such as adding, subtracting, multiplying, or dividing two simple fractions, but also to perform more complex arithmetic expressions such as the one shown in Figure 6.28. It is recommended to highlight, at each step, the part of the arithmetic expression that is concerned with the particular step of the procedure, in order to keep on track.

Do not forget that these are suggestions and that you should find the best methods and tools for the child you are working with. As much as possible, embed these exercises into games to motivate the child and find way to reward his/her progressions to keep the motivation high.

$A = (1\frac{1}{3} - \frac{1}{2}) \times (2 - \frac{1}{5}) + 2 \div (1 + \frac{1}{3}) - \frac{\cancel{18}^{3}}{\cancel{12}_{2}} \div 2$	Simplify
$A = (1\frac{1}{3} - \frac{1}{2}) \times (2 - \frac{1}{5}) + 2 \div (1 + \frac{1}{3}) - \frac{3}{2} \div 2$	Convert all terms into fractions
$A = (\frac{4}{3} - \frac{1}{2}) \times (\frac{2}{1} - \frac{1}{5}) + \frac{2}{1} \div (\frac{1}{1} + \frac{1}{3}) - \frac{3}{2} \div \frac{2}{1}$	ⒷE MD AS Start with the operations within the Brackets
	B⒠MD AS No Exponents exist, so move to the next operation
$A = \frac{\cancel{5}^{1}}{\cancel{6}_{2}} \times \frac{\cancel{9}^{3}}{\cancel{5}_{1}} + \frac{2}{1} \div \frac{4}{3} - \frac{3}{2} \div \frac{2}{1}$ $A = \frac{3}{2} + \frac{\cancel{2}^{1}}{1} \times \frac{3}{\cancel{4}_{2}} - \frac{3}{2} \times \frac{1}{2}$	BE⓪⒟AS Perform all multiplications (simplify if possible) and divisions
$A = \frac{3}{2} + \frac{3}{2} - \frac{3}{4}$	BEMD⒜⒮ Perform both additions and subtractions starting from right to left.
$A = \frac{6}{4} - \frac{3}{4}$	BEMD⒜⒮
$A = \frac{3}{4}$	The final fraction cannot be simplyfied.

Figure 6.28 Simplifying a complicated arithmetic expression with rational numbers by using the fractions heuristic model.

References

Bailey, D. H., Hansen, N., & Jordan, N. C. (2017). The codevelopment of children's fraction arithmetic skill and fraction magnitude understanding. *Journal of Educational Psychology, 109*(4), 509–519.

Bailey, D. H., Siegler, R. S., & Geary, D. C. (2014). Early predictors of middle school fraction knowledge. *Developmental Science, 17*(5), 775–785.

Ball, D. L. (1990). Prospective elementary and secondary teachers' understanding of division. *Journal of Research in Mathematics Education, 21*, 132–144.

Bonato, M., Fabbri, S., Umiltà, C., & Zorzi, M. (2007). The mental representation of numerical fractions: Real or integer? *Journal of Experimental Psychology: Human Perception and Performance, 33*(6), 1410–1419.

Butler, F. M., Miller, S. P., Crehan, K., Babbitt, B., & Pierce, T. (2003). Fraction instruction for students with mathematics disabilities: Comparing two teaching sequences. *Learning Disabilities Research and Practice, 18*(2), 99–111.

Connolly, A. J. (2007). *KeyMath-3 diagnostic assessment: Manual forms A and B*. Minneapolis, MN: Pearson.

Cooreman, A., & Bringmans, M. (2016). *Eureka Wiskunde. Kameel 1 basiskennis algrebra*. Leuven: Eureka Expert.

Cooreman, A. (2017), *Rekentrappers 3HR Module 5. Tafels van 4,8 en kwadraten en breuken deel 1*, 56, 58–59. Leuven: Eureka Expert.

Desmet, L., Grégoire, J., & Mussolin, C. (2010). Developmental changes in the conceptions of decimal fractions. *Learning and Instruction, 20*(6), 521–532.

DeWolf, M., Bassok, M., & Holyoak, K. J. (2015). From rational numbers to algebra: Separable contributions of decimal magnitude and relational understanding of fractions. *Journal of Experimental Child Psychology, 133*, 72–84.

Durkin, K., & Rittle-Johnson, B. (2012). The effectiveness of using incorrect examples to support learning about decimal magnitude. *Learning and Instruction, 22*(3), 206–214.

Durkin, K., & Rittle-Johnson, B. (2015). Diagnosis misconceptions: Revealing changing decimal fraction knowledge. *Learning and Instruction, 37*, 21–29.

English, L. D., & Halford, G. S. (1995). *Mathematics education: Models and processes*. Hillsdale, NJ: Lawrence Erlbaum.

Fuchs, L. S., Malone, A. S., Schumacher, R. F., Namkung, J., Hamlett, C. L., Jordan, N. C., ... Changas, P. (2016). Supported self-explaining during fraction intervention. *Journal of Educational Psychology, 108*(4), 493.

Fuchs, L. S., Schumacher, R. F., Long, J., Namkung, J., Hamlett, C. L., Cirino, P. T., ... Changas, P. (2013). Improving at-risk learners' understanding of fractions. *Journal of Educational Psychology, 105*(3), 683–700.

Fuchs, L. S., Schumacher, R. F., Long, J., Namkung, J., Malone, A. S., Wang, A., ... Changas, P. (2016). Effects of intervention to improve at-risk fourth graders' understanding, calculations, and word problems with fractions. *Elementary School Journal, 116*(4), 625–651.

Fuchs, L. S., Schumacher, R. F., Sterba, S. K., Long, J., Namkung, J., Malone, A., ... Changas, P. (2014). Does working memory moderate the effects of fraction intervention? An aptitude-treatment interaction. *Journal of Educational Psychology, 106*(2), 499–514.

Ganor-Stern, D. (2013). Are 1/2 and 0.5 represented in the same way? *Acta Psychologica, 142*(3), 299–307.

Geary, D. C., Boykin, A. W., Embretson, S., Reyna, V., Siegler, R., Berch, D. B., & Graban, J. (2008). Report of the task group on learning processes. Retrieved from http://www.ed.gov/about/bdscomm/list/mathpanel/report/learning-processes.pdf

Geary, D. C., Hoard, M. K., Nugent, L., & Bailey, D. H. (2012). Mathematical cognition deficits in children with learning disabilities and persistent low achievement: A five-year prospective study. *Journal of Educational Psychology, 104*(1), 206–223.

Hamden, N., & Gunderson, E. A. (2017). The number line is a critical spatial-numerical representation: Evidence from a fraction intervention. *Developmental Psychology, 53*(3), 587–596.

Hecht, S. A. (1998). Toward an information-processing account of individual differences in fraction skills. *Journal of Educational Psychology, 90*(3), 545–559.

Hiebert, J., & Wearne, D. (1983, April). Students' conceptions of decimal numbers. Paper presented at the Annual Meeting of the American Educational Research Association, Montreal, QC.

Hiebert, J., & Wearne, D. (1985). A model of students' decimal computation procedures. *Cognition and Instruction, 2*(3–4), 175–205.

Hiebert, J., & Wearne, D. (1986). Procedures over concepts: The acquisition of decimal number knowledge. In J. Hiebert (Ed.), *Conceptual and procedural knowledge: The case of mathematics* (pp. 199–223). Hillsdale, NJ: Lawrence Erlbaum.

Hurst, M., & Cordes, S. (2016). Rational-number comparison across notation: Fractions, decimals and whole numbers. *Journal of Experimental Psychology: Human Perception and Performance, 42*(2), 281–293.

Iuculano, T., & Butterworth, B. (2011). Understanding the real value of fractions and decimals. *Quarterly Journal of Experimental Psychology, 64*(11), 2088–2098.

Jordan, N. C., Resnick, I., Rodrigues, J., Hansen, N., & Dyson, N. (2017). Delaware longitudinal study of fraction learning: Implications for helping children with mathematics difficulties. *Journal of Learning Disabilities, 50*(6), 621–630.

Karagiannakis, G. (2015). Οι αριθμοί πέρα απ' τους κανόνες. Αθήνα: Διερευνητική μάθηση.

Kloosterman, P. (2010). Mathematics skills of 17-year-olds in the United States: 1978 to 2004. *Journal for Research in Mathematics Education, 41*(1), 20–51.

Krowka, S. K., & Fuchs, L. S. (2017). Cognitive profiles associated with responsiveness to fraction intervention. *Learning Disabilities Research and Practice, 32*(4), 216–230.

Lafay, A., & Helloin, M.-C. (2016). *Examath 8–15*. Published on internet https://www.happyneuronpro.com/.

Lortie-Forgues, H., & Siegler, R. S. (2017). Conceptual knowledge of decimal arithmetic. *Journal of Educational Psychology, 109*(3), 374–386.

Manalo, E., Bunnell, J. K., & Stillman, J. A. (2000). The use of process mnemonics in teaching students with mathematics learning disabilities. *Learning Disability Quarterly, 23*(2), 137–156.

Martin, T., & Schwartz, D. L. (2005). Physically distributed learning: Restructuring and reinterpreting physical environments in the development of fraction concepts. *Cognitive Science, 29*(4), 587–625.

Mazzocco, M. M. M., Myers, G. F., Lewis, K. E., Hanich, L. B., & Murphy, M. M. (2013). Limited knowledge of fraction representations differentiates middle school students with mathematics learning disability (dyscalculia) versus low mathematic achievement. *Journal of Experimental Psychology, 115*(2), 371–387.

McCloskey, M. (2007). Quantitative literacy and developmental dyscalculias. In D. B. Berch & M. M. Mazzocco (Eds.), *Why is math so hard for some children? The nature and origins of mathematical learning difficulties and disabilities* (pp. 415–429). Baltimore, MD: Paul H. Brookes Publishing.

Meert, G., Grégoire, J., & Noël, M. P. (2010). Comparing the magnitude of two fractions with common components: Which representations are used by 10- and 12-year-olds? *Journal of Experimental Child Psychology, 107*(3), 244–259.

Meert, G., Grégoire, J., Seron, X., & Noël, M.-P. (2012). The mental representation of the magnitude of symbolic and non-symbolic ratios in adults. *Quarterly Journal of Experimental Psychology, 65*(4), 702–724.

Meert, G., Grégoire, J., Seron, X., & Noël, M.-P. (2013). The processing of symbolic and nonsymbolic ratios in school-age children. *PLOS ONE, 8*(11), e82002. doi: 10.1371/journal.pone.0082002

Misquitta, R. (2011). A review of the literature: Fraction instruction for struggling learners in mathematics. *Learning Disabilities Research and Practice, 26*(2), 109–119.

Mix, K. S., Levine, S. C., & Huttenlocher, J. (1999). Early fraction calculation ability. *Developmental Psychology, 35*(1), 164–174. doi: 10.1037/0012-1649.35.1.164

Newton, K. J. (2008). An extensive analysis of preservice elementary teachers' knowledge of fractions. *American Educational Research Association, 45*(4), 1080–1110.

Ni, Y., & Zhou, Y. D. (2005). Teaching and learning fraction and rational numbers: The origins and implications of whole number bias. *Educational Psychologist, 40*(1), 27–52.

Noël, M. P., & Grégoire, J. (2015). *TediMath Grands, Test diagnostique des compétences de base en mathématiques du CE2 à la 5ᵉ.* Montreuil, France: ECPA (Editions du centre de psychologie appliquée).

Resnick, L. B., Nesher, P., Leonard, F., Magone, M., Omanson, S., & Peret, I. (1989). Conceptual bases of arithmetic errors: The case of decimal fractions. *Journal for Research in Mathematics Education, 20*(1), 8–27.

Rittle-Johnson, B., Siegler, R. S., & Alibali, M. W. (2001). Developing conceptual understanding and procedural skills in mathematics: An iterative process. *Journal of Educational Psychology, 93*(2), 346–362.

Sackur-Grisvard, C., & Léonard, F. (1985). Intermediate cognitive organizations in the process of learning a mathematical concept: The order of positive decimal numbers. *Cognition and Instruction, 2*(2), 157–174.

Saxe, G. B., Guberman, S.R., & Gearhart, M. (1987). Social processes in early number development. *Monographs of the Society for Research in Child Development, 52*(2), 216.

Saxe, G. B., Diakow, R., & Gearhart, M. (2012). Towards curricular coherence in integers and fractions: A study of the efficacy of a lesson sequence that uses the number line as the principal representational context. *Zdm Mathematics Education, 45*(3), 343–364.

Shin, M., & Bryant, D. P. (2015). Fraction interventions for students struggling to learn mathematics: A research synthesis. *Remedial and Special Education, 36*(6), 374–387.

Siegler, R. S., Duncan, G. J., Davis-Kean, P. E., Duckworth, K., Claessens, A., Engel, M., ... Chen, M. (2013). Early predictors of high school mathematics achievement. *Psychological Science, 23*(7), 691–697. doi: 10.1177/0956797612440101

Siegler, R. S., & Lortie-Forgues, H. (2017). Hard lessons: Why rational number arithmetic is so difficult for so many people. *Current Directions in Psychological Sciences, 26*(4), 346–351.

Siegler, R. S., & Pyke, A. A. (2013). Developmental and individual differences in understanding of fractions. *Developmental Psychology, 49*(10), 1994–2004.

Siegler, R. S., Thompson, C. A., & Schneider, M. (2011). An integrated theory of whole number and fractions development. *Cognitive Psychology, 62*(4), 273–296.

Stafylidou, S., & Vosniadou, S. (2004). The development of students' understanding of the numerical value of fractions. *Learning and Instruction, 14*(5), 503–518.

Stigler, J. W., Givvin, K. B., & Thompson, B. J. (2010). What community college developmental mathematics students understand about mathematics. *Mathematics Teacher, 1*(3), 4–16.

Test, D. W., & Ellis, M. F. (2005). The effects of LAP fractions on addition and subtraction of fractions with students with mild disabilities. *Education and Treatment of Children, 28*(1), 11–24.

Tian, J., & Siegler, R. S. (2017). Fractions learning in children with mathematics difficulties. *Journal of Learning Disabilities, 50*(6), 614–620.

Tian, J., & Siegler, R. S. (2018). Which type of rational numbers should students learn first? *Educational Psychology Review, 30*(2), 351–372.

Tirosh, D., Fischbein, E., Graeber, A. O., & Wilson, J. W. (1999). Prospective elementary teachers' conceptions of rational numbers, 1–17. Retrieved from http://jwilson.coe.uga.edu/Texts.Folder/tirosh/Pros.El.Tchrs.html

Wang, Y. Q., & Siegler, R. S. (2013). Representations of and translation between common fractions and decimal fractions. *Chinese Science Bulletin, 58*(36), 4630–4640.

Index

Note: Page numbers in *italics* indicate figures and page numbers in **bold** indicate tables

abstraction principle 41
acquisition: of sequence of number words 39; of verbal numerical chain 38
Adams, A. 206, 207, 216, 220, 221
Addition Fact Retrieval subtest 129
ANS *see* approximate number system
Ansari, D. 4
approximate number system (ANS) 2, 36–38, 73, 74, 119; accuracy to 50; acuity test 55; arithmetic skills, training of 122–123; and dyscalculia 44–45; 'mental number line' 43; numerical magnitude encoded 42; training of 48–50
Arabic code 65, 73, 97–98; positional system of 82, 90; unique string of symbols in 237
Arabic numbers 3, 36, 51, 60, 64, 90–100; associated with verbal number 54; comparisons 45, 48, 52, 53, 55; difficulties in understanding 28; errors in writing 90; number line intervention involved placing 53; ordering of triplets of 49; place-value system of 6, 83; and verbal number 79
area model, of multiplication 175–177, *177, 178*
arithmetic/arithmetic skills: assessment of 128–131; basic operations 106; complex additions, strategies for **113, 114**; complex calculations 112–118; complex multiplication and division, strategies for **117**; complex subtraction, strategies for **114**; counting-all strategy for simple addition and subtraction 108; counting-down strategy for simple addition and subtraction 110; counting-min strategy for simple addition and subtraction 109; counting-on strategy for simple addition and subtraction 108–109; counting-up strategy for simple addition and subtraction 110–111; decomposition strategy for simple addition and subtraction 110, 146–153; development of 107–118; and difficulties observed in dyscalculia 118–121; digit-based strategies for complex calculations 114; estimation in, role of 118; number-based strategies for complex calculations 114–115; overview 106–107; retrieval strategy for simple addition and subtraction 109; simple addition and subtraction 108–111; simple multiplication and division 111–112; training and intervention studies 122–128
Auerbach, J. 1
Aunio, P. 48

Baccaglini-Frank, A. 25
Bailey, D. H. 241, 260
Bala, S. 81
Ball, D. L. 11
Baroody, A. J. 116
Barrouillet, P. 79
Bartelet, D. 4
Barterian, J. A. 88, 93
base-10 composition transparency 147
base-10 decomposition transparency 147
base-10 positional system 97–98
base-10 system: bubbles structure to subtract 13, 14, *21*; and calculations 82–84; competence assessment 93–94; development of 75–77; influences of language on development of 78;

magnitude representation 73–74; numerical systems 72–73; positional system 77–78; training studies 85–93; transcoding 78–82
basic numerical skills: approximate number system 36–38; development of 36–44; enumeration and counting principles 40–41; learning cardinal value of number words 41–43; mapping numbers to spatial layout 43–44; object tracking system 37; overview 36; verbal counting 38–40
Basili, A. 73, 74, 79, 80, 90
Bassok, M. 242
Becker, J. 77
Beeres, K. 3
Bell, D. 7
BEMDAS *see* brackets, exponents, multiplication and division, addition and subtraction
Bermudez, V. 122
Bevan, A. 45
Bientzle, M. 53
Blomert, L. 4
Bonato, M. 240
Bottge, B. A. 9
Bow-Thomas, C. C. 46
brackets, exponents, multiplication and division, addition and subtraction (BEMDAS) 16, *18*
Brannon, E. M. 42, 49, 122
Briars, D. J. 39–41
Bryant, D. P. 252
Bryant, P. 7, 75
Bull, R. 52
Bunnell, J. K. 247, 248
Burns, M. K. 123, 132
Butler, F. M. 252
Butterworth, B. 45, 242

Camos, V. 79
Caramazza, A. 73, 74, 79, 80, 90
cardinal principle 40
cardinal value of number words: enumeration rehabilitation 58–59; learning 41–43
Carey, S. 42
Carraher, J. 7
Caviola, S. 127
Chang, C. M. 81
Changas, P. 11
Cheng, F. S. F. 84, 87, 93
Cheng, Y. L. 88, 93

Circling, Organizing, Sketching, Modelling, Operating, Scanning (COSMOS) 16, *17*; for word problems 221–222, *222*
Cirino, P. T. 23, 24, 124, 132, 134, 204, 217, 221
Clayton, S. 44
Clements, D. H. 47
Clever chart 99, *100*, 135; addition and subtraction on 145, *146*
Coban, L. 3
Codding, R. S. 123, 132
Cohen, D. 48
Cohen, L. 48, 120
Collignon, O. 54
competence assessment, of base-10 understanding 93–94
concrete-representational-abstract (CRA) 252
Cooper, R. G. 37
Cooreman, A. 5
Cordes, S. 242
COSMOS *see* Circling, Organizing, Sketching, Modelling, Operating, Scanning
'count-by-tens and ones' conceptual structure 75, 76
counting-by-ten task 84
counting-large-numbers task 84
counting-principle knower 42
counting principles 40–41; abstraction principle 41; cardinal principle 40; one-to-one correspondence principle 40; order irrelevance principle 41; stable order principle 40
CRA *see* concrete-representational-abstract
Cragg, L. 44
Cress, H. 53
Crollen, V. 54

Dal Martello, M. F. 73, 79–81
De Brauwer, J. 82
decimal numbers 258, *287*; arithmetic operations on 286–290; arithmetic with, challenge of 242–243; assessment of 259–261; calculations converting into fractions **288**; comparing, difficulties in 238–239; interrelation of *282*; interventions on 246–249; understanding of 282–286; visual representation of *283*, *284*, *285*
decimal position system, training of 87, 87–90, *88*

decomposing numbers 63–64, *64*; task 84
Degroote, V. 54
Dehaene, S. 2, 48, 73, 120
Delazer, M. 127
Deloche, G. 79, 81
De Smedt, B. 3, 16, 53, 113, 128
Desmet, L. 238
Devine, A. 7
De Visscher, A. 4
DeWolf, M. 242
Diakow, R. 253
Dienes blocks/materials *88*, 92, 95, *95*, 282
Dirkx, G. S. M. A. 85
Doabler, C. T. 15
Domahs, F. 127
Dots Comparison 55
Dowker, A. 81
Dupoux, E. 73
Durkin, K. 246, *247*
dyscalculia 1–2, 196; approximate number system and 44–45; arithmetic skills and 118–121; basic number processing deficit 2–4; causes of 2–8; children with, difficulties in 84–85; cognitive profiles of students with **27**, 27–28; counting and enumeration 45–46; deficit in one or several general cognitive processes 4–8; difficulties encountered in 44–46; and difficulties with rational numbers 244–246; effective instruction practices in 9–10; instructional strategies for 10–24; language skills and 4–5; mathematical profiles 24–26; memory and 5–6; number positioning on line and 46; prevalence of 1; procedural 119; reasoning skills and 7–8; subitizing and 45; visual-spatial processes 6–7; word problem solving and 202–204
Dyson, N. 241, 243, 244, 270

Early, M. C. 10
Early Numeracy test 55
effective instruction practices 8–10
Eibl, G. 127
Elen, J. 53
Ellis, M. F. 249
enumeration 40–41; and dyscalculia 45–46
enumeration rehabilitation 56–58; child's performance **57**; clinical example of 56–57
enumeration subtest 55
Epinat-Duclos, J. 7
equal-to-one fractions 263–265

equivalent fractions *268*, 268–270
Ermakova, A. 78, 83
Evans, D. 7
Examath 8–15 55, 129
explicit instruction, for dyscalculia 12–15; basic-level, example of 13, 14; instructional sequence of 14; teaching components 12

Fabbri, S. 240
Farkas, G. 8
Faux, G. 99
Fayol, M. 80, 81
Feigenson, L. 55
Fennema, E. 75, 76, 82
Fias, W. 82
Fien, H. 15
fingers, as tool for number representation 59, *59*
'fingers and toes' strategy: for additions 139, *140*, 142; for subtractions 141, *141*
Fischbein, E. 237
Fischer, U. 53, 54
Fletcher, J. M. 23, 24, 124, 132, 134
Flexplicit intervention strategy 11; components of 12–24; explicit instruction 12–15, **26**; heuristics 15–16, **26**; math flexibility 16–20, **26**
fraction(s) 258–259; assessment of 259–261; comparison of, difficulties in 239–241; as a division 270; division of fractions 279–282, *280*; equivalent 268–270; heuristic model of operations on, verbal explanation of **289**; heuristic model of operations on, visual representation of **290**; interrelation of *282*; interventions on 249–257; like, addition and subtraction of 270–273; multiplication with 277–279, *278*, *279*; as a number 262–263; as part of whole or of a single object 261–262; as part or subset of collection 265–268; proper, improper, and equal-to-one 263–265; representations of 239–240
Fraiteur, S. 91
Frensch, P. A. 113
Friso-van den Bos, I. 53
Fuchs, D. 23, 24, 124, 132, 134, 203, 208, 210, 211
Fuchs, L. S. 11, 23, 24, 124, 132, 134, 203, 204, 208, 210, 211, 217, 221, 253, 254, 256
Fuson, K. C. 39–41, 74–76, 82

Gabriel, F. 7
Gallistel, C. R. 40, 41
Ganor-Stern, D. 242
Garcia, A. I. 202
Gardner, J. 7
Gardner, S. 7
Garin, A. 77
Gattegno chart 99–100
GCF *see* greatest common factor
GDI *see* general strategy instruction
Gearhart, M. 253
Geary, D. C. 46, 113, 119, 120, 241
Gelman, R. 40, 41
Gelosia method 184
general strategy instruction (GDI) 207
Gerotto, G. 127
Gersten, R. 9
Gervasconi, A. 77
Ghesquière, P. 16, 113
Gilmore, C. 44
Ginsburg, H. P. 84, 196
global numerical processing programmes 47–48
Göbel, S. 5
Grabner, R. H. 128
Graeber, A. O. 237
GraphoGame-Math 48
greatest common factor (GCF) 273
Greeno, J. G. 197, 198
Grégoire, J. 41, 238, 241
Griffin, C. C. 206, 207, 216, 220, 221
Groen, G. J. 108
Gross-Tsur, V. 1
grouping model, of division *171*, 171–172, *172*
Gunderson, E. A. 257

Hachigian, A. 78, 83
Halberda, J. 55
Hamden, N. 257
Hamlett, C. L. 11
Hanich, L. B. 10, 245
Hansen, N. 241, 243, 244, 260, 270
Hardiman, P. T. 199
Haria, P. 206, 207, 216, 220, 221
Hasselbring, T. S. 9
Heller, J. I. 197, 198
heuristic model: BEMDAS 16, *18*; COSMOS 16, *17*; for long division *186*; of operations on fractions **289**, **290**; for times tables and corresponding divisions *174*; of word-problem solving *16*, **221**, 221–222, *222*
heuristics, and dyscalculia 15–16

Hickendorff, M. 114, 115
Hiebert, J. 75, 76, 82, 237, 243
Ho, C. S. H. 74, 84, 87, 93
Holyoak, K. J. 242
Honoré, N. 51, 54
Huber, S. 54
Hulstijn, W. 85
Human, P. G. 75, 76, 82
Hurst, M. 242
Hyde, D. C. 50

Ifrah, G. 72
Imbo, I. 82
improper fractions 263–265
instructional strategies, for dyscalculia 10–24; dimensions to integrate 20–24; explicit instruction 12–15; heuristics 15–16; math flexibility 16–20; motivation factors 23–24; multiple instructional examples, use of 22; peer-assisted mathematics instruction 23; providing on-going feedback 22–23; student's verbalization 21; visual representations 20, *20*, *21*
'integrated tens and ones' conceptual structure 75, 76–77
intervention, in base-10 system 94–102; Arabic code 97–98; base-10 positional system 97–98; exchange, equivalence, composition, and decomposition *96*, 96–97, *97*; exercises in representing number 92; generalization of big numbers up to millions 100–101, *101*, *102*; positional chart 97–98, *98*, *99*; verbal numbers and Arabic numbers 99–100; verbal numbers and base-10 material, use of *95*, 95–96
intervention studies: children's numerical development 46–47; global numerical processing programmes 47–48; targeted numerical interventions 48–54
Iuculano, T. 125, 242

Janssen, F. 85
Jenkens, E. 110
Jeong, Y. 78, 83
Jiménez, J. E. 202
Jitendra, A. K. 206, 207, 216, 220, 221
Johnson, S. 44
Jordan, N. C. 11, 203, 241, 243, 244, 260, 270

Kaduvettoor, A. 206, 207, 216, 220, 221
Karagiannakis, G. 5, 25, 221
Kaufmann, L. 83

KeyMath-3 55, 93, 129, 131, 259; Problem Solving' subtest in 217
Khanum, S. 50
Kim, C. C. 81
Koponen, T. K. 124, 135
Koppel, H. 76
Kreps, G. 75
Krinzinger, H. 82, 85
Kroesbergen, E. H. 53
Krowka, S. K. 256
Kucian, K. 123

Lai, W. F. 78, 83
Landerl, K. 45, 46
language skills, and dyscalculia 4–5
language transparency 147
large written numbers task 84
Laski, E. V. 78, 83
least common multiple (LCM) 273
Le Corre, M. 42
Lee, K. 211
Leh, J. 206, 207, 216, 220, 221
Lemaire, P. 112
Léonard, F. 238
Léone, J. 7
Lewis, A. 199
Lewis, K. E. 245
lexical errors 80
'lexicalization' 81
Link, T. 54
Lloyd, D. 81
Lochy, A. 127
Long, J. 253, 254, 256
Lonnemann, J. 85
look, ask, pick (LAP) strategy 249–252
Lortie-Forgues, H. 243, 244, 278, 280
Lubienski, S. T. 11
Lucangeli, D. 48
Lukito, G. 123, 132

Ma, L. 10
Maczuga, S. 8
Maertens, B. 53
magnitude representation 73–74
Malone, A. S. 11
Mammarella, I. C. 7, 127
Manalo, E. 247, 248
Manor, O. 1
mapping numbers, to spatial layout 43–44
mathematical profiles, and dyscalculia 24–26
mathematical skills, associated with domain **25**
mathematical verbalization 252, 258

Math Flash programme 132
math flexibility, for dyscalculia 16–20
math learning disability *see* dyscalculia
MathPro test 93, 129, 217
Mawart, C. 122
Mayer, R. E. 199
Mazzocco, M. M. M. 10, 55, 245
McCloskey, M. 73, 74, 79, 80, 90
McCormack, T. 1
McGourty, J. 1
Meert, G. 241
Mehler, J. 73
memory **25**; and dyscalculia 5–6
'mental number line' 43
Merz, S. 3
Mestre, J. P. 199
Mewborn, D. S. 11
Miura, I. T. 78, 81
Mix, K. S. 88, 93
Moeller, K. 53, 54, 83
Montessori cards 87, 93, 97, *98*, 99, *99*, *151*
Morgan, P. 8
Morsanyi, K. 1, 7
Moura, R. 85
motivational environment, for students with dyscalculia 23–24
Multi-Digit Number Comparison 93
multiplication chart *166*
Multiplication Fact Retrieval subtest 129
Murphy, M. M. 10, 245
Murray, H. G. 75, 76, 82
Mussolin, C. 238
Myers, G. F. 245
Myers, T. V. 50

Namkung, J. 11
National Mathematics Advisory Panel 15
natural number bias 236
natural numbers 237
Next and Previous Number subtests 55
Ng, S. F. 211
Nobes, A. 7
Noël, M. P. 4, 45, 51, 54, 80, 81, 120, 121, 241
non-symbolic tasks/training 3, 51
Nuerk, H. C. 53, 54, 73, 83
number line 43–44; mental 43; positioning numbers on 43, *43*; priority to working on 53; training 51–52
Number Line subtests 93
number positioning on line 43, *43*; and dyscalculia 46
number processing deficit 2–4
Number Race 48–49

number representation, fingers as tool for 59, *59*
Numeracy Screener 55
numerical development, children's 46–47
numerical systems 72–73
Nunes, T. 7

Obersteiner, A. 48
object tracking system 37
Oettinger, T. 203
Okamoto, Y. 81, 85, 93
Olivier, A. I. 75, 76, 82
one-knowers 42
one-to-one correspondence principle 40
order irrelevance principle 41
ordinality 60–62

Park, J. 49, 122
Parkman, J. M. 108
partial products method 184
peer-assisted mathematics instruction, for dyscalculia 23
Perruchet, P. 79
Peters, G. 16, 113, 121
Piaget, J. 46
Piazza, M. 2, 120
Pinel, P. 120
Pinheiro-Chagas, P. 85
Pixner, S. 82, 83
'place-value tens and ones' conceptual structure 75, 76
playing cards: comparison-to-five task with 63; as revision materials 60, *62*
Poisson, A. 7
positional chart 97–98, *98*, *99*
positional system 77–78
Powell, S. R. 9, 23, 24, 124, 132, 134, 204, 217, 221
Power, R. J. D. 73, 79–81
Prado, J. 7
Prentice, K. 203, 208, 210, 211
problem-solving transfer (PST) instruction 210–211
procedural dyscalculia 119
proper fractions 263–265
Pyke, A. A. 243, 244
Pylyshyn, Z. W. 37

Ramani, G. B. 51, *51*, 52, 54, 64
Räsänen, P. 48
rational numbers 237; ability to process, assessment of 259–261; addition and subtraction of like fractions 270–273; addition and subtraction of unlike fractions 273–277; arithmetic operations on decimal numbers 286–290; arithmetic with decimal numbers, challenge of 242–243; arithmetic with fractions, challenge of 243–244; and children with dyscalculia 244–246; comparing decimal numbers, difficulties in 238–239; comparison of fractions, difficulties in 239–241; decimal numbers, interventions on 246–249; division of fractions 279–282, *280*; equivalent fractions 268–270; fraction and decimal numbers together, working with 290, *291*; fraction as a number 262–263; fraction as part of whole or of a single object 261–262; fractions, interventions on 249–257; fractions as a division 270; fractions as part or subset of collection 265–268; intervention strategies on 246–259; learning challenges 236–244; multiplication with fractions 277–279, *278*; overview 236; proper, improper, and equal-to-one fractions 263–265; rehabilitation paths 261–291; understanding of decimal numbers 282–286

reasoning skills **25**; and dyscalculia 7–8
rehabilitation, of basic numerical skills 55–66; cardinal value of number words 58–59; connecting symbolic numbers 59–60; counting string 55–56; decomposing numbers 63–64, *64*; enumeration rehabilitation 56–58; number representation, fingers as tool for 59, *59*; numbers up to 100 64–66; relationships between numbers 60–63
rehabilitation and teaching, in arithmetic: addition 132–133, *133*; complex addition and subtraction 144–153; complex calculations on multi-digit numbers 174–181; decomposition strategy for multiplication and division *178*, 178–179, *179*, *180–181*; multiplication and division by powers of ten 174–175; relationship between multiplication and division 172–173, *173*, *174*; simple addition and subtraction 134–144; simple divisions 169–172; simple multiplications 159–169, *160*, *161*; stimulate flexibility 179, 181; subtraction 133–134, *134*; written calculation algorithms 182–187; written calculation for addition 153–156,

154, 155, 156; written calculation for subtraction 156–159, *157, 158, 159*; written division algorithms 184, 187; written multiplication algorithms *183*, 183–184

rehabilitation paths, in rational numbers 261–291; arithmetic operations on decimal numbers 286–290; division of fractions 279–282; equivalent fractions 268–270; fraction and decimal numbers together, working with 290, *291*; fraction as a number 262–263; fraction as part of whole or of a single object 261–262; fractions as a division 270; fractions as part or subset of collection 265–268; like fractions, addition and subtraction of 270–273; multiplication with fractions 277–279; proper, improper, and equal-to-one fractions 263–265; understanding of decimal numbers 282–286; unlike fractions, addition and subtraction of 273–277

Reiss, K. 48
representational-abstract (RA) 252
representation-of-place-value task 84–85
Resnick, I. 241, 243, 244, 270
Resnick, L. B. 238
Restle, F. 73
Revkin, S. K. 48
Reynvoet, B. 53
Richards, J. 39–41
Rightstart ('Head Start') programme 47, 48
Riley, M. S. 197, 198
Rittle-Johnson, B. 246, *247*
Roberts, R. C. 122
Robinson, K. M. 116
Rodgers, M. A. 9
Rodrigues, J. 241, 243, 244, 270
Roman code 73
Rourke, B. P. 7, 120
Rousselle, L. 45, 121
Roussos, P. 25
Rusinek, S. 122
Russell, R. L. 84, 196, 203

Sackur-Grisvard, C. 238
Salminen, J. 48
Sasanguie, D. 53
Saxe, G. B. 253
schema-based instruction (SBI) 207
Schiltz, C. 82
Schleifer, P. 46
Schmidt, S. S. 3
Schneider, M. 3, 6, 241, 253

Schumacher, R. F. 11, 253, 254, 256
Schwartz, F. 7
Seethaler, P. 124, 132, 134
Seethaler, P. M. 23, 24, 204, 217, 221
self-regulated strategies (SRL) 210–211
Sella, F. 48
Seron, X. 79–81, 241
Shalev, R. S. 1
sharing model, of division 169, *170*
Shin, M. 252
Siegler, R. S. 51, *51*, 52, 54, 61, 64, 110, 119, 241–244, 253, 278, 280
Simms, V. 44
Sinclair, A. 77
Singapore method, for word problem solving 211–216
Single-Digit Number Comparison 55
single-digit numbers 85, 132, 135, 142, 173, 178; addition of *141*; basic arithmetic operations 106; multiplication 163–164, *165*; subtraction from whole tens *150*; unitary conception of 77
Skagerlund, K. 4
Smith, L. B. 88, 93
SNARC effect *see* spatial numerical association of response codes effect
Soltesz, F. 7
spatial numerical association of response codes (SNARC) effect 43
Spelke, E. S. 37, 50
Squire, S. 75
stable order principle 40
Stafylidou, S. 239
Starkey, P. 37
Steere, M. 81
Stevens, E. A. 9
Stillman, J. A. 247, 248
Stockton, J. D. 88, 93
Strang, J. D. 120
Stricker, J. 3
student-centred instruction 8
student's verbalization, for dyscalculia 21
subitizing, and dyscalculia 45
Subitizing subtest 55
Sullivan, K. S. 90
Sullivan, P. 77
Symbolic Magnitude Processing Test 55
symbolic numbers 59–60, 63
symbolic training 51
syntactic errors 80
Széminska, A. 46
Szmalec, A. 4
Szûcs, D. 7, 50

targeted numerical interventions 48–54; involving body, importance of 53–54; number line training 51–52; priority to working on number line 53; representation of magnitude, training of 51; specific training of ANS 49–50; training of ANS 48–49
teacher-directed instruction 8
Tedi-math battery 55, 93, 129, 216
TediMath Grands battery 55, 93, 129, 130, 216–217, 259
Temple, C. M. 121
Tempo-Test-Automatiseren (TTA) 129
Tempotest Rekenen (TTR) 129
Test, D. W. 249
Thompson, C. A. 241, 253
three-digit numbers 81, 85, 89, 92, 100, 145; addition of *151*; decomposition strategy for dividing *180*; positional value concept 87–88; subtraction of 12, *151*
Tian, J. 242
Tièche-Christinat, C. 77
Tirosh, D. 237
Tompson, I. 152
Torbeyns, J. 16, 113–116
Tournaki, N. 123
Träff, U. 4
training, of arithmetic/arithmetic skills 122–128; based on ANS or magnitude representation 122–123; complex calculations 127–128; simple arithmetic 123–127
training, of base-10 system 85–93; decimal position system *87*, 87–90, *88*; encoding 10ness for number magnitude 85–86, *86*; remediation programmes of transcoding 90–92
transcoding, base-10 system 78–82; definition 78–79; development of 79–81; errors 79–81, **80**; influence of language structure on 81–82; models 79; remediation programmes of 90–92
Tressoldi, P. 48
Trick, L. M. 37
Triple Code model 120
Tronsky, L. N. 113
TTA *see* Tempo-Test-Automatiseren
TTR *see* Tempotest Rekenen
two-digit numbers: 'count-by-tens and ones' conceptual structure 75, 76; decomposition of 20, *20*; 'integrated tens and ones' conceptual structure 75, 76–77; magnitude, improvement in 86; magnitude of 73; 'place-value tens and ones' conceptual structure 75, 76; unitary conception of 75, 75–76; 'X-ty group and ones' conception 75, 76; *see also* base-10 system, bubbles structure to subtract
two-knowers 42
typologies of word problems: additive and subtractive problems 198–199; multiplicative problems *199*, 199–200, *200*; proportional or ratio problems 201–202, *202*

Ufer, S. 48
Umiltà, C. 240
unbreakable chain 39
unit transparency 147

Vaessen, A. 4
van Bers, B. M. C. W. 1
Vanden Bulcke, C. 82
Van der Elst, G. 80
Van der Linden, L. 4
Van de Walle, G. 42
Van Loosbroek, E. 85
Van Luit, J. E. H. 53
Van Nieuwenhoven, C. 41
Van Rinsveld, A. 82
Varelas, M. 77
Vasilyeva, M. 78, 83
verbal counting 38–40; bidirectional chain 40; breakable chain 39–40; numerable level of string 40; stable and conventional 38; unbreakable chain 39; unstable and unconventional 38
Verschaffel, L. 16, 113–116
Vilette, B. 122
Visscher, A. 120
visual representations, for dyscalculia 20, *20*, *21*
visual-spatial processes **25**; and dyscalculia 6–7
visual-spatial working memory (WM) 6
Vosniadou, S. 239

Wang, Y. Q. 242
Wearne, D. 75, 76, 82, 237, 243
Weger, U. 73
Whyte, J. C. 52
Wiley, J. G. 113
Willmes, K. 73, 85
Wilson, A. J. 2, 48
Wilson, J. W. 237

Wood, G. 85
word problem solving: addition and subtraction word problems 212, 223, *223–229*; building progression in 218–220; change problems, examples of *223–226*; cognitive skills for 197; combine problems, examples of *226–227*; compare problems, examples of *228–229*; didactical programme for 211–216; difficulty in 195–198; and dyscalculia 202–204; equalize problems, example of *227*; experimental intervention or instruction programmes 204–216; four-step strategy for 207; helping student in 218–233; heuristic models for **221**, 221–222, *222*; multiplication compare problems, examples of *229–232*; multiplication compute problems, example of *229*; number combination programme 204; overview 195; problems of percentages, examples of *232–233* ; research on intervention or instruction programmes 204–211; RUN strategy for 205, 206; same problem structure 209; Singapore method 211–216; skills for, assessment of 216–218; supporting mathematical modelling 220; synthetic representation of analysis of difficulties in 218; typologies 198–202; *see also* typologies of word problems
word-problem tutoring 206
Wynn, K. 107

Xu, F. 37

Yao, Y. 46

Zamarian, L. 127
Zhang, Y. 85, 93
Zorzi, M. 48, 240
Zubern, J. 83

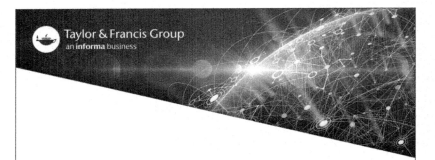